PENGUIN CANADA

BEYOND BELFAST

WILL FERGUSON is a three-time winner of the Stephen Leacock Medal for Humour. His previous travel memoirs include *Beauty Tips from Moose Jaw*, covering his travels in Canada, and *Hitching Rides with Buddha*, a critically acclaimed account of Ferguson's end-to-end journey across Japan by thumb as he follows the cherry blossoms north. His novels include *Happiness*™, a satire set in the world of publishing about a self-help book that actually works, thus causing the end of the world as we know it, and *Spanish Fly*, a coming-of-age story set amidst the con men and jazz-club grifters of the 1930s.

ALSO BY WILL FERGUSON

FICTION

Spanish Fly
Happiness™

TRAVEL MEMOIRS

Coal Dust Kisses: A Christmas Memoir

Hitching Rides with Buddha:
A Journey Across Japan

Beauty Tips from Moose Jaw:
Travels in Search of Canada

HISTORY/HUMOUR

Canadian History for Dummies
How to Be a Canadian (with Ian Ferguson)
Why I Hate Canadians

AS EDITOR

The Penguin Anthology of Canadian Humour

AS SONGWRITER

Lyricist for the songs "Con Men and Call Girls, Part One,"
"Losin' Hand," and "When the Carnival Comes to Town,"
on the Tom Philips *Spanish Fly* album

BEYOND BELFAST

A 560-Mile Walk Across Northern Ireland on Sore Feet

WILL FERGUSON

PENGUIN
CANADA

PENGUIN CANADA

Published by the Penguin Group

Penguin Group (Canada), 90 Eglinton Avenue East, Suite 700, Toronto, Ontario, Canada M4P 2Y3
(a division of Pearson Canada Inc.)

Penguin Group (USA) Inc., 375 Hudson Street, New York, New York 10014, U.S.A.
Penguin Books Ltd, 80 Strand, London WC2R 0RL, England
Penguin Ireland, 25 St Stephen's Green, Dublin 2, Ireland (a division of Penguin Books Ltd)
Penguin Group (Australia), 250 Camberwell Road, Camberwell, Victoria 3124, Australia
(a division of Pearson Australia Group Pty Ltd)
Penguin Books India Pvt Ltd, 11 Community Centre, Panchsheel Park, New Delhi – 110 017, India
Penguin Group (NZ), 67 Apollo Drive, Rosedale, North Shore 0745, Auckland, New Zealand
(a division of Pearson New Zealand Ltd)
Penguin Books (South Africa) (Pty) Ltd, 24 Sturdee Avenue, Rosebank, Johannesburg 2196, South Africa

Penguin Books Ltd, Registered Offices: 80 Strand, London WC2R 0RL, England

First published in Viking Canada hardcover by Penguin Group (Canada),
a division of Pearson Canada Inc., 2009

Published in this edition, 2011

1 2 3 4 5 6 7 8 9 10   (WEB)

Copyright © Will Ferguson, 2009

Manufactured in Canada.

LIBRARY AND ARCHIVES CANADA CATALOGUING IN PUBLICATION

Ferguson, Will
Beyond Belfast : a 560-mile walk across Northern Ireland on sore feet / Will Ferguson.

ISBN 978-0-14-317062-4

1. Ferguson, Will—Travel—Northern Ireland. 2. Ulster Way (Northern Ireland)—
Description and travel. 3. Walking—Northern Ireland. 4. Northern Ireland—
Description and travel. 5. Authors, Canadian (English)—20th century—Biography.
I. Title.

DA990.U46F37 2011   914.1604'824   C2010-906087-3

Visit the Penguin Group (Canada) website at **www.penguin.ca**

Special and corporate bulk purchase rates available; please see
www.penguin.ca/corporatesales or call 1-800-810-3104, ext. 2477 or 2474

CONTENTS

A Note from the Author

"When you take a path, the path takes you."
—IRISH SAYING

I first walked the Ulster Way in the fall of 2000, at the dawn of the new millennium, as a fragile peace settled over Northern Ireland. Thirty years of bloodshed, of punch and counterpunch, of death and counterdeath—that apocalyptic chain of events known with uncharacteristic understatement as "The Troubles"—had finally come to an end, and travellers were beginning to rediscover the North. I returned to Belfast in 2008 to reclaim my family's lost estate—such as it was. This is the story of those two journeys, the first across a landscape and the second into the past.

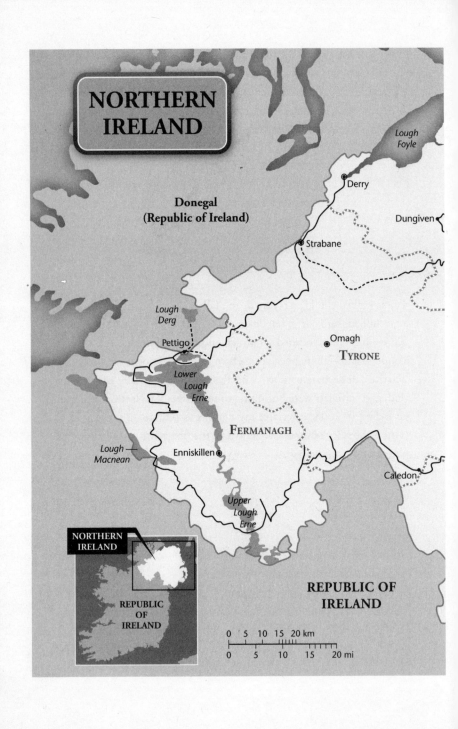

NORTHERN IRELAND

Lough Foyle

Derry

Dungiven

Donegal (Republic of Ireland)

Strabane

Lough Derg

Pettigo

Lower Lough Erne

Omagh

TYRONE

FERMANAGH

Lough Macnean

Enniskillen

Caledon

Upper Lough Erne

REPUBLIC OF IRELAND

NORTHERN IRELAND

REPUBLIC OF IRELAND

REPUBLIC OF IRELAND

0   5   10 15   20 km
0   5   10   15   20 mi

Part One

THE ULSTER WAY

STARTING OUT

from Whiteabbey to Larne

At the Belfast airport, watching the carousel turn, playing a game of "match the luggage to the tourist," I placed my bets.

Lumpy duffle bags: a tangle of young men as loosely packed as their belongings, shirts untucked and hair uncombed. A scuffed and bestickered guitar case: the goatee in the corner. A canvas rucksack, well travelled, with bandana tied on by way of identity: that would be hoisted onto the tanned shoulders of an athletic and lonely-looking young woman with hair pulled back—and there she was now, looking sun-creased and beautiful. Down the chute slid a procession of cardboard boxes rigged up with packing tape and binder twine. These were pulled off, one by one, by a family—a large, motley family that was apparently using the airport as a postal service. There was a frazzled mother in a far corner, slumped in a chair, surrounded by a nest of diaper bags and blankets and various pieces of apparel, as though she and her toddler had decided to bed down right there. The largest, most unwieldy bag would be hers.

And now, coming down onto the carousel in shiny unblemished nylon, a sleek, high-tech, space-age backpack with superfluous straps and a metal frame sewn right into the fabric for maximum efficiency in weight-load distribution. This was the sign of a naïve and doomed endeavour. This was the sign of someone on a collision course with reality.

I wrestled my backpack off the carousel, dragged it outside.

IT WAS BILLED as "the longest waymarked trail in the British Isles." Stitched together over the 1970s and early '80s, the Ulster Way turned a slow circle through the six counties of Northern Ireland, beginning and ending in Belfast, following coastlines and country lanes, forested paths and moorland heights, old canals and ancient pilgrimage routes. Depending on which source you consulted, the Ulster Way was anywhere from 520 to 630 miles long, a discrepancy that should have raised more alarm bells for me than it did.* *If they can't agree on the length, how can they agree on the actual route?*

Fewer people had walked the Ulster Way than had climbed Mount Everest, and I couldn't wait to end up in a bar somewhere next to a mountain climber. "Oxygen tanks, Sherpa guides, frostbite, snow blind, lost yer toes, had to cannibalize your team leader. Blah blah blah. Well, let me tell you something, buddy, *I've* walked Ulster."

Northern Ireland is the last archaic rump of British occupation on Ireland's sacred soil—or the final defiant bastion of subjects loyal to the Crown, depending on your point of view. (As I would learn, both interpretations are correct; it just depends which pub you happen to be sitting in at the time.) Many places claim to be "a world apart." Ulster, as Ireland's North is historically known, truly is. Physically, culturally, politically, it is the inevitable asterisk in Irish history, where every assertion seems to be followed by the aside "*Exception:* See Ulster."

In his overview of Irish history, geographer J. H. Andrews emphasized "the tendency for the north to stand aloof from the rest of the

---

*As part of the UK, the Ulster Way is marked and measured in miles. It was in miles that I walked, miles that I thought, miles that I dreamed at night. By the end of my journey, kilometres seemed alien and coldly mathematical. For those of a more metric persuasion, simply multiply the miles by 1.61. The route I followed was roughly 900 kilometres in length, though I ended up walking almost a thousand by the time I was done.

country," adding that "much of the north … is really a maze of tightly packed small hills known as drumlins, low but quite steep, and patched together with fragments of bog or lake. For much of their history the drumlin belts have made a surprisingly effective obstacle." I jotted this down, made careful note of it: *aloof, isolated, remote, culturally distinct.* What I SHOULD have noted was the reference to bogs. That too should have set off alarm bells, considering I was planning to walk across the very landscape Andrews was describing.

Sheared off from the rest of Ireland in 1921, Northern Ireland was a modern attempt at solving a centuries-old standoff, with the six most "British" (read "Protestant") counties lumped together to form a separate entity. "A Protestant Parliament and a Protestant state," in the words of one particularly myopic leader, wilfully overlooking the fact that a third of the population of this new state were Catholics.

British, yet not part of Great Britain. Irish, yet not part of Ireland. The Six Counties of the North are a cornerstone of the UK (officially: the United Kingdom of Great Britain *and* Northern Ireland— emphasis mine). With Northern Ireland included in the mix, though, there really ought to be quotation marks around "United." As noted, the historical name for the nine rebellious, independent, warring counties of the North is Ulster. The term is also used, however, to refer to the Six Counties that were set apart during partition in 1921. In this sense, "Ulster" is simply a richer, more culturally laden synonym for the somewhat sterile designation "Northern Ireland."

In the Republic, Northern Ireland is seen as the missing piece of the jigsaw, an unruly breakaway statelet, the Taiwan to its China. In Britain, Northern Ireland has been a self-sustaining headache, a famously cantankerous province where even the "loyal" citizens are abrasive and needling in their demands. *"We're British!"* is the apocryphal demand made by one Unionist politician, *"and you British better remember that!"*

There is no politically neutral way of referring to the North. Northern Ireland has the traits of a country, in the sense of being a distinct region with a separate political boundary and a unique character—as Scotland and Wales are considered countries, while still being part of the UK—but Northern Ireland is rarely referred to in this way. It is also "Irish" in the larger context of geology, climate, social traits, past events. The region had a great deal of history prior to the schism of 1921—most of it soaked in blood, true, but still. Northern Ireland is a recent invention; Ulster is not. The long struggle between Protestant and Catholic is part of that history, that heritage; the two sides are so entwined in their sense of identity as to be inseparable. "We're stuck with each other" is how one fellow explained it to me. "Who else would want us?" Certainly, the Republic of Ireland had been having second thoughts about absorbing such a hard-headed bunch of Northerners, Catholic and Protestant alike, into the mix. The cry of "One island, one Ireland!" has seemed oddly muted of late.

MY INITIAL IMPRESSIONS of Belfast were fleeting at best; I arrived at dusk, left just after dawn. But even in that short time, I came up against two defining aspects of the culture, things that would confound and beguile me for much of my trip: the Ulster Fry and Ulster craic. That is, the obscenely large breakfasts people eat and the clipped rhythm of their banter.

For those of you who have so far managed to avoid an Ulster Fry, I warn you now: just reading about said repast can make your arteries clog. The thing is, I *like* big greasy breakfasts, or at least I thought I did. That was before I was faced with the full might of Ulster's culinary prowess: eggs not so much fried as basted in grease and sausages prepared the same way, often in an array—pork sausage, black sausage (i.e., congealed blood) and white sausage (also made from congealed blood)—along with half a fried tomato, a whack of fried mushrooms, a goop of baked beans, some fried potato bread and, as often as not, I swear, a little packet of low-fat butter. Ulster hospitality demands you not be permitted to leave until oil is oozing from your pores and your belt has snapped like a Lash LaRue bullwhip. And then? They smile at you, the bastards, and say, "We'll just sop up this last bit of grease with some more bread, shall we?" At this point they usually bring out a plunger and begin stuffing the food directly into your gullet. The whole time I was in Northern Ireland I never once saw anyone from Northern Ireland actually eat blood sausage; they just feed it to visitors, apparently—part practical joke, part rite of passage.

The morning had started innocuously enough. I was down early, before the other guests at the B&B. An older fellow shuffled in soon after, and the lady of the house sent out some toast and tea for us. The toast arrived quickly and pre-cooled, an art the Northern Irish would appear to have learned from the English, who have long mastered the art of producing cold toast directly from the toaster.

The tea and toast were just a feint, though I didn't know it at the time. While the owner prepared an Ulster Fry in the kitchen, I sat out front, gnawing away, muttering darkly about the corrosive influence of English cooking on the world. The butter was frozen, wouldn't even begin to melt. I commented on this to the other guest, but he took it as a warped sort of compliment. "Aye, it takes a good chew." "This isn't toast," I said. "This is bark. And I'm from Canada. I know bark."

The lady and her helpers hurried about setting the tables and getting everything ready for the rest of the guests. As they bandied back and forth, I fiddled with my tape recorder. It was a mini-dictaphone, newly purchased, and I was still trying to figure out the various settings. As I worked on it, I slowly became aware of the rhythms around me, the quick tempo. It was strangely … familiar. Craic is about rhythm and music rather than set-up and punchline. It needs to be heard. If you were, say, to tape-record a round of craic, then later transcribe it, hoping to transfer the wit from pub to page, or street to sentence, you would, as I was, be disappointed. Case in point: that B&B in Belfast.

One of the people helping out that day was a young man with a broken wrist. His hand was plastered up in a cast, and as they hurried about, the lady of the house teased the lad—a handsome young lad, I should note—with that slightly serrated, wryly flirtatious manner older women reserve for such moments.

The more I listened, the more fascinated I became, and, like Margaret Mead among the islanders, I quietly hit RECORD. Here's what I got:

"How'd you do that really, then?" asks the lady, referring to the lad's cast. Having teased him about everything else, she had moved on to his injury. "Drinkin' was it?"

"Not a drop."

"Several drops, then?"

"Nah, just fell down is all."

"Aye, the Guinness will do tha'."

"Was no Guinness involved, I swear."

"My mistake. Harp, was it? Or Tennent's?"

"Wasn't. Dead sober, I swear. I was just messin' about with my girlfriend, standing on my head, just for a lark, like."

"And yer girl pushed you, then? Finally came to her senses?"

"Was no pushing involved. Fell and twisted it on my own, so I did."

"No help required?"

"No help required. Didn't realize it was broke till next morning, when I woke and saw it swollen like. Went in, and doc there says it's split. I didn't cry once, not a peep, even as he set it."

"So you're a big boy, then?"

"That I am."

At which point I cut in with all the subtlety of a North American, a big grin already plastered on my face. "Well then!" I said. "I guess we can't, heh heh, 'twist your arm' if we need something."

They turned, as though noticing me for the first time. Silence. My grin suddenly seemed very strained; I let it slide off my face.

"Can I get you a cup of tea?" he asked. ("Cuppa tay?" in the original.)

I said no, I was fine, thanks, and he waded back into the banter as I watched from the sidelines. The Ulster Fry appeared soon after.

PROTESTANT STOCK

I grew up in Canada's northern forests, in a former fur-trading post closer to the Arctic Circle than to the American border, but Ulster was always there, in the verbal tics, the turns of phrase, the endless cups of milky tea, the magical thinking, the constant ribbing, the easy laughter, the fear of long pauses, the sense that every silence needed to be filled, quickly. Conversations in our family were not so much carried forth as held aloft, like the birdie in a game of badminton where the goal is not to score points but simply to keep it in the air as long as possible. I was one of six kids in a sprawling single-parent family that included various configurations of foster children, local outcasts, semi-nomadic friends and dogs of dubious lineage, all of us raised—or rather herded along—by the daughter of a Belfast orphan.

When my grandfather left Belfast as a child, the North was still part of Ireland, and Ireland was still part of the British Empire. He arrived in the New World with a cardboard suitcase and a small collection of stories, tales he held in his palm, tales that he polished till they gleamed. Tales he passed on to his children. If my grandfather knew the full details of his past, he never revealed them. Doled out fables instead, warm memories and sad glimpses of who he was before he arrived in North America. There were rumours, though. Whispers among his children of fanciful truths and wondrous secrets. My grandfather had landed as a Protestant, but, my mother told us, "We always thought he was Catholic. There were gaps we couldn't quite fill." She and her siblings often wondered if there was something their father was holding back. "He was so young when he came over that he may not have known himself."

One of my mother's first memories was of her father's boots. "Knee-high, almost army-issue. I remember him rubbing dubbin into the leather so they'd last, the smell of that." She was placed inside one of those boots as a toddler, remembers everyone laughing at how small she was, how big his boots were.

"He would joke about the size of his feet," my mother recalled. "How it wasn't the shoes but the boxes they came in that fit him. I remember him pulling a tooth of mine that was loose, his huge hands and the fact that they were stained with tobacco and tasted bitter."

He was a handsome man. And tall, too, over six feet. "Very strong as well," my mother said. "He could balance his entire body on one open palm. He would lie out perfectly straight, with his body suspended in air." It was an acrobatic trick he performed to entertain his children. "Even late in life he could balance himself like that. His ears stuck out, too, and he used to wiggle them."

Oversized and strong, yet thin. Very thin.

"I don't think he ever recovered from the malnourishment and illnesses he suffered as a child," my mother said. "He had this skin condition as well, hereditary. His skin was very loose, and he could pull it up anywhere on his body. He'd pull it up from his neck and cup his chin with it to make us laugh. He used to say, 'I was meant to be a much larger man. I never really grew into my own skin.'"

My grandfather died long before I was born, but echoes of him ran through my childhood. We came from Protestant stock. Or did we? There were so many unanswered questions. Details that didn't line up. Dates that didn't jibe. And one photograph in particular that my mother came across in an album of his. It showed him as a little boy, well dressed and smiling, standing in a garden at the bottom of a sweeping staircase. Where was that photo taken? No one seemed to know. Among my mother's siblings and cousins the tales grew of a tragic love affair, of hidden Catholic roots, a family dispossessed, an estate forfeited. A young Catholic girl and a Protestant lord, perhaps? A lost manor, a lost title, even? In the absence of evidence the imagination soars.

My grandfather was an Ulsterman: John Richard Bell, known as Richard. A good Protestant name, that. Only problem was, as we would later discover, John Richard Bell didn't exist. The name "Bell" had been given to him by the orphanage; that was what his children suspected. Another possibility, of course, was that he wasn't a long-lost lord at all, but simply a street urchin rescued from the back alleys of Belfast, a gypsy perhaps. This was the version I favoured when I was young and aching to travel.

Northern Ireland held the key to my grandfather's past, to my family's past, to my past. It was always there in the background, and my desire to walk across the hills and valleys of Ulster, to walk my way into an understanding of where I'd come from, bubbled for years like a kettle on low heat. When my wife, baffled by my fixation, asked me why it was so important, I said, "It's about *family*. It's about home."

It was also about denial.

We all wake up at some point, I suppose, and realize that our days of hitting the road, fearless and free, are coming to an end, and any trace of gypsy we might have claimed for ourselves is fading, and fading fast. I wanted to fool myself into believing in a younger narrative, into believing I had one more adventure inside of me, *that I was meant to be a much bigger man.*

I hadn't wanted to do it alone. Tackling the Ulster Way seemed a daunting undertaking. Being sociable by nature, I would have much preferred a companion, maybe even a Sherpa guide or two, or a plump team leader, but any friends with eight weeks to spare (layabouts, in other words) balked once I explained the route to them. "Ireland!" they'd say. "Terrific! Count me in." "Great," I'd say. "We start just outside of Belfast ..." and that would be that. *Belfast?* "C'mon," I'd say. "It's not like the world changes into a grim black-and-white photograph when you cross the border. As long as we don't wave a Union Jack in Republican areas or an Irish tricolour in Unionist areas, we'll be fine." But nothing doing. You'd think I was asking them to go for a stroll through Baghdad.

Nor am I especially athletic. When I went to get my passport renewed, I had to run up two flights of stairs to make it to the immigration office before it closed. I arrived red-faced and out of breath. As I stood, bent over, hands on knees, gasping for air, the clerk asked, "Purpose of visit?" After a moment, I replied, "I'm going to ... to walk across the, ah ... the north of ... *wheeze* ... of ... Ireland."

There was a long pause. "*Why?*"

It was a question that would haunt me often over the course of the next two months.

A PARTIAL CONQUEST

On the train out of Belfast, past the docks and along the lough, I see the twin profiles of Samson and Goliath slip by. They signify to visitors that they have entered a land of battling giants. Those two shipyard cranes, so named, sit above the city docks, defining the harbour skyline. The *Titanic* was built in the shipyards of Belfast; it sailed from those docks, down this lough. Still a sensitive topic, that, and even today, when asked about the *Titanic*, people in Belfast will tell you, "*It was fine when it left.*"

I'd arrived in Northern Ireland late in the season, and the hills beyond the city wore the last days of summer like a cotton dress, loose and light and moving on the wind. I got off the train at Carrickfergus, on the shores of Belfast Lough. It was from this deep saltwater inlet that the fifth-century Celtic chieftain Fergus first set sail, crossing the North Channel and taking Gaelic customs and language to that far shore. The nation he founded would become known by its Roman name: *Scotti*. It was from Carrickfergus that the Gaelic colonization of Scotland was launched, and it was into this lough that Fergus returned, homesick for the hills of Ulster, only to founder on the rocks that now bear his name. My father's family claims a direct kinship with Fergus of Scotland—and through Fergus, back again to Ulster. Both sides of my past, Irish and Scots, seemed to have conspired to bring me here, to this shore.

At Carrickfergus an eight-hundred-year-old castle juts out into the water on an outcrop of rock, seems like a rock itself: a solid mass with a square keep and rounded guard towers. When Irish historians speak of "eight centuries of English oppression," they begin with the Norman invasion of 1169 and the clash between chain-mailed foreign knights and wild Gaelic chieftains. One small band of invaders rode north from Dublin in 1177 under John de Courcy to claim Ulster. They fought their way in, brought the Celts to heel, held back challenges from competing Norman conquerors, and built a series of stone defenceworks along the coast, the most important of which was at Carrickfergus. It's the finest surviving castle of its era in Ireland and the only intact Norman keep in the North.

The Norman invaders never conquered the entire island, and they weren't exactly English, either. They were, rather, the French-speaking descendants of Viking marauders who had settled in northern France and then branched out into Wales. Even worse, they had been *invited* onto the island, by an Irish chieftain no less, a man who was feuding with one of his rivals over a wife he had seduced—or abducted, depending on which version you were partial to. He sought aid from Henry II, a French-born, French-speaking, French-Norman king for whom England was only one part of his empire. Henry II had earlier been granted a charter to subjugate and "civilize" the Irish by Pope Adrian IV, who was—*aha!*—an Englishman. (Trace any thread of Irish history back far enough and you will eventually come to an English villain. Nationalists are particularly good at this.)

The Normans would settle and be absorbed into Irish culture, would become *Hibernis ipsis Hiberniores*, "more Irish than the Irish themselves." They would be known as the Old English, though, really, New Irish would have been more accurate, and the area of "English" control would shrink over the centuries until it was little more than the region around Dublin known as The Pale (whence comes the phrase "beyond the pale"). The Anglo-Norman conquest of Ireland was anything but.

It was under the Tudors that the subjugation of Ireland began in earnest, became systematic, reaching its peak with Elizabeth I. Though she *said* she preferred to "bring in that rude and barbarous nation to civility by discreet handling rather than by force," her actions belied that, and under her reign Ireland was hammered into submission. By the time of her death in 1603, Gaelic resistance appeared to have been crushed.

Ireland has always presented a problem for England, too distant to be fully assimilated, too near at hand to be ignored. It was a back door that needed barring. The danger that England's enemies would use Ireland as a base was very real. Irish rebels often turned to Spain, Germany, France—and later, to the United States—to help them in their struggle, and it became a self-fulfilling phobia on the part of the English: the more they clamped down, the more the Irish rebelled, and the more the Irish rebelled, the more they sought help among England's enemies.

The last region to defy English authority was Ulster, and this remains one of the great ironies of Irish history: the final stronghold of Gaelic society would become the most staunchly British area of Ireland. It was in the North that the chieftains made their stand, and it was here that Gaelic laws, religion and customs survived the longest. Which is why the Protestant Plantation of Ulster, as the colonization of the North was known, became such a violent and contentious undertaking. The North had to be subdued, and its Gaelic leaders checked. It was precisely *because* Ulster was so defiantly "Irish" that England undertook a relentless colonization of that region. When the Gaelic earls fled in 1607, sailing for continental Europe, abandoning their estates and leaving the native Irish leaderless and adrift, England pounced. Entire counties were confiscated and redistributed.

The Plantation of Ulster saw a massive influx of Protestant colonists arrive, many of them Old Testament Scots Presbyterians, dissenters with stubborn defiance woven into their DNA. Together with the old-money Church of Ireland Anglicans, they left an indefatigable mark upon the land. Most of Northern Ireland's towns—and virtually all of its inland communities—were either founded or redesigned by Plantation Protestants; they shaped the Ulster we see today. It is a contribution that is often undervalued.

Theirs was an incomplete conquest, though, and the Plantation of Ulster was a messy patchwork of opposing claims. There was no clear Protestant-Scots/Catholic-Irish divide, no Hadrian's Wall to separate the two. The displacement of the old order was intermixed with the arrival of the new, and Ulster's competing loyalties remain, the two sides as interlocked and interlinked, as segregated and divided, as unconquered and unconquerable as ever. Had the Plantation failed utterly, or succeeded fully, the North would be a much quieter and more peaceful place. As it was, the Plantation was a *partial* conquest, the worst possible outcome. A religious standoff became enshrined as a way of life, and it would set the template for much of what was to come.

My father's family were Cape Breton coal miners who had left Scotland almost en masse, an entire contingent of Fergusons setting sail. My Irish side consisted of a single orphan, travelling alone to the New World, his brother waiting for him on the other side.

History had brought me here, to County Antrim, to the shores of Belfast Lough. It was from this lough that my grandfather had once sailed, had left Belfast behind, had shed Ireland, shed Ulster. I stood, face to the wind, looking out across the water. Had it been at night? I wondered. Had he seen the castle at Carrickfergus slip by? Seen the sea open up ahead?

FOUR KINDS OF CLOUD

In the bedroom community of Whiteabbey, I sat on a park bench adjusting my pack. It was raining back in Belfast, I could see it in the distance, and I watched Samson and Goliath dissolve into the mist. A sign posted nearby warned walkers to "Beware Unexpected Waves," which struck me as not particularly helpful. One might as well put up notices advising people to "Avoid Unexpected Bomb Blasts."

I slung my pack up and onto my shoulders, stumbled backward, lurched forward. Waymarkers beside the road pointed me inland, to the Knockagh hills. The Ulster Way signs featured a cartoon-like silhouette of a walker, pack on back, stick in hand. It was an image that would guide me, entice me, betray me and taunt me throughout the next five hundred–odd miles. No matter. I had taken that first lunging step. Like John de Courcy, I too would conquer Ulster.

The route draws you in slowly. Past a pale church, I followed a wooded stream along a path veined with roots, then scrambled up, out of breath, into the middle of a grim housing estate where sectarian slogans were scrawled across backyard walls. Churches, quiet greenery and simmering political standoffs, all within the first ten minutes on the trail.

I trod on, feet feeling thick, trying to find a plodding pace I could call my own, along a gummy track beside a bus yard depot. A huddle of teenage schoolboys were crowded around a single cigarette, puffing furtively. I sniffed the air: just tobacco. Girls in a flurry of knees and tossed hair swarmed by. Showing a lot of leg, those demure lassies, and I don't imagine schools in Northern Ireland are issuing miniskirts as part of their uniforms, so they must have been hitching them up—the better to torment the boys.

They say that every ounce of gear you pack in the morning equals a pound at night. By the time this day was over, I would be carrying a small Ford Pinto on my back.

Onward I hobbled. Mist, turning to rain, falling softly. Ah, but I was ready for that: I knew it was the rain that gave Ulster its lush, almost tropical feel. It was the rains that kept the rivers rolling, peaty but clean, and it was the rains that threw rainbows across the landscape. I stopped. Slung my backpack onto the side of the road, unzipped the top, removed the pouch with my rain gear in it, unfolded the jacket and pants, pulled them on, buttoned them up and then tightened the shoulder straps on my pack to compensate for the shift in volume—at which point, it stopped raining. Just as quickly, a stifling humidity set in. I took off my pack, removed my rain gear, folded it back into its prearranged pouch, reattached myself, tightened the hip brace on my backpack, adjusted the shoulder straps to compensate for the shift of weight onto my hips, then adjusted the hips to relieve the shoulders. At which point, it started to rain. I had wrestled my rain gear back out and taken two steps forward when, right on cue, the sun burst out again like an actress milking an ovation. Cursing loudly—scatological references and blasphemy, mainly—I stuffed my rain gear away again, punching it down when it wouldn't fit, and stomped onward.

So it went: rain, heat, humidity, rain, *refrain*, as I entered the forests of Knockagh, climbing upward along a narrow road.

From the castle at Carrickfergus the day before, I'd seen the County Antrim War Memorial on its bald cap of hill above the trees, obelisk sticking up like a pushpin. Near at hand, it had seemed, though today I wasn't so sure. The memorial had long slipped out of sight, but I knew it was up there en route, on the summit, the first leg of the first day of the rest of my life. A cement farm track branched off toward the top. All that stood in my way was one final steep climb. A mere trifle! A warm-up for what was to come. I cinched my pack tighter and headed up.

By the time I reached the war memorial, I was clinically dead. I stumbled out into the clearing on the top of Knockagh Hill, legs buckling with every farcical step, face flushed and chest heaving like the bosom of a pulp-novel heroine. My NASA-designed backpack had revealed its true intent and was trying to drag me down onto my knees. It succeeded. I collapsed in front of the obelisk, rolled over onto my pack, tortoise-like, grappling feebly with the various straps that were holding me captive.

Above: clouds on a field of blue.

Back home at my kitchen table, maps bespread and confidence high, I had studied meteorological guides to clouds, had memorized the different formations one might see, had familiarized myself with the sort of weather they forebode. By cleverly reading these signs in the sky, my guidebooks assured me, I would be able to predict the future. Cumulus clouds, for example, when white and rounded, indicate good weather. If they are *anvil-shaped* and cumulus, however, they are a portent of bad weather. Stratus clouds, thin and layered, bring light showers *if* they become hazy. Cirrus clouds, or "mare's tails" to those of us in the know, are wispy and high-altitude; if they start to descend—and you will know they are descending when they appear to thicken—they signal a coming change in air temperature that can cause sudden rain bursts and quick winds.

That day at the Antrim War Memorial, on my back and looking up, I saw every one of those major cloud formations: fluffy white clouds, both rounded and anvil, with a haze of stratus to one side and wispy white cirrus behind. *Welcome to Northern Ireland.*

Groping at my clasps, I eventually popped the right combination and managed to slither free. My shirt was plastered with sweat.

"Eight miles down," I wheezed. "Four hundred and fifty-two to go."

The Antrim War Memorial was a lot less heroic up close. It seemed to be made of discount cinder blocks, and the attached message, commemorating the County Antrim men who had died with "knightly virtue," displayed the dates "1939– 945," the second "1" having fallen off and never been replaced. Or maybe it was never there to begin with; maybe the memorial was counting backward into time. In Northern Ireland, where the past looms so large in the rear-view mirror, always closer than it seems, that too would be apt.

From the hill I'd scaled, I had a full panorama of Belfast Lough, from the city to the sea, with green fields laid out across the hills and the castle at Carrickfergus crouching on the shore below. I had done John de Courcy proud. Indeed, part of me was tempted to quit while I was ahead. Go back into town, ensconce myself in a pub, tell people, "The Ulster Way? Well, I've walked *part* of it."

But no. Onward I went, through the forest, past the squishy edges of a woodland reservoir, aiming for the next valley across the next hill. I found it, but not without tribulation.

NOW, I'D EXPECTED to get lost on occasion, had expected to lose the trail at times, but not on my very first day. I had arrived well armed, after all. I was toting several guidebooks and every relevant Ordnance Survey map, with their many contours and elevations drawn in detail; the Ulster Way was often marked in a Morse code of red dashes. They really are remarkable, those Ordnance Survey sheets:

so detailed they show individual houses. So detailed they even have *telephone booths* marked, which would prove to be my salvation on that first day when I took a wrong turn in the forest. Because, as I quickly discovered, all the meticulous cartographic details in the world won't help if you don't know where you are on the map. Intersections that looked so crisp on the page were maddeningly messy up close. Trails branched and then branched again without a waymarker to aid me—leading me deeper into a dark forest of spruce and pine, as a niggling suspicion grew that I was Off Route. This is not a good state in which to find yourself. Off Route sounds better than Utterly Lost, but it amounts to much the same thing.

I came out at a lonely road unrolling through the forest, studied my map, the road. Nothing matched. I could see a sole farmyard in the distance, carved out of the woods, and I walked toward it, thinking I might ask the (assuredly beautiful) daughter within for directions, maybe enjoy a cup of sun-dappled tea, some flirtatious chitchat, but no one was about, beautiful or otherwise, and I continued down the road.

The valley below presented a view of green fields and rolling hills, with rounded dark headlands rising up beyond them, barren-topped and ominous. But where was I? At a T in the road I came upon another farmhouse. Again, no one home. Where were Ulster's daughters when you needed them?

So. Which way to go? I was just about to flip a coin when I saw it, set back on a grassy verge in the forested hill: a telephone booth. Inexplicable, but very useful. A key point of reference, that. I checked the Ordnance Survey, found the phone booth as marked, and everything clicked into place. I could now line reality up with the map, and vice versa. *You gotta love that attention to detail. Thank you, Ordnance Surveyors!*

Man, was I Off Route.

I followed the road down a gentle slope that might have been pleasant were it not for the moments of sheer terror that punctuated my walk. The drivers in Ulster always seemed to be fleeing the scene of a crime. A quiet road, but what it lacked in numbers it more than made up for in speed, with drivers hurling themselves madly around corners and over blind crests, airborne for the most part, never expecting to come across a lone backpacker and, as such, refusing to accept my existence. The road I was walking had high hedges on either side, so my options were limited. Too narrow for pedestrians—too narrow for cars, really—it squeezed traffic through like pigs down a python as I flung myself into the underbrush on every passing.

Along the way, I passed a waymarker showing me where I *should* have come out of the forest, and I adjusted the tally accordingly: *a five-hundred-and-sixty-TWO-mile walk across Northern Ireland.*

The skies had cleared, and the late-afternoon sun was hitting the heights ahead, lighting up forests and fields alike. The entire landscape was glowing green, almost fluorescent. I took a deep breath and smiled—smiled in spite of everything, in spite of the dead weight of my backpack, the clammy damp of my clothes, the ache in my back, the pain in my knees. *Life was good.* And then it started to rain.

"Now where the hell did that come from?" I shouted, staring up at the sky. In Northern Ireland, I realized, you didn't need clouds for it to rain.

THE PRIDE OF BALLYNURE

An Ulster Way waymarker guided me along the last few yards into Ballynure in much the way ground crews will bring an airplane in after it's already crossed the Atlantic.

The first pub I came across, I entered: the Ballad Inn. The establishment had a single interior but two different doors, one marked "lounge" and the other "bar." After downing a pint of lager in one extended gulp, I asked the lady behind the counter what the distinction was.

"Lounges're more for evenings, right? More for entertainment, like?" She spoke with a rising lilt, as though she herself were not sure. "Bars are more for drinking?"

"Well, then," I said. "I came to the right place," and I ordered another pint.

The heart of Ballynure was a small clutch of buildings, mostly grey, mostly stucco. The downtown, such as it was, consisted of a barber shop, said pub, a large Presbyterian church and a HUGE butcher shop, brightly lit and with a sizeable parking lot beside. Union Jacks were all aflutter over Ballynure, marking it as Protestant territory, in case the oversized church were not evidence enough. I knew Ballynure mainly from swashbuckling tales of old as the home of legendary eighteenth-century bounty hunter John McRea, who once chased cutthroats and highwaymen across the moors. I hadn't counted on JACKSONS BUTCHER SHOP being the prime attraction.

I went inside, admired the meat on offer: slabs of pork, wads of beef, splays of poultry. *Surely the people in this small village can't consume all of this,* I thought.

"Must be hard being a vegetarian in Ballynure," I said.

"Aye," said the young man behind the counter, ruddy of face and large of hand, as he pushed a pork shank through a saw blade. He looked over at me with a grin even as the blade was cutting bone. (Not his, thankfully.) "We're famous, so we are. The pride of Ballynure."

"Really?"

"Aye. They come t'Ballynure from all over."

"All over?"

"Aye, from Ballyclare, Ballymena, Ballymoney even."

I had no idea if I should be impressed by this. "You cut 'em thick," I said.

"Really?" he asked, his interest piqued. "I would have thought yer steaks in America would be bigger." My accent had already outed me.

"Canada, actually. I'm, ah, Canadian."

"I see," he said, and the conversation sort of fizzled.

Being a Canadian in Europe is a lot like being Welsh in North America: no one really cares. It's not that they hold it against you. If anything, they have a vaguely positive image, a sort of benign lack of interest, as it were. "Canadian? That's terrific." "*Welsh, you say? Good for you.*"

"Back where I'm from we tend to eat our meat in thinner slices," I said. Like, under four inches.

"Aye? Well, we have to cut 'em thick over here. No choice, really. We cut 'em to fit the size of our mouths, you see."

Was that a quip? Had I just been quipped?

"What are you for then?" he asked.

Much as I'd have loved a fat raw steak, I had a bus to catch to the next town and a backpack to lug. "Can't," I said. "Just window shopping." And then, suddenly, "I'm walking the Ulster Way. The entire thing in one go."

"Are ya? And how's that workin' out?"

"So far, so good."

He nodded.

"Except for the rain," I said.

"Rain? There's been no rain."

I looked outside at the puddles. "But it rained," I said. "Three times on the way in."

"Tha' wee mizzle?" he said. "That wasn't rain."

"Well," I said. "There was water, and it was falling from the sky. I don't have a dictionary handy, but I'm fairly sure—"

"That wasn't rain," he insisted, all empirical evidence to the contrary.

Turns out, in Ulster, unless you are drenched to the bone and facing imminent hypothermia, it doesn't count. Nor was it cumulative, as I'd discover. Three "showers"—those anemic, namby-pamby Percy pants of the meteorological world, hardly worth commenting on—did not combine to equal one "rain."

An older man, rounder and even ruddier, chuckled at this. He was feeding meat into a grinder and had been listening in. "If yer plannin' to be hikin' up here, get used to being wet," he said. "And anyway," he wiped his hands on a towel, "there's no such thing as bad weather, just the wrong clothing."

"Is it hard unnerstannin us?" the younger fellow wanted to know. "The accent an' all?"

"Well, you do speak fast in Northern Ireland."

"*Ach*," they brushed this aside. "We don't talk fast. You lot listen slow."

The door jingled and a customer came in. "Michael!" cried the older butcher. "How many sausage pies today?"

Michael was a thin young man in a road-crew fluorescent vest, off the job and looking sleepy. He said, "Just the six. I have to watch my diet."

"We hardly see you out and about anymore. New wife has you whipped, does she?"

"Just tired is all. Six pies, then."

"Tired?" said the older butcher with a laugh. "Try cuttin' meat for a living."

Michael of the road crew scoffed at this. He'd been working split shifts, early mornings and late afternoons. "Listen," he said, "I'm out working while youse are still asleep."

"Now then, Michael, I take umbrage at that. It's dark when I get up, I can tell you."

"Sure, it's dark," said the crewman. "Till you open yer eyes."

This, they decided, was a fine piece of craic, and they laughed their approval.

"He's got you there, Da," said the younger butcher.

And on it went, the longest possible route from point A to point B: Ulstermen in conversation. In times gone by, the English upper crust amused themselves by coming up with cute collective names for certain groupings: a murder of crows, a bevy of girls. Had they gotten around to this island, I have no doubt it would have been "a banter of Irish."

Here's the thing, though. That B&B back in Belfast? Protestant. That butcher shop in Ballynure? Protestant.

In Northern Ireland, the Prods have a reputation for being prickly, for being personally reserved but politically belligerent, businesslike yet frugal, both tight-lipped and tight-fisted, as it were, while the Catholics are perceived as warmly garrulous and mystically

Celtic. These aren't stereotypes imposed from outside, they are self-perpetuated. There are those who would claim the Protestants of Ulster are not even Irish at all, but "British," though I'm not sure what that means culturally. It certainly doesn't mean English; the Northern Protestants are far closer in culture and character to the Scots than the English, as their shared roots attest. Many of the Plantation Protestants who came over from Scotland spoke Gaelic. And it's important to note that the Irish Sea and the North Channel were not barriers, but part of a highway, one that joined a shared "culture province" encompassing southern Scotland and northern Ireland. It was a culture united rather than divided by the sea. To some, the arrival of Gaelic-speaking Scots was seen almost as a homecoming. The key difference? The Scots had been swept up in the Reformation; they arrived as Protestants. Their Gaelic cousins in Ulster had remained Catholic, and this would prove a fatal divide, reflected today in the political divisions between those in Northern Ireland (predominantly Protestant) who want to remain in the UK, and those in Northern Ireland (predominantly Catholic) who want to join the Republic. Nationalists in Northern Ireland will tell you, adamantly, that they themselves are *not* British. Not in the least. But the money is pound sterling, the distances are in miles, the British prime minister is their prime minister and so on. The citizenship, the laws, the passports—British. More importantly, the 1998 Good Friday Agreement, overwhelmingly supported by the Nationalist community, explicitly recognizes the people of Northern Ireland as British citizens. It seems to me you can't cherry pick. To accept the Good Friday Agreement and then dismiss one's British citizenship is a bit much, no?

Many Unionists insist just as adamantly that they are *not* Irish, not in the least—which is sort of like denying gravity. After four hundred years in this beautiful corner of this beautiful isle, they are as much entangled in and defined by Ireland as anyone else. *Northern Irish*, to be sure, but Irish nonetheless. To be a colonial is to be born into exile. Such is the case of Britain's Ulster outpost: to visitors it is painfully evident that the people here are Irish. Protestant Irish. Ulster Irish.

Unionist Irish. Loyal Irish. *British* Irish—however you want to slice it. But Irish still.

The average Protestant is taciturn. Perhaps. But if so, he is taciturn ... *for an Irishman*. In the same way that I would be considered svelte ... *for a sumo wrestler*. Or tall ... *for a pygmy*. A "taciturn Irishman" is still very chatty. As I would discover, it is a friendliness that is guarded at times, but always sincere. *Tersely chatty*, as it were. Over the course of my trek, the one thing I learned to rely on, other than the unpredictability of the weather, was the kindness of the people, whether Protestant or Catholic, Prod or Fenian. Why they couldn't show this same generosity of spirit to each other was something I never was able to reconcile. "Aye, we love visitors and hate our neighbours" was how it was explained to me.

The father and son in that Ballynure butcher shop: surely they were Irish too? British citizens, Northern Irish. Seems self-evident, and yet ... entire wars have been fought over that point. Families have been slaughtered for it.

SLOGANS AT NIGHTFALL

I arrived at dusk, as the lights began to glow, burning deep within the homes.

"You Are Now Entering Loyalist Larne," the handpainted signs warned, or reassured depending on your background. I'd had to go Off Route (intentionally, this time) in search of accommodation—to the harbour town of Larne. I was wondering if I'd made the right decision ...

The Ulster Way gave Larne a wide berth. It was a grim town with a grim reputation, not all of it undeserved. A haven for bigots, was what I'd been told. A town that had been "ethnically cleansing" its neighbourhoods of Catholics in the same way that Carrickfergus now was. In the same way that Republicans along the border had been systematically cleansing their areas of Protestants—and in much the same manner: threats, beatings, fire bombings, deaths.

Graffiti for the UVF (the Protestant answer to the IRA) stained the sides of many a wall in Larne. All part of the alphabet soup of paramilitary organizations that plagues the North. It made your head spin trying to keep it straight: UVF, UDA, UFF, LVF, IRA, INLA, IPLO, CIRA, RIRA. I knew that, generally, a U (for Ulster) signified Protestant thugs, while an R (for Republican) signified Catholic thugs, but the ongoing internecine feuds among them were a tangle of Gordian proportions, and one I would never be able to sort out.

When the Irish get together, there is nothing they enjoy more than forming a secret society. From the Whiteboys and Oakboys of the 1760s, to the Catholic Defenders and the Protestant Peep o' Day Boys of the 1780s, from Ribbonmen to the Molly Maguires, through to today's IRA and UVF, clandestine societies have been a defining aspect of Irish history. Many of today's public organizations, such as the Orange Lodge and the Ancient Order of Hibernians, began as semi-secret societies. If you get four Irishmen together, it's said you will have five cabals, six conspiracies, seven secret handshakes, a dozen blood oaths and at least two feuds. That sounds like an exaggeration, until you start reading Irish history, especially that of the North. If anything, those numbers are conservative.

Indeed, the first thing that strikes visitors to the North is the stark binary nature of the society. You can chart it out, map the either/or nature of it like a field guide:

Protestant	Catholic
Unionist	Nationalist
Loyalist	Republican
Prods	Taigs

Although the terms "Unionist/Loyalist" and "Nationalist/Republican" are sometimes used interchangeably, "Loyalist" and "Republican" have a nastier edge, suggesting armed paramilitary resistance more than simply a political stance. And as for "Prods" and "Taigs," these would be the insults hurled, the term "Prod" being self-explanatory and "Taig" being an obscure reference to an Irish name. You also hear Catholic nationalists referred to as "Fenian" (usually followed by the word "bastards"), a reference to a failed nineteenth-century rebellion that was named after the legendary *Fianna*, warriors of ancient Irish mythology. Long memories, up here. On it goes:

the Queen	the Pope
Union Jack	Irish tricolour
the red-white-and-blue	the green-white-and-orange
London as distant capital	Dublin as a distant capital
of the heart	of ditto

and, of course, the colour code:

orange	green

Unless the orange is that of the Armagh Gaelic football team—then it is most definitely a *Catholic* orange.

Ironically, the Irish national flag—the green, white and orange— was designed as a unifying emblem, a fact apparently lost on the Loyalists who still burn the Irish flag every July at the bonfires of the Twelfth. These would be the bonfires lit to celebrate the victory of the Protestant King William of Orange over the Catholic King James—in 1690. *Long memories, up here*.

Speaking of which, another important split would be:

1916	1916

These two dates may look the same, but I assure you they refer to two very different 1916s. The *Protestant* 1916 refers to the blood sacrifice at the Battle of the Somme, when the brave boys of Ulster advanced across no man's land into death and glory—and in doing so helped secure the North for Britain. After the sacrifice of the Somme, the loyal Protestants of the North could hardly be shunted aside. This should

not be confused with the *Catholic* 1916, which refers to the blood
sacrifice of the Easter Rising in Dublin, when brave nationalist boys
led a doomed but heroic revolt, one that ended in death and glory—
and in doing so sparked the war that would eventually free Ireland
from British rule. (Never mind that many of the boys who died at the
Somme were Catholic, or that many of the leaders of the 1916 uprising
were Protestant. The binary code doesn't allow for overlap.)

"The Sash"	"The Soldier's Song"
No surrender!	*Tiocfaidh ár Lá!* ("Our Day Will Come!" pronounced *Chucky ar la!*)

Those would be the anthems and respective battle cries.

UVF	IRA

As noted, these would be two of the main armed militant groups,
both illegal, both ruthless.

The UVF (Ulster Volunteer Force) was named for past glories: in
this case the volunteer army that was formed to fight Irish Home Rule
and that later marched off to the Somme. The IRA (Irish Republican
Army) was also named for past glories, in this case the guerrilla army
that fought the British in the Anglo-Irish War that ended with the
formation of the Irish Free State in 1921. Which is to say, the strug-
gles of yesteryear are used to justify the pipe-bomb massacres of today.
In Ulster, the past is always present. Memories don't die in Northern
Ireland, they ferment.

I found it exhausting. It would get so bad that there were times
when, asked "Coffee or tea?," I would think, *Is coffee Protestant? Or
Catholic? And what about tea? Which one should I choose?* (Correct
answer: tea. The coffee is bloody awful.)

I'd been warned that in Northern Ireland slogans had long since
replaced discourse and that most political debate could be reduced to
a mural or a slash of graffiti, a tattoo across knuckles, a cry of "No

surrender!" or "Chucky ar la!" I didn't know if that was true; the people I would meet during my walk seemed relentlessly well informed, but I did notice the powerful shorthand that symbols provided in Northern Ireland. You could scarcely *not* notice it. The most evocative of these symbols, one claimed by both sides, was ancient: the Red Hand of Ulster. It too was flying at Larne as I walked the streets of the harbour town looking for a room. The Red Hand is a historic pan-Ulster emblem, and though the Loyalists have been trying to appropriate it as exclusively their own, it has proven too enduring for that. Forget the Irish tricolour of the southern Republic or the Union Jack of Great Britain: the true flag of Ulster is a severed red hand, held up in an act of stubborn defiance. Its meaning can be traced to a tale of rival clans rowing hard toward the coast of Ulster, each determined to claim the land ahead as their own. They had agreed that whichever band touched the shore first would take possession, and as they drew near, the chieftain on one of the boats hacked off his own hand and flung it. Cut off your nose to spite your face? That's nothing. This is Ulster; they will cut off their hand to win a race.*

The man behind the desk at the hotel had slab arms and Loyalist tattoos, the type of tattoos the IRA sometimes cut off and mailed back to the families of the men they had kidnapped and killed. I walked out into the quiet streets of Larne, looking for a meal. A tang of sea air was blowing in. Lights shone behind drawn curtains. Empty streets. Painted slogans everywhere.

And you wonder …

You wonder what dark loyalties, what secret grievances, what hidden resentments and long-stoked desires for revenge are simmering behind those closed doors, those shuttered panes.

---

*When I told my twelve-year-old son this story, he said "You know what would suck? If you missed."

Part Two

THE GREEN GLENS
OF ANTRIM

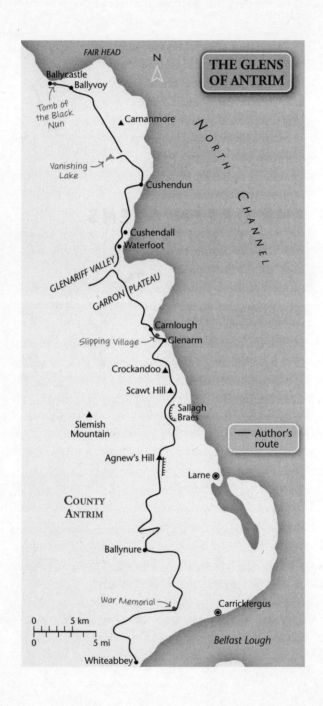

THE GLENS
OF ANTRIM

FAIR HEAD

N

Ballycastle
Ballyvoy
Tomb of
the Black
Nun

Carnanmore ▲

NORTH CHANNEL

Vanishing
Lake

Cushendun ●

Cushendall ●
Waterfoot ●

GLENARIFF VALLEY

GARRON PLATEAU

Carnlough ●
Slipping Village
Glenarm ●

Crockandoo ▲

Scawt Hill ▲

Sallagh
Braes

Slemish ▲
Mountain

Agnew's Hill ▲

Larne ◉

—— Author's
route

COUNTY
ANTRIM

Ballynure ●

War Memorial

Carrickfergus ◉

0   5 km
0   5 mi

Belfast Lough

Whiteabbey ●

BALLYNURE TO BALLYCASTLE
Along the Northeastern Coast

After a deep sleep, enlivened only by charley-horse knots in my calves that knocked me out of bed at one in the morning, I returned to Ballynure quasi-refreshed. It was stiflingly hot, the rains of Belfast having missed the Antrim Glens. If anything, the complaint out here was that the summer had been too hot, too dry—not something one often hears in Ireland, north or south.

I left the bungalows of Ballynure behind, walking my way out of the valley in angled ascent. The road I was following was being very coy, climbing upward on long zig and slow zag. A maddening way to cross a mountain, back and forth on the same flank, ending up only slightly higher after each turn. Even with the oppressive weight of my backpack, I wished the route were more decisive. I would rather have walked straight over the top than follow this slow upward slalom.

I passed a rural schoolyard and, beyond it, limp in the heat, a sag of Union Jacks and droopy Red Hands. This would be the Ballyboley LOL Hall, a squat stucco-on-stucco arrangement on the side of the road. Elsewhere in the world, LOL might be a txt mssge 4 "laugh out loud," but not in Northern Ireland, where it refers instead to the Loyal Orange Lodge. The Orange Order, barely known outside the UK, is a tradition deeply entrenched among Unionists. A fraternal order known for its marches and large Lambeg drums, its orange sashes and bowler hats, it was founded in 1795 after a clash in County Armagh between Catholic Defenders and Protestant Peep o' Day Boys that left dozens dead. Created in the aftermath of a sectarian brawl, the Orange Order has never quite outgrown its roots, try though its moderate members may. Dedicated to the memory of King William of Orange, the lodge aims at preserving the Union and maintaining the Protestant Ascendancy. This is not editorializing on my part; these are the official goals as stated in the Orange Oath.

The Catholics have their own version of the Orange Lodge in the Ancient Order of Hibernians, but the Hibernians have never managed to ignite the same passions—or animosities—that the Orange Order has. For Orangemen, the lodge is a cultural institution, a keystone of Protestant identity, one that defends rather than attacks. To Catholics, it is little more than a society of bigots whose never-ending processions are aimed at reminding them who's in charge. "It's triumphalist," is the complaint one hears. "It provokes." "It's traditional," is the response. "It protects." Personally, I found it hard to see what the fuss was about—on either side. But then, I wasn't raised in Northern Ireland, was neither steeped in Protestant traditions nor threatened by them.

If nothing else, the parking lot out front of LOL No. 458 had a terrific view of quilted fields, sheep drifting across like slow-moving confetti. In the distance, the Key of Hell highlands rose up above Belfast, pale in the haze. (That would be "Cave Hill" as pronounced with an Ulster accent, something that always unnerved me. "Been t' Key of Hell yet? Ye have to go t' Key of Hell. Ye can't come to Norn Iron wit'out goan to Key of Hell!")

The fenceposts in the parking lot at the Ballyboley LOL were painted red, white and blue, and the half-slap of flags on a lacklustre wind was the only sound, save that of my back groaning and my knees whimpering.

I continued my ascent, stopping now and then for a swig of water. With each switchback the vista below got slightly headier. At the

entrance to Ballyboley Forest, I slid my backpack off, knuckled my knotted shoulders. It is not a good idea, unencumbering yourself every time you stop, and I knew it. You should become one with your pack, Zen-like. But Buddha never had to face a muggy Ulster day with a sadistic rucksack clinging to his enlightened shoulders.

I staggered onward, breathing in bugs and walking with the sort of Frankensteinian gait that makes you pity the monster rather than fear him. I had been looking forward to the coolness of the forest, but the humidity followed me in, sapping what little reservoir of strength I had.

The trail wound its way steeply upward, and I passed other hikers coming down. "A brave day," one of them said, and I nodded.

"A very brave day," I replied, not sure what that meant exactly. A grand day? horrid? difficult? imminent thunderstorms and lightning strikes? balaclava gunmen on the road ahead? Brave it was, though, and I tried my best to live up to it.

Another pair of lightly packed daywalkers skipped by. "Have enough gear do you?" they asked.

"Going to Glenarm," I said—gasped, really.

They took a couple of steps, came back. "You're nowhere near Glenarm."

"I know," I said. "Painfully aware of that, in fact."

Okay then. As long as I knew. They wished me the best and headed off.

I eventually emerged at a car park where a highway cut through the forested heights. I was about to stride across when a transport truck cannonballed past, shattering any sense of forest solitude. Having scampered back to the side of the road, I listened ... Waited. Nothing. Gently, gently, I put one toe on the tarmac, and immediately a station wagon flew by, followed by several trucks in hot pursuit that shrieked like Luftwaffe dive bombers in tight formation. I almost ran into myself that time, so quickly did I beat a retreat. I waited. Nothing. I was caught in a real-life game of Frogger, with no do-overs. So I turned, casual-like, hands in my pockets, whistling as though to say,

"I could really care less about crossing," then bolted across without warning, backpack galumphing, before any Ulster drivers caught me in their crosshairs. No bears or snakes in Ireland, but the drivers were doing their part to keep things interesting.

Ahead lay the next challenge: Agnew's Hill, the highest point of the day's hike at 1,555 feet. I secured my pack, guzzled some more water—which seemed to spout instantly from my pores—and set out.

Fortunately, I'd climbed so high by this point that I was looking almost straight across at Agnew's Hill, rather than up at it. What I soon discovered, though, was that this was a blind summit. What I could see was just the first hump. The true summit lay beyond. A cruel trick of topography, that. You drag yourself up the side of a hill, thinking you've made it, and are just about to congratulate yourself, thinking *That wasn't so bad!*, when you're faced with another slog.

The guidebooks I'd entrusted my life to had warned that waymarkers were "scarce" along this section, and by scarce they meant "nonexistent." No problem. I could see a summit rising up in a barren swell; I had only to aim for that, then follow the ridge northward. How hard could it be? I left the forest for the moorlands.

The day was swimming with humidity, and the ground was suction-cupped with patches of mud. Muggy and boggy: *moggy*. It was exhausting picking my way along, not just physically, but mentally as well. I couldn't allow myself to fall into a mindless stupor. I had to focus on every step. If I let my gaze drift upward toward the horizon I would inevitably trip, backpack lurching on my shoulders like a Bedouin astride a camel. And so, I teeter-tottered along, eyes trained four feet in front of me the entire way.

When I reached the final cairn on the final summit, I slouched off my pack, cricked my neck. A haze of heat had settled on the hills, but through it I could see shapes of things to come: the rolling heights ahead that still needed crossing.

I set off across the top of Agnew's Hill—more mountain than hill, really—and soon succeeded in losing the "trail" (heavy, heavy, *heavy* editorial quotation marks on the word "trail"). The heights were

overgrown in heathery bracken, as tiring to wade through as the rock and bog had been earlier. It was like running in deep water, and I floundered about, starting and stopping, balking then backtracking, picking up what I thought was the route only to lose it again. I finally stopped, hands on hips, frowny-face to the wind, utterly befuddled.

No problem! I whipped out my newly purchased compass and adjusted for True North. (I had come prepared.) I watched as the needle swung slowly one way, then *sloooowly* the other, before pointing back toward Ballynure. I shook the compass, took another reading; this time it pointed toward Greenland. Nothing worse than an indecisive compass. I split the difference, adjusted my direction accordingly, strode off ... and immediately toppled down a cliff. Well, no. But I did find myself on a hillock of heather, surrounded on three sides by bog water and wondering what I'd done wrong. Now I knew why people carried walking sticks up here. It wasn't so much for pace as it was to act as a dipstick of sorts, prodding puddles to see how deep the damage would be.

Fortunately, I had another trick almost literally up my sleeve, certainly up my pocket. I pulled out a pair of collapsible binoculars (we're talking *really* prepared) and scanned the horizon. Here's the thing about bogs: the horizon line looks more or less the same whichever way you turn. Picking out the elusive line of waymarkers was no easier for my trouble, so I put the binocs away. I didn't need them to see Slemish Mountain, though. It was unmistakable even in the distance; a volcanic nub rising straight out of the plains, it has one of the most distinctive profiles of any hill in Ireland. It was there, on Slemish, that a young slave boy named Patrick toiled as a shepherd. He was a Christian from a family of aristocratic Britons on the edge of the crumbling Roman Empire, and he had been captured by Irish raiders and sold into servitude. He tended his herd on the slopes of Slemish for six years, and when the time presented itself, he escaped, barefoot, through the howling depths of winter. He escaped Ireland, escaped Ulster, returned to his family estate. They had been praying for his return from pagan captivity. God had guided young Patrick home ... and yet, Ireland had gotten hold of him. That island out there beyond the realm, that island on the edge of the known world, was calling to him. In dreams, voices whispered, beckoned: "*Come back again and walk among us.*" Patrick would heed that call, would return to Ulster, would convert an island, would become Ireland's greatest saint.

If he could make his trek through the howling depths of winter, surely I could cross the same hills in aerodynamic hiking boots. The summit of Agnew's Hill was barren and spongy. Sticky and hot. I'd been hoping for more of a wind at the top, but even the faintest breeze acted like a cooling balm.

A lonely road disappeared into a fold of hill below. I began my descent, but any sense of a path was soon lost in a maze of sheep trails, and when I reached the barbed-wire fence at the bottom I was off track and had to walk along the fence until I found a stile.

It was only then, at the bottom, that the truth about Agnew's Hill slipped into view. Looking up, I could see a sheer dead-drop embankment of stone, a great gash of rock that had been hidden from view at the top. I'd been walking along the edge of a cliff without realizing it. *Good thing it was so clearly waymarked!*

MY COMPASS may have failed me, but the ancient pre-Druidic religions of Ulster did not.

I was heading now toward a standing stone marked on the map, across muggy moorlands with trickles of stream running through. It was as though the landscape itself were perspiring.

The standing stone I was seeking rose up from the moors like a single canine tooth, and I had to admit there was something intrinsically hip about using a Neolithic stone marker as a point of reference. Ulster is scattered with these ancient monuments, most of them pre-Celtic Stone Age and early Bronze. They later became focal points for Gaelic rituals, with Druids using them in sacrificial rites that are lost now in a haze of history. Having arrived at my first such standing stone, I celebrated by drinking what turned out to be the last of my water.

Flinging my pack over the barbed-wire fence between me and the road, I followed the pack over, carefully, using the cross-beams to swing myself across, delicately. You don't want any sudden shifts in mid-manoeuvre, and you certainly want to avoid getting scrotally entangled in barbed wire. I crossed the road and came to the fence running along the other side. This one was even trickier, because the wires were older and slack. Not just barbed wire, but *rusty* barbed wire. I found a boulder I could use, and high-stepped over. Not much farther along, I had to do it all over again. Another fence, another missing stile. Another scrotally endangering high-wire act. More fences appeared, this time fieldstone, built without mortar or brick— or rulers, apparently.

Beyond them, past a purply rise of heather, lay the reason for the day's hike: the cliffs at Sallagh Braes. Coming in from behind, across the moor, there is no indication of the sheer drop that lies on the other side. But when you arrive, there it is. At Sallagh Braes, the world drops away. Below the dramatic horseshoe escarpment, a latticework of green fields spreads out toward a small harbour. A sweep of blue, and beyond that, the coasts of Scotland, milky in the haze.

I'd fought my way along sheep trails, through heathery bracken, over fences barbed and rusty. I'd fought my way across the moors, and it was worth every cursed step. I'd met no one on the trail since I crossed the highway, not a soul, which was a shame. Having arrived at Sallagh Braes—aching and sweaty—I would have loved to have had someone to nudge and say, "Can you believe this?!" You aren't supposed to approach the cliff edge, but how can you not? If you fell, at least you'd die with a hell of a view.

I rummaged around in my backpack, found some beef jerky, ate it while looking out at the vista below. Turns out, and you may want to jot this down, salted dried beef is probably not the best thing to eat when you've run out of water. Had I really finished both canteens already? Answer: yes. Didn't I have a juice box somewhere? Oh, right. I'd drunk that in one fisted squeeze back atop Agnew's Hill. I found the husk of it and wrung a few drops out onto my tongue, but that just made it worse, like flicking water onto a sun-parched desert.

I pushed on, with only the faintest updraft of wind to cool me. My thirst went from niggling to nagging to "Hmm, that pond water doesn't look so bad." I had brought some magic tablets that supposedly turned the murkiest of sludge into pure spring water, but when I rooted for them in the various pockets and secret compartments in my pack, I found nothing. (They were in my jacket pocket, as it later turned out—for easy access, you see.)

Over a headland hump, and another valley opened up below. That would be the oxymoronically named Drains Bog, a smaller version of Sallagh Braes, one that swoops down not to cultivated fields but to scruffy scrublands. I could see the outlines of an ancient fort below, and beside it a parking lot. A parking lot with a *car* in it. Even better, I could see two daywalkers ahead of me picking their way down along a different route. I started hurrying at this point, desperately trying to close the gap, and I burst onto the parking lot waving my arms as the two young men were getting into their car, a small red hatchback.

"Wait!" I croaked.

They turned, watching me as I came stumbling over. "Lost, are you?" they asked.

"No. Not exactly."

"Need a lift, then?"

"I need water."

"Water?"

"I'm very thirsty."

They exchanged looks and then, in that kind Ulster way, laughed at me. "This isn't the bloody Sahara."

"Sure enough," his friend chimed in, "this is Ireland. Stand in a field long enough with yer mouth open and it'll soon fill with water."

"Hasn't … rained much … up here," I said, my throat parched. I wondered if I was getting heatstroke.

"Oh, it'll rain. Death and taxes."

Still, they gave me a bottle of water, warm but unopened, that they had on the floor in the back seat, waved away my offer of money, and drove off shaking their heads.

Just trying to make everyone's day a little more surreal: that's my motto. *"D'ye not remember the time that Yank came ou' from behind a rock pleading for water?"*

THE DAY WAS bleeding away, and I worried about losing light.

Ahead lay Scawt Hill. I pushed on, following a fence up the first hump and over. Waymarkers, sparsely paced: if you squinted one eye and stuck your tongue out the side of your mouth, you could just about see the next one lined up. I followed a trail (maybe even the one I was supposed to be on) out onto the open heights. It was finally starting to cool off. The winds had shifted, in from the coast, and a musky smell came up from the land, as sweet as silage. I was atop an immense thumb of land that pushed forward into the sea. Below me was the wooded cleft of Glenarm Valley, inviting and green. My long day's walk was almost done.

On Ulster's northeast coast a series of valleys fan to the sea. Gouged from the headlands by glaciers, these glens form isolated, fjord-like notches with villages clustered at their mouths, closer in culture and distance to Scotland than to the rest of Ireland. So close to Scotland, in fact, that the chieftains on the Antrim side often lit bonfires to signal their Scottish cousins when they were in trouble. From Scawt, the Mull of Kintyre was so close I could almost run my hand down its sleeping flank.

The Ulster-Scots identity, so central to the Glens, developed largely in isolation. Gaelic-speaking Scots Catholics settled here *before* the Protestant Plantations, and until a coast road was blasted through in the 1830s, these Glens really were a country unto themselves. I'd been prepped by a colleague from Belfast on what to expect when I entered the Glens. "When you get there, turn your clock back fifty years. The men are all seventy-eight years old. They all have tweed hats, a pipe and one tooth. Usually on the bottom."

On the bottom?

"Standard issue."

Antrim was Ireland's Scottish corner, I'd been told by many people. "Go to Ballymena or Ballymoney, you could be in Scotland."

"What," I joked, "the people are tight with their money, are they?"

"Yes. Very Scottish. They know how to turn a penny into a pound."

A trick I have never mastered, alas. I may be Scottish on my father's side, but I've not acquired that particular knack.

The Glens of Antrim are among the most celebrated coastlines of Europe, and I was about to enter them almost by stealth, down the side of Crockandoo Hill and into the wooded valley below.

I descended into a nightmare of bracken. The slopes of Crockandoo were overrun with thorn bushes, and a narrow trail wended its way through. Cattle used this path as well, and it was soon pockmarked with hoofprints and thick with cow flops. This was a good sign, actually. Cows are lazy; they don't meander about if they don't have to. Sheep will happily chew their way in and out of cul-de-sacs, but cows take the line of least resistance. I stuck with the cow flops and came out at a gate, where an Ulster Way signpost congratulated me at having made it through.

Evening always comes so quickly in valleys. At the top of the hills there had still been some light; in the forest below it was already dusk. A church steeple above the trees. A cleft in the headlands, opening onto a sea the colour of moonlight. I couldn't think of a finer way to enter the Glens.

THE BANSHEE OF GLENARM

Down from the hills and the heather, headlong into civilization, into Glenarm, a village of art galleries, cafés and craft shops—the change was as stark as it was sudden. I came in along the pastel-painted homes, powder blues and pale yellows, to where the storefronts formed a continuous wall on either side, with archway passages into backyards. One moment I was a trekker, the next a mere stroller, albeit one with burrs in his hair and mud on his hems.

I can't tell you how happy, how *elated*, I felt to be back among shops and humanity. So elated, in fact, that I walked right through town and was on my way out before I noticed. When I did, luckily, I was standing in front of the last pub in Glenarm. I entered said establishment, downed a flagon of their finest ale and ordered (apparently) the Worst Meal Possible. "*Spare no expense! I want something really horrid.*" Now, I'm not a finicky eater, but I know bad when I see it. My one foray into restaurant reviewing back home had ended when I submitted a too-honest assessment. ("If you've ever wondered what pig saliva tastes like, here's your chance!" Ah, the joys of journalistic anonymity.)

I had passed other cafés on my stroll, and another pub or two, but I have unerring instincts when it comes to this sort of thing. I now faced a chicken that had clearly been drowned and then dispatched with a flame-thrower and a large mallet. The skin was not so much cooked as it was cremated, while the inside, I quickly noted, was a cheerful salmonella pink, the meat still clinging stubbornly to the bone.

"How is it?" asked the lady of the pub.

"Lovely!" I said.

I HAULED my backpack up the main street of Glenarm to a family B&B. They weren't expecting me and didn't have a bed ready, but I finessed my way in using what I admit is a bit of a dirty trick. When I set out to conquer my Ulster Everest, I never quite knew how far I would make it on any given day, even with my route paced out in advance on what would prove to be a wildly optimistic five-week schedule. "What if I wanted to keep going?" I asked myself—aloud, so as to justify the use of quotation marks. "Why, I'd be forced to stop early just because I had a reservation somewhere! Would be a shame if I'd wanted to keep walking." Not that this ever happened. But still. The point is, I never knew with certainty how far I'd get and thus couldn't book my lodgings ahead of time. Instead, I would simply show up at the nearest B&B—in essence, someone's home, B&Bs often being a side business in Northern Ireland, where a family has an extra room or two to let. I would arrive, unannounced, and say, "Hi! The Northern Ireland Tourist Board gave me your number," thereby immediately shifting all responsibility onto them. It wasn't an out-and-out lie, because I had indeed contacted the Northern Ireland Tourist Board before I left, and they had indeed given me a list of B&Bs, hostels and inns along the Ulster Way.

At Glenarm, the lady of the home was very gracious, given that I'd arrived smelling of the bog and dragging a backpack of vaudevillian proportions into their entryway.

"Really?" she asked. "The Tourist Board?"

"Absolutely."

"Aye? Well then, come in, I'll make up a wee bed for you in the back."

Of Ulster's many verbal tics, the ones I found most charming were "aye" and "wee." "Aye" is especially wonderful. It has the scent of the sea about it; it's wizened and wise and sounds so much more intelligent than "yup." Put an "aye" in front of something and it instantly becomes weighty, gains solemn credibility. "*Aye, t'was the leprechauns that killed JFK.*" And you think, *Of course!* Palm slap to the forehead. *That makes perfect sense.*

Likewise with the indiscriminate use of "wee." I'm not sure what "wee" means, but I do know it doesn't mean "small." That's what it *seems* to mean; certainly the room they found for me in the back was a bit "wee," but when I told her I was hiking the Ulster Way, all five hundred and sixty damn miles of it, she said, "A good wee walk then." (No doubt, in Ulster, King Kong would be referred to as "a great wee monkey," Everest as "a tall wee mountain.")

While the lady of the house prepared my bed—I think it may have been one of the children's rooms—I rubbed feeling back into my shoulders, cricked my neck, and tried not to let my body seize up into one extended charley horse. It had taken me all day to get from

Ballynure to Glenarm, and it had almost killed me. I knew there was no way I could keep lugging my entire pack across the Glens, over the highlands, up one valley and into the next. So I made a decision, right then and there, one that would complicate things greatly but would ease the pain in my knees and shoulders considerably. Instead of taking all of my gear with me, I would, wherever possible, take a small day pack instead, setting up base in a town and then making day hikes along the trail from there. After all, did I really need four changes of clothing and a library of guidebooks with me at every moment?

I used Glenarm as my base for the next few days, tackling the Ulster Way in segments, falling back to the village after each walk. This involved taking buses up and down the coast, which was an unexpected bonus—it allowed me to see the Antrim shores in many lights: in early dawn, in evening's glow, in turbulent winds and in calm, in sunshine and in mist, the colours shifting from white chalk to black basalt, from red sandstone to blue-grey clays. I went up and down that coast eight or nine times, and I never got tired of the view. Every shift of light, every change in weather revealed richer nuances of sky and sea and coast.

I was sometimes forced to take a taxi back to where I'd left off the day before, often a rural crossroads or an arbitrary gap in the under-brush. "Let me off ... right ... *there!* By that tree!" I spent hundreds of pounds I had not budgeted for and left behind some very confused taxi drivers. We'd be up on some bogside road, with me leaning forward, and suddenly I'd shout, "Wait wait wait ... *there!* Beside that rock."

Back at the Glenarm B&B, I'd dump my day pack in my bedroom and join the other guests for a cuppa. A full moon outside, a warm milky drink inside. Life was good.

An older couple and their grown son were also staying at the B&B. The parents, expats of Antrim, were on a nostalgic trip through the Glens.

"I was born here," said the mother. "We moved away some forty-five years ago. But you never truly leave a place like this, do you?" She had been telling the lady of the house about a plane crash, years before. "Like it was yesterday."

The plane crash?

"Was during the war, and me mother was down in Larne doin' the shopping, and me brother Morris, he was in charge, even though he was just a wee boy himself. We saw it coming in low, with smoke spewing out, down across the water, right for our house it seemed. I remember wee Morris pushing us back inside and then standing there, holding the door shut as though he could stop it." A soft laugh, a softer sigh. "Missed us. The pilot died. He pulled up, tried to clear the hill past the old quarry, but he didn't quite make it. The wing caught the edge and he burned. The shriek of it, the plane coming in like that, sounded like a banshee."

Her husband, as stocky and earth-rooted as she was wistful, leaned in, asked me, "You've heard of the banshee, then?"

The banshee?

"Of Glenarm. The one stalks Lord Antrim and his family. You know it, then?"

I didn't.

"You've heard of it?"

I hadn't.

"The banshee, it will only follow those who have O' or Mac in their name. The Earl of Antrim and his kin, descended from the MacDonnells, so they are. The banshee of Glenarm, oh, it's got an awful wail, it does. That scream, it cuts right through you."

"You've—you've actually heard it?" I said, trying to mask my incredulity.

"Heard it?" said the father. "Heard it?"

His son rolled his eyes in anticipation of what was coming. "Da ...," he said. But the old man swatted his son's objections aside like a fly. "Heard it? I've *seen* it."

It was like meeting someone who'd spotted Nessie or had a beer with Bigfoot. "You've seen a banshee?"

"Looked like a small wee woman with wings folded back. It was walking along the dockside, waiting for a death so it could start its terrible wail. Say what you want—laugh like my son here—but the Glenarm Banshee is real. Back when I was a lad, the tough boys used to gather at the corner at night. Loud craic and bullyboy words. Aye, they thought they were tough—till a banshee landed in their midst one night, screaming for a soul. And believe me, tough guys or not, they scattered."

"Been drinking, were they?" asked the son. "That's usually when the banshees and fairies start appearin'. Ever notice that, Da?"

The father levelled his gaze at me, challenging me to balk, to smirk. "I saw it," he said. "The Banshee of Glenarm. With me own eyes."

They really do say "me" for "my," I thought. And there really are banshees stalking the Glens of Antrim. This was the moment I realized I had indeed crossed over to the other side of the looking glass.

That night the streets were besieged by the screams of younger banshees: children, setting off fireworks long into the night, amid shouts and squeals and anticlimactic pops. The lighting of them—and the scramble to get away before they went off—was cause for more laughter than any actual pyrotechnics. I lay there, in my wee bed, listening to the banshees, trying to will myself to sleep, trying not to think ahead to when I would next be alone on the moors, or to that quirky family fact: our name was originally MacFergus.

THE CARTOGRAPHY OF PUBS

I liked Glenarm. It had a medieval feel to it. Not in the architecture, necessarily, but in its atmosphere. I suspect it was because, the pastel-painted houses and livelier storefronts aside, the town's more imposing structures—the churches and halls—were slate-grey and sombre. Were you to turn a corner in Glenarm and run into a chain-mailed Norman knight galloping past, you'd hardly blink.

The village had a castle, a lord, several resident ghosts, an old stone bridge or two, and a "whistling wood"—wherein, according to the walking map they hand out, "*on a dark windy night the voices of lost souls may lament their tortured state.*" This in their tourist map, mind you.

Glenarm's roots were certainly medieval. It had long been a MacDonnell stronghold and even now was the site of the Earl of Antrim's estate, making it the hereditary "capital" of the Glens. When you read the history of the Glens, it sometimes feels as though the landscape was merely a backdrop for the raucous rivalries of two great families: the MacDonnells and the O'Neills. The antics of Sorely Boy MacDonnell and his nemesis, rival and sometime ally, Shane O'Neill "the Proud," raged up and down these coasts.

Glenarm Castle was hidden from view, leaving me to stand at the Barbican Gate instead, puzzled as to why I wasn't on the other side of the wall. How was it that I was not among the landed gentry? A mystery for the ages. I would have hammered on the door, maybe challenged the current earl to a duel, but the Barbican Gate had a series of murder holes in it, used to pour burning liquid down on would-be invaders, and I decided, discretion being the better part of valour, to move on.

It was a manly sort of place, Glenarm. Nothing fey or feminine about it, and as I kicked around town on my second day there I fell in with a stocky Englishman named Kim who had moved to Glenarm to open a restaurant.

"You came in through the forest?" Kim asked. He was a sturdy man, ex-army, a walker as well from the looks of it. "It's good you did. Those forests are one of the last major stands of broad-leaf native Irish oak in Ireland. The Earl of Antrim owns those woods. It even has a resident falconer."

Falconer?

"By order of the Earl of Antrim himself."

"That's still a job?"

"It is."

Man. I wanted that on my business card: *W. Ferguson, Resident Falconer.*

Kim took me on a rambling tour of Glenarm, pointing out the homes of various eccentrics and oddballs and giving me a crash course in local history. He explained the cartography of pubs in Glenarm as well. There was an Anglican pub, quite modern; a Catholic pub, which was more traditional; and a Presbyterian pub, filled, when I popped in, anyway, with dour, unsmiling patrons. Which is to say, it was traditional Presbyterian. There was also a middle-ground pub where both sides could drink and eye each other warily across pints of dark ale. Glenarm was considered a mixed community—mixed, but not intermingling, to judge by the pubs.

Kim turned to me. "You've heard the joke?" And indeed, I had. It should almost come in caps: The Joke. "An American—but you could just as easily tell it of a Canadian," he said quickly. "A tourist. A Canadian tourist, let's say. He's walking through Belfast at night, and he feels a gun barrel push against his back, and a voice whispers, 'Are ye a Catholic or a Protestant?' The quick-thinking American—or Canadian—replies, 'I'm Jewish!' 'Never mind that,' says the Irishman. 'Are ye a Catholic Jew or a Protestant Jew?'"

I'd heard another version involving an atheist: "Are ye a Catholic atheist or a Protestant atheist?" Both rang true.

"The interesting thing," said Kim, "is that it's a joke the Irish tell about themselves. They think it's funny. It's an acknowledgment that they *are* insular, and they know that they are, and yet—"

"They don't care," I said.

Kim smiled. "Perhaps … I'm sure there's a lesson there somewhere."

I countered with a joke of my own, one Kim hadn't heard before. In fact, as I travelled, I told it again and again—and no one ever seemed to know it. It got a warm response, from laughter to sage nods of agreement: "*Aye, that's us all right.*" I like to think I introduced this joke to Northern Ireland. So, next time you're in the northern reaches of the Emerald Isle and someone tells you the following tale, you will know whence it came.

An Irish farmer finds a genie and is granted a single wish. "Anything you desire," says the genie. "There is but one condition. In the spirit of reconciliation, whatever you ask for, I will also give to your neighbour—double."

The Irishman thinks long and hard, and then says, "Can you put out one of me eyes?"

KIM AND HIS WIFE were raising twin girls in Glenarm, and he took a certain proprietorial pride in the town. Wherever we went, he was constantly stooping to get litter, like someone picking lint from a sweater. As we tromped through the tall grasses of a graveyard, the sound of one of his footsteps came back as a crinkle, and Kim stopped to pull the reeds away. He disentangled a two-litre plastic Coke container and carried it with him until he could discard it.

On an earlier walkabout, I had spotted great, straight-backed letters painted across a building inside the Catholic church grounds: LOVE. This stopped me. I had seen similarly painted Loyalist tags, UVF and UDA and LVF ... but LOVE? What kind of paramilitary militia would choose an acronym that spelled LOVE?

As it turns out, this was a subversion of subversion. It was, as Kim explained, a turnaround. "Protestant extremists had painted UVF on the side of the building. The local priest, Father Henry I think his name was, climbed up on a scaffolding and—rather than paint over the original graffiti—simply added an L at the start, and then turned the U into an O, the F into an E. It changed U-V-F into L-O-V-E."

On the edge of town, the Glenarm police station stood barricaded behind high walls and barbed wire. The IRA had long ago declared war on the Royal Ulster Constabulary, Northern Ireland's legendary—or infamous, depending on your point of view—police force. As a result of the Republican campaign, police barracks, even here amid the quiet rural calm of Antrim, had been transformed into fortresses: the modern equivalent of Norman keeps. I would never get used to the jarring sight of these barricaded stations, or to the astounding fact that, in Northern Ireland, the same police officers who went about writing traffic tickets and investigating stolen bicycles were locked in a death battle against IRA gunmen. That the RUC managed to maintain any semblance of normal police work was astounding. In Northern Ireland, there was a clear distinction between what the police wryly called "ODC" (Ordinary Decent Crime) and the uglier political forms of violence. Someone gets drunk, picks a fight with a bouncer: that's ordinary decent crime. Someone breaks into a home and steals a telly: that too is ordinary decent crime—unless, of course, the burglar is a Catholic and the target is a Protestant (or vice versa), in which case it is "ugly sectarianism at its worst" and denounced as such by the appropriate political spokesperson.

Although often demonized in Ireland, the RUC had gained an international reputation as one of the best-trained police forces in the world. They were among the most highly decorated as well, and during the height of the Troubles they were the police force with the highest fatality rate *in the world*. The second most dangerous place to be a police officer at that time? El Salvador. And the fatality rate among police officers in Northern Ireland was *twice* as high as that in El Salvador. The RUC were predominantly Protestant, though the fact that the IRA and other Republican groups had declared the RUC "legitimate targets" and had threatened to kill any Catholics who joined the force might have had something to do with the low levels of recruiting among the Catholic community. To many nationalists, the RUC were cartoonish villains, in cahoots with Loyalist paramilitaries. There were certainly cases of RUC officers—especially within the Special Branch—feeding information to the Loyalists, using them as assassins by proxy, or even pulling the trigger themselves, just as there were cases of Garda officers in the Republic feeding information to the IRA. (One pair of officers in the Republic of Ireland was suspected of helping to arrange more than a dozen murders, with many of the victims RUC.) But to claim that the RUC were in collusion with Loyalist paramilitaries was hyperbole, akin to saying all Catholics are terrorists and all Protestants are bigots.

I had arrived during a pivotal moment in history, when the RUC were preparing to stand down. Under the terms of the Good Friday Agreement, the force would be reorganized and renamed: it would actively recruit and reserve spots for Catholics (the IRA had agreed not to kill them if they did) and would rid itself of the term "Royal" and of any overtly British symbolism. It would become the Police Service of Northern Ireland (PSNI) and would focus as much as possible on ordinary decent crime.

In Northern Ireland, however, the barricades were still up. Officers had to be careful even when having a drink at their local pub, Protestant or not, and still could not talk openly about what they did for a living for fear of ambush and execution. They still served, often-times lived, behind steel doors and watchtowers, under siege. There was no LOVE written on RUC walls.

MOSCOW JOE AND BOBO THE BRAVE

Unencumbered, carrying a mere shoulder-toss of a day pack, I continued my walks from glen to glen. Breezy strolls, were it not for the extra fifty pounds of food I carried in my gut. With stomach thus packed, they sent you waddling out into the world. "*Let's see you cross a hill with that in your gullet!*" The good news in this was that it often took me the better part of a day to walk off an Ulster Fry, so I rarely needed lunch, just a power bar or two along the way.

One morning, free of my main pack but still weighted down with Ulster hospitality, I headed for Carnlough, following the old Straidkilly Road above the coast, as cars competed to see how close they could come without actually hitting me. I was still getting used to the narrowness of Ulster roads and the recklessness of its drivers. An odd species, that: equal parts derring-do and death wish, yet with an odd veneer of calm. Three tractors roared by in quick succession, driven by fourteen-year-old boys who had not yet had to grapple with either the proper shifting of gears or the heavy implications of human mortality, specifically my own. A short while later two more tractors careened by the other way, kicking back clods of mud at me and leaving a waft of diesel fumes in their wake.

The road led through Straidkilly proper, just a handful of houses really, old and new, scattered along the road. I'd been keen on visiting Straidkilly ever since I'd heard that it was sliding into the sea. "You go to sleep at night, and you could wake up in the morning on the Bay Road" was how the lady in the corner store at Glenarm had put it. The buildings were built atop packed clay that was slowly shifting underneath. Straidkilly is called the "Slipping Village," and let me tell you, is it ever *not* worth visiting. The houses aren't sliding into the sea right before your eyes or anything; the rate is roughly one inch per year. I stood awhile, trying to will some sort of stop-motion visual effect, hoping maybe for a sudden lurch from one of the bungalows, but no, the houses were most definitely not creeping downhill like architectural triffids. I wasn't even sure I was in the right village. If it was North America there would have been a huge billboard: "Welcome to the Village that is SLIDING INTO THE SEA!" with a painting of houses whisking down slopes as the inhabitants leapt from their windows. There would have been a Slide-o-Rama Amusement Park and souvenir shops selling apparel emblazoned with messages like "My Mom and Dad went to the Sliding Village and all I got was this stupid T-shirt" and risqué postcards for the parents: "Did the Earth move for you too?"

A sign posted at Straidkilly advised motorists ROAD LIABLE TO SUBSIDENCE, which showed a laudable confidence in the education of the average driver, trusting them to catch and understand, as they zoomed past, both "subsidence" and "liable." They don't dumb things down in Northern Ireland. I liked that.

Up here, brewing illegal moonshine was once a popular pastime. Old potato peelings, spoiled beer—anything, really—was boiled and distilled into *poteen*, a drop of "the hard stuff," as it was known. Poteen was a form of alcohol so pure it was said to appear on some periodic tables. "*My Mom and Dad bought me some poteen, and all I did was go blind!*" A secret subculture grew up around it, with illicit drinking dens known as *shebeens*. I mention this because one of the local shebeens was out here, along Straidkilly Road, and maybe that's where the legend of the sliding village began, not from geological slippage but delirium tremens. "*Jaysus, man. Is it jest me, or is this entoire feckin' town startin' to sloide!*"

As I walked down from Straidkilly the next glen appeared, soft and impossibly green. Hedges lay over the hills like a net, loosely thrown. White-painted warnings on the surface of the road greeted visitors, the competing messages crossed out and repainted several times over, creating a palimpsest of tribal demarcations: UVF STAY OUT OF CARNLOUGH! And over this: IRA STAY OUT OF GLENARM! which was in turn crossed out with UVF OUT! added.

Somewhere between Glenarm and Carnlough I had crossed an invisible divide. Whereas Glenarm was a mixed community (hence the wariness of its pubs), Carnlough and the coastal towns beyond were Catholic. Scots Catholic. As close to neutral as the binary code allowed. As the paint-splattered road-top messages attested, it wasn't "Up the 'RA!" or "UVF Forever!" It was *stay out*, both of youse.

I walked in to Carnlough along a perfect arc of shore, past a harbour bobbing with boats. The village had the feel of a walled city, with the white slab of a stone archway forming a gate that the coastal highway squeezed through.

In the valley behind Carnlough, I could see isolated hawthorn trees in the middle of open fields—"fairy thorns," as they are known, left undisturbed by wary farmers. Fairies in Northern Ireland are not the Disneyesque Tinkerbells of modern lore; they are dark and deceitful, magical, cruel, cunning. One does not chop down an isolated fairy tree without consequence. Few would risk it, and those who did would often find their axes drawing blood, not sap. Chop down a fairy thorn and your family could be cursed. On an earlier walk, I'd asked an Antrim farmer about these gnarled trees dotted along the landscape. "Surely you don't believe in fairies and spirits?" I'd asked. "I don't," he said. "But that may not matter." It was, I must admit, both a sensible approach and rather sound theology to boot.

Speaking of fairies …

On my way into Carnlough I'd spotted a sign, handpainted and taped to a pole. It read:

MUST C 1 old pensioner spreading happiness

Farther along, another handpainted sign:

CUM C mi wee rubbishy but happy irish cottage

An arrow pointed down a side street. With curiosity well piqued, I left the coast road and entered Carnlough's quieter side lanes. On the way in, I passed a dishevelled elderly man, clad in tweed and grey stubble, coming down the other way. He was humming to himself as he walked. I asked him about the sign I'd seen. "Is it some sort of Bed and Breakfast?" I guessed.

The old man gave me a sad smile. "Wish it were. No, the wee house is just up there, on your right. A bloody load of rubbish is what it is." He twirled a finger near his temple. "The man's a loony."

Oh.

"Well, then," I said. "Should I even bother ..." My voice trailed off.

"Worth seeing? That rubbish?" I thought this was a rhetorical question, that he was being sarcastic, but no. "Oh, aye! Worth a visit. It's a local landmark, you can't pass through Carnlough without stoppin' by and takin' a wee peek."

Tolerant of their loonies up here in Antrim.

"We have a soft spot for eccentrics," is how the white-haired man put it.

"In Ireland?"

"In the Glens. Aye, the Glens are crawling with eccentrics. Something about the isolation, y'see. Now, Joe, he's in a class by himself. Y'can't miss it. Off you go now." And he left, humming the same soft tune I had interrupted.

Joe, I discovered, was Joe McKinley, a retired milkman—"Moscow Joe," as he was styled—and his front yard was home to the world's most ironic junkyard. It was, I mean this in all seriousness, a profoundly postmodern arrangement of found artifacts and anti-art. Not that any such theories were at play there. In fact, the only thing at play there was Joe; it was a junkyard collage, an al fresco museum-cum-oddity-hut of the unusual and the everyday—all lovingly arranged and labelled. But junk nonetheless. I'd never seen anything like it.

Here is just a partial inventory:

- A "genuine" foot bone from a dinosaur found in the old Carnlough quarry.

- The shoe of Finn McCool, legendary Irish giant. ("Weighs a ton!" said the note attached to a size 14 boot.)

- A pair of "300-year-old shoes" which had been found at a "1,000-year-old house."

- An old baby pram and assorted children's toys, including Joe's daughter Fiona's tricycle. (Fiona had grown up and was long gone, a note said, but her widowed father still had her mementoes on display and carefully catalogued. It was sad, sweet and strange—at the same time.)

- Dozens of transistor radios, splayed open, wires exposed.

- Fishing nets draped across fence posts and rotting into mulch.

- A ratty stuffed toy that Joe claimed to have won in a Moscow circus tent.

- An assortment of flotsam (shoes, shovels, boots and sea buoys) that Joe had found while walking along the beach, usually in the early hours of the morning. The exact time he found each item was given, right down to the minute—but not the month or year. ("Fishing net: Found at Beach at Cullyback 3:21 a.m.")

~ A rusty hubcap that had fallen off Adolph Hitler's Mercedes-Benz in Berlin in 1935 as the car sped along the Kaiserplatz. The hubcap, y'see, was smuggled out of Germany by Joe's grandfather, who at the time had been selling "Irish seed spuds" on the streets of Berlin when *der Führer's* motorcade went speeding past, spiralling a hubcap onto the cobblestone street. Joe's granddaddy had stuffed the hubcap under his coat and taken it back to Ireland with him—and now it hung, in its rusted dubious glory, outside Joe's home in Carnlough, County Antrim. The entire story of the hubcap was told in Joe's distinctive cartoon lettering.

There was also an indistinguishable relic of some sort supposedly snatched from the *Titanic*, a couple of blacksmith tools, an old bucket from 1920 (taken from "my Granny's farm in lovely Ballycastle"), loads of old pots, the jawbone of a horse, a deflated football and—as the centrepiece of the entire arrangement—two complete junkyard cars, fully decorated with glued-on bric-a-brac.

This and more—much, much more—were crowded into the front yard of a small bungalow. I wanted to rap on the front door and see if crazy old Joe was in, but the front gate was twisted shut with barbed wire, and the gaps between were clogged with stinging nettles growing thick among the artifacts. The yard looked like it hadn't been tended to for a long time.

I managed to piece together Moscow Joe's background from the quotes beside the various items. A milkman turned beachcomber, he was born in 1931 and self-named after his favourite city: Moscow. He was a descendant of the assassinated US president William McKinley and had drawn a pair of pictures that were now on display in Carnlough's Londonderry Arms Hotel. Joe was, apparently, a regular fixture at the hotel bar.

That settled it. I had to visit the Londonderry Arms and find Joe.

But then, as I was taking one last marvelling gander at Moscow Joe's magnum opus, I noticed a small sign that stated: "Will you be sad to now know that after 34 years here I am going to live with my only son and Kathryn in Nottingham? It's just too, too lonely on my own all the long dark winter …"

Damn.

I'd been looking forward to meeting my first genuine Antrim eccentric. As I was walking away, two women called out from the other side of the lane.

"Looking for Joe?" they asked.

"I was," I said. "But he's gone away to live with his son."

"And leave all that rubbish behind? I don't think so. Just go up to the house and give a good shout, he'll come out."

"Really?"

"But mind you, don't take anything Joe says too seriously." She tapped her temple. "He's right friendly, but he's not all there."

Back I went to the rubbishy yard to holler awhile. *"Joe? … Moscow Joe? … Hello?"* Nothing. So I went to the hotel instead, determined to track him down.

There's no need to name it; if you say "hotel" in Carnlough, it can only mean one thing: the Londonderry Arms. Musty carpets in the halls. A stuffed, marble-eyed moose head mounted in the foyer. It had the air of older days, of handlebar moustaches and upper-crust hijinks, a place both elegant and elegiac. The windows had panes of "bullseye glass" with ripples frozen in them like the circles from a pebble dropped in clear liquid, or a bullet fired into gelatin.

When I asked at the desk, they told me Joe had just left. "You probably passed him on the way in." I ran out, but the streets were empty of eccentrics.

"He'll be back," the desk clerk assured me when I returned, so I decided to wait Joe out at the bar. I ordered a pint of lager and a plate of pan-fried salmon on a bed of leeks. It came with something called "champs." Champs, for those of you who haven't had them, are mashed potatoes with flecks of green in them, which does not at all look like a chef's sneeze, so put that thought right out of your head.

"I'm waiting for Joe," I said to the waiter, a well-turned-out chap in a starched shirt.

"Joe McKinley?"

"That's the guy. Lives in town, a bit eccentric."

"Eccentric? Aye, that's one word for it. His yard, now, y'seen that, did you? The Council will go in, clear it out, but he just starts up again. He was just in—"

"A moment ago, I know. What does he look like?"

Well now, slap me with syrup and feed me to the bears if the description he gave didn't match almost exactly the man I had stopped at the very start, the one who said Joe was "a loony" and that the yard was rubbishy but worth a visit. Had that been Joe himself? Was it a self-evaluation?

I made the long walk back out to Moscow Joe's yard, having completely forgotten about the Ulster Way, only to find the gate still closed, the wind still blowing, and the day fast falling into dusk.

I never did track down the elusive Joe McKinley; it was like trying to catch a leprechaun.

WHEN I RETURNED to Carnlough by bus the following morning to complete the next leg of the Ulster Way, I stopped at a small shop to pick up some snacks for the hike. The man behind the counter, barrel-chested like so many of the men in the Glens, was named Gabriel. His dog, Bobo, a blond Newfoundland retriever, gave me a perfunctory once over, then curled into sleep on the floor.

Gabriel was taciturn, but helpful. When he discovered I was walking the Glens, he pulled out a folder of various clippings from beneath his counter. Among the clippings was a story about the Londonderry Hotel. He gave it to me for reference.

"You've been to Garron Tower?"

I hadn't.

"You have to."

But it wasn't on my route.

"I'll arrange a ride with the next person who comes through the door."

That sounded awfully cocky to me, but sure enough, a young man stopped by and was immediately roped in to act as my driver, running me out along the coast and up the winding road to Garron Tower, hidden in among the trees. It was once the summer residence of the Marchioness of Londonderry, the same lady who built the Londonderry Arms as a coaching inn (her estate later passed to one Winston Churchill); it now housed an elegant private school.

Plopped back outside Gabriel's shop, I stuck my head in to say thanks, but he would hear nothing of it.

"You've been to the waterfalls?"

The waterfalls?

"The ones in the glen. You've been?"

I hadn't.

"You have to."

He didn't say this belligerently; it was more a simple statement of fact. If you came to Carnlough, you went to see the waterfalls. Cranny Falls, as they were known.

In this case, a fortunate congruence of circumstances occurred. The Ulster Way from Carnlough turned inland, went right past Cranny Falls. I showed him the Ordnance Survey map, but he brushed that aside as inadequate. *Surveyors, what did they know?*

"I'll draw you a wee map," he said. And so, armed with directions from Gabriel, I set off.

I walked into the glen, and the hills came to meet me halfway. The road turned into a concrete path, pocked with the hoofprints of cattle that had crossed the surface years ago while the cement was drying. The hoofprints had filled with water, Lilliputian lakes cast in stone.

A trail branched off, through a sheep-infested paddock littered with Glosette chocolate-covered peanuts, and entered a river gorge clad in hazel and elm, wet with moss and layered with ferns. A pocket of rainforest hidden from view.

I watched the waterfall thunder through in rich peaty brown, and the morning's planned hike slipped farther and farther into the distance. I could see myself staying in the Glens, maybe forever. "*It's the weirdest thing,*" my son would say, years later. "*My dad walked into a valley one day and never came out the other side.*"

Having frittered the morning away, I abandoned my original plans and headed back toward Carnlough. Hearing a bark and a holler, I turned, and coming up quickly was a blond dog at full gallop. Behind him, Gabriel. Ah, yes, my guardian angel. Or—I tried to dredge up memories of Sunday schools past. Was Gabriel a guardian angel, or was he one of those avenging angels? The ones with the fiery swords. The Angels of Death. I looked around. I was utterly alone. The Irish are experts at ambushes; they study the lay of the land, know just where to pounce. As Gabriel strode down the path directly toward me, I frantically flipped through the conversational quips I had made at the shop, realized I'd lobbed a few good-natured jibes about the IRA and the UVF. The phrase "bunch of idiots" may have cropped up at some point. Surely Gabriel hadn't sent me up to the waterfall just so he could follow me in to pummel me alone and at his leisure?

"Hello!" he said. "Thought you could use the company."

I felt embarrassed for having doubted him. Or at least I did until the pummelling began …

I'm kidding, of course. Bobo had needed a walk and Gabriel had decided to join me. "Closed the shop for the afternoon. Fine weather like this, a shame to waste it." He pointed to a pebbled track cutting across the fields. "That's the old quarry line. Narrow-gauge tracks. They would run limestone from the quarry—*there*—to the docks—*down there*. The railway's gone, but where the tracks were has been maintained as a footpath. It crosses the old bridge, the one in the middle of town."

It was the centrepiece of Carnlough, that wall-like archway, cutting across the coast road.

"So that wasn't a defensive wall?" I said, genuinely disappointed. "No castles or cannons?"

"Limestone," he said. "It connected the quarry with the harbour." And then, with no small amount of disapproval: "You didn't read the clippings I gave you? About the hotel and the quarry?"

I hadn't. But no matter. The three of us followed the path back into Carnlough, with Gabriel pulling Bobo in on a lead whenever we passed sheep in a field. Bobo would woof and try to yank free, but Gabriel kept him close at hand. "He likes to chase 'em. He's just playing, but the sheep don't know that."

"Woof," said Bobo.

He was an exuberant dog, full of motion and misdirections, big and loose like big dogs always are. If anyone was going to protect us from sheep, it was Bobo.

By the time I arrived back in Glenarm, it was almost dusk.

"You still here?" said Kim when I ran into him on the street.

According to my schedule, by now I was supposed to be rounding the wind-lashed heights of Fair Head on the northern coast.

"Um, it's been slower going than I expected—I haven't actually made it past Carnlough."

He nodded. "The Glens will do that."

QUEEN OF THE GLENS

To cross the Garron Plateau is to become acquainted with the wind. On Agnew's Hill I had prayed for a breeze; now, I was hit full force. The winds buffeted me back, pushed me forward, filled my mouth, drowned my ears, circled around, pulled me off balance, this way and that, jostling me like a drunken uncle at a wedding. It was aggravating. It was exciting. It was exhilarating. It was, unfortunately, not waymarked.

The headlands of the Garron Plateau contain the most extensive region of blanket bog in Northern Ireland, and the term "blanket" is apt. A deep layer of peat, overlaying a bedrock of basalt, is draped across upthrusts of ancient lava, spongy, open and trackless. These are *raised* bogs as well, a peculiarly Irish phenomenon in which the sodden earth is pushed upward without ever draining, remaining wet even at the heights. It's strange: you don't expect swamp grass and open water on a summit; you certainly don't expect vertical puddles. But that's what you find. It's a landscape that produces "will o' the wisps," bog vapours that have an intoxicating effect and are said to have inspired nighttime revelries and tales of the wee folk. *Drunk on a landscape*: I liked that. It almost made up for the sudden pockets of pungent water and the constant eye-watering winds.

Lakes of shadow were moving across the moors. I followed what I thought was a path but turned out to be just another sheep trail. It meandered through the heather awhile before simply … vanishing, as though the sheep in question had either lifted off or been sucked under. This was definitely sheep-swallowing terrain, so I suspect it was the latter.

An hour into the hike, I looked around, realized I was lost. Not hopelessly lost. I had only to push onward and I would eventually fall off one side of the plateau or another. I was lost not in the sense of orientation but of isolation. The emptiness rolled away from me in every direction, with not another soul in sight. There was just me, the open highlands and the wind. And hours of bogwalking still ahead.

Past squishy ponds, pooled atop the peat, I eventually found a trickle of water, which turned into a creek, which turned into a stream that suddenly plunged through a cleft—and down to the valley beyond. I now stood high above Glenariff Valley, self-anointed "Queen of the Glens."

One shouldn't squander one's supply of superlatives before getting to Glenariff. At Glenarm, you think, "spectacular!" At Carnlough, "incredible!" At Glenariff, you need to sing it.

It was laid out before me. Headlands pushing into the sea, a perfect, U-shaped scoop of valley between. Forested meadows below and ladderwork fields—those thin-strip farms bordered by hedges—sloping up the far side, giving each farmer an equal slice of lowland, glen-side, and hill ground. You could almost imagine someone skateboarding down it, up the other side with a hang-time over the hills … and then back down again.

The early afternoon sun was filling the valley, and the fields beyond were a deep and abiding green. It's a colour with real mass, real weight. In my younger days, as a film student, they'd taught us about colour saturation, a concept I'd never quite understood until now. The greens I'd grown up with were thinner, slighter. They didn't penetrate the surface, but lay like a faint coat of paint along the top. Ulster green is green to the core, green to the bone. It's a wet green, too. Damp clothes look darker; so too does a damp landscape. I'd never seen such colour saturation before, and I wanted to find the nearest road, flag down a taxi, go to the airport, jump on a plane to Toronto, track down my old film prof and say, "Remember when you taught us about the different properties of colour and light, and how I thought it was a bunch of malarkey? Well, I know better now. For I have walked through the Glens of Antrim, have seen maximum colour saturation, *maximum green*—and can you please bump my grade up from a B–?"

If you die in the Glens, it must be a short step to Paradise.

From those heady heights—and yes, I was drunk on the landscape—I began a slip-footed, perilous and at times acrobatic descent into the valley. I came down so quickly my ears popped, finishing the last stretch at a near jog, through a sloping sheep paddock and out onto the side of a road.

I opened my map, considered my options. If I turned right, I would reach the coast road, where I could catch a bus back to Glenarm; if I turned left, walked inland instead, I would enter the deepest reaches of the valley.

I was tired, more from the wind than the walking—my face burned from it—but how could one come to Glenariff and not walk the valley itself? I measured the distance on my map, using the sophisticated bent-thumb technique, and concluded it was only two miles or so, as the crow flew. I was neither a crow nor flying, but no matter. I turned left and walked in, along the bottom of the glen. Forest gradually squeezed in the fields. It felt as though I were walking into a canyon. The vanishing point came nearer. And as the cliffs on either side closed in, they also grew higher. Thin trails of what looked to be waterfalls were misting down the sides, falling but never landing. Disappearing into thin air, so it seemed, evaporating en route.

The road I was following came at last to a forested wedge where a parking lot, a souvenir stand, a restaurant—*I bet they have beer!*—and the entrance to a scenic walk greeted me. I had reached the celebrated waterfall trail at the head of Glenariff Valley, and the beer tasted very good indeed. It was almost dinnertime, but I still had a valley to conquer.

"Aye," said the waiter, an older man of relaxed mien. "There's a waterfall just behind the restaurant, the trail goes up from there. It's a fine walk. Famous, so it is."

Somewhere, in the far recesses of my brain, a flag was raised. "Up?" I asked. "As in, *north*? Or up, as in uphill?"

"Uphill," he said.

"Do most people do it that way?"

"No," he said, "most of them are sensible, like. They start at the other end and walk down."

I was suddenly so tired. I couldn't face another uphill trek through the forest. I wanted to flow downhill, like a lazy river. I'd thought I'd been on the start to the valley walk; I was really at the end. The restaurant and souvenir stand were a net to catch tourists as they emerged; the interpretive centre was at the top of the valley.

"Maybe I'll just call it a day," I said. "Take a taxi back to—"

"Oh, but it's a brilliant walk, so it is. And you've come all this way, from America like."

Another fellow in the restaurant, a friend of his, agreed. "You have to walk it." He was firm about that.

"Now, Gavin here is goin' that way," said the waiter, volunteering his friend's services. "Headin' to Ballymena, Gav?"

"Aye, kin give yer man here a run around."

It was settled, then. I would not have to summon taxis or helicopters but would be dropped off at the top of the trail and would then walk my way down. Just in time for supper.

"You'll eat more after a long hike," the restaurateur joked. "Work up a proper appetite, like."

WELL, THANK GOD I got a ride. It was a long way around, turning on a hairpin and then climbing uphill into Glenariff Forest Park. I could see the Garron Plateau across from us, and I thought, *I walked that.* I was going to mention this, but then realized it would have made me look very wimpy indeed, to have crossed the heights of Garron only to complain about a footpath.

My Ballymena-bound benefactor drove me in to the trail head and dropped me off at a vast spread of parking lot in front of the Nature Reserve Interpretive Centre.

"That's you, then," he said. "Off to it. Just take that first step, let gravity do the rest."

Ah, the joys of a downhill hike.

This was a much more civilized and ambler-friendly route. Other hikers were out in force. Germans in pressed shorts, laces tightly tied. Elderly birdwatchers. Cacophonous school groups, fit couples, pensioners on a stroll—and me.

There were several trails to choose from; I made my choice based on "whimsy." The beauty of marked paths meant I didn't need compass or Ordnance Surveys or emergency flares. Take that first step *and let gravity do the rest* ...

The air was wet with the scent of green—a real scent that, one of clover and earth—and I was soon in among a rich mix of trees: Sitka spruce and Douglas fir, larch and pine, conifer and broadleaf—even a few palm trees thrown into the mix. The river the path followed spilled into feathery green overgrowth of tropical ferns and moss-fallen trees. The water pooled and then tumbled, collected, fell again. I passed high above one waterfall and then lower along another, more delicate than the first, a "mare's tail," as they say. Like the cloud. The path grew narrower, ran across thick arterial roots and through damp shadows. A pair of drowsy teenagers, fishing lines angled into the river like a scene from *Huck Finn*, were startled when I walked by. They watched me disappear along the rapidly diminishing path.

It was a pleasant stroll. Very pleasant. It was also, unfortunately, a dead end.

The sides grew closer, the path grew thinner. It was like an optical illusion, in which the lines of convergence are skewered to create a sense of perspective where none exists. I felt as though I were growing larger as I walked. The path shrunk, the vanishing point was suddenly underfoot, and I found myself wading through nettles and overgrown grass. I stopped. Looked around.

I had done it. I had gotten lost on one of the most well-travelled routes in the Glens. Retracing my steps, past droopy fishing poles and sleepy teenagers, I found the waymarker that had pointed me into the wooded cul-de-sac. The sign had been turned around. Intentionally. And I just knew it was those two ne'er-do-well teenagers I'd passed earlier. I considered going back to give them a proper finger-wagging, but the fact that (a) they might, possibly, be innocent and (b) I could very well end up with both fishing rods inserted up my backside helped dampen my determination.

I did rejoin the main trail, though—the elderly birdwatchers had pulled ahead—and I did eventually reach the Ess-na-Crub Falls behind the restaurant.

"We were about to send a search party," was the greeting I received.

"I took the scenic route," I said.

"Aye? Thought we'd lost you. Were going to send someone out w' bread crumbs."

"Me?" I said. "Lost? Naw. I'm from the Great White North. We can track polar bears across ice in the middle of a blizzard. We're trail-finders, it's in our blood. I was just taking my time, exploring all avenues. I didn't want to rush through, you see. I wanted to savour the experience."

"So," he said. "You got lost, then?"

"Yup."

After supper, and a fine meal it was, he called a taxi for the long run back. The day was winding down, and my feet ached in a manly sort of way.

"I walked in," I shouted to the driver as we sped, windows down, along the coast road. "Across the Garron Plateau."

"Aye? And how was that?"

"It was a great wee hill," I said. And I meant it.

A CONVERGENCE OF RIVERS

One doesn't simply enter the O'Neill Family B&B in Cushendall, one swims in, through chaos and confusion. A wedding was under way in the village—a local girl was marrying a boy from across the water, and the town was under siege by English accents. Every guest house and B&B was booked solid, and I was lucky to get a room at all. I know that because Mrs. O'Neill told me. "You're lucky to get a room at all," she said. And then: "What is the Tourist Board doing giving out our number when we're full up?"

I planned to use Cushendall as my base for the next series of walks, and I was put in her son's room, right at the top of the house—in the attic, practically—amid many apologies and counter-apologies on her part. A counter-apology, I'd learned, is a distinctly Ulster art form, wherein you apologize and then immediately withdraw it. In this case: "Aye, I'm terribly sorry, puttin' you way up here at the top of so many stairs—but you're a walker, you shouldn't mind. Think of it as exercise, trainin' for your big trek." She stopped on the stairs. "You shouldn't complain!" That last line was delivered as a scolding.

"But—but," I stammered. "I wasn't complaining. You—you were apologizing."

"Aye?" she said. "And why should I be apologizing, you're the lad with the legs of steel. Now, leave your bags and come downstairs. You'll have a cuppa." It wasn't a question. Of course I would have a cuppa.

I was herded into the kitchen and introduced to cousins, in-laws, neighbours, nephews, nieces and Colette, who was a category unto herself, apparently.

"Colette here, oh no, she isn't a relation, she works here, but she might as well be a member of the family, God forbid." Mrs. O'Neill spoke only with commas, her sentences strung along in a laundry line procession. "Oh, but I'm only joking, she's like a sister, Colette is, sit down, sit down, Colette pour the poor man some tea, you look starved, oh and take no notice of him, that's Paddy and he's just being daft, will you not have some sweets with your tea then, what wi' you walkin' all the way from Belfast?"

I pondered the layered negative syntax of that last query ("Will you not have some sweets?"), trying to decide whether one was meant to answer in the affirmative if one wished to have some sweets: "Yes, I will not." Or in the negative: "No, I will *not* not have some." Either way seemed incorrect. By that point a plate of sweets had already appeared, though, and Mrs. O'Neill spilled more introductions into my lap. The kitchen table was the central gravity well of the household. Everyone seemed to make at least one turn of it, in much the same way pilgrims will circle the stone at Mecca. In such a manner was I introduced to half the O'Neill clan and most of Cushendall.

I fell in love with Mrs. O'Neill. How could you not? She was constantly laughing and shaking her head, Our Lady of Bemused Laughter. The wedding guests—men in ill-fitting suits, tugging on their collars, bridesmaids in frilly dresses and astonished pink blush— were crammed into the O'Neill family home. In my grubby clothes and mucky boots I felt excruciatingly out of place, but no one took much notice. There were bigger things to fret about. Phone calls to make, details to coordinate, long-winded uncles to outwait. The most pressing problem, though, was "What are we going to do with all these strawberries?"

The Problem of the Strawberries was vexing indeed. Mrs. O'Neill had sent Colette down to the grocer's earlier to stock up on something sophisticated with which to ply her out-of-town wedding guests. But in all the commotion, she'd forgotten to serve them.

"Why not serve them for breakfast?" I suggested, but this elicited cocked heads and puzzled looks. Fruit? For breakfast? In Ulster? I mean, really, son, you can't fry strawberries in lard, so how could you possibly serve them for breakfast?

"An' anyway," said Mrs. O'Neill, shooing away her husband and her brother (or maybe it was her husband's brother; there were too many supporting characters for me to keep up with). "The strawberries will be gone by tomorrow morning, the way these lot are eatin' them."

"Here," she said, laughter in every breath. "Take these, take as many as you'd like, they'll give you energy for your great walk." She scooped up handfuls of strawberries into a paper towel. I placed them in my day pack and promptly forgot about them. Turns out, paper towel is not the best choice for the containment and transportation of strawberries. Days later, I would be dining on slightly fermented strawberry jam, mashed in between various stained and soggy pieces of apparel, but all the sweeter for it.

TO MRS. O'NEILL, my quest was both quixotic and amusing. I'd missed the gap between Glenariff and Cushendall, and when I took a taxi out the next morning, only to turn around and walk back in, she found it eminently entertaining: me heading out and then showing up forty minutes later for mid-morning tea.

Waterfoot, where I started, was little more than a line of shops strung across the mouth of the Glenariff Valley. Stucco buildings, several standing derelict with windows dutifully broken, crowded a road that was anchored on either end by pubs. There was a fish-and-chips shop and take-away Chinese food and Irish tricolours above the pubs. (So that was *Catholic* Chinese food they were serving in Waterfoot.) The village had a rundown feel to it, but its stunning location, with Glenariff sweeping up on either side and the sea just a stroll away, made up for what it lacked in architectural charm.

On the short walk back into Cushendall, I passed broken shards of wall on an outcrop of rock: the ruins of Red Bay Castle. Outlined against the sky, they looked more Neolithic than medieval, a standing-stone balancing act perched above the sea, near a stone arch tunnel. The arch at Red Bay is famous; it's featured prominently on postcards and souvenir tea-towels throughout the Glens. The coast road plunges right through it. A footpath circles *around*, outside the arch, but where's the fun in that? This was one of Antrim's landmark formations: how could I not walk through it? A couple of decent-sized strides would be all it took—never mind that it was on a blind corner. I waited for an ebb in the traffic and then stepped briskly through, feeling not unlike Wile E. Coyote in those moments just before he gets flattened by a truck.

The ruins of Red Bay Castle now teetered right above me. Built in 1563, on the site of an even older fortification, the castle was once a key stronghold of the MacDonnells. It stood all of two years before Shane O'Neill showed up. He torched the interior, knocked in the walls, looted the store rooms. Sorely Boy MacDonnell just as quickly rebuilt it, and the O'Neill–MacDonnell feud/alliance rollicked on. Red Bay Castle was once again destroyed, once again rebuilt. It was finally gutted, for good this time, by Cromwell's humourless Puritan army. *All that history crowded onto a single outcrop of rock.* The ruins might have been little more than a slab of wall, but they were an evocative slab nonetheless, with sheep lining the ridge above, silhouetted heroically against the clouds—insomuch as sheep can ever be considered "heroic."

The texture of things: that sandstone outcrop of rock, pitted with caves, that the castle sat upon had a reddish, almost purple tinge to it, with pebbly rocks embedded. I ran a hand along it, and a piece of gravel came loose. It was all soft and crumbly. Not a particularly firm foundation to build a family dynasty on. The miracle was that these Gaelic ruins were standing at all.

IN CUSHENDALL, the mossy heights of Lurigethan Mountain are ever-present. A dramatic volcanic plug dividing one glen from the next, Lurigethan is a stark reminder of the corrugated nature of this landscape, one that crests and falls, headland after headland, valley following valley, opening, as always, onto the sea.

Beyond Lurigethan lay the fairy-infested heights of Tievebulliagh, one of the most famously haunted hills in Ulster. Otherworldly lights are seen at night on Tievebulliagh, and it is said that the songs of the *Fianna* can yet be heard, echoing still. The Fianna were a race of giants, warriors semi-mythical and faintly historical, whose exploits are of Homeric proportions.

The leader of the Fianna was Finn McCool (Fionn Mac Cumhaill), father of the warrior-poet Ossian—"warrior-poet" being a distinctly Ulster Irish mix of bloodshed and balladeer. Ossian's fame lay in his eloquence as much as in his skills with spear and shield, and the Queen of the Otherworld fell in love with him. She enticed Ossian into crossing over, into her realm, out beyond the western sunset to Tír na nÓg, "Land of Youth," a kingdom where time stood still and no one ever grew old. Ossian spent his days there in languid love, but his heart eventually tugged him homeward. The green hills of Ulster were whispering, calling him back. "Just for a visit," he promised. "No good will come of this," she warned. But Ossian persisted, and his goddess lover gave him a horse to travel back upon. She cautioned him, however, that fairy time was fragile. "You must not set foot on Ulster's soil," she said. "Stay always upon this horse." He agreed, and returned to a changed land, one he scarcely recognized. The pagan gods were gone; the Fianna were mere folklore. St. Patrick had overthrown the Druids, replaced the standing stones with stone crosses. The men and women of Ulster had grown smaller, somehow, weaker, their souls sapped, bodies enfeebled. From his horse, Ossian watched with disgust as three of them tried to move a boulder. He finally leaned over to help. His foot slipped ... touched the Ulster green. And in that instant, time collapsed. The great warrior-poet, last of the Fianna, had his youth sucked out of him as the years returned with a vengeance. Ossian was left a withered old man, and in some versions, even turned to dust. Ireland's Orpheus, Ireland's Adonis, gone.

Ossian's grave sits on the lower slopes of Tievebulliagh, not far from Cushendall. Some claim that the grave is actually a Neolithic tomb, whose connection with the warrior-poet is "largely romantic." But those of a scientific bent are missing the point: something larger than bone is buried there.

THAT EVENING, I went for a walk, past the RUC station with its floodlights and prison-high chain-link fence, into town.

Cushendall is shaped by the flow of water. But although it's on the sea, it doesn't feel like a seaside town, even with its picturesque harbour. The heart of the town is a forested grove where three rivers converge to form the River Dall. Small birds darted about, quantum equations made manifest: neither mass nor energy, but something in between. The correct birdwatching term for these little bursts of feathers is, I believe, "lbj's." Little brown jobs. In Cushendall the lbj's are actually *dippers*, white-breasted birds that perch on river rocks, bowing and curtseying, short tails bobbing up. Dippers nest under bridges, and they can swim—and even *walk*—under water, neither fish nor fowl but a bit of both.

Cushendall is a nice place for a stroll. (A short stroll, admittedly, as one soon runs out of Cushendall to stroll through.) It was quiet that evening, almost as though under curfew—and perhaps it was, considering the solid square presence of the centrepiece tower. The village was once owned by a gentleman named Francis Turnley, who undertook many a varied improvement, the most enduring of which was a sandstone tower built at the crossroads. Known as the Curfew Tower, it was intended to be "a place of confinement for idlers and rioters." What a splendidly imperialistic time that was, I thought, when a gentleman might simply "purchase" an entire village, lock, stock and peasantry. A time when "idlers" were a real concern. A forelock-tugging, "yes m'lord" era. It must have been a great time to be alive—if you were the tuggee and not the tugger, of course.

Sullen teenagers (a redundancy, I know) were hanging around out front when I got to the tower. Which is to say, the loathsome "idlers" were with us still. *Damnation, where is my walking stick with which to scatter them!*

"Is the tower open?" I asked.

They stared at me with bovine gaze, shrugged. Ah, to be young and burning with lassitude and apathy.

I tried the door. "Closed," I chirped. Like they cared.

Drawing on all their inner resolve, they managed to shrug again, barely able to lift their shoulders, so great was the weight of their existence upon them. One took a weary drag on a cigarette. Another attempted to bring his can of cola to his lips but gave up halfway, the effort being simply too much for him. He clearly had larger, metaphysical issues to grapple with.

"You know," I said—and no, I don't know why I was trying to make conversation with them—"this tower, it was built to lock up loiterers and riff-raff, such as yourself."

The irony was lost on them, alas, and I wasn't rewarded with even a shrug this time, but only heavy-lidded, morose stares.

"Well, see ya later!" I said.

I sought out a quiet pub, where I filled myself with warm fare and cold lager. Thus fortified, I walked out again into the warm September night. A full moon had cast its spotlight on the town, and the sea winds had shifted, were coming in across salt water now. At that moment, I couldn't think of anywhere I would rather be than in Cushendall in County Antrim with sore feet and a belly full of beer.

THE VANISHING LAKE AND THE BLACK NUN

In the week or so I'd spent on the Antrim coast, I'd become fascinated by potato chips and the sheer variety of them available. The array, the buffet, the cornucopia, as it were, went far beyond Salt & Vinegar or Bar-B-Q. No, these were crisps of a higher order, and I spent an inordinate amount of time making my selections. The potato chips produced by the Tayto Company were especially tasty. Pickled Onion, Smoky Bacon, Roast Chicken, Prawn Cocktail, Ham & English Mustard, Strong Cheese & English Mustard, Mature Cheese & Spring Onion, Smoked Ham & Pickle, Sausage & Tomato, Roast Beef & Mustard, Worcester Sauce, T-Bone Steak, Sizzling Chilli Beef,

Flame-Grilled Steak: all real flavours, on sale in the small shops and vending machines of the North.

So many wonderful varieties, and they all tasted exactly the same— like salt and MSG. The first bite was amazing. You'd think, "Wow! That *is* roast chicken with pickled onion. That *does* taste like aged cheddar and spring onion!" But by the second bite, and those that followed, whatever artificial stimulus your taste buds had received had been neutralized. It was just salt and MSG after that. To differentiate between Worcester-flavoured potato chips and Roast Beef & Mustard required a palate more refined than mine.

Still, it was great fun selecting my daily packet. The next morning, having made my choice (Prawn Cocktail, because I was near the sea and wanted to enjoy the bounty therein), I set off for the next glen.

From Cushendall, the Ulster Way hugged the hillside above Port Vinegar, along a coastal footpath that felt suspended above the water. A decent puff of wind might send you over. You certainly wouldn't want to trip. Above the path, bay windows looked out across the water: views, with homes attached.

The trail then turned inward, winding its way toward the roofless ruins of an ancient medieval church set back among woods where tombstones leaned at improbable angles, moss-covered and lichen-stained. A tower at one end had a tomb-like passage beneath it, a chambered crypt of mysterious intent. The plaque out front suggested that the purpose of the chamber was unknown, though I can attest that it was as quiet and dark as a grave.

As I walked down the hill into Knocknacarry, a collection of houses in search of a town, a horse-drawn two-wheeler wagon clattered past. The constant incongruities of Ulster were much in evidence that day, and I soon found myself walking behind a tractor loaded down with cut peat. A sleek Mercedes-Benz inched along, unable to get past. The driver of the Benz gave me a puffed-cheeked sigh as I pulled alongside him, as though he and I were allies of sorts—this in spite of the fact that, as a long-distance walker, I was actually *less* efficient than the peat farmer causing him such vexation. The tractor eventually turned off, the Benz pulled away, and I was left to walk into Cushendun alone.

It was in Cushendun that I ran into the first major problem of my trip.

Cushendun is the village in Ireland that's closest to Britain. Scotland's Mull of Kintyre sits just offshore, so it seems; a short run and a hop would probably get you across. Cushendun is where Shane O'Neill "the Proud" finally met his end. That was in 1567, when Shane had—unwisely, as it turned out—sought refuge among the MacDonnells. Having irked Queen Elizabeth one too many times, he'd fled north, into the Glens. Never mind that Shane O'Neill had taken Sorley Boy captive, and never mind that he'd let Sorley Boy's father die in a cold cell. And never mind that whole "leading a campaign of pillage and war against you and torching your family castle back at Red Bay" thing. Shane O'Neill returned Sorley Boy to his clan. *"Bygones be bygones, eh, Sorley Boy?"*

The wonder is that the MacDonnells didn't kill Shane O'Neill on the spot. The code of hospitality in the Glens dictated that shelter be given, and the MacDonnells were an honourable clan. They even held a banquet for Shane and his men, with meat and ale and many a raised glass. A couple of drinks in, however, and Shane started to get lippy. The MacDonnells simmered, said nothing. But when Shane decided he should marry Sorley Boy's sister, thereby making a claim on MacDonnell territory through wedlock rather than battle, Hell—having been barely contained—broke loose. A brawl quickly turned into a massacre. Shane escaped but was chased down. (Another version of events has the melee starting when one of Shane O'Neill's retainers made a comment about Sorley Boy's mother. Either way, the results were the same. Ulster history is essentially one extended donnybrook.) Not only did the MacDonnells kill Shane O'Neill, they cut off his head, and not only did they cut off his head, they pickled it, and not only did they pickle it, they sent it back to the English as a present.

Castle Carra at Cushendun is where Shane O'Neill was feted just before he was killed. I walked out to the ruins—a corner wall with archway windows in a quiet meadow north of town—and wondered how far he had made it before they caught him, before they hacked him down, wondered how close he had been to slipping free once more. It was here at Cushendun that the luck of Shane O'Neill finally ran out.

Cushendun is an anomaly in several ways. Small-scale and architecturally distinct, the village is a casually eclectic mix of slate-clad Cornish-style dwellings and "chocolate box" cottages with oversized Mansard roofs and undersized window panes. Even the grander homes of Cushendun have a cottage-like feel to them. Stranger still, most of the village—the cottages, Cornish homes, even the beach—is owned outright by the National Trust.

I stopped in at the National Trust tea room, opened the crumpled accordion of my Ordnance Survey map. Ahead of me lay my first real test. Beyond Cushendun, the Ulster Way as marked on the map crossed Mount Carnanmore and then ran down to the far cliffs of Fair Head. According to the guidebooks, however, the right-of-way was being contested by local farmers, who refused to grant access to hikers. My first instinct was to go anyway.

"I've crossed fences before," I'd boasted to Belfast colleagues.

"Have you now?" (This would be the same colleague who advised me on the single-tooth allotment of Antrim men.) "And when a farmer sees you traipsing across his land? Tells you to turn back?"

"I figure I'll charm my way through."

"You can outcharm a bullet, can you?"

Having now arrived at Cushendun, my conundrum could no longer be deferred. One of the guidebooks suggested I abandon the Ulster Way and follow an inland path called the Moyle Way instead.

Seeing my map and books open, and my tea growing cold, the fellow clearing the tables said, "He's here, you know. That's his bar on the other side of the river."

Pardon?

"Randal McDonnell. It's his book you've got there."

Of the various references I had in front of me, the most entertaining by far was a touring guide to the Glens written by one

Mr. McDonnell of Cushendun. Although not geared toward walkers per se, it was filled with wonderfully tart opinions. Tourist Board pamphlets assured visitors that the Antrim Glens offered "a wonderful selection of culinary delights," including, but by no means limited to, "award-winning sausages and unique ice cream." (What exactly was unique about Antrim ice cream, or which governing bodies oversaw the aforementioned Awards in the Field of Sausage Excellence, was not elaborated upon.) But here was Mr. McDonnell's take on Antrim's "culinary delights":

> *A few good cafes and restaurants do exist, but you will be unlikely to find them. Don't waste too long looking; just go to the first place you see and treat eating as a utilitarian activity.*

And this, from his entry on Turnley's Tower back in Cushendall:

> *It is really a fake of no particular antiquity, having been built about 1800 for [an] eccentric landlord who was of dubious mental stability ... Nothing memorable has ever been associated with the tower.*

I half-expected to find a cranky old grump minding said bar. I found instead a soft-spoken gentleman with a trim grey beard and a habit of not looking at you directly when he spoke, which was, I admit, a tad disconcerting. I kept trying to move into his line of sight, only to have his gaze slip away. In fairness, he may have found it equally disconcerting to have a hiker show up waving his book and out of breath from having run across from the tea room. (I was determined not to have another Moscow Joe moment. "*Randal? Aye, he just left.*")

I explained my predicament to him: I needed to get from Cushendun on the east coast to Ballycastle on the north, but the route as marked was both vague and possibly blocked.

He scoffed at this. "How could they deny access? It's just a bog. It's open fields and ... here—" he unrolled a detailed development map, one that charted proposed projects, planned works, budgetary daydreams. "This," he said, running a finger along the map. "This is the old road. It's overgrown now, but still a trail. That will take you up the west side of Carnanmore. It joins another road—*here*. Follow that down, you'll be fine."

I spotted a placename on his map, one sure to send a tingle of excitement up the spine of even the most jaded of travellers: *the Vanishing Lake*. My route would take me right by it. I'd heard of it, the fairy lake that swallowed stage coaches, confounded scientists, was often cloaked in an inexplicable mist. Could see it in me mind's eye: ghostly shapes moving across the water, the eerie sound of—

"Lake?" said Randall. "Hardly a lake. Just a puddle, really."

"A puddle?"

"Limestone underneath. The water drains away slowly, fills up after a rain and then drains away again."

No mysterious ladies proffering swords? Fairies or dragons, that sort of thing?

"No. Just drownings, I suppose. Now then." He started to roll the map back up. "Take the corkscrew out of town, you'll come across the old road. Follow that north. It'll take you over Carnanmore."

"The corkscrew?"

"The corkscrew."

THE CORKSCREW, as it happened, was a series of sharp hairpin turns north of Cushendun that switchbacked up and over the hills beyond.

Sure enough, the old road was right where Mr. McDonnell had said it would be. It cut straight over, slicing across the zig-zag of the main road and heading directly for the heights with an admirable disregard for topography. I followed it upward and was soon alone on the moors, surrounded by a beautiful emptiness of heather and hillocks: rich browns and dark greens, with the purply wine-stain of thistles growing in clumps along the hills and tufts of bog cotton amid rust-red leaves. I was carrying my full gear with me, so it was well I had a firm trail to follow. I couldn't have made it otherwise.

Although Ireland had never been conquered or occupied by the Roman Empire, the old road felt like an ancient Roman byway, half-forgotten, overgrown. I leaned into the wind, felt it push back. The air chilled, the sky darkened. *Prime banshee weather*. I crossed a rock-jumbled stream and went over a rise, and when I was within striking distance of the Vanishing Lake, I left my Roman highway and pushed across the boggy bramble. It was like trying to navigate an inflatable bouncy castle at times, so spongy was the terrain. Black-faced sheep watched my clumsy progress with a curiosity not usually ascribed to their species.

I was out of breath by the time I arrived. The lake had (of course) vanished, and I was left to admire magnificent mud flats as I followed its high banks around. The main road across Carnanmore actually cuts *through* the lake, and it was hard to imagine that this muddy puddle could flood the causeway at times.

A rent-a-car couple had pulled onto the side of the road and were waving me over like I was a ship on the horizon. They were Americans, had seen me coming across the hills, a man of the moors apparently, and they'd assumed—erroneously, considering the fact that I was stumbling and slipping, not striding in full flight—that I was someone who might be able to help them.

So, what the hell: I donned an Oirish accent and spouted a bit of gibberish at 'em—"Aye, 'tis a wee fine day far'a tap o' the cairn"—and I soon had them convinced that the lake appeared only under a full moon and when the winds were just right. Not that fooling tourists is difficult; I thought of all the times *I'd* been duped, up to and including the idea that the Ulster Way was "waymarked."

They were swell folk, Bob and Marge (or Tiff and Tipper, or whatever their names were), though they did seem to think they were on a theme ride at Disneyland, waiting for the next diorama to wheel into place. I understood their disappointment; in North America there would have been souvenir shops, T-shirts, a neon sign announcing, "SEE the Amazing Mystifying VANISHING LAKE! One of Nature's SEVEN WONDERS!"

Bob looked at his watch, frowned. "Let's go, honey. That lake isn't doing anything."

"Just a sec!" She was videotaping a lake that wasn't there. She was videotaping mud.

They assured me it was a great little country I had.

"Aye," said I, "and may the wind o' the heather be lashin' the Mournes afore the devil shakes yer sausage."

"Thanks!" They sounded so sincere in their appreciation that I felt a twinge, an actual twinge, though ever so small, of guilt.

Off they went in their rent-a-car over the hills, and immediately it began to pour. Karma in action. I considered waiting to see if the lake would fill up.

AS THE DOWNPOUR thinned into spits and spats, I made my way back, past the same puzzled sheep, onto the old Roman road. I could see a farmhouse ahead, and I wondered, idly at first, then with growing apprehension, if it had been *that* farmer, out here in these empty moors, far from any witnesses—if it had been *that* farmer who had blocked walkers from crossing his land. *Can outcharm a bullet, can you?*

The trail came up right into the farmyard. I stopped. Watched. The windows were dark and no dogs were prowling the perimeter, so I tiptoed—as much as one can in heavy boots—right past the farmhouse and out through the front gate.

A country lane unrolled across the landscape like a tattered ribbon over scrub fields. As I walked down, the fields gave way to meadows, and the meadows to quilted green. I had crossed Carnanmore.

The Carey River churned through a deep cleft below; I'd hopped across the same river back when it was a mere trickle in the moors. Farmhouses began appearing closer together now, and traffic started to pick up, mainly in the form of tractors driven, as always, by fourteen-year-old boys. At the crossroads of Ballyvoy, I was greeted first by a pub, then by a church. All that was required now was a SPAR, the convenience-store chain that all communities are, by law, required to have. (I would become something of a connoisseur of SPAR sandwiches over the course of my trip. I'm not sure what the name refers to—"Sandwiches Priced At Reasonable Rates," perhaps. Sometimes instead of a SPAR, the store would be called "Costcutters" or "Vivo," but the prepackaged sandwiches were more or less the same.) I passed a second church—this being Northern Ireland, after all—but shockingly, still no SPAR. The guidebook said there was a shop in Ballyvoy, but damned if I could find one, and I left the village sandwichless. *I really should report them*, I thought.

I could see the lights of Ballycastle shimmering in the dusk, but before I could reach them I passed a golf course. And beside the golf course—in it, really—lay the bones of an ancient monastery. At the Ballycastle golf course, ghosts are probably considered standard hazards, like sand traps or water ponds.

Depending on which source you consulted, the Bonamargy Friary was built somewhere between 1480 and "around 1500." Headstones, sinking into mossy neglect, listed drunkenly, as though leaning into the wind. The earthly remains of Sorley Boy and the MacDonnells, rulers of the Glens and Isles, lay mouldering in a vault. More lurid still, and the real reason I stopped by Bonamargy, was that it was also where the Black Nun rested. A prophetess and holy woman, the Black Nun had asked to be buried under the doorway of the chapel, so that feet might tread upon her as penance down through eternity.

Darkness was falling by now. I had fully planned on stomping across the Black Nun's grave—in the spirit of Ulster, you understand, sort of like kissing the Blarney Stone if you're in the Republic—but in the eerie half-light, I chickened out. For one thing, although the guidebooks said it was marked, it wasn't evident exactly *which* threshold her bones were buried under; I would've had to stomp around on each to be sure. More to the point, though, I didn't want to be followed on my journey by any spirits I might rouse. If I believed in such things. Which I didn't. It was just that, as the Antrim farmer had pointed out, whether or not I believed might not matter.

THE TRAFFIC PUSHED ME along into town. The lights of Ballycastle might have been those of the Vegas Strip, so enticing and exciting did they appear after the moorland heights of Carnanmore. There were people *everywhere*. I felt like a hillbilly, agog at the sight of it. (In my memory, Ballycastle is roughly the size of, oh, Tokyo.)

I checked myself into a hotel on the Diamond, as the town squares of Northern Ireland are inevitably called, regardless of their shape. I'd been in trapezoids, rhomboids, ovals: all were designated as their town's Diamond.

"I've come from Belfast," I said, signing the hotel registry with a flourish. "On foot."

"Aye? That's grand." He looked at the address I'd written down. "We've got a couple here who are from your neck of the woods." The clerk waved them over. "This gentleman's from Canada," he said.

It was Bob and Marge.

Part Three

GIANT'S CAUSEWAY

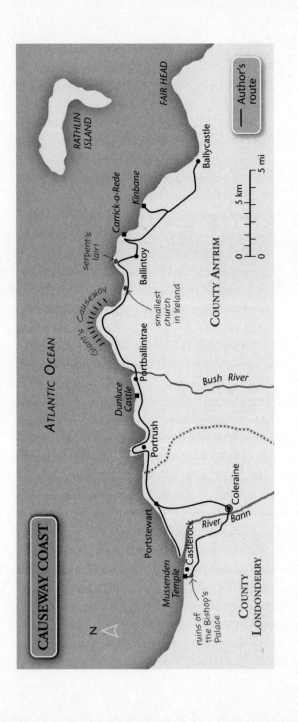

BALLYCASTLE TO CASTLEROCK
Along the Northern Coast

Ballycastle in the early hours.

I was desperate to get away before I ran into Bob and Marge again. As it was, I'd left a pair of puzzled tourists in my wake. (Having adopted a stage Irish accent, I couldn't very well stop. You could see the bafflement in their faces. "*They talk like that in Canada? Really?*") The desk clerk, meanwhile, having checked me in under one accent only to hear me address the Americans in another, seemed equally confused. Fortunately, it was such a *bad* Irish accent he didn't recognize it for what it was meant to be. He probably thought I'd either been drinking or had suffered a mild stroke.

I liked Ballycastle. It had a summery feel to it even in early September, and as I walked down from the Diamond, full pack on my back, the town of shopkeepers and traders gave way to one of beaches and seaside strolls. I followed the curve of sand past the marina and looked out at the headlands beyond, where the full weight of the Fair Head cliffs fell into the sea.

Rathlin Island lay anchored off the coast amid whirlpools and riptides. Rathlin moves. I'd read that some days it felt near at hand, and on others it drew back, into a haze of distance. At times, the island seemed near enough that you could skip stones across, while at other times it receded so far you needed a boat to reach it.

Rathlin—that Viking-bedevilled, ghost-imbued island—stood in high relief the morning I left, its lighthouse beacon turning, a cluster of homes low along the shore of its one sheltered nook. Rathlin forms a high plateau, and its cliffs were clouded with seabirds. Guano aside, the island is soaked primarily in history, which is to say, blood. Rathlin was where the Vikings first launched their attacks on Ireland, and the ensuing years saw mayhem and massacres on the island at regular intervals, from those first Norse raids to Elizabethan troops who tossed women and children from the cliffs while the MacDonnell men watched in horror from the shore; they had sent their families to Rathlin for safety and were now powerless to save them. Another massacre at Rathlin was later carried out by the Campbells, and not to cast aspersions or anything, but you ever notice how, whenever there's a massacre, the Campbells seem to show up? They must be on a mailing list or something.

Mist was starting to spill over the top of Fair Head like smoke poured from a pitcher. When it curls over the cliffs like that, it is said to take the shape of the Grey Man. He lives on those heights, takes form in the fog, *is* the fog. And now Rathlin began to pull back as well, retreating into cold vapour.

Time to go.

Ballycastle was waking up, lights were flickering on. The homes in the heart of town were staggered, uphill and down, and every-thing seemed to have been folded to fit. I followed North Street on a steep climb behind the marina and the town fell away. A sea mist was blowing in through the trees and across the road. *At what point exactly does mist become fog?* I opened my map, compared what it showed to the milky, whitewashed world I now inhabited. I could hear the mournful lowing of cattle, but couldn't see any. The world was slowly being swallowed, and I had to stand aside—far aside—whenever traffic crept through, headlight beams reduced to soft orbs.

It's better not to know some things, isn't it? Like, for example, that the high road you're walking along in a fog-drowned world is where the bodies of famine victims were once abandoned, unshrouded and unblessed, their spirits left to wander the moors. It would be better not to know something like that, yes? Why I had read the ghost stories I had the night before was beyond me. Because I knew exactly where I was. I'm not sure I exhaled the entire time.

Gradually, the fog turned into condensation, and the condensation began to fall, softly at first and then pelting down in volleys. The rain washed away the fog—*now there's an Irish sentence*—and the landscape revealed itself. I had made it through, had passed over the unmarked graves unscathed.

I must say, the Irish really know how to build ruins. They did a terrific job at Kinbane, where the shards of the castle were set amid white and black cliffs of basalt and chalk. Waves broke on submerged rock. Seagulls and ravens sparred in the air above. The tableau was a study in contrast: the constant motion of the sea, the solid mass of the cliffs. When you turned the corner, from the eastern Glens of Antrim to the northern coast, the land went from wide valleys to sudden cliffs, craggy and crest-fallen (in the geological sense). Two of the finest coastlines in Europe: back to back. I celebrated by popping open a packet of Pickled Onion potato chips. *Mm-mmm.* MSG and salt.

From Kinbane, I rejoined the main road as the sun burned away the last wisps of mist. The day turned hot, sultry even, and I began a slow striptease, stopping every few feet to peel off another steam-soaked layer. Fields ran down to the edge of the cliffs, with the sea beyond and Rathlin Island ever present. Out here, it must feel as though you were farming on the very edge of the earth. At one point, cars veered over and people got out, stood hands on hips, agog. It really was a traffic-stopping view. I recognized some of the cars; they had tried to run me over earlier, but we now shared the bond of a landscape mutually admired. Take the most hardened IRA and UDA gunmen, plonk them down in front of that view, and all they'd be able to do is grin at each other in their shared good fortune at being *here*, in Ulster, calling this home.

The sightseers drove off still smiling, giving me a cheerio wave as they went. I was sure I'd see them again; they would no doubt be lying in wait for me farther down the road.

Over the next hill, the village of Ballintoy appeared amid green fields thick as felt. But before I walked down into Ballintoy, there was a detour to make, to the edge of the cliffs at Carrick-a-Rede, to what I dubbed "The Swinging Bridge of FEAR!!" (The Northern Ireland Tourist Board really should be talking to me about this sort of thing.)

I could hear the ongoing squabble of seabirds—the accusations and protestations, the continuous unresolved arguments that constitute seabird society—long before I arrived. Past a parking lot, near full, I followed the path down to where the plank-and-rope footbridge made its daring leap across to a cliff-high rise of rock offshore.

Carrick-a-Rede means "rock in the road," and that is exactly how the island works, the boulder-like blockade squeezing the water around it. There had been a salmon fishery at Carrick-a-Rede for more than three hundred years, and for the last two hundred of those, fishermen had used the same type of bag net stretched across the same channel. Two hundred years, and the fish never caught on.

To get to that knuckle of rock each year, the fishermen would string a swaying footbridge across the sheer-drop gap of what was actually the mouth of an extinct coastal volcano, the sides having collapsed, letting in the sea. The bridges were put in for the summer and taken down again in early autumn, and though the historic salmon fishery was now coming to an end, the bridge at Carrick-a-Rede had become an inadvertent tourist attraction all on its own. When I arrived, there was a traffic jam of bodies waiting to get across. A group of Italians—over-expressive as always—were shouting at a poor woman who had frozen in the middle, hands clenched on either side. Their frantic urgings and flailing *"Deus deliver us"* arm gestures did nothing to calm the situation, but the lady did eventually inch her way across, not realizing, of course, that she would have to come back the same way. What the bridge failed to do, the wind almost accomplished, trying hard to sweep at least a few tourists into the sea. They must have to scoop a couple out from there every year.

Close to shore lay the impressive mass of Sheep Island, and farther out, the backdrop of Rathlin. Beyond that, Scotland the Brave. *Throw a couple of ropes across, a plank or two ...*

IN VILLAGES like Ballintoy, pubs often act as a sort of communal living room. They may not always be jovial, but they are inevitably well lived in. That evening, I checked in to the Sheep Island View Youth Hostel—aptly named: you can see the rounded hump of Sheep Island peeking up behind Ballintoy's iconic white church—and then went off in search of beer. The streets of Ballintoy (or rather, *street* of Ballintoy, there being only the one, really) felt deserted, but if you stepped inside one of the pubs, life was in full swing. The bar I wandered into had been taken over by an impromptu music session, with participants sitting around a table as though they were in someone's kitchen.

I bought a pint, wedged my way in. More people kept crowding in, so I introduced myself to the fellow I was jostling up against. I figured if I was going to be that physically intimate with someone, I should at least know his name. The crowd may have been mixed, and the music may have been traditional, but the instruments were Catholic. You think I'm kidding, but no. Northern Ireland's binary nature went beyond mere political allegiances. In that Ballintoy pub, the use of *bodhrán* drums marked this as Catholic music.

Lambegs are the large thundersome drums lugged about by Protestant marching bands. *Bodhrán* are the smaller, traditional Irish drums. You can't lug a Lambeg into a pub, so they were (thankfully) absent from late-night music sessions. Advantage: Catholic.

The ongoing list of either-ors encompasses one's choice of athletic activity, drink—name, even—with Protestants on one side, Catholics on the other. And when it comes to the sports that both sides play, such as soccer, you can divide by one's choice of team.

Lambeg	vs.	bodhrán
cricket	vs.	hurling
Rangers	vs.	Celtic
Guinness	vs.	Guinness (Okay, so some things they do agree on.)
Billy	vs.	Seamus

Billy is a Protestant name. Seamus, like Sean or Eamon, would be considered Catholic. I grew up as Billy, my older brother was Sean. That would have messed with their heads over here.

Cricket, considered "British," is Protestant almost by default, while hurling—a riot disguised as sport—falls under the auspices of the Gaelic Athletic Association, which is another way of saying "Catholic," in fact if not in name. And Rangers vs. Celtic in football? Odd, no, considering that neither team is located in Northern Ireland? I'd asked about this. "Ah," it was explained to me, "but these are Ulstermen you're talkin' about. We'll travel for a fight if we have to." It is a battle by proxy: the Glasgow Rangers are a Protestant football team, while the Glasgow Celtics are Catholic. Wear a Rangers jersey in Catholic Belfast on a Friday night and you will be beaten. Wear a Celtic jersey in Protestant Belfast, same thing.

Up on the northern coast, in the tiny village of Ballintoy, things were less dire. "We all get along up here," the man next to me said. And when he found out I'd be walking the coast come morning, he leaned closer, asked, with a mischievousness that bordered on the malicious, "You've heard of Lig-na-Paiste?"

I had. A serpent that dwelled in a cave below Ballintoy, St. Patrick having apparently missed it when he cast the snakes out of Ireland. It was a dark, monstrous creature, Lig-na-Paiste, one that could be defeated but never destroyed. *Defeated but never destroyed.*

"The creature returns once every hundred years," my new friend noted. "Can only be stopped by a man with the surname of McCurdy. Now the cave, you'll be walking right past it tomorrow."

"When did Lig-na-Paiste last appear?" I asked.

"Oh," he said. "About a hundred years ago."

A young woman with loose curls and a soft voice was singing sad and sweet to the accompaniment of squeeze-box and fiddle: ballads mainly, with the usual carnage they entailed. Irish ballads, like Irish history, are strewn with bodies and broken hearts. These dirges soon melted into upbeat tunes about rebels and revenge, and from there became quicker still, flying jigs and reels. The roots of country and western music lie in Ireland—in the North particularly. The Ulster emigrants took a great many ballads to the United States with them, and you can trace the music of the American plains back to these hills, these pubs.

I hesitated to join in. I recognized several of the sing-a-longs, but even I knew that the inclusiveness of Irish music had its limits. Besides which, there is a court order against my singing in public. My wife took it out, had it notarized and everything. Still, after a few drinks, how could I not join in on "Danny Boy," especially as I had been the one calling out for it? And then, well, hell, it was the "Green Glens of Antrim." Having walked those very glens, how could I not? I had earned the right, nay, the *obligation*, to stand up, arms outstretched, and belt that one out mournfully and with the greatest of conviction.

The crowd started to thin after that.

THE OLD GUY IN THE YOUTH HOSTEL

I woke before dawn and walked out into an indigo world.

In Ballintoy's hidden harbour, boats lay tethered and sleeping. Sheep Island, that double-humped rise of rock where sacrifices had once been left—sheep for Viking marauders and cave-dwelling serpents alike—seemed closer than ever. Ballintoy is, technically speaking, part of Norway, at least according to the arrangements made between the Norsemen and the villagers, wherein sheep were paid out and the village made a Norse protectorate. I'm not sure how much weight that would have in a court of law, should the Norwegians ever press the matter, but there is no record of the treaty ever having been suspended. If nothing else, Ballintoy was behind in its rent.

Among the harbour's limestone and basalt cliffs, I spotted a dark cave hollowed out by the sea. In the chill of early morning, it was expelling a dragon's breath of mist, and I wondered, idly, if that was the cave in which Lig-na-Paiste dwelled as I tripped over myself trying to get away.

Not that I believe in such things …

THE ULSTER WAY follows the Causeway coastal path around cliffs, past rocky coves and over sudden slashes of rock. Islands, looking like shards of pottery, were shredding the sea as I picked my way around a rocky headland and came out on the pure crescent of White Park Bay, a mile of soft sand with another knotted headland at the other end.

I followed the beach down, came to the jut of rock. At low tide you can get around it, but at high tide, the sea cuts you off. I, of course, had carefully studied the relevant tidal charts and had scheduled my crossing with exact precision … In fact, I'd completely forgotten about the warnings until that very moment. *Oh, right. Something about the tide.* Luck was with me, though, and the sea had pulled back just enough for me to get by, scrambling over sea-slicked surfaces. Slowly, and with a singular lack of nimble-footedness, I made my way over ankle-twists of rock and boulders tangled with dulse, past a single knife blade of stone rising from the water.

I stopped for lunch at a large blockade of boulders at the bottom of a cliff. The sea was back where it belonged, and I took my seat on a clean slab of stone. Odd, that. There was no seaweed dripping from the stone, and its corners were sharp and clean. I asked myself, "Self, how do you figure such large and sharply edged boulders as these ever managed to get washed up on shore?" I looked up—at the overhang of the cliff directly above me and then quietly packed up my lunch. "Maybe I should be moving along."

Around the next bend in the shore lay one of the most visually arresting villages in Ireland: Portbraddan. If Ballintoy's was a hidden harbour, this was a hidden village. I counted nine buildings in total, flattened against the cliff walls like prisoners trying to avoid a search-light. Unfortunately, Portbraddan was closed the day I went through. Not a soul was stirring inside any of the homes, though a few power walkers did blast past, slinky Spandex pants flashing purple and red.

The pride of Portbraddan is its church: the smallest in Ireland, so they claim, and I can't imagine how you could make one any smaller. It was a stone building, about the size of a shed—a really *small* shed. Even more remarkable, this shed-like church came complete with a steeple, a church bell, and a tiny, stained glass window on one end for gawkers like me to peer through. Inside was a tiny pulpit but no pews. It would have been standing room only during services, I imagined. A miniature village with a miniature church; I felt like the Friendly Giant. I felt like Gulliver in the land of Lilliput.

"Tiny church!" I called out when a pair of power walkers strode by in a strideful manner. They barely flickered a look in my direction.

Past Portbraddan, around the next corner of the cliffs, everything was jumbled together magnificently: the sea, the coast, the rocky meadows. The whole landscape was in motion. The rise and fall of the sea, the wind in the grass. Endless variations on a theme. A shallow stream slipped over mossy rocks, into a tidal pool that emptied into a cove and then spilled into the sea. A pair of fussy ducks pecked at the stream-side grass like a deacon and his wife picking at a salad.

In a secluded nook, I interrupted a pair of teenagers in mid grope. Flustered and flushed, they broke from their embrace with a wet suction-cup effect. "Hello there!" I said. "Wonderful day!" The boy, blushing to the bone, nodded. The girl wouldn't meet my eye, was intent instead on tucking her blouse back in.

The path turned, came to an access trail where a band of elderly women had gathered for their day's hike, walking sticks at the ready like soldiers on parade. They marched off, single file, toward Portbraddan with a confidence that bordered on bravado. If that young couple thought they were embarrassed before, wait till this parade of ladies passed by.

AT DUNSEVERICK, slabs of stone, scarcely still standing, marked what was once a crucial axis in Irish cartography, one both mythological and historical. Dunseverick Castle was where the road from the ancient capital of Tara reached the northern sea. It was, quite literally, the far edge of the Irish world. A knight from Dunseverick was at the Crucifixion, saw Christ die, was so close a drop of blood splashed his brow. It was this same Knight of Ulster who rolled the stone aside so that the body of Christ could be entombed—or so the story goes. (It's been a while since I've been to Sunday school, but I don't recall any mention of Ulstermen at Calvary that day.)

Warnings were posted at Dunseverick. Warnings about high winds that could sweep you right off the heights. And after Dunseverick the coast grew even more dramatic, more ... *heroic*. Stone archways. The jagged peak of Benadanir, where falcons, riding updrafts, turned lazy, lethal circles in the air. The trail wound its way upward, firm-packed but precarious, as the sea thrashed in tantrum among the rocks below.

It was off this coast that the Spanish Armada of 1588 came to its ignoble end. Scattered by English ships, forced up and around the top of Scotland, the Armada finally foundered. One of the Spanish ships, *La Girona*, dangerously overloaded with officers, noblemen, sailors and soldiers, struck a reef and went down near here in the midst of a wild gale. Of the 1,300 men on board, only a handful survived—some sources say nine, others as few as three. Either way, the death toll was comparable to that of the *Titanic*. Bodies washed up along the shores for weeks. The remains of one soldier were discovered on the east Antrim coast with Spanish chestnuts in his pockets. He was buried as found and years later a chestnut tree grew from his grave. Treasure from *La Girona* has been recovered, but tales persist of hoarded gold, scavenged from the wreck, hidden below floorboards even now, and for the cost of a pint, it is said you will find someone who'll let you in on the secret. (If as much gold came ashore as is claimed, this coast would be inhabited entirely by millionaires.)

"Fine day!" said a man with a walking stick, coming the other way.

Another walker, and then another. Omens of the Giant's Causeway began to appear: striated cliffs, marked by the sort of claw marks a back-hoe leaves in wet earth. On the slopes where the moss-like vegetation had peeled back, honeycombs of rock were exposed.

The Ulster Way arrives at the Causeway in the most *bravo!*-inducing fashion possible, from behind and on high, past the stone pillars of an organ-pipe formation, and then down, down, down to that most remarkable of coastlines, where a pavement of mainly hexagonal basalt pillars, as tightly packed as tiles, marches into the sea. The Giant's Causeway was created by the lovesick giant Finn McCool as stepping stones to reach a beautiful lass on the Scottish shore, or so it's said. Another version—more believable, perhaps, given McCool's Ulster heritage—is that Finn McCool built the road in order to fight a Scottish giant. (The Giant's Causeway does seem to resurface in Scotland, albeit on a much smaller scale, at the island of Staffa.) These are the mythological explanations. The scientific one, which involves lava spreading out in a pool, then cooling slowly in geometrical fissures, is nowhere near as entertaining.

The Causeway is Northern Ireland's biggest tourist draw, appearing on countless brochures and postcards. Throngs of people were scampering around and across the honeycomb, past formations with names such as "the Giant's Chimney," "the Giant's Harp" and "the Amphitheatre," and over onion-skin rocks that looked like blisters, and boulders, smoothed by a thousand years of sea, dubbed "the Giant's Pebbles." There was even a curved stone known as "the Giant's Shoe." (Using the dimensions of said "shoe," they have calculated Finn McCool's height at exactly fifty-two feet, six inches.)

This coastline is a World Heritage Site, the only one in Northern Ireland, but a common reaction on arriving at the Giant's Causeway is disappointment. When asked if the Causeway was worth seeing, Samuel Johnson famously replied, "Aye. Worth seeing, but not worth going to see." This type of response may have been based on the standard manner of approach to the Causeway: through the main entrance and then *plop!* right into the midst of it. When you come in along the coast instead, seeing the Causeway appear like something clawing its way out of the earth, the coastline and formations revealing themselves in staggering proportions around every bend, *that's* a prescriptive against disappointment.

I'd been told of the "tourism explosion" in the North—not the best choice of words when discussing Northern Ireland, perhaps—but hadn't seen much evidence of it until now. And yet, the coast was so expansive, the formations so endless, it didn't feel overrun; the crowds just added to the excitement. (Though that may have been the loneliness of the long-distance walker speaking.)

I spent the rest of the day on the Causeway. The only awkward moment came when, as I headed to the souvenir shop, I was suddenly forced to leap, cat-like, to one side, pirouetting in mid-air to hide my face. It was Bob and Marge, on their way to the parking lot. They didn't spot me, fortunately, so I was spared having to converse once again in my patented Oirish accent.

An empty stretch of road ran back toward Ballintoy. The light was fading, but traffic was steady. I found a spot, raised my thumb like Caesar passing a verdict—and almost had it taken off. The car that passed practically spun me on my heels, like a top.

Vehicles were filing out of the parking lot, and I walked backward just outside the exit, arm out, expectant, smiling. Nothing. Drivers wouldn't even make eye contact with me, and as time trickled by and the traffic thinned, I faced the awful prospect of walking back to Ballintoy on legs already rubbery and worn. Not. A. Single. Person. Stopped.

An hour passed. Darkness fell, not unlike an executioner's cloak. I had backward-walked several miles, it seemed, thumb aloft, and all for nothing. I was stranded and tired, and my temper began to bubble.

Fuck it. I turned, was about to stomp back to the Causeway centre, try to catch the last of the staff before they left, maybe beg a ride or call a cab, when, in the gathering night, a bus appeared, pushing the light of its headlamps toward me. I waved my arms above my head, stepped out almost directly into its path.

"We're not supposed to pick up on the road," the driver muttered once I'd climbed aboard.

The bus was fucking empty. What did he care? I sat in the back, fumed.

It was late by the time I arrived at the hostel. I came in to silent looks in the common room, brewed myself another fucking cup of instant fucking noodles, ate them noisily. "Foul" didn't begin to describe my mood.

"What's the deal with this country?" I asked the first people unfortunate enough to wander within range. "I tried to hitch a ride back from the Giant's Causeway. Simple, right? One road, everybody was going my way. No one stopped!"

My captive audience, a pair of young American college boys, tanned and tousle-haired, nodded sympathetically.

"That's tough, dude." (Yes, yes, yes, he bloody well said "dude.") "Me and my buddy?" he confided. "We hitched up from Dublin this afternoon, wasn't a problem."

I stopped. "Really?"

They nodded.

"Well, what am I doing wrong, then?"

"Prob'ly nothing, dude. It's just, you know, you're *old*."

His friend agreed. "No offence, but people driving by are thinking, 'What's with this guy? He's *old*, but he doesn't have a car?'"

"But ... but ... I'm not old." My voice was lost somewhere between whimper and whisper. And that's when it hit me, full on like a bag of bricks: *I was the creepy old guy in the youth hostel.* There's always one. He's always alone, he's always making noodles in the common room, always trying to talk to people. I remembered those guys. I remembered thinking, "What's he doing here? He must be, like, in his mid-thirties—at least!"

I ran to the washroom. Stared hard at my face. It was the face of someone closer to forty than to thirty, someone who'd long since left his Tír na nÓg, who hadn't seen twenty since it slipped away in the rear-view mirror a long, long time ago. It was the face of the creepy old guy in the youth hostel.

I packed up, left first thing the following morning, and haven't been back to a youth hostel since.

ANOTHER DINNER PARTY RUINED

I caught a bus back to the Giant's Causeway, pushed on, following the headland around. I could see the earth's curve in the sea. On the coast ahead: a slender arc of sand, and then Portballintrae, an early-morning arrangement in soft whites and pale peach. Beyond Portballintrae: darker headlands reaching out into the sea. That would be Donegal, in the Republic. It's one of the quirks of Irish geography that the South actually wraps around and stretches farther north than the North does.

There is a soft, minimalist quality to Portballintrae. Poised above its harbour, the town does not run to the water's edge but remains up from it, slightly aloof. The horseshoes over the doors of a thatched-roof cottage, arranged by size and upward-turned to catch the luck, echoed the shape of the town itself, for Portballintrae is a horseshoe, turned north to catch the waves, if not the fortunes, of a cold sea.

Many harbour towns have a rough-and-tumble charm about them, but not Portballintrae. "The life of the village is of a very quiet kind, and the inhabitants seem steeped in the dreamy sadness of the sea": this was the description I'd found in an 1869 travel book. The author commented on the clean, whitewashed modernity of the village, adding that he would have preferred a little "greenery" to make it more pictur-esque. "Even a little ivy trailing here and there," he suggested. The people of Portballintrae had not heeded his advice, I was happy to see, and little had changed in the interim: the town was still whitewashed and clean, and without trees for the most part, at least along its harbour.

The Ulster Way followed residential streets in among beige bunga-lows to what looked like a dead end. A sign pointed to the right, however, along a public footpath that ran directly behind the backyards of several homes. A "burglar's delight" sort of path, it turned—fled, in effect—across a hedgerow meadow and then emptied onto the busy A2.

I rounded the hangman heights of Gallows Hill, where many a soul had come to an end at the sudden snap of a noose, and there in front of me—draped across its rocky heights above the sea—lay the cliff-top ruins of Dunluce. "Mouldering upon the summit of a gloomy crag," as that 1869 travel guide put it. "A savage looking piece of solitude." The walls of the castle formed an open-air maze, with crumbling towers still standing guard on the landward side. Dunluce even had a resident banshee named Maeve, a young woman who drowned while fleeing her father's iron-fisted tyranny. Maeve's ghost now dwelled in the tower that bore her name, could be heard at night sweeping the floor. Although originally a stronghold of the fighting O'Flynns (an especially bruising Celtic clan), Dunluce was later claimed as an Anglo-Norman bastion and then—almost inevitably—by Sorley Boy and the MacDonnells.

The walls surrounded a Scottish-style manor home built by the Earl of Antrim to appease his Scots-born wife. It didn't work. She hated Dunluce. Hated the cold and damp, the constant crash of the sea, the sense of being perched upon the edge of an abyss. Her fears, as it turned out, were well founded, for during the preparations for a winter feast in 1639, while a howling storm battered the black basalt cliffs below, the castle's kitchen sheared away and fell into the sea, taking the back wall and several servants with it. (And you just know that Lady MacDonnell's first reaction was "Great! Another dinner party ruined!") A young tinker, sitting on a ledge, watched in horror as it plunged. He survived, and the windowsill he was sitting on now faces open water.

The tour buses arrive in convoy at Dunluce. I followed the crowds to the ruins, across the gap of what had once been a drawbridge, keeping a watch for Bob and Marge as I went. I could see the Skerries—a ridge of flat-slab rock that slants up, out of the Atlantic—

and beyond them, along the coast, the hook of land where the seaside resort of Portrush now beckoned with its multi-coloured homes. I took a last chestful of air from the heights of Dunluce and left the place to its modern-day siege.

A road led down to the sculpted cliffs of White Rocks: limestone arches, high pillars and standing columns, mesas and caves contoured by the sea, with the castle ruins of Dunluce rising up like stalagmites behind. Waves were rolling in along the shore, lips of water curling over, then crashing down. Curran Strand, the beach I was on, has an odd shape. The Skerries had created a back current that pulled the coast *outward*, forming an unusual convex bulge. As I walked in toward Portrush, the town slipped out of view, lost behind this curve. The Skerries, though, were closer than ever. Moss-clad and treeless, they looked more like a Japanese rock garden than a chain of islands. Seals sometimes bask on the Skerries, but there were none that day. Porpoises frolic in these waters as well, apparently, but there were none about when I went through. Eider ducks were out in full force, though, confounding the Skerries with their commotion.

I stripped my boots and socks from raw feet, walked along the tide-line on sand as soft as talc. Around the bulge of Curran Strand, I reached the boardwalk promenade on the Portrush waterfront, where tourists milled about, ice creams in hand. I felt as if I had come ashore from a shipwreck, pant legs turned up, legs wobbly, face salt-burnt and red. Somewhere along that swath of blond sand, I had passed my one-hundred-mile mark. I felt *virile*. Forget those low-slung, overpriced sports cars; you want to deal with a mid-life crisis, strap on a backpack and head for the north Antrim coast.

I sat on the promenade among the holidayers and tried to brush off the sand stuccoed to my feet. (An impossible endeavour; sand between one's toes is more impervious to movement than a Unionist politician.) Cherry-red blisters were blossoming, and I poked at them, fascinated. You could've used images of my feet to cure people with foot fetishes once and for all. My toenails had taken on a strange, bluish tinge, and the less said about my calloused heels, the better. I strapped the swellings down with bandages and hobbled (heroically) into town.

RUSTY PLASTIC

Portrush is a peninsular town, surrounded by sea on three sides; walk five minutes in any direction, and you'll soon come upon waves.

Elegant Victorian houses had been painted over in jellybean colours, limes and powder blues—lurid pastels, if such a thing is possible. Every second home seemed to be a B&B with a VACANCY sign posted. I had arrived at the end of the bathing season, though I suspect that Portrush is one of those seaside towns where it is always out of season, even when the streets are crowded, even when the tourists are splashing about. It reminded me of a saucy English postcard, where ruddy-faced men in bathing suits eye a lady's knickers, saying things like "Cor! I'd give her a lolly!" Portrush is caught in a constant crosswind, the sea always present. Pleasant in summer, perhaps, but it must be bone-chilling in the wet depths of winter.

Seagulls mewed and cried. The town was filled with their din. I wandered past T-Shirt City (one-upped by T-Shirt World farther along the street). A "tuppence arcade." Game centres, gaping and loud. The inevitable KFC. Trinket shops and souvenir stands. And eateries everywhere, offering a rich array of menu items: "Bacon, chips and sausage," "Sausage, chips and eggs," "Fish, chips and sausage," "Sausage, eggs and sausage" and, of course, "Sausage, sausage and sausage." Not to mention the ongoing libel of Northern Ireland's "steak" burgers.

I did find a few expensive restaurants, but in the plebeian middle ground, it was Death by Sausage. I suppose I could have gone for quail pâté and braised pheasant, but eating alone in such regal environs would have been far too expensive and far too depressing. I went for the sausage, eggs and sausage instead.

The main square at Portrush featured a tower clock that didn't work. It had taken me a while to realize that in Northern Ireland clocks are mainly decorative. I wandered past looming Biblical billboards that

nagged passersby with hectoring gospel creeds: "All have sinned &
come short of the glory of God." "Christ Died for the Ungodly." "It is
appointed unto men once to die, but after this the Judgment." It sort
of took away from the fun, which was the whole entire point, I
suppose—to ruin the mood. *"Okay, then, you lot go off and enjoy
yourselves—but you'd better not enjoy yourselves while you're doing it!"*

After all that hellfire, it was a relief to get back in among the
tawdrier shops and the slot machines, the souvenir stands and antique
stores cluttered with kitsch. The kitsch in Portrush is not only wide,
but deep. I sought warmth inside a tea room, where I huddled over a
cuppa beneath a breathtaking collection of ceramic teapots. Teapots
commemorating various Royal Family non-events. Teapots shaped
like rabbits and cottages, piglets and hens. There were clowns (happy)
and clowns (sad) and even one slightly demonic clown with a glint in
its porcelain eye. I was admiring the collection, had found a matching
set shaped like Laurel and Hardy, was trying to remember which one
was Hardy and which one Laurel, when I realized that the lady behind
the counter—a sweet dear who looked not unlike a porcelain teapot
herself—was deep in discussion about an armed robbery that had
happened the week before.

"He had a knife, came up to wee Nigel. Now Michael, he grabbed
the man and wrestled him down behind the counter. Then the other
fellow, he puts on as though he's helping us, but was actually with'm.
Was with a girl as well, so there was three of them. Michael was bitten—
he went to the hospital and noticed another cut on the back of his arm.
Must have been from the knife. Oh, it was past midnight by the time
they got home. Police caught most of them, they're in court today."

She was telling this story to a neckless man and his small, wiry
sidekick. The larger man leaned in, said in an intentionally ominous
tone, "They should be taken care of."

"Oh, no," the lady said quickly. "Couldn't do that."

"Our people never do. That's the problem."

It struck ice to my bone when I heard him say that; it seemed such
a leap, from teapots with pictures of the Queen to vigilante knuckles.

Around about then, the door jingled and a woman came in, a traffic warden who had, apparently, given the man a ticket earlier.

"Was my fault," he said, but he was clearly still pissed off about it. "You're from Scotland," he said.

"From Fife," she replied.

"Well, you should go back to Scotland," he said, "and stop writing up tickets so zealously."

"I'll take that as a joke," she said, without even a flicker of a smile.

"Take it how you like," he said.

"Scotland, y'say?" the smaller man cut in, trying his best to relieve the tension. "Been here long?"

"Too long," she said.

"Well, you've hung on to your accent," he replied, congratulatorily.

I'd been there too long as well, I realized. It was just a matter of time before they noticed me, and this was a conversation I did not want to be part of.

I paid and slipped out. Found a room in one of Portrush's pastel B&Bs. It was on Eglinton, a residential street that had reinvented itself as a commercial lane, and was run by a stout young couple with a dumpling of a baby.

"I'll show you to your room," said the wife.

The house rambled up three flights of stairs and down two. I followed along, hallumphing my pack. "Walkin', are yis? Well then, we'll have to give ye a full breakfast tomorrow." It was more a threat than a promise. "Aye ... a full ... Ulster breakfast." I knew what that meant: Death by Sausage.

It was pelting rain the following morning, and I could smell the Fry wafting up already.

Now, there are, by my estimation, 287,042 different types of shower fixtures in Northern Ireland, no two of which are the same. Most are made of plastic, in colours that haven't seen light of day since the 1970s: weird shades of orange and green. They come pre-broken, I believe, to save time and effort. The bathroom in this particular B&B featured a large round knob that turned one way, with a rim on the outside that turned the other way, and a metal doohicky in the middle that went up and down to no evident effect. Turning the oversized knob released a dribble of water. Turning the rim released a trickle. So those were my options. It was like being a talentless safecracker: no matter what combination of the three components I employed, the water flow never increased, and after I'd spent the better part of an hour trying to figure this out, I realized that it had been provided primarily for my amusement, a sort of early-morning brain-teaser to be played nude and shivering. That sort of thing had happened many times already: *Let's see. The large ring turns one way, the central knob turns the other way … and nothing much happens.* I kept expecting to find—indeed, was surprised I never did—shower fixtures in Northern Ireland that came in the shape of a Rubik's cube. And yes, since you asked, North American plumbing is of the highest quality known to man, with fixtures made of ivory and unicorn horns, and water that runs as clear and warm as the tears of an angel.

Having survived the trial by ordeal that is an Ulster Fry, and the dribble by tap that is an Irish shower, I set out to walk Ramore Head, the rugged hook of land that Portrush is built upon.

The rain was coming down in gusts by now. A safety rail and posted warnings advised people to stay back from the edge, but I scoffed at this. I was the Hundred Mile Man! Safety rails were for mere mortals. I strode right up to the edge and admired the view (which was slightly better from there than it was from two feet back behind the rail, thereby more than justifying the risk involved). With my rain jacket hood pulled tight, I peered over into the agitation of sea below. The town might be a cheesy postcard, but its setting was anything but.

From Ramore Head, I walked back along the other side of the peninsula, past a mass of intestinal tubing. A sewer system? No, it was the backdoor view of the Waterworld Amusement Park. *Rusty plastic*: sounds impossible, perhaps. But this was Northern Ireland; up here even plastic rusted eventually.

In the harbour, tall masts swayed drunkenly on wind and tide. The gusts were picking up, an annoyingly persistent companion that hurried me along, down the street and back to my B&B. The husband greeted me when I came in, and as I dried my glasses on a tug of shirt, I told him about my walk around Ramore Head.

The husband said, "Aye, every year someone gets dragged off. Just three weeks back a man fell in, washed up in the harbour later that day. Self-selecting, like. Sort of an IQ test. You didn't go near the edge, did you?"

"Do I look like an idiot?" It wasn't a rhetorical question. I really wanted to know.

"Once at Ramore," he said, "a wave took a father but left the wee child who was standing right beside him. Untouched. The father was the son of a fisherman. It was like the sea was hunting him."

"Really?" I said. "Pull my other leg, it's got a bell on it."

He laughed. "It's all true, I swear." And by true, he meant, of course, not true. I was starting to get the hang of this.

"Are they calling for rain tomorrow?" I asked.

"Sorry to say. Mind, there's no such thing as bad weather," he noted. "Only the wrong clothes."

To threats from his wife about tomorrow's breakfast (it would be a "right proper full breakfast," she warned), I excused myself and went upstairs to soak away some of the day's chill. Nothing like the dribble of lukewarm water to revitalize one's spirits.

CROSSING THE GREAT DIVIDE

I left Portrush the following morning with a day pack and a gut filled with Ulster Fry. In defiance of the forecasters, the sun had come out, though the day was still blustery. At a public square, amid a half-circle of cement columns, kids tried and failed at skateboard moves. Tried and failed, tried and failed. Has anyone anywhere ever seen a teenager actually complete a skateboard move in any public square—ever? Waves were rolling in. A cold day, but a few diehard surfing enthusiasts in wetsuits were bobbing in the water. They paddled out, fell off. Paddled out, fell off. Surfers and skateboarders must get along great.

No sooner had I left Portrush than I crossed into County Londonderry. The Ulster Way hugged the coast, following a path alongside a golf course, thus exposing walkers to random balls and wind gusts both. Hares played hide-and-seek in among tufts of grass. I kicked up a golf ball as I went, and soon after another arced out of the sky, bounced down in front of me. This was followed by a hearty "*Feck!*"—the Ulster equivalent of "Fore!" apparently.

This was different from the "fook" of Antrim and the "fack" of Belfast. It seemed to me that you could chart Northern Ireland's dialects through that single word—the Feck, Fack, Fook Theory of Linguistic Regional Identity. There was a research grant in there somewhere, I was sure.

The homes along the coast grew larger and closer together as I neared Portstewart. An elderly couple caught up and passed me, followed by a dog hobbling along on arthritic legs. This did nothing to bolster my confidence.

The path eventually ended and I followed a seawall into Portstewart, past faded painted messages: "British Citizens Demand Democracy!" "Smash the Cowards!" "God Save the Queen!" The same hectoring spirit I had seen on the gospel billboards earlier.

Graffiti aside, Portstewart was a more restrained, more dignified version of Portrush. It was an attractive town, with reflexology clinics and aromatherapy centres and small shops selling overpriced wooden toys. I found a quiet doorstep, pulled off my boots. My feet immediately puffed up to ten times their normal size, much in the manner of a life raft, and as I was sitting there, pushing at one of the larger blisters with an undue interest, a young colleen, sun-kissed and red of hair, stepped around me. "Hello there!" I said in my best American accent, smiling up at her. Turns out—and here's a cultural tip for you—the girls of Northern Ireland are not attracted to men with blisters. She looked at me as though I were something she had scraped off the bottom of her shoe. I rewrapped my blisters, wedged my feet back into my boots and pushed on.

West of town lay the sweeping sandbar of Portstewart Strand. I followed its graceful curve alongside grassy dunes. A lone horse rider galloped past, leaving a perfect trail of cookie-cutter prints. Waves were sliding up the shore in veils of water. Soggy islands of dulse lay stranded, and I squelched through, stirring swarms of flies as I went. *Flies really like dulse*, I thought, which is another reason to avoid eating the stuff.

Along the water's edge, tiny sandpipers hurried by like overwound commuters, little briefcases tucked under their wings. "Gotta go." "Gotta go." "Sorry." "Watch out. Coming through."

I wrestled my feet out of my boots again, soaked them in cold water with a satisfying hiss, and walked awhile on wet sand, avoiding the high-tide lines of flotsam.

At the end of Portstewart Strand, a stone seawall jutted out, holding back the beach to keep the mouth of the River Bann from silting over. I rebooted my sore feet, clambered over a tumble of blackened boulders, looked across at the seawall on the other side. Such a narrow slice of water; I could almost wade across. Heck, I could probably pee across. The smallest of gaps—and yet, it might as well have been a chasm. The only way to reach the other side of the Bann and rejoin the Ulster Way was to turn inland, walk down to Coleraine, cross a bridge and then walk back up again.

A pair of swans drifted past, unaffected by my conundrum. I'd reached one of Northern Ireland's Great Divides. Historically—and certainly psychologically—when you crossed the Bann, you crossed over from the Protestant side to the Catholic. The reality is much more complicated, of course: there are staunchly Loyalist Protestant towns west of the Bann, just as there are staunch Nationalist communities to the east of it. The Glens of Antrim were not Republican, though they were certainly Catholic. But the River Bann is a divide just the same, a mental block as much as a river.

It was apt, then, that it proved to be such a barrier. I turned, headed back to Portrush.

I RETURNED to Portstewart the following day with a cunning plan, though it wasn't *my* plan per se. It was from one of the Ulster Way guides I was using. And it wasn't so much cunning as it was completely daft. Instead of road walking, the guide said, why not arrange for a boat to ferry you across the mouth of the Bann? Maybe ask one of the fishermen.

Which is what I did.

I went down to the dock, explained my predicament, tried to hire someone. The man I spoke to had yellow rubber pants and was standing in a boat. From this, I deduced he was a fisherman.

"Across the Bann?" he said.

"That's right."

"To the other side?"

"Yes, all the way."

"To Castlerock?"

I checked the map. "Yes. To Castlerock, on the other side."

"But where would you land?" he asked.

I hadn't thought that part through.

"There's nowhere to dock," he said.

"No?"

"I suppose I could drop you off in the water, and you could wade ashore like MacArthur."

So.

Road walking it was. Down one side of the River Bann, and then up the other, through the inescapable bottleneck city of Coleraine, which sat astride the Bann like a gatekeeper of the bridges. Coleraine had a handsome central square with a grand town hall presiding; a fine place, no doubt, but I stomped through in an irritated mood. It had taken me the whole morning to get there, when all I wanted was to cross the river.

I put Coleraine behind me as quickly as I could, walking up Cranagh Road to a crest on the hill. The landscape ahead was suddenly laid out before me like a map: Donegal and the Atlantic Ocean, right where I'd left them, and the River Bann as well, twisting through the sand dunes. I could see Portstewart in the distance, could see where I'd been forced back and around, could see that narrow slice of water, the banks on either side looking like the pieces of a jigsaw puzzle that don't quite fit. Could see it all. Twenty feet of water, ten miles of road.

The train to Castlerock rattled past across the plains, and with a martyred, well-practised sigh, I started the long walk down.

I reached the Bishop's Palace just before it rained. You'd think that would be fortuitous, except for the fact that said palace had no roof. It lay across the hillside in all its Ozymandian glory, a magnificent shell. The rains turned into a steady grey drizzle, and, with my hood pulled up, I wandered through the palace as though it were a life-sized game of Clue. It had a certain regal emptiness. The walls, though, were overlaid with scratched-on graffiti, letting you know, in case you were wondering, that Fran had been there, as had Micky and Paige, and that Dave was "a perv." Such plebeian banalities etched into the very skin of the building's interior! What a downfall from glory! The eighteenth-century palace, known also as Downhill Castle, must have been splendid in its day, with lounging rooms and libraries and domed ceilings, a winter garden, drawing rooms and courtyards. Now gone. All gone.

That cheered me up considerably. If I hadn't been born an earl or a duke, with a palace of my own, I could at least take joy in the downfall of others. In this case, one Frederick Augustus Hervey, Earl of Bristol, Anglican Bishop of Derry—the "Earl Bishop," as it were, combining as he did the secular and the spiritual, though with a clear preference for the former. An eccentric and by all accounts engaging figure, the bishop was a man of fine tastes, well travelled and well learned, with a love of good wine and food, who kept, as a sort of hobby, one supposes, several mistresses in high style. (That would be the "earl" side of the equation.)

A dilettante and a rebel—and more to the point, a dilettantish rebel—he was also admirably ecumenical in his approach, offering support to the proscribed Catholic Church and earning both the respect of Voltaire and the contempt of King George. Today, the Earl

Bishop is remembered mainly for (a) his assortment of architectural follies and (b) the donkey races and other such contests—hopscotch and leapfrog—he held on the wide strand of beach below his home, contests that pitted his own often overweight clerics against those of the Presbyterians in comic events staged primarily for his own amusement. His courageous stance against sectarianism, meanwhile, is all but forgotten. Such are the vagaries of fame.

Monuments and ruins were scattered like spare change across the grassy heights of Downhill: the remnants of a walled garden, the earl's palace, the "Mausoleum" (a tower dedicated to his brother) and, at the edge of the cliffs, the Mussenden Temple.

The Mussenden Temple is probably the single-most photographed structure in Northern Ireland. A lonely domed rotunda looking out over the moody blue of the North Atlantic, balanced on the very edge of a 120-foot drop, it was meant to be a gift for the bishop's cousin, the wonderfully named Frideswide Mussenden, a young woman with whom he shared a deep and—to judge by the rumours that linger even now—deeply unhealthy affection. The temple was designed as a library wherein she might read books and gaze out upon the ever-changing seascape, though sadly she died before the building was completed in 1785. That the design was based in part on the temple of the Vestal Virgins in Tivoli—a reference to Frideswide's "virginal" character—does suggest that the good bishop failed in any alleged attempts at seduction. (Though one is tempted to scratch "Bishop Hervey's a perv" on the tower's side.)

Donegal, across the water, was so close now you could have bounced pennies off it. Alas, having spent a day getting to this point, I now had to turn around and go back. My gear was still in Portrush. And so, to the saucy postcard and rusty plastic I now returned, by train and bus and, finally, by taxi. It was dark by the time I got back.

It had been very much a Sisyphean day. *Two steps forward, one step back.*

Part Four

LOST IN THE SPERRINS

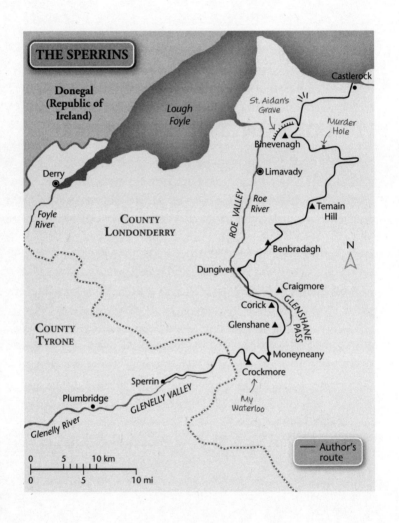

CASTLEROCK TO THE GLENELLY VALLEY

Through the Interior

Want to know the secret of Ireland's lush, green riches, the magic pixie dust that makes the Emerald Isle so emerald? It's not the blood of patriots, or the morning dew or evening mists. No, it's a simple recipe, really: take equal parts sheep shit, cow manure and rain. Mix thoroughly. Spread with a lavish generosity. Let steep.

I know this, for I have walked the wild heart of Ulster. I have hiked the Sperrin Mountains in rain and mud and rain again, a boot-sucking, soul-swallowing experience that took me through every kind of shit Ulster has to offer—figuratively and not—and I have lived to tell the tale.

LAND OF THE O'CAHANS

It started with clammy pillowcases and sheets that smelled faintly of mildew. That didn't bother me, as most of Ireland smells faintly of mildew. Throw in some cigarette smoke, maybe a waft of spilled beer, and you have the essence of any good pub.

In this case, though, it was more troubling. I'd checked in at a faded guest house where an elderly lady showed me to a dank room with dank sheets, and I woke the next morning feeling itchy.

I spent most of the morning getting back to where I'd left off: the gates of the Earl Bishop's Downhill estate. *Downhill.* Was ever there a more alluringly named locale for a walker? Unfortunately, Downhill soon turned uphill, plunging inland through a canyon-like gap in the cliffs. This was Bishop's Road, another project by pervey Hervey, and it angled upward, above sandy shores, past farms and fieldstone fences, into wilder heights of stunted forest.

When I finally reached the crest of Bishop's Road, the view beyond opened up as though a curtain had been parted. And what a view it was. A dizzying sweep to sea and shore, it provided a striking study in contrasts: of curves and colours and competing textures. Tablecloth fields below, spreading out toward the sandpaper arc of Magilligan Strand—longest beach in Ireland. The metallic sheen of Lough Foyle with the bruised blue of the North Atlantic and the humped back of Donegal beyond.

A viewing platform had been cut into the cliffs, and spires of stone fell away into forest and plain. Tidy farms, tiny fields. I could hear a train rattling across the flatlands below, and suddenly the entire landscape felt like that of a model railway, idealized, miniaturized.

Updrafts were carrying mist along the cliffs. I was standing at the boundary between climate zones, where currents of wind and rain met to battle it out. I was walking upward into colder climes. The mist grew heavy, turned to rain. My waist was now itching and raw; from the damp and the friction of my jeans, I assumed. By the time I reached the edge of Binevenagh Forest, I'd had enough. Several hours of slogging had left me clammy from the condensation that builds up inside rain gear, no matter how "breathable." My feet were more swollen than usual. Walking on blisters is never fun, and my midriff was burning too. I unhitched my belt and dug in with both hands, but it was an itch that grew with the scratching. I pulled up my shirt: a suture line of welts had formed at an angle across my stomach. I needed some sort of cream. I needed a long bath, a good bowl of soup. I needed to get off this mountain.

On the Ordnance Survey map I spotted an escape route: a road that slanted sharply to the plains below. I followed it down, coming out of the mist as though descending from a cloud. Three of my blisters burst, pop-pop-pop, like bubble wrap. The only thing worse than hiking on blisters is hiking on broken blisters; it's like fire-walking, but without the high-fives at the end.

I hobbled along, down to the base of Binevenagh and around, until I came to St. Aidan's Church and Holy Well. I knew that "holy well" meant Catholic, and Catholic meant miraculous cures. I considered going into the chapel, maybe reciting a prayer for people like me—*"O Abstract Concept in which I truly wish I could believe ..."*—but I decided to seek out the well instead. It was a "wart well," as it turned out, and blisters being a subspecies of wart, I felt I might soak my aching feet in Holy Goodness, be cured Lourdes-like before going on, maybe splash a bit of water discreetly down my trousers to ease the welts that had formed there as well.

The well was near a grotto dedicated to the Virgin Mary. Rosaries were draped across Mary's hands, which were held out in prayer, and her feet were adorned with fresh flowers. Of all the things Protestants discarded—the Pope, the saints, the relics, the bones—the one thing we really should have kept was the veneration of Mary. She has such a softening effect, giving a glimpse of deeper, more feminine forms of worship, far beyond the rigid stone-carved commandments and Thou Shalt Nots.

Binevenagh Mountain rose straight up behind St. Aidan's in a black wall, the upper reaches lost in a sea of mist, cliffs rising directly into the overcast. There was no one about save a workman who was wheeling plaster into the graveyard and putting the final touches on a headstone. He saw me, nodded as he passed, and I decided not to soak my feet in the Holy Water of Christ, in case there was some taboo I didn't know about. Wet bandages were wadded into the stones around the well like papier mâché mortar, and the water was cool and clean, which meant you could see the debris on the bottom: coins and leaves, mainly, but a few wayward bandages as well.

"Tea cup's jest there, like."

I turned, startled. It was the workman, in overalls, dusted in plaster. "For the war."

"The war?"

"Aye. T'drink like or wash wi'."

Ah yes, water. The "t" was silent, apparently.

"Need t'rub yer hands inna durr."

"Inna durr?"

"Aye, a' St. Aidan's grave. It's wha' we say anyway. C'mon. I'll show ye."

His name was Kevin O'Neill. A sturdy-built man of middle years, with a salted moustache, a gentle demeanour and a thick mouthful of accent. You know how when someone speaks Dutch, even though you don't know the language, you can sort of pick out every second or third word? That's how it was for me. I missed a lot of what he said on the impromptu tour that followed.

Mr. O'Neill built monuments, was finishing up his day's work, and he walked me up to the medieval ruins behind the current church. In one crumbling corner stood a nook the size and shape of a bread oven. But it wasn't an oven. It was an open grave.

"Reach in," said Mr. O'Neill.

The idea was to rub your hands in the dirt and then walk down to the well to wash it off. It was really my feet that needed tending, but I couldn't think of a polite way of soaking my blisters in the well. Especially as there was a cup. I didn't imagine pilgrims would want to be drinking from my foot bath. I laid my palm inside the grave instead. The soil was cool to the touch and the sensation vaguely spooky, as though a hand might lunge out and grab me by the wrist.

We walked back to the Holy Well so I could wash the dust off.

"Y'kin drink from it as well, if ye like."

I looked at the bandages along the bottom. "Maybe next time."

Two of Kevin O'Neill's sons had appeared, though I wasn't sure from where. Strong Ulster lads, both of them, and they took their da's role of tour guide in stride.

"Where ye gettin' to then?" they asked me.

The nearest town on the map was Limavady. "Limavady?"

"Ah," they assured me. "Ye don't want Limavady."

I don't?

"Naw. We'll give ye a ride inna Dungiven."

Even better. Dungiven was on route.

"We'll show ye the ol' priory," the father said.

They piled their small pickup with wheelbarrows and shovels. I offered to ride in the back, with the wheelbarrows, but they squeezed me in up front instead.

Mr. O'Neill popped the truck into gear. "They've been helpin' out. I ha' three sons an'a darr'r."

They corrected him. "Four sons, Da."

"Aye, tha's right."

"Hard to unnerstann'm?" asked the younger son as we drove along, the truck bucking from the weight. "Our da?"

"A bit," I admitted.

"Ah, is worse in Derry," the father said. "They doan speak there, they sing."

"Honestly, it's not so bad," I said to Mr. O'Neill. "I probably understand about eighty percent of what you're saying." I was being generous in my estimate.

The sons laughed. "Doin' better'n we are then," the older boy said. "We doan unnerstann half a wha' he says."

I'D CROSSED a political divide, and IRA signs and Irish tricolours greeted me as we drove into the mountain pass of Dungiven. It was a reminder that in Northern Ireland *altitude* determines both the nature of the landscape and the communities therein. In his seminal study *God's Peoples*, historian Donald Harman Akenson notes that in the North you can tell whether an area is predominantly Catholic or Protestant simply by its height above sea level, Catholics having been pushed out of the fertile valleys and plains into the hills. Dungiven, in the heart of the Sperrins, was a case in point.

The town is located in a saddleback, with bald mountains above and rolling hills below. The Sperrins all but encircle the town, adding an ominous backdrop to every view. This is the Land of the O'Cahans. What the MacDonnells were to the coast, the O'Cahans were to the hills and valleys, and after Mr. O'Neill dropped off his sons, he ran me out to the old priory, principal burial site of the O'Cahans.

I knew about Dungiven Priory, had circled it on my map. It was one of the oldest ecclesiastical stone-and-mortar structures in Ulster, with a nave that was built in the early 1100s on the site of an even older pre-Norman monastery. The O'Cahans built their manor home here at the priory, uniting religious and political power, making Dungiven their stronghold. Once a centre of power and intrigue, the priory now slumbered quietly in its wooden grove among the fields, like an old man dreaming of campaigns past.

The headstones were on hilly ground, and we tramped in through high weeds.

"Used t' play here when a'was a wean," Mr. O'Neill said, "wean" meaning child, from "wee 'un" I imagine. I wondered if it had influenced his choice of vocation, playing among tombstones like that.

"The Seven Sons," he said. "Are'n there."

We entered the nave, now a roofless ruin, and Mr. O'Neill showed me the mausoleum at the back. Its heavy doors were bolted shut, but you could peek in through wire mesh, and as my eyes adjusted to the dark, details emerged.

"This used t'be open," he said. "W'played in there as well."

It was the finest tomb of its kind in Northern Ireland, the final resting place of the great Cooey-na-Gall O'Cahan, who died in 1385. The lid of the chieftain's coffin featured a stone effigy of a king lying in rest, with a line of soldiers carved below in what looked to be kilts. Those would be the Seven Sons. I counted them.

"There's only six," I said.

Mr. O'Neill peered in. "Aye? Well, one of 'em must be out."

"Popped down to the shop?" I asked.

"Maybe."

The Sons were in fact Scottish mercenaries, gallowglass warriors as they were known, who fought alongside the O'Cahans.

As we walked back from the priory along a wooded lane, Mr. O'Neill pointed to a turreted rooftop peering above the trees. "Dungiven Castle," he said. "Ye kin stay there. They rent rooms, like." And here I'd been preparing to sleep in a bog. A castle sounded dandy, but *dammit*, this itch wouldn't go away; I needed to sort that out first.

Mr. O'Neill passed me on, baton-like, to a lady who was tending a grave at the current church in front of the old priory. He wanted me to see a modern monument: the grave of Francis McCloskey.

"First person t'die inna Troubles," said Mr. O'Neill. "Beaten t' death by the RUC." The starting casualty of what would become a thirty-year civil war.

The lady agreed. "You think that oul priory is history?" she chided me. "Real history began in 1968."

Mr. O'Neill had to be going, and I thanked him profusely.

"Ye'll be all right then?" he asked.

"Oh, he'll be fine," said the lady. She was a well-tended woman in skirt and modest heels, and she took me over to see a grand headstone: that of a local IRA member who had starved himself to death during the hunger strikes of the 1980s. A tour of the graves of Dungiven wouldn't be complete without it. We'd driven past banners of the emaciated hunger strikers on our way in, Christ-like in their depictions, hung high along the wide streets of Dungiven. Ireland was converted to Christianity without producing a single martyr, unique in the history of the faith in Western Europe. But they have more than made up for it since; indeed, the island has become something of a factory for modern-day martyrs, Republican and Unionist alike.

"If you need a place to stay …," the woman said, concerned that a stranger might be without shelter in her town.

Try as I might, I was never able to reconcile the politics of Northern Ireland with the kindness of its people. Or overcome the unease I felt when the conversations drifted toward sectarian shoals. *Catholics are not all terrorists, any more than Protestants are all bigots.*

Of course not. But it was the tacit approval given to terrorists and bigots respectively that I found so disconcerting. This woman was almost maternal in her concern for me, even as she took dark delight in the tales she related. Ghost stories have a long pedigree in Ireland, North and South—ghoulish deaths and ghastly debts repaid from beyond the grave—and the recent Troubles had produced a wealth of new versions. As we walked through the graveyard, she spoke in a musical lilt, pointing out and explaining each death in turn. Horror stories of a woman shot in front of her children, of a man whose face was chewed off by guard dogs when he tried to escape from prison. "They set the dogs on him, caught him in the river, so they did. It was awful."

And why was he in jail? Oh, let's not get into that.

My stomach burn had turned into a low-grade rash, and my feet needed a serious soak, so I declined the woman's offer to stay in her home. She gave me a phone number and address for when I got to Belfast. "They'll explain the history better'n I can. They'll have lots of information. Be careful though," she said. "It's near the Shankill, and the Prods are on a rampage."

The number in Belfast she gave me was for the main Sinn Féin office, political wing of the IRA.* Was I being recruited? Did I look like Republican material? A Sinn Féin sympathizer?

I knew why. It was because I hadn't said anything while she spoke of the brave IRA men. In saying nothing, I had in fact acquiesced. In Northern Ireland nothing is neutral, not even silence.

DUNGIVEN WAS a classic Irish town, the type you might see North and South, with shops lining up along a single main street, the storefronts creating one continuous wall, and a river running past that was more or less ignored. (The lack of interest Irish towns show in their river fronts is a defining trait. It's only recently that rivers have begun

---

*Sinn Féin, of course, denies any association with the IRA, with a wide-eyed innocence that isn't fooling anyone.

to be appreciated, with riverside paths and parks put in. For the most part, they have been dumping grounds at worst, benevolently neglected at best. Often, if you made your way behind the shops on the main street, you would discover a quiet river flowing past, untended and cheerfully undervalued.)

I counted at least five pubs as I walked down from the priory, which reflected well on the town, I thought. Along the way, I came upon an engraved stone set in the sidewalk marking the exact spot where Francis McCloskey was killed on July 14, 1969, "murdered by the RUC," according to the town's plaque. The police would tell a different story, no doubt.

The RUC station farther down was, not coincidentally, a fortress with corrugated steel walls and a watchtower. The town's Presbyterian church actually backed onto the police station, with mesh over its stained glass windows to protect it against projectiles, stones, history. Siege and counter-siege; the ongoing waltz that is Ulster.

The Ulster Way ran straight through Dungiven, but the only evidence of this was a single waymarker pointing in the general direction of the Sperrin Mountains.

I had more immediate concerns to deal with. I could no longer pretend that the line of welts on my abdomen was simply a rash from rain and friction. The welts now extended well below my beltline, and in the hazy recesses of my brain, I remembered a story my brother Sean had told, of a charming hotel in Paris and the charming guests he had picked up there. I found a phone booth.

"Hullo," Sean said, groggy-headed in Montreal.

Oh right, time zones. This was an emergency, though.

"Sean," I said. "It's me."

"Billy?" (When he's tired, he forgets I've graduated to Will.)

I explained my situation. "Do you think it's bedbugs?" I asked.

"Oh no," he said. "It's not bedbugs."

Whew!

"It's scabies. Much worse. When did they come to the surface of your skin?"

"Just today."

"Good, so you haven't infected any bedding. You have to do something right away. You know the line of sores? Those are scabie tracks."

"And?"

"They're heading for your crotch."

Words to send a shiver through the most stout-hearted of travellers. "Oh my God, what do I … "

"Permethrin lotion," Sean said. "And lots of it."

I ran to the first chemist's I saw. Dungiven girls are known for their beauty, and the young woman who was about to lock up was no exception.

"Just closing," she said with a smile. "Sorry."

"No, please, I just need to—it'll just take a second. Two seconds, tops."

"Shall I time you, then?" she asked, stepping aside to let me in. "American, are you?"

"Even better," I said.

"Not Irish?" she laughed.

I hunted down said liquid, grabbed two enormous jars of it, took them up to the counter, smiling rakishly. "What did I say? Two seconds, am I right?"

Her smile had disappeared. And when I looked down at the label, I realized why. FOR SCABIES, BEDBUGS & PUBIC LICE.

An awkward moment passed between us. I considered blurting out, "I don't have pubic lice!" but it seemed that would only add to the awkwardness. Instead, I paid and hurried out, eyes down and face burning.

The lady at the B&B must have thought I was a germaphobe of the first order. I stood in the very centre of the room, equidistant from everything, touching absolutely nothing as she went over the details. As soon as she left I ran for the bathroom, disrobed, stared in dismay at the advance my parasitic invaders had already made. You have to smother them alive, and I used a towel soaked in permethrin to blot my entire body from nose to toes. I washed my face with the stuff, leaned over the sink and trickled it through my scalp, soaked a facecloth in it and wrung it over my shoulders, let it run down my back. I looked like a chalky ghost by the time it had dried.

I changed into clean clothes, then threw the ones I'd been wearing into the family's washing machine on the hottest setting, adding three times the recommended amount of detergent. Bubbles began to ooze out the top, and I stood over the machine expecting an eruption of foam at any moment. My clothes spun dry with soap bubbles still on, so I ran them through again to make sure they were thoroughly rinsed. Suds were still clinging to them, so I ran them through again. The lady passed by half an hour later, saw me maintaining my grim vigil, said nothing. *"A germaphobe who washes his clothes three times in a row and stands over the washer protectively as though a dingo might steal his underwear at any moment. Why'd the Northern Ireland Tourist Board give him our number?"*

MURDER HOLE

You'll be happy to know it worked. The wee critters never made it to the tropical forest of my pubes, nor did I infect that guest house in Dungiven.

Being a long-distance hiker means being a cheap drunk. You walk until your legs ache and your soles hurt and your inner monologue starts to drive you mad—you walk all day like that, starting at dawn, and you fade with the sun. Hit the bar at the end of a day's hike, and a single pint will be plenty; by ten o'clock you're falling asleep at the counter like the town lush. Dungiven is a centre for Irish music, but after only a single session I had crawled back to the B&B and into bed. Having doused myself with lotion, I now hid like a vampire in my room. Just as well, because I had a long day ahead of me and needed all the rest I could get.

Having been whisked down to Dungiven by Mr. O'Neill and sons, I would have to do the next leg in reverse, across the Sperrins and back to Bishop's Road. I would be carrying all of my gear with me and camping on the trail, pitching my small tent when darkness fell. I would be at the mercy of imminent weather—and in Northern Ireland the weather is always imminent.

Sure enough, the clouds above Dungiven that morning were set on slow boil, the meteorological equivalent of a foreboding chuckle. My blisters had deflated—praise be to St. Aidan!—but my feet were still tender. I stepped as lightly as one can with a Ford Pinto strapped to one's back, eyeing the clouds all the while, trying to read the winds.

I'd become obsessed with my feet and with the sky: the silly and the sublime. And tonight I'd be sleeping in the hills.

FROM DUNGIVEN, the Ulster Way ran up and over Benbradagh Mountain, across hardscrabble slopes suitable only for rough grazing— and Catholic farms. The Roe Valley was laid out below like a loose blanket. Fields and undulating farmland, tidy meadows and wooded lanes falling away with every step. This would remain the most striking aspect of the Sperrins: how pastoral farmlands gave way so suddenly to barren heights strafed by wind and rain.

A cold mist was coming down. It was as though the mountains themselves were exhaling steam, and I walked into it, was swallowed whole. Dark shapes. Spectral sheep. Ghostly outlines of stunted thorn trees. By the time I reached the flattened summit of Benbradagh, the world below had been erased. A metal gate appeared, and I slung my backpack over, following it across. The winds at the top didn't so much howl as moan. *Banshee weather*.

I crossed one hump, then another, began the long descent out of the mists again. The far side of the mountain was even lonelier and emptier, with lichen-stained boulders scattered across heathery slopes. I could see a single farmhouse on the road ahead, perched on the edge of dark forests, and when I passed, a silhouette in the window stopped and watched as I went by. I came to Legananam Pot—"pot" being the name for a phenomenon in which the ground collapses in on itself, taking a pocket of forest with it, creating a sunken garden effect.

Another farmhouse sat almost on the edge of this pothole; an unnerving place to live, I imagined.

A waymarker pointed me into an impenetrable wall of bush, so I improvised, charting my own route along a half-forgotten trail through the trees that was, nonetheless, marked on the Ordnance Survey. I came out onto open fields, crossed a swaybacked fence and—*splat!* Laces deep in ripe wet cow flop. I'd let my gaze drift upward, had forgotten that it's the immediate foreground one needs to be wary of. I found an open bit of bog water and sloshed my boot around, trying to wash off the worst of the manure. I succeeded only in adding a piquant peaty aroma to the already intoxicating bouquet of cow patty perfume. It was a combination that would follow me like an unwanted guest for days to come. I had never stepped over, around, or in so much cow shit. It was the price you paid for fields that green, but still.

When I came to a natural stone amphitheatre on the side of a hill, I huddled there for lunch (SPAR sandwiches and Oriental Rib potato chips), a kingly repast tainted only by the aforementioned aromas. It's really hard to enjoy a sandwich when the smell of cow shit has filled your mouth. The road beyond led me to the miracle of a rural crossroads pub: The Pot Bar (in reference to another sinkhole nearby). It wasn't open, alas, and no amount of door-rattling *Hallooos* could rouse the owners. I went on with thirst tragically unslaked.

The Ulster Way led me through forests and then up the grassy sides of Temain Hill. Cattle, black and tan, ambled over to see me as I walked along the road. Horses, skittish and mane-tossing, bolted as I passed. A lone driveway led down to a farm at the edge of the forest; these would be their cattle, their horses. Bony knuckles of rock were now showing through the grass. A gate drawn across the road had a "Children at Play" sign attached, and someone had been using the silhouettes of the two small children as target practice, the dings and dints in tight clusters on the heads and hearts. A disconcerting sight, to be sure, though probably a testament more to boredom than anything else. Still … I hurried through the gate, cast a sidelong glance at the farm below, picked up my pace.

A cat's cradle of grey communication towers rose in the distance, the satellite dishes on the side as large as Lambeg drums. A sign identified them as "Electricity Radio Telephone Stations," which seemed to cover all the bases.

Wisps of mist clung to the hillside, but I could see Donegal in the distance. The clouds began to pull apart like wool, letting the sun break through, and a wave of light swept toward me, across Lough Foyle and over the valley, illuminating each meadow, each hand-drawn square of green in turn, moving up the very heights I was standing on. Every hillock, every cluster of grass stood out in bright relief—and then it was gone. The clouds resealed, the mists returned.

I longed to follow the road down into that tea-cozy landscape below and leave the lonely barrens behind. But no. I had moors to cross, forests to thread and miles to go before I slept. I picked my way across the boggy landscape, hitting water with every third step. An alpine fog had settled upon the hills, and the fence posts I had been following marched off into nothingness. With a growing sense of being lost at sea, I turned, considered going back, but the towers behind me were now only faint Etch-a-Sketch renderings—and then they were gone as well. I wondered whether a person could drown in fog, if fog might ever grow thick enough to suffocate a man. I walked on. Rows of wind turbines were faintly visible, blades appearing and disappearing as they stirred the swirling mists.

A line of trees began to take form ahead of me. I had reached the edge of Cam Forest. I found a gap and followed it in, down to a forestry road, letting gravity do the rest. I came out at a busy highway that cut through the woods; I'd heard the traffic long before I arrived. In a nearby paddock, a pair of thoroughbreds snorted steam, regal in their chess-piece profiles.

Having made it across open moors, through bog and fog, having threaded my way unaided through the darkest forests, having done all that, I was now greeted by an Ulster Way waymarker. The waymarkers, I realized, were more congratulatory than purposeful. A sort of pat on the back for having made it through. *"Yes, you are still on the Ulster Way. Well done."*

I followed the edge of the highway for a mile or so and then—between bursts of traffic—ran across to the other side, where a second Ulster Way sign pointed me back into the forest. This would be the pattern for the rest of the afternoon: passage through dark woods, an exit onto sudden highways, a bone-rattling walk alongside traffic, and then a plunge back into dark woods.

The day bled away. A caravan campsite was marked on my map about two miles off route. But if I kept going, if I pushed on, I would reach a second campsite farther away, but on route. That seemed the better plan. I studied the maps. Looked at the sky. I had an hour of light at most, so I would have to hurry. I traced the route I would need to take to the second campsite: up Formoyle Hill, past Murder Hole, into Grange Park Woods and then—hang on. Murder Hole? An unusually descriptive name, that. Vaguely familiar-sounding, as well. I rummaged in my backpack, came up with a guide to local lore, found the entry for Murder Hole.

> *This lonely road was once the site of an infamous highwayman who preyed on lone travellers, slicing their throats and taking what little money they had before burying their bodies in unmarked graves. It's said the ghost of that highwayman yet stalks Murder Hole Road, and in the still of night you can hear his mournful—*

Well, that settled it. A four-mile detour it was.

I had no intention of spending the night in any area marked "Murder Hole." So off route I went, along forestry trails to the first caravan site. I'd been hoping, foolishly as it turned out, that other campers might show up, but no. It was just me. I'd bivouacked on trails in other places, in Okinawa and in the foothills of the Rocky Mountains, where snakes and bears respectively make a middle-of-the-night pee a nerve-racking adventure. Ireland had no snakes,

St. Patrick having ethnically cleansed the island of them. No bears, either. It did, however, have banshees and fog and phantom highway-men, and that was bad enough. I felt spectral myself, still powdery pale from my self-anointment rites the day before. You can't shower for twenty-four hours after application, so I also had a manly, musky aroma about me, to put it euphemistically. You know how they say people's olfactory senses are designed not to find their own body odour repugnant? That isn't true.

The small tent I was carrying was really just a glorified sleeping bag with a cover that forked over it. And though my backpack was theoretically waterproof, I dragged it inside to be safe. I woke to find myself embracing it, which was too symbolic for words. I had passed the night in dead slumber. Condensation was beaded on the inside of the tent. The droplets grew, trickled into each other.

I crawled outside, cotton-mouthed and shoulder-stiff, watched dawn break across an empty world. It was that time of day when only the wind is awake. I would have killed for a cup of coffee. I'd planned to purchase a small stove when I first arrived but had forgotten about that until the very moment I needed it. I rolled my sleeping bag up, or rather tried to; sleeping bags are the snakes-in-a-peanut-can novelty item of camping gear. I ended up punching the bag back into its ridiculously small nylon sack. I ate an ironically named "power bar"— compressed cardboard and old newsprint from the taste of it—then packed up my equally ironically named "tent."

A cool morning, rich in mist. Where the other forests had funnelled me more or less straight through, this one, Springwell, was a confusing labyrinth of rutted tracks and planted trees. I retraced my steps to where I'd left off, turned north on what I hoped was the right trail. Every fork in the path required a lengthy consultation with my map. It was hard enough to find my way through rested and in daylight; thank God I hadn't tried this at dusk. I came out past a church and a clutch of farmhouses onto a desolate road that ran through a high gap in the hills toward—I took a deep, steadying breath—Murder Hole.

The "hole" was little more than a dip in the road where a derelict building now stood amid nettles and tall grass. Empty windows, staring outward. Stone walls, crumbling inward. A backdrop of dark forest behind. These, presumably, were the ruins of the Ram's Horn Coaching Inn, whose owners had once been in murderous cahoots with the cutthroats who prowled the hills. A chill hung in the air— one not entirely related to temperature. In this hollow many a solo traveller's journey had come to a premature end. I pushed on, walking a little faster than was necessary.

The heights of Binevenagh were shrouded in fog—permanently so, apparently. The Ulster Way offered a scenic detour around a summit-top lake located, improbably, on the edge of the Binevenagh cliffs. I made the long walk in, even though the murky mop-water of fog I was trudging through allowed views only of the ditches on either side and a few feet of the gravel ahead. When I finally reached the reedy edge of Binevenagh Lake, water and mist had merged into a blurry grey, as though the lake didn't have a far shore but simply dropped off the edge of the unseen cliffs. *This must be what it was like at the edge of the world,* I thought. *Back when the world was still flat. This must have been how the oceans ended.*

Details emerged, like smoke given form. I could see the silhouettes of shore-side fishermen casting lines into the ether. Boats were not permitted on Binevenagh Lake—just as well, you wouldn't want to sail off the end of the world—so it was fly fishing and spinners instead.

As I walked past, a fisherman said, "Be careful now. The cliffs are just there, like." He pointed into the sea of grey ahead.

With no views available and no reason to risk tumbling off the sides of Binevenagh, I turned around instead, started on the long trudge back to the main road. Plonks of water began to tap me on the shoulders, insistent, as though they had something to tell me. I started my descent, coming down out of the mists once again like a hermit from the hills. My glasses, beaded with rain, created watercolour starbursts of light: halos and prisms, fleeting rainbows. I was travelling through Ulster in a fog. Literally, figuratively, meteorologically—any way you care to take it.

I needed a bath. I needed a bed and a warm room. I needed a ride, is what I needed.

Still chastened from my experiences on the Causeway coast, I slogged on, head down, not wanting to hold out my thumb and give drivers the satisfaction of not stopping. Which is when I discovered a certain Zen-like quality to hitching rides in Northern Ireland. Hold out a thumb, and drivers eye you with suspicion. Turn your back on them, and they stop.

A car pulled over. One of the fishermen from the lake.

"A damp day," he said, as I crawled in.

I agreed. It was a damp day indeed.

He drove me down and around, past St. Aidan's, below the cliffs I'd skirted earlier. Looking up, I realized that I had never actually *seen* the top of Binevenagh.

The driver laughed. "Well, it's up there somewhere," he said. "You'll have to take our word for it."

THE MANY WALLS OF DERRY

I set my sights on Derry, catching a bus from Limavady, off route and heading for Northern Ireland's second-largest city.

Its formal name is Londonderry. The locals call it Derry (after the original name, Doire, from the Gaelic meaning "oak grove"). Londonderry is its Protestant name, Derry is its Catholic name, something that throws visitors and politicians into no end of verbal contortions. "*It's nice to be here in the City of Derry, in the County of Londonderry.*" The city's largest, most staunchly Protestant organization, the Apprentice Boys of *Derry* (emphasis mine), protested angrily when the city's municipal government changed its name to the Derry City Council, even though the city itself is still officially "Londonderry." And even though one of the most beloved Unionist songs is a ditty known as "*Derry's* Walls" (again, emphasis mine). If you're not confused by this point, you're not paying attention. The newspaper columnist and radio host Gerry Anderson, meanwhile, refers to it as "Stroke City," in reference to the stroke (i.e., slash) that is so often employed: Londonderry/Derry. But even that is fraught with political undertones. Which name do you put first? Should it be Derry/Londonderry? This is Ulster: there are no easy answers.

The Old City really ought to be called Londonderry, though. It was Protestants who built it, defended it, named it. With the modern city having spilled out, far beyond the original gates, Londonderry today is the walled district *within* the city of Derry. I'm a sucker for walled cities: Quebec, York and now the Old City in Derry. (The corrugated steel "peaceline" walls of Belfast don't count.) The first wholly planned city in Ireland, Londonderry was a classic example of Renaissance city planning, with its central Diamond and iron-grid pattern of streets radiating outward with a geometric clarity.

In 1689, Londonderry's walls withstood a siege that lasted 105 days, the longest in the history of the British Isles, when the Protestant population inside held out against the forces of the deposed Catholic king, James II. James had been ousted in a bloodless coup—the "Glorious Revolution," as it is known—when a group of British parliamentarians invited the king's daughter Mary and son-in-law, the Dutch prince William of Orange, to come to England and claim the throne as co-monarchs.* This was done to counter recent moves toward Catholic emancipation that James had launched and to block the possibility of a Catholic dynasty on the throne of England. (Even today, the head of the British Royal Family is explicitly forbidden from ever marrying a Catholic. And they wonder why Catholics in Northern Ireland have been tepid in their support of the Queen.)

With James Catholic, and William and Mary Protestant, the stage was set for an epic battle, a clash of the kings, James II vs. William III,

---

*William's title refers to the Principality of Orange in southern France, where William's family had been based before shifting their focus to Holland.

Catholic resistance vs. Protestant ascendance. Or, to put it in proper Ulster terms, Jimmy vs. Billy. It was part of a larger continental game of chess aimed at blocking the imperial and territorial ambitions of France's Sun King, Louis "*L'état c'est moi*" XIV. (The hapless James, having been chased off his throne, had sought refuge and support in Louis's court.) Ireland was the battleground, and there it would be perceived very much as an ethnic-religious war, one that pitted Planter against Gael. Never mind that many of the Planters were themselves Gaelic Scots.

When the Protestant garrison inside Londonderry was ordered to evacuate in the winter of 1688 to make room for incoming Catholic troops, the people inside sensed a massacre in the making, and a band of thirteen apprentice boys slammed shut the gates of the city, locking the doors and rallying the populace.

The following spring, James himself appeared outside the city walls and demanded that Londonderry surrender. Instead, he was fired upon. So he sat on his horse in the rain, a forlorn figure, waiting for the people inside to change their minds. They never did. James left, and the siege of Londonderry began. Mortar bombs and cannonballs fell; famine and pestilence stalked the crowded streets. People were reduced to eating candles and shoe leather, as well as rats and dogs that had fattened from eating corpses. At one point a hollowed-out cannonball was fired into the city, carrying a message outlining possible terms—the first known example of "air mail," as it's been called. The reply from inside the city walls was adamant. *No surrender!*

It's a cry that echoes still.

The siege of Londonderry stands with the Battle of the Boyne as a defining moment in Protestant Irish history. Londonderry held on, the siege was lifted, and the following summer, on the banks of the River Boyne, the two kings finally met face to face. James lost, William won, and the Protestant Ascendancy was affirmed. Ireland's notorious Penal Laws soon followed, with their punitive restrictions on the Catholic faith and, more to the point, on Catholic land ownership.

Never mind that the Pope was on the side of King William and had even helped fund his campaign (an embarrassing fact, that): the Siege of Londonderry and the Battle of the Boyne have long since left the realm of history and entered that of myth. The Orange Order, the Apprentice Boys, the Lambeg drums and the endless, endless marching have seared these received mythologies into the collective memory. Catholics view the marches as triumphalist braggadocio; Protestants see them as a cultural touchstone, marking defiant survival in the face of overwhelming odds. The possibility exists that both interpretations are correct. Never mind that William's army contained a vanguard of elite Catholic troops, and never mind that the Pope celebrated when James was defeated, and never mind that James himself had wanted to proscribe the Irish language and replace it with proper English; this isn't about history, it's about tribal lore, about memories that move just below the surface, like a vein under skin.

Derry, as it is now known, is also where the modern Troubles began.

Following the partition of Ireland in 1921, Catholics in the North were considered treasonous almost by definition, and their communities were systematically ground down and ghettoized. The unabashed, wholehearted exclusion of Catholic citizens in Northern Ireland was entrenched at the local level for more than forty years. The voting system itself was rejigged to give Protestants an inflated and permanent majority, and the gerrymandering of electoral boundaries and the allocation of public housing to favour Protestants was almost breathtaking in its audacity. If Unionists could have denied Catholics the vote outright, they would have. As it was, the property requirements for enfranchisement achieved much the same thing: you couldn't vote unless you owned property, and far more Protestants than Catholics owned their homes. The system even allowed some individuals to have *multiple* votes, granted overwhelmingly to Protestants. It was as though the Penal Laws had never been revoked.

By 1966, in Derry, twenty thousand Catholics were represented by eight city councillors; half that number of Protestants, meanwhile, were represented by *twelve* city councillors. This gave Protestants a permanent grip on the city—even though they were now very much in the minority. For the great irony of Derry is that the Catholics have indeed captured the city, and the cry of "No surrender!" has long since been swamped by brute demographics. Today, Catholics make up more than ninety percent of central Derry's population, the Protestants having moved (fled?) to the other side of the river.

By any logic, the city should have been ceded to the Republic; it's on the far side of the Sperrins, and on the other side of the Foyle, with Donegal as its hinterland. The natural border between the two states runs down the Foyle, and even at the time of partition, Derry had a Catholic majority. But logic has nothing to do with it, and for Unionists to have surrendered the city to the South would have been unthinkable, a betrayal of the pact that Protestants have made with their past. Bad enough that the Boyne was now in Republican territory; Londonderry could not be handed over as well.

I ARRIVED in Derry without a plan, unless you call having a drink as soon as humanly possible a plan.

A pint at a corner bar, and I felt cheered on my way. I had decided to splurge on my accommodation. After a night in the hills, I felt I owed myself as much, so I checked into an elegant Georgian guest house with high ceilings, generous stairwells and superfluous drawing rooms featuring chairs so uncomfortable you just knew they had to be expensive. I was put in the smallest room in the house. My room was, in fact, higher than it was wide. A sort of glorified broom closet, though with more tasteful decor, admittedly. I wondered why I had been shunted aside like that till I saw myself in the mirror, fresh from the bogs, unshaven and unbathed, twigs in my hair, mud on my boots, face still powdery pale. I was practically emitting stink rays. The miracle was that they'd rented me a room at all. *"Covered in muck, tramping his great wee boots across our carpets. Why did they give him our number?"* The owner was lovely nonetheless, a lady of grace and good manners. She dropped by my room, asked if I'd care for some tea. "Though perhaps you'd like to freshen up first?"

I showered and shaved, washed the Sperrins from my hair, and thus recivilized, set out to walk the city's walls. I started at the soaring landmark of the Anglican cathedral, where the hollowed-out cannon-ball used to fire the terms for surrender into the city sits on display like a holy bowling ball. Also on display are the four oversized padlocks that were used to lock the gates in 1688, relics as venerated as any shard of bone in a Catholic chapel.

Across from the cathedral, beyond city walls bristling still with cannons, one looks out into the small, beleaguered enclave of the Fountain, the last Protestant neighbourhood in the cityside of Derry. Row houses, many of them derelict, with sad, defiant murals painted on; faded Union Jacks and curbs painted in red, white and blue. The Fountain has its back to the wall, literally. Embattled and tattered, and still under siege.

Walk farther along the walls of Derry, and the Bogside spreads out below you on the reclaimed marshlands that gave the neighbourhood its name. It was down there, in the Catholic ghettos outside the walls, that the 1960s civil rights movement ignited and caught fire. It was down there that thirty years of bloodshed began.

Disenfranchised, marginalized, the Catholics of Derry had taken to the streets. Protest marches became confrontations, confrontations became riots, riots became running street battles. Residents estab-lished "no go" zones and painted a sign on the gable wall of a Bogside row house that read YOU ARE NOW ENTERING FREE DERRY. By the spring of 1969, the main electoral and housing reforms demanded by the civil rights movement had been granted and a system of "one person, one vote" had been installed, but by then it was too late. The genie was out of the bottle. That summer, as the annual Apprentice Boy marches were about to begin, the Bogside boiled over. Bricks and Molotov cocktails rained down, and the RUC waded in, swinging batons and cracking skulls. The crowds broke and the police pursued, shouting "Come out and fight, you Fenian bastards!" This did not endear them to the Catholic populace. Residents of the Bogside barricaded themselves in, and the three days of rioting that followed became known as the Battle of the Bogside. It ended with British troops being called in to restore order. The soldiers were welcomed by the police, who were overextended and physically exhausted, and—surprisingly—by the Catholic community, who saw the army as a stabilizing force. They cheered the arrival of troops because it meant the withdrawal of the RUC.

The honeymoon soured, though, when a military clampdown was launched against Republican (read "Catholic") neighbourhoods in Belfast and elsewhere. Internment without trial was introduced, and hundreds of Catholics were summarily rounded up (very few of them IRA, unfortunately). Protests against internment turned violent, and on January 30, 1972, a day that would go down in history as "Bloody Sunday," British paratroopers opened fire on protestors in Derry, killing thirteen people. A fourteenth died later from the wounds he received. It was a watershed moment in Northern Ireland's history, one memorialized in Nationalist mythology and U2 lyrics ever since.

After Bloody Sunday there was no turning back. The cry *Tiocfaidh ár lá!* rose in crescendo, and the IRA lashed out. On Bloody Friday, July 21, 1972, more than twenty bombs exploded across Belfast in the space of an hour, killing nine people and injuring one hundred and thirty more. One bomb went off in a crowded bus station, and charred torsos and burnt limbs were littered along the pavement. You never hear much about Bloody Friday, though. It hasn't been mythologized the way Bloody Sunday has. Funny, that. (*Hey, Bono!* We're still waiting on that "Friday, Bloody Friday" song.)

What began as an emergency intervention by the army became a war of attrition, and during the conflict, British soldiers would often use the seventeenth-century walls of Derry as cover, creating a strange continuity with the past. By 1980, it was estimated that thirty percent of downtown Derry had been bombed or burnt out. The "Free Derry" sign still stands, however. The gable it was painted on has been preserved, and you can see it from the city walls today.

Farther along, and just inside these walls, you come to the Apprentice Boys Memorial Hall, a handsome nineteenth-century Baronial-style building. It sits ringed with security cameras, and the windows facing the Bogside are covered in wire mesh as protection against bottles and bricks. The sides of the Memorial Hall are paint-splattered and scorched where Molotov cocktails have hit.

I left the walls and walked down into the Bogside, trying to retrace the route the British armoured cars had taken on Bloody Sunday, using a map of that day. A stocky man stood watching, beefy arms crossed over his chest, as I paced it out.

Not long after, I passed a pub. Stopped. Went back. I recognized the name. It had been in its day a notorious IRA drinking hole, though if you didn't know the history you'd never have guessed; it looked like any pub on a sleepy afternoon. *If you didn't know the history, you'd never have guessed.* It was an observation that could apply to much of Northern Ireland, actually. Curiosity got the better of me. And what the hell—I could use a drink.

A handful of regulars sat at the bar. I collected my pint, pulled up a stool. They nodded, didn't smile.

The boys at the bar that day were baiting Seamus, a heavy, fleshy-faced fellow who was a source of endless amusement for the others. One of the patrons, a man with tattoos across his arms, kept surreptitiously dialling the bar with his cellphone. He'd then pick up the receiver at the bar, shout, "Seamus! It's for you. It's someone here wantin' to apologize to you about something." Gullible Seamus would take the phone and—nothing. "The fecker hanged up!" he'd say. The first fellow would then secretly redial, call the bar again. *"Seamus! It's for you."* And so on.

If Seamus got up, even for a moment, one of them would kick over his stool and yell, "Seamus! How much'a you been drinkin'?" They'd then grab him as though they were trying to steady him up, when in fact they were pushing him this way and that. "See! W'ya look at tha', he can't barely stand. Right full, so he is."

"Am not!" Seamus would yell, pulling away from their rough-housing. "Mind the Rolex!"

"Rolex?" the others laughed. "That's no Rolex, that's a Bollocks."

Even the bartender, an older avuncular figure, got into it. "Seamus," he'd say when the stool clattered over, "stop that fer feck's sake."

Seamus sputtered and roared. A big, dim-witted patsy.

Among the patrons was an older gentleman they referred to as "Sergeant." Every time they did, he would correct them. "It's Major," he'd say. So they split the difference, started calling him Sergeant-Major. "And you call yourself a Republican!" they laughed.

The other men were in their mid- to late fifties, greying hair, slightly balding. It dawned on me that they might well have been in the thick of things during the Battle of the Bogside, might have been hurling Molotov cocktails, might have taken blows from police batons.

Their humour soon took an even darker turn, with the tattooed instigator referring to Seamus as "fatso."

"W'ya look at him?" he'd say. "The fecker's carryin' forty pounds on his head alone. Big-headed fecker, he is."

"That's enough," said the bartender, reining him in.

When Seamus purchased a bag of chips (Roast Beef & Onion), his tormentor sweetly asked, "Can I have some, please?"

When Seamus said yes, the fellow reached in, took the entire contents in one big paw.

"I said, *that's enough*," barked the bartender.

"Just a bag of crisps," said the fellow. "Y'heard him say I could have some."

"Doan be takin' his food from 'm," said another one. "He's a growing boy, Seamus is."

"Aye, growing each way. Fat-headed fecker."

I realized, in a flush of goose bumps, that my presence was egging them on, that they wanted to see my reaction. I finished my beer, departed quickly.

They fell silent as I left, heads turning like turrets on a tank when I went past.

The guest house in Derry was behind an RUC station. As I walked past on my way home, day pack slung over my shoulder, I came upon a tense scene unfolding. Police lights were flashing, without the accompaniment of sirens and somehow eerier for that. The street out front of the station had been blocked off, and the fortress doors of the front gates now rumbled open. RUC stations really are medieval, with watchtowers and turrets and drawbridge-like doors, razor wire acting as their moat. An armoured Land Rover rolled out, with officers in helmets and flak jackets jogging next to it on either side. The armoured vehicle suddenly turned, angled itself across the street, and the men in the flak jackets took up position, automatic rifles held tight against their hips. I heard later that a rocket had been fired at the station in some sort of attack; their manoeuvre may have been a response to that, though I'm still not sure. I didn't see any smoke or damage as I walked by, mesmerized as I was by the operation taking place before me. *They seem to be targeting compact cars* ... So caught up in this street-side drama had I become that I overshot my destination and missed the street to my guest house. I turned, came back—and that's all it took.

"Can I have a word with you, mate?"

Shit. "Yes, officer?"

One RUC officer blocked my path; a second stood back to one side, just out of my sight line.

"You appear to be lost," he said. His hand was held against his gun, finger flat along the side.

Now, I'm not one of those death-wish travellers. You know the kind, the ones who walk barefoot across Papua New Guinea or go rooting around in the underbelly of the Moscow crime scene. I've had my run-ins: hauled off a bus in Ecuador, made to kneel; robbed at knife point in Amsterdam (I know, who *hasn't* been robbed at knife point in Amsterdam?); arrested and then released by the Japanese Highway Patrol for hitchhiking on an expressway; interrogated by national security in South Korea (I paid a "fine" and was finally allowed to leave). But this was particularly unsettling. The RUC were, technically speaking, a civilian police force. A *British* civilian police force, and the image of the British policeman is generally benevolent. But in Northern Ireland, they're not bobbies. They are armed; they are dangerous.

"Why so nervous?" asked the officer. He was smiling, but not with his eyes. "No reason to be afraid of us."

I stammered out a long answer, but once he heard my accent, everything started to change. The smile became more sincere, the shoulders relaxed.

"Okay then," he said, stepping back.

My face was burning. I felt like such a girly boy. I started to say something else, but he waved me off, turned his eyes back to the street.

A well-trimmed older gentleman, another guest, I presumed, was in the drawing room when I returned.

"And how was your day?" he asked.

"I was stopped," I said. "Just now, by the police."

He waited for the rest of the story, thinking there must be more to it, but no.

"He had a gun and everything," I said, but the gentleman in the drawing room just shrugged as though it were an everyday occurrence.

"I walked the walls as well," I said. "Went down into the Bogside."

He raised an eyebrow. "And how did that work out?"

"Well, I went for a drink and wasn't beaten up."

"Aye," he said. "That's about all you can aspire to in the Bogside."

I'D BEEN LOOKING forward to my Derry interlude because it meant I could finally stay up late, experience a bit of the Northern Ireland nightlife. I'd seen evidence of it in the towns I'd passed through, mainly in the form of broken glass outside pubs as I walked by in the early morning, heading into the hills. It was as though the Broken Glass Fairy had come through during the night (along with the Vomit Splatter Pixies). Towns often seemed hungover and bleary-eyed come daybreak.

I'd been told there was only one Protestant pub left in the Old City. Most of the Protestants who still worked downtown drank at "mixed" pubs, though in Derry a mixed pub didn't exactly mean "non-sectarian," as I would find out. It meant "Prods tolerated—but you'd better toe the feckin' line."

In a pub just off the Diamond, a group of lads took notice of my notebook. They were involved with cross-community something-or-other. I'd tried to be discreet, but they'd caught me scribbling and had deduced I was "an important journalist from America." That's how they introduced me to the barmaid, anyway, who remained singularly unimpressed.

One of the boys bought the next round, meaning I was now trapped. Aggressive hospitality, something of a Derry specialty. The ringleader introduced me around the table—"Tha's Kev, tha's Sean, tha's the other Sean, tha's Ryan, tha's Kieran, don't put any attention in wha' he says, it's all shite"—and when I asked him what he did for a living, he said he was an inventor.

"Really?" I'd never met an inventor before. "What are you working on?"

He leaned in, voice dropping to a conspiratorial whisper. "You won't say to any'n?"

I nodded.

"Promise?"

Yes.

"A waterproof teabag." Nod and a wink. "Aye, think of the savings. Tha' one teabag'll be all y'ever need. It brews a wee bit weak, but once we get past that … "

I'd heard of the waterproof teabag before—in Newfoundland, actually, which made sense, Newfoundland being an outpost of Ireland after all.

Derry's answer to Edison had more than mere teabags on the go, though.

"Solar-powered flashlight," he said. "It's the next big thing. You'll see. Now Kev here, it's twenty-five years he's been pursuing his lifelong dream."

Which was?

"To become a child protegé. He's very determined, so he is."

Another round of drinks appeared—I hadn't finished the previous one—then another, and another. I tried to buy the next round, but they pulled me back down. I was in this for the long haul.

The conversation took an unexpected *Mars needs women!* tack, with the boys insisting that we Americans were "hoarding" the world's supply of blondes. "Write tha' down. The men of Ireland are in dire need of blondes. Send us yer excess, y'got more'n yer share in the States, out there in California. We'll send you some of our girls in return. They're sick of us anyway, I'm sure you'll get a good number volunteering."

Seemed a fair trade. I'd never been in a city where the women were so consistently beautiful. Not that I noticed that sort of thing. But it is worth pointing out that the beauty of Derry women was cited several times to me as the origin of the town's moniker "the Maiden City." In fact, the nickname came from the walls having never been breached, "maiden" originally having the nuance of "virgin." But who was I to argue? "Fetching," that was the word. The women of Derry were fetching. And as far as I was concerned, the men of Derry could have all the collagen-injected, pneumatic Barbie blondes they wanted.

The beer was sloshing around inside my brain, and they were asking what I thought of Derry. "It's a grand city," I said, but the paint-splattered wire mesh and scorched walls of the Apprentice Boys Memorial Hall niggled away at me. "Why can't you let it go? Does it matter that much? I mean—you've won. It's just a bloody march, a parade with some flutes and a drum. It's not like they're burning your women and raping your churches."

I know. You're not supposed to ask questions like that. Bringing up politics in Northern Ireland is like poking a bear to see if it's dead or just sleeping. And here's me saying I'm not one of those death-wish travellers. But feck it. I was tired of being neutral, of having silence forced upon me by unstated threats. I wanted them to explain this shite to me.

"The marches?" they said. "Y'wanna know about those, do you?"

What I hadn't realized was that I was at a mixed table, four-to-one advantage: Catholic.

"Ryan? You hear that? Sure the Yank here is doin' a write-up on yer culture. No surrender and all tha'."

"Feckin right, no surrender," said Ryan. "Not with you lot around."

The first fellow turned back to me, grinned. "Y'see? One big happy family. Write that down. Oh, the Irish are a close-knit bunch. Now Ryan here, he even has a Catholic name, so he does."

"Feck off."

"Now, now, Ryan. Yer Billy was a poofter, y'know that, right?"

"Get stuffed," said Ryan.

"It's a known fack. Yer Billy was a bum banger. Wee small, too. A reg'lar midget, he was. It's why he was always astride tha' horse a' his, couldn't see above their heads otherwise."

The others laughed.

"I'm forgiving you a beatin'," warned Ryan.

"It's a God's truth, Ryan. Yer man was a wee gay midget."

"And what does that say about you lot? Gettin' yer arses whipped by a midget?"

A fairly good riposte, I thought. But the others laughed it aside, and Ryan pulled on his jacket. "Right. Had anaffa youse." He stood up. "They're doing this for yer benefit," he said to me, more by way of accusation than explanation.

"C'mon, Ryan. Sure a'moany kiddin'. C'mon back, buy us one, doan run out on yer round. Jest havin' a bit a barney. Doan be makin' the Yank here write us down as mean."

Ryan gave me a terse Ulster nod. "Right," he said to the others. "I'm off to the chippy."

His tormentor turned to me, said with a sad shake of his head, "These Prods. Always arrangin' to be offended when it's their turn t'buy. Write that down—they're very cheap. It's the Scotch innim."

I finally managed to buy a round. It took some doing because—apparently—Derrymen have a reputation for being generous. I'd never heard that before, or since, and for all I know they just made it up on the spot, but even a concocted reputation is something that needs to be lived up to. "Yer money's no good!" they kept telling me, until at last they allowed me to buy. The barmaid was ignoring us by this point, and as I waited my turn at the counter I wondered ha ha if Ryan might be coming back later. Toss a bomb through the window ha ha. Maybe spray the room with bullets ha ha. This ridiculous fear, once rooted in my brain, refused to let go. It was like an evil weed, with deep roots. I decided to bolt, was desperate to bolt, but I couldn't. *I needed to buy my round.* It was a cultural imperative. I didn't want them to think we Prods were cheap. I decided I would buy my round and then get out. I would move the drinks to the table, fake left, feign right, head to the washroom—and then run like hell. Even then, it took several trips for me to get the drinks over to them (I never did master the Irish art of holding upwards of a dozen glasses between two hands), and right about then Ryan reappeared, somewhat sheepishly, and to much laughter and a new volley of jibes.

"Back are ya?"

"So soon, man?"

"Feck you, forgot ma bag, so I did."

Broken glass on the sidewalks. Broken glass in the alleyways, broken glass atop the walls themselves. Broken glass, catching the light. Broken glass everywhere, it seemed, in the lanes and walkways of Northern Ireland, crunching underfoot. *This is a country that walks on broken glass every day of its life*, I thought, as the voices and the laughter grew distant and blurry.

ON MY SECOND DAY in the city it began to rain. Hard. The water washed through the streets, sluicing the gutters, running between the cobblestones. I didn't know it at the time, but this marked the start of what would be the wettest autumn in one hundred years. It would set records. For rainfall. In Ireland.

"Heavy rains tomorrow as well," the lady of the manor said as I checked in for another night.

"Aye," said the same inexplicable gentleman. (He never seemed to leave; I believe he lived in the drawing room.) "Now the Sperrins, where you're going," he said. "They're like a big sponge. Hold the water, so they do."

"But they are still hills," I said. "And water eventually runs downhill, right? Right?"

He and the lady of the house exchanged sad looks.

The lady had a pair of teenage daughters—true Derry beauties, willowy and long—whom I kept running into on my way up and down the stairs. I smiled every time, and every time they looked straight through me. *Oh right*, I recalled. *I'm old now. I don't exist. Not really.*

In spite of the rain and the cloak of invisibility I wore when it came to the women of Derry, I liked the place. I was in no rush to get back to the hills. I could wait out the rain.

THE ART OF UNSOLICITED ADVICE

It took several days, but the rains eventually lifted long enough for me to dash back to the Sperrins.

I still had several more mountains to cross, and I knew that if I was going to be sleeping in the hills, I'd need to bring some warmth along with me. So before I left the city, I stopped by a camping supply store and purchased a collapsible Coleman stove with a screw-on butane canister.

"How long will it last?" I asked the man at the counter as he handed my purchase over to me.

"Oh, it's sure to last as long as you'd wish." This was a completely Irish statement.

"And how long would that be, exactly?" I asked.

"As long as you'd wish."

I see.

"Well," I said, slowly, carefully. "I *wish* it would last till the end of time itself. But what I would really like to know is how long it *will* last."

"It'll last as long as you want."

"And how long would that be?"

"As long as you'd wish."

It was no use. I was trapped. Trapped in the treacle of Irish logic. Doomed. I cleared my throat. "Now listen to me, you bog Irish Mick, either you start giving me some straight answers or I'm going to insert this canister up your ass, turn it sideways and ignite it."

But of course, that wasn't what I said. What I said was, "Well, how about four days? Will it last four days?"

"Aye, it will."

"Okay. How about five? Let's go for five. Will it last five days?"

"Oh, if it can last four days, it's sure to last five."

"How about six?" I asked.

"I can't see why not. If it will last five days, what's another day? Sure it'll last six."

"And seven?"

"If it'll last six, it's sure to—"

"You see where this is leading?" I said desperately. "We will eventually approach infinity."

"Aye. As I said, it'll last as long as you could wish."

I gritted my teeth. No jury on earth would have convicted me. Justifiable homicide, that's what they'd say. I thanked him and was on my way.

I returned to Dungiven to pick up the trail again. A thick mist had settled in the valley beneath the town, blanketing the lower landscape, leaving the hills above stranded like islands. A beautiful view—if only I didn't have to walk into it.

This time around I'd booked a room in the castle. A narrow manor house anchored with great round oversized towers on either end, Dungiven Castle advertised "inexpensive lodging." It looked suspiciously like a youth hostel.

"Not a hostel, budget accommodations," I was told when I checked in. *Communal* budget accommodations, which is sort of the definition of a youth hostel, I would have thought.

It certainly smelled like a hostel. It had a musky aroma of unwashed socks, and an interior decor that did not mirror the grandeur outside. The place was filled with muddy-booted backpackers plotting their next move. I hadn't met a single soul on the trail since I'd turned inland at Castlerock, yet here were hikers in abundance. Doing day walks, mainly, and most of them were giving up even on that. "Not in this weather."

There was the usual fellow telling everyone about the time he trekked Kathmandu and how it had been much worse than this. In youth hostels, there is *always* someone talking loudly about how they had trekked Kathmandu and how that had been much worse than this—further evidence I was in fact in a hostel. There were Germans, smiling in that vaguely condescending way they have, as though they are in on a joke no one else is privy to. A handful of Americans. A Dutch couple. Australians, of course. (Walk into any hostel anywhere in the world, throw a stick and you'll hear an "Ow! Crikey!") And then there was me, alone in my endeavour.

"You're hiking? In this?" they'd ask.

"No choice, really."

Stare at the sky long enough and you can convince yourself of anything. I saw portents of clear weather with every roll of cloud, and the next morning, when the rains slowed to a drizzle, I made my move.

Corick Mountain was one of those places that paradoxically grew smaller the closer you came; what began as a brooding mass of mountain became a rounded height and then a grassy knob. I thought of Agnew's Hill, back in Antrim, and how in Northern Ireland the mountains are hills, and the hills are mountains. I wondered what that said about Ulster.

I climbed over a rusted, fecal-splattered cattle fence, followed the track upward and came out onto the mountain's exposed flank. Boulder erratics lay scattered about, scaled with lichen, sinking slowly into the heathery expanse.

I was now walking high above the Glenshane Pass. In the valley below, the highway threaded through the hills, with Dinky Toy traffic zipping along it. On the far side of the pass, quarry-work machines were taking great bloodless bites out of Craigmore Mountain. I pushed on, climbing several more gates before I came upon some empty cement-walled animal pens, which I huddled beside, shivering with cold and feeling tired. But ah! In my day pack, I had my handy new Coleman stove with the screw-on butane canister. I brewed me up some noodles, warmed my hands by the flame, was about to leave when I thought, *What the hell?* I brewed up some Nescafé as well, sloshing a bit of water around first to rinse out the mug. The coffee had a nice chicken broth aftertaste. A few pelts of rain could not discourage me; I just turned the flame higher.

Around the grassy slopes of Corick Mountain and then into the sudden darkness of Glenshane Forest, where tall stands of evergreens blotted up the light.

Here I had a decision to make. If I turned right, I would cross higher, windier terrain. Turn left, and I would descend to the highway below. Somewhere down there, in the lonely Glenshane Pass, stood the Ponderosa Roadhouse, the highest altitude pub in all of Ireland. I told myself the direction I chose would depend entirely on what the weather was going to do. At which point it started to pour, resolving my dilemma instantly. Down I trudged, onto the side of the highway. The rain was coming down so hard now it was bouncing off the asphalt.

I'd expected to have a pint at the roadhouse, call a taxi from there, but I'd misread the map and had come out on the wrong side. The only pub—the only *building*—in the Glenshane Pass, and I had missed it.

I made the long walk back to Dungiven as cars hydroplaned past, and I arrived back at the castle in a foul mood. I spent the evening at John T's pub, which was crowded and loud with country music. Ordered a beer and proceeded to fall asleep, head down on table, until I was prodded awake.

"Not drunk," I said. "Walking."

"In this weather?"

The next day, I tried again, going up the side of Corick Mountain only to be chased back down by rainy winds, banshee-like in their ferocity. I stumbled ass-over-teakettle several times, and a pair of forestry workers who'd been checking on the entrance gates took pity on me. "We'll run you into town," they said.

As the wipers flailed back and forth, the fellow behind the wheel said, "We watched you coming down. You seemed to have picked the boggiest route."

"Yes. I do seem to have a knack for finding water."

"Should put a divining rod on you," said his friend.

Like you'd need help finding water in Ireland.

The driver hunched forward, willing the wee pickup through the rain. "Y'need to work on your technique," he told me.

"My technique?" What technique? You put one foot in front of the other, and then repeat if necessary.

"Aye," his friend agreed. "Your technique is terrible."

Jeez. They sounded like my wife.

"You see," explained the driver. "You can't just chug along like that. You're steppin' too heavy. Y'need t'find a rhythm, like. Maybe get a stick as well, for balance. Way you're doin' it, yer sure to take a tumble."

"I never tumble," I said.

This would not be the last piece of unsolicited advice I received in Dungiven. Indeed, free advice seemed to be something of a local specialty. Despite Tourist Board images to the contrary, Irish pubs— and those in the North in particular—can be sullen places at times, hostile, even. If you come barging in talking loud and grinning big, as we North Americans are wont to do, you're apt to get a chilly response indeed. I'd seen it happen. Fortunately the tourists in question, as well as being brash, were also oblivious. I'd found the best strategy was to come in scowling, then spread out a wet map and start muttering darkly to myself. This always drew a crowd. There was something about an Ordnance Survey map and a hiker in a bad mood that the average Ulsterman simply could not resist.

Dungiven had an array of pubs along Main Street, all of them well suited for waiting out the rain. Right across from the castle was O'Hagan's Bar, established in 1889 (and not vacuumed since, I believe. Kidding! Sort of!). A homey enough place, but often filled with the very German backpackers I'd sought to escape, so I usually ended up farther down at Murphy's Pub instead, established in 1897 and thus not nearly the venerable institution O'Hagan's was.

After a drink or two at Murphy's one evening, I slopped down to another pub, past the IRA signs and hunger striker memorials, where I sat, scowling as always at my maps, as though somehow they were to blame. The Gaelic sports paraphernalia in the bar left no doubt I was in a Nationalist drinking hole. Friendly enough, though. Several of the patrons took an immediate interest in my quest.

"He's walkin' all Six Counties, so he is."

"Really? That's grand."

"And how's that working out for you?" they wanted to know.

"Well," I said through teeth well gritted. "Fine, except for the fact that the Ulster Way doesn't really exist." The Ulster Way, I'd come to realize, was more an idea than an actual trail, more a notion than a fact, a sort of "*Wouldn't it be great if ...*" type of idle musing. The Irish seemed to be under the impression that drawing a line on a map would somehow conjure a trail into existence. "The route seems to exist primarily in the imagination of those who designed it," I said.

"Aye? So that aside, it's going well?"

It was a wonder that the beer glass didn't break in my fist. "Oh, it's going swimmingly," I said.

"An' anyway, the best trails are the ones you find yourself."

"No," I said, "the best trails are the ones that, marked on a map or in a guidebook, actually exist in the real world." I muttered something blasphemous under my breath, went back to my map.

"The Ulster Way, is it?" said another fellow, throwing himself down beside me. "I walked that myself."

"No, you didn't."

"Not all of it, no. But I have walked the Sperrins. It's wet up there, y'know."

"Thanks for the tip."

I was at a loss as to what to do next. I'd studied the Ordnance Survey map, knew that the next stretch of the trail was tricky. I could easily end up stranded in the barren heights above Glenshane Forest in the rain, far from any shelter. Camping in the midst of a downpour held little appeal. I looked at the map again … Maybe a better approach would be to take a taxi *out*, to the end of the forestry trail, and then walk *back*, into Dungiven. That thought depressed me even more, though. I wanted to put Dungiven behind me, had started to feel as if I was trapped in an Ulster version of *Groundhog Day*.

The lads in the pub had taken up my cause, though. What was the problem? they wanted to know.

"Well," I said, "I need to get to Glenshane Forest."

"Oh, aye. That's nine miles. You take the main road, past the old priory—"

"Actually," I said, "I'd be coming the other way, from the forest *into* Dungiven."

"Aye? A bit trickier, that, but you can still do it. From there back t'here it'd be eight miles or so."

I'll stop right there.

You caught that, no? Let me summarize the ensuing conversation, then, to spare you the merry-go-round that followed.

Me: "So, A to B is nine miles?"
The other fellow: "Aye."

Me: "But B to A is eight miles?"

The other fellow: "Aye."

I cleared my throat. "Do you see the problem?"

"Well," he said, "it's downhill comin' the other way, innit?" He explained this to me as though I were the dumbest kid in daycare.

It made no sense. Of course it made no sense: this was Ireland, and I was in a pub. But it did give me reason to pause. Walking downhill sounded appealing. True, downhill through boglands, with their cruel combination of soft turf and steep angles, was a torment on already swollen joints, but this would be on a firm-packed forestry trail.

"Walking downhill *is* faster," I admitted. "But it can be hard on the knees."

"Aye," said a low voice behind me. It belonged to a barrel-chested man—barrel-legged and barrel-shouldered as well; less a man than an oak cask, really. The sort of man who shows up at key moments to warn you about The Curse of That Which Ye Seek. "It's the downhill walks that'll do you in."

The others nodded at this. The man had spoken A Great Truth.

"The human legs, y'see," he said. "The knees and tha', they're designed for walking uphill."

"Uphill?"

"Aye, they're not designed for walkin' downhill."

"But—but, but. Surely if you walk *uphill* you will eventually need to walk back down, right?"

"I suppose. Aye."

"I mean, it's just common sense. If you go *up*, you'll have to come back down again at some point. Right?" I had a few pints inside me, and I could hear my voice, shrill but oddly distant, rising as I spoke, as though someone had turned up the treble by remote control. "You see the flaw in your logic, yeah? You do see how preposterous that is? You do, right? *Right?*"

When one is drinking in an IRA pub in an IRA town, it's best not to provoke the locals. But I was gone. My knees were throbbing, my feet hurt, and every second or third word seemed to come out as a shout. "It's a DESIGN FLAW is what it is! Our knees should bend BOTH ways—I mean, that would make a lot more SENSE. *Completely bendable knees*—THAT'S what humans NEED. I mean, it makes NO goddamn sense. Why would they be designed for walking uphill ONLY, huh?" I didn't know what the hell I was saying.

The Irish, of course, are masters of the veiled threat, and my barmate, having endured my increasingly bizarre harangue long enough, leaned in, levelled his unblinking gaze at me, and said, "Well, if it's a design flaw, you'll have to take that up with the Designer Himself." The subtext clearly being: *"And if you'd like a personal meeting with Him, it can be arranged."*

I looked down at my drink. "I'll shut up now," I said.

He nodded at this.

And then, after a long pause, I said, by way of explanation, still looking down at my drink. "I'm just tired is all."

"No need to apologize," he said.

THIS STRANGE EDEN

Back into the Sperrins, up the side of Corick Mountain, scattering sheep, watching the skies.

The rains had stopped, and the heavy ceiling of cloud had lifted. Oh, it was still wet all right, and cold, but I had my stove. I stopped often for coffee and noodles, or to warm my hands when needed, a luxury I enjoyed at great length.

In the early morning, and under a full pack, I crossed the open heights above Glenshane Forest and then came down the other side, toward the next stretch of trees. A barbed-wire fence blocked the way, but I followed it down till I found a narrow and—considering I had to straddle it—disconcertingly rickety stile. Even with the stile, the wire was very high, almost at crotch level, in fact. Once again I was forced to risk scrotal entanglement in barbed wire. *Rusty* barbed wire. I didn't see a path on the other side, but no one puts a stile over a fence without a reason, and sure enough, when I got across and then ducked under a thick overhang of branches—down onto my hands and knees, backpack swaying—I came out onto a trail. Overgrown, but faintly visible.

I had to wade through thorn bushes and stinging nettles—my legs would burn for days, the hi-tech fibre of my hiking pants having proven ineffective in the face of Ulster undergrowth—in order to reach a forestry road farther down. From there, I turned navigational guidance over to gravity, let my own momentum take me along.

I came out of the forest near a picturesque stone bridge, beside a wide grassy clearing. Perfect. I pitched my tent beneath a stand of poplars, and with stomach growling, assembled my Coleman stove, lit the flame, and then watched as it sputtered and died. I lit it again. Again it sputtered and died. I shook the canister. Empty.

I didn't know whether to curse, laugh or cry. I believe I may have done all three at the same time. I ate the noodles uncooked.

That night the winds picked up, and I woke to the sound of fingers drumming on nylon. The rain had worked its way through the canopy of trees and was tapping mad Morse code messages on my tent. I crawled out, groggy-headed, decided I needed a cup of hot coffee, remembered the empty canister, cursed the Irish and all their kin accordingly, then stuffed my Amazing! Expanding! Sleeping Bag back into its case. I slung my pack over my shoulders and started the long trudge down into Moneyneany.

Moneyneany had a shop, a pub and a great, bloody big church. An impressive building, and weirdly out of scale, it seemed, for such a small community. I passed Celtic crosses in a graveyard, turned right. Set my course for Crockmore Mountain.

My Waterloo ...

IT STARTED with another long slog up another long farm lane.

The higher I got, the worse the weather became, rain and wind in equal parts sweeping relentlessly across bog rocks and tufted grass. The earth had fallen away in places, revealing the black peaty darkness below, the oily soil now slick with rain. The lane was running with water, and I was forced to cross several cattle grids, those metal pipings you sometimes see laid across to keep livestock from straying. The pipings, often loose, acted like mini log rolls. More so since I was carrying a heavy, poorly packed rucksack on tired, jerky legs, with my head down into the wind. I slipped several times on those damnable cattle grates during the climb up Crockmore, my invective lost in the swirling rain.

The hike became an ordeal of false summits, with the top of Crockmore never seeming to come any closer. Gusts of rain forced me to turn around at times and walk backward, and the wind harried my steps, shoving against me as if I were a drunk at closing time. *"Have you no home to go to? Ou' wit'ya!"*

When I finally reached the top of Crockmore Mountain, I was too exhausted for elation. I could see the next of the Sperrins lined up ahead, wind-swept and barren, remote.

Under clouds so low I could have reached up and run my fingers through them, I began my slow descent. I'd been warned that the Sperrins were moody, that "it can be lashin' on one side of the mountain, and sunny on the other." Well, I'm here to tell you it was lashing on both friggin' sides. The rain—well, *attacked* is not too strong a word; it came pelting down, out of the mist like bullets through smoke.

The lane ended.

I looked for a waymarker, found none, followed a line of fence posts, until those too abandoned me. The trail as magically drawn on the Ordnance Survey sheet had failed to materialize, and I was left to pick my way down the side of the mountain, through a boot-sucking minefield of steep bog. Which is when it happened—I stepped forward, sank to my shin in mud. *Shit!* This was bog of a thicker nature, and it vacuum sealed around my foot. I wedged my other boot against a rock, pulled hard, spouting wild profanity all the while. I felt my foot shift inside my boot, ever so slightly, and I froze. The rain was pounding down now. Losing a boot to the bog would be horrible beyond belief. I stopped, forced myself to relax and then slowly worked myself free. My boot was covered with a thick, inky peat that proved impossible to scrape off, and I pushed on, my muck-heavy boot adding a lopsided weight to my descent. At one point I tripped, fell face-down in the mud, came up sputtering, tasting bog.

I tugged a bit of sweater from my raincoat sleeve, wiped my face as best I could, wondered again at the wisdom of printing maps that featured mythical songlines marked cheerfully in red, purporting to be a hiking route. I don't know. Maybe it was just me. Maybe the Northern Irish didn't need waymarkers. Maybe signposts were for sissies up here among the hearty men and women of Ulster. Maybe they were born with a knack for aligning the sun and the moon, needing only to sniff a clump of heather, prod a piece of sheep spoor before striding off confidently across the trackless moors—but somehow I doubted it. I suspected the reason I had met no Irishmen along this route was because the Irish knew better. They knew that bogs were God's way of saying, "Don't come through here. Go around, fool!"

For a moment, I could see a road far below. Then it disappeared, lost in the rain, and there was only me and the mountain.

My laborious descent took me to the cement walls of a sheep pen, where I tried to find shelter, but no matter which wall I huddled behind, the wind found me. A few soggy sheep watched in wonderment, asking, "*We have to be here. What's your excuse?*"

The road reappeared, suddenly very close, almost within reach, it seemed, but as I slogged toward it I found the way barred by a rain-engorged stream—one that clearly aspired to riverdom. *Dammit.* Fortunately, someone had thrown a jerry-rigged bridge across it: wooden pallets on an iron frame. The planks looked rotted, but the bridge was being used by someone, presumably to get to the cement sheep pen. *Let's hope it's a big, strapping Irish boy who weighs more than me and my backpack.* I took my first tentative step ... and the wood broke underfoot. I lurched backward, regained balance, arms propelling on either side. The threat of dropping through the wooden pallets, getting shards of wood embedded in places they shouldn't be, kept me light on my toes. I tried again, shuffling across high-wire style on the iron edge of the frame.

Once I'd conquered the stream, I dragged myself up onto the side of the road—but now what? I was lost in the empty heart of the Sperrins. The mountains swept down one side of the valley and up the other, and the road ahead was just one long, lonely stretch of nothing. I unfolded my damp map, got my bearings. There was only the one road marked on this side of Crockmore. I knew I had to follow it to the town of Sperrin, then cross a bridge and climb another series of mountains. I wasn't even halfway through the day's hike.

I followed the road as it unspooled into the upper reaches of the Glenelly Valley, one of the most remote regions in Northern Ireland. Along the way I crossed over from one county to the next. I entered County Tyrone in the most ignominious of fashions, in a defeated mood, harassed by hectoring rains. This coloured my whole perception of Tyrone. It's the county known as "the Heart of Ulster," but I referred to it in less charitable terms.

I'd never been so tired. On the edge of Goles Forest, a single white-washed cottage stood, windows dark and no one home. I headed through the forest and out again, the Glenelly River running unseen through marshy grass below. An hour or more of walking, and the valley slowly began to open. Farms, misted in the rain, now swam into view, and the river grew cleaner, faster. Fields thick as felt and green as any billiard table took shape, with fieldstone fences running between. It was beautiful, I suppose.

I arrived at last at the town of Sperrin.

That's what it said on the map, anyway. There wasn't a lot to Sperrin. Considering it was the namesake of the mountains that surrounded it, I was expecting … something. I don't know, a shop, maybe. A pub, certainly. But it wasn't even a village, let alone a town. Just a cluster of homes at a crossroads with a metal Quonset hut past the intersection. I spotted a company truck out front of the hut and a deliveryman who was dropping something off, a piece for a tractor or something, to a man in coveralls. They'd taken shelter under the entrance while the second man signed for it.

I slopped up toward them, smeared in mud.

"Please, can you tell me where the nearest bus stop is?"

I was supposed to turn south at this crossroads—I could see the next series of obstacles the Sperrins had thrown before me, the next line of mountains I was expected to cross. But I couldn't do it. I couldn't face any more of this.

"Buses?" they said. "Along Glenelly?"

I nodded.

"There's none."

"No buses?"

"No, none a'tall."

"Taxis, then?"

"No, no taxis."

"Well," I said, "any four-star hotels with saunas and all-you-can-eat buffets?"

They laughed. "Not yet. We're working on it."

I stood there until the awkward silence guilted the deliveryman into offering me a ride. "Tell you wha', sit tight a few minutes, I'll run you in. I'm on my way to Strabane. There's buses there'll take you anywhere—anywhere you'd like."

"Anywhere except Glenelly," I said.

"Aye."

As we drove in, I fell half asleep, head against the window, drifting in and out. Across the valley were the serrated mountaintops I was now supposed to be walking across. The Sperrins Cultural Centre floated by on one side like a hallucination. Brand new, from the looks of it. *A museum dedicated to emptiness.* Catholic hills, Protestant valleys. A village called Eden flitted past, and with it the Eden Loyal Orange Hall, flying its inevitable Union Jack. The facade was splattered with paint from past attacks. This strange Eden.

I fell asleep for good somewhere around Plumbridge and was woken much later by a shake of the shoulder from the driver.

"This is you," he said. I stumbled out. Thanked him. This was me.

A FORTY-MINUTE bus ride took me back to Derry. I arrived still covered in mud, checked back into the Georgian guest house, tracked down the bastard who had sold me the stove.

I slammed the empty canister on the counter. "It died," I said. "Explain that to me, would you?"

"Aye," he said. "The canisters only last forty-fifty minutes at fifty-one kilopascals per inch." (Or some such.) "Now, the *stove*, that'll last you years, as long as you'd wish for. But these canisters? They need to be changed regularly, you stupid shite-for-brains Yankee feck." I'm summarizing, of course. That last bit was implied, though.

He smiled at me. "Another canister, then?"

I raised my chin high, straightened my back, squared my chest, said, "Yes, I believe so."

The same gentleman was ensconced in the drawing room at the guest house. He hadn't moved since I left, it seemed.

"And how were the Sperrins?" he asked.

"Wet."

The forecasts were equally dismal. "Heavy rains," he said, "is what they're calling for, up in the Sperrins. It'll take weeks to drain, so it will. It's one big sponge, aye. One big sponge."

"I'LL SEND FOR YOU!"

Would you rather be a gypsy or a lord? A carefree soul, stepping lightly on the earth, or a landowner, rooted in wealth and living in a manor? These are questions to ponder when you're housebound under an Arctic cold front, with the northern lights rippling outside and snow lying heavy across the land, windows iced with frost as you warm yourself around a communal teapot.

The unconnected dots of my grandfather's past allowed any number of constellations to be drawn, from tragic to triumphant, from Dickens to Horatio Alger, and the green fields of Ireland never seem quite so alluring as when you've been swallowed whole by a monochromatic Canadian winter. Were we the offspring of tattered gypsies or the lost heirs of landed gentry? The version of the past you prefer depends on where you are in life. As I pulled at the tether of our small town, it was the gypsy possibilities that appealed the most. The restlessness wasn't my fault, you see, it was the Roma blood in me stirring. My brother Ian, meanwhile, said he would settle for a mansion, "and maybe a summer house on the French Riviera." These were the sorts of sacrifices we were willing to make.

My grandfather had been a Barnardo boy, one of a generation of orphans rescued from the streets by an Irish evangelist named Dr. Thomas Barnardo who'd set up his first homes in London during the darkest days of the Industrial Revolution. The conditions in the Barnardo's Homes were austere, often cruel, though by the standards of the day their approach was considered enlightened. Thousands of children were fed, clothed, given shelter and trained to perform menial tasks. As often as not, they were shipped to the colonies as indentured servants—serfs, in fact if not in name.

My grandfather was admitted to a Barnardo's Home in 1910, along with his older brother, William.

If my grandfather really was a Catholic, why did his brother have such a staunchly Protestant name? Well, maybe their *mother* had been Catholic and their father Protestant, with William named after his father's side. There was another possibility. Richard and William were strikingly different in appearance and in temperament. Whereas my grandfather was tall and thin, William was short and stocky. My grandfather was a born storyteller; his older brother was quiet and reserved. Even their ears were different: William's were small and close to his head, in stark contrast to my grandfather's jug handles. The two boys sounded so different, in fact, that I often wondered if maybe they weren't brothers at all but had met in the orphanage; perhaps William was simply an older boy who had befriended my grandfather—always a sickly child—and had watched out for him. That certainly would explain what happened on the Belfast docks.

As soot and cinders filtered down, a group of Barnardo children were led single file through the mob toward a waiting ship, headed for a new life in North America. The horn sounded, the crowd shoved forward, but just as the boys were about to reach the gangplank, a hand fell on my grandfather's shoulder.

"Richard, what are you doing here?" It was an official from the Barnardo's Home. He pulled my grandfather from the line as William and the others were swept ahead. "You're not going with them," the man said. "You didn't pass the medical."

The Barnardo's Homes had a policy of not separating siblings, and yet there was my grandfather, with his little pack, watching helplessly as William was pushed farther and farther away from him, the distance between them opening up. And now the horn was sounding and the gangplank was being raised and William was on deck, frantically trying to find his brother. He spotted him on the pier below, leaned over the side, was yelling, "Richard! I'll send for you! I'll send for you, Richard!"

As the ship pulled away, my grandfather was left behind, sobbing, on the Belfast docks. He was eight years old.

THE BARNARDO'S HOMES had a program for "genteel orphans," children who were well mannered, better behaved, less rough-and-tumble than the others. These children were placed with foster families rather than in group workhouses. After being separated from his brother, my grandfather was sent to live with one such family, and he had warm memories of that time. Unfortunately, his health continued to deteriorate, and he was removed to a Barnardo's Homes sanatorium on the Jersey Islands.

The men in charge of the Barnardo's Homes were often low-level retired officers who ran the orphanages with a military rigidity. On Jersey, the boys were caned regularly, often till their hands or backsides bled. This was considered salubrious.

"It was orchard country," my mom told us. "He used to talk about how the men from the farms would hire the Barnardo boys to help with the harvest. One of the farmers let Dad and the other boys who were working that day fill their shirts with apples to bring back. He always remembered that, walking in, beaming, his shirt full of apples for everyone."

When they got there, though, he and the other boys were accused of stealing and were caned "quite brutally," as my grandfather told it. "The man who ran the home," my mother noted, "was a sadist."

When the orchard farmer heard about this, he loaded an entire wagon up with apples, drove it straight onto the Barnardo soccer pitch, called the children over, started filling all of their shirts with apples.

Christmas came and went, that year and the next—Father Christmas never seemed to make it to the orphanage. My grandfather was on the third floor of the sanatorium, recovering from another respiratory illness and watching from the window as the boys played soccer below, when a letter arrived. A photograph, to be precise, one mailed as a postcard and postmarked "Orillia, Ontario." It showed a grinning farm boy, no more than thirteen or fourteen years old, with his arm thrown around the neck of a calf and a message on the back written in large, untutored letters: "I guess you will know your brother William."

My grandfather ran from the room in his nightgown, down the stairs, out onto the middle of the playing field, yelling, "Canader! A picture from Canader!" as the other boys crowded in.

William was working as a farm boy in "Canader," was saving his money. Richard was still considered too sickly to travel overseas, though, and instead of going to Canader, he was sent to a manor house to work as a servant.

"A 'butler's butler,' that's what he called himself," my mother remembered. "He actually worked for the housekeeper; that was who he was indentured to. She was very hard on him."

The lord of the house was puzzled by my grandfather, wanted to know more about his background. "You're not like the other ones," he said to the boy. "Where did you come from?" But my grandfather's memories were hazy: stories of an officer father killed in battle, of a mother dying young. Nothing he could peg a past to. Maybe it was just natural grace, but there was something in my grandfather the lord recognized. Of all the staff, Richard was the only one not required to address the lord as "sir." The men who had abused the children on Jersey Island had demanded the boys call them "sir" even as they were being caned, and my grandfather had vowed he would never again use that term of address.*

My grandfather was still a servant, however, a "butler's butler," and the housekeeper treated him like her personal lackey, ordering him about, making him sleep in the smallest room in the basement. Feral cats roamed the estate, and having spent most of his remembered life sleeping in large dormitories, my grandfather suddenly found himself alone as feline eyes peered down at him from the window. He spent many nights terrified, hiding under the blankets.

The lady of the house owned expensive china plates, and she provided the housekeeper with a fund to replace any that became chipped or broken. If none did, the housekeeper would pocket the money—which is why my grandfather was forced to carry each plate separately when he brought them to the scullery after meals, up and down the stairs, again and again and again, while the housekeeper yelled at him for being so slow.

My grandfather was sixteen by the time his brother William was finally able to buy out his contract, helped a little by the scraps of money my grandfather had managed to squirrel away. On his last day at the manor, he stacked up the plates—every goddamn one of them—and carried them down to the scullery, stepping hard, plates bouncing as he went. When he came in, the housekeeper saw him, began shrieking, "Richard, Richard! The plates!" He let them go and they fell, one on top of the other, shattering onto the floor in a glorious crash.

"And which plates would those be?" he asked.

---

*He never did, not until years later, as an adult, when he found a friend and father figure in a Canadian United Church minister, Reverend Galbraith. He was the only man my grandfather would refer to as "sir."

MY GRANDFATHER sailed to North America in 1918, on one of the first troop ships carrying servicemen home after the war. It was crowded with soldiers and British emigrants.

William had travelled west on the CPR and was working on a homestead in Saskatchewan when he sent for Richard. My grandfather packed what few clothes he had in a single case, along with a small tuck box filled with photographs and addresses, souvenirs and secrets. He had built it himself, in fine decorative woodwork, and he called it his "treasure box." He was travelling in steerage, and while at sea he discovered the clasp on his suitcase had been forced open and his treasure box stolen.

Still small for his age, my grandfather was hiding under a lifeboat tarp, "blubbering away," as he put it, when a burly-necked serviceman found him. When he heard what had happened, the serviceman stormed through the decks, my grandfather in tow, grabbing people by the collar and demanding to know if they'd seen the treasure box. "Whoever has that box is in trouble," he warned.

"Of course," my mom said, "whoever had it threw it overboard after that."

When the past was small enough to fit into a tuck box, it was easily lost at sea.

The big fellow asked my grandfather where he was going. "Saskatchewan," he said, "to see my brother." "Really? Where in Saskatchewan?" "Roleau." The big fellow grinned, said, "That's where I'm from. Roleau."

And so, in one of those strange moments of synchronicity, my grandfather was taken under the wing of a returning soldier and more or less adopted by a farm family in Roleau. A train across the continent, under the care of his prairie protector, took him to a new life on the Great Plains, where his brother William was waiting.

"The reunion," my mother said, "was joyous."

In North America, William and Richard became Bill and Dick. It was a fresh start in every sense. "When Dad got off that boat, he said he never felt he was British again."

Bill gave his brother a photograph of their father, a formal portrait showing a stern-looking man with a beard and a well-pressed suit. Their father had died in the Boer War, Bill explained. And their widowed mother, left to care for four children, had slowly unravelled. One child had died of fever; another, just a toddler, had overturned a cauldron of boiling water on herself and never recovered. After the second child died, their mother had turned to face the wall, had willed herself to death. It was then that the two boys, William and Richard, were thrown into the world as orphans.

One photograph had survived the journey over. My grandfather had carried it with him in his jacket. It showed him as a small child, before the death of his parents, before the orphanage, before any of that. In it, my grandfather was standing in the garden of a beautiful estate, at the bottom of a sweeping staircase flanked by ornamental urns, looking very happy, very much at ease.

My grandfather never went back to Ireland, never wanted to. Bill did, however. He returned to Belfast years later, on some undisclosed matter, and returned with bad news: the official records of their family had been destroyed in a courthouse fire. After that, the past became a closed book, an open question.

Gypsy? Lord? Or something in between?

Part Five

THE LONG ROAD
TO LOUGH DERG

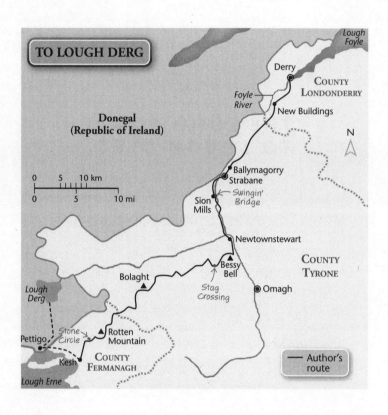

DERRY TO PETTIGO
Along the Western Border

Rains pursued him, cold winds seared his flesh ...

The Sperrins had defeated me. I admit that readily. I couldn't face going back into those mountains. I couldn't.

Back in Derry, as rain washed down, I watched the forecasts unfold: a large cloud had apparently formed, cartoon-like, directly over the Sperrins. I couldn't go back up there, considered quitting my trek altogether. *"Did I ever tell you about the time I walked one-third of the Ulster Way?"*

Fortunately, while moping around the Derry Visitors Centre, I came upon a guide to scenic walks in the Foyle Valley—and discovered an alternative route. If I walked south from Derry, through Sion Mills, I could reconnect with the Ulster Way *on the other side* of the Sperrins. If I had to walk in the rain, I'd much rather it be along country lanes and through picturesque villages serving picturesque beer in their picturesque pubs than through open bogs that were, let's face it, not known for their proliferation of pubs.

I justified this change in plan by two arguments I felt were unassailable. Firstly, the Ulster Way had proven to be a far from seamless route; the break between Cushendun and Ballycastle had already forced me to plot my own path. Secondly, the route I was now going to follow would actually *add* miles to my walk. I wasn't shortening it, I was lengthening it.

The sun dripped through on the day I left—in Ulster, even the sunshine is wet—and I took this as an encouraging sign from above.

You are now leaving Free Derry.

AN ODE TO STUCCO

It's surprisingly difficult to differentiate between cow shit and common mud. I found this out as I walked through Bolies Glen, south of Derry. I was following a mucky path that was mixed with— I stopped, sniffed the air—cow flops, definitely. Not horses. Certainly not sheep. I was becoming something of a connoisseur of odours. Visual clues helped too: flies were the key. If you saw flies crawling on mud, it wasn't mud, step around.

Somewhere along the way, I heard a swing, a *thwack* and a "Feck!" As I fought my way through a cloud of midges, I almost tripped over a dead hare caked with mud by the side of the lane. Done in by an errant golf ball, no doubt.

I entered the town of New Buildings, through the back door as usual, walking straight into a suburban-style subdivision. Suburbs are all the more confusing for their logic; I marched purposefully into one cul-de-sac, marched just as purposefully out again. There were, naturally, very few new buildings in New Buildings. The Methodist church was made of leftovers, it seemed—stone, brick, stucco.

I'd crossed another invisible divide: the street lamps of New Buildings were painted like candy in red, white and blue. The curbs and bus shelters, too. I boomeranged in and out of town, past tattered Union Jacks and angry Red Hands and grim Loyalist graffiti that staked out territory as surely as a dog does: UDA, UVF. It was jarring to come upon these splashes of sectarian rage in the quiet of the Ulster countryside. Where I'm from, gang-tag graffiti is an urban phenomenon. To find it along secluded country roads and in small, sleepy towns was like coming across a squirrel with a handgun: it didn't fit.

I crossed back into County Tyrone, was greeted by the Cullion Orange Hall, complete with a raised portrait outside of King Billy astride his white stallion, sword pointing ever forward.

Time for some coffee. Rummaging around in my pack, I found the butane canister, but no stove. Sitting somewhere on the wrong side of Crockmore Mountain, no doubt. Damn.

Soon after, a large farm dog appeared and tried to pick a fight with me, woofing loud and low as I passed. (And you just know if you could translate what he was barking, it would have been "*Catholic? Protestant? Catholic? Protestant?*") A pair of workmen came to see what the commotion was about, paintbrushes clenched in fists and ready for trouble, but as soon as I called out to them they realized I was just some dunderheaded Yank tramping along the road to no apparent purpose.

Using the Ordnance Survey maps and my own unerring sense of direction, I had plotted a route along a dismantled railway beside the Burngibbagh River. This would take me over an old bridge and into the village of Ballymagorry (which I'd chosen solely because it sounded so quintessentially Irish). Unfortunately, I couldn't see any river, and that had thrown me off.

One of the workmen came over, drawn irresistibly to my unfolded map and puzzled brow.

"The river?" he said. "It's over in among those high reeds, I imagine. Not even sure if it's still there."

Hard to misplace a river, no?

"Just a wee stream, really."

With all the rain, it was hard to imagine any stream disappearing.

"Aye," said the fellow. "But it hasn't rained so much here, been more up in the Sperrins like."

You don't say.

He called back to his mate. "Tommy! W'ye go down and see if tha' stream is still there?"

Tommy stopped what he was doing. "And how am I t'do that?" he yelled back.

"Just hop the hedge and walk over to the other side like, and if yer toes get wet or you disappear, we'll know it's still there."

"I think not," said Tommy.

The first man gave me a shrug that said, "Well, I tried."

I thanked him anyway. When I got to the bridge, the truth was exposed. The Burngibbagh River did not exist. Shocking, but true. The Ordnance Survey needed to know! I made a note to call the information in at the next opportunity. The river was on the map, all right, but it wasn't there in real life. (I imagined alarms going off at the OS HQ, "A'oogha! A'oogha!" with surveyors running out, still chewing their toast, throwing their gear in and roaring off in Land Rovers to confirm this earth-shaking announcement.)

I walked back to where the workmen were crouched beside a gate. "It's not there," I said. "The river."

They looked at me.

"Just so you know," I said. "In case anybody else asks." I felt I had to tell *somebody*.

The first fellow nodded. Slowly. "I'll keep that in mind then, plan accordingly."

There was an awkward pause. "Well," I said. "Guess I'll be on my way then."

He nodded. Said nothing.

THE PATH I WAS following, known as the Friar's Walk, cut a lazy S through a grove of trees and over a stone bridge that crossed another vanished stream. A bridge over nothing, out of place and out of proportion for such a simple landscape. Perhaps it had been built as an object of meditation for the friars who had once walked here, hands behind their backs, heads down. Or maybe, like the Burngibbagh, the river below had simply disappeared.

The old railway line that had once run through the valley was gone, but you could still see where it had been, a raised bed, now overgrown. A horse followed me awhile on the other side of his fence. Piano music drifted across green fields. Someone, somewhere, was practising, was working their way through a tricky bit.

The road curved around a sleepy nook. In a row of stucco townhouses, one of the units had been attacked and then abandoned; charcoal scorch marks fanned out from broken windows. The townhouses on either side were intact, though, with doily-like curtains and flowers out front. Someone had been burnt out of their home, and as much as I hoped it was a faulty electric kettle or an errant cigarette—a house fire followed by vandalism—I suspected there was something darker at work. *The Irish eat their own.* I'd heard that more than once. A Catholic family who got uppity? A Protestant family who needed to be taught a lesson? Did it really matter? You'd need a score card to keep track.

I crossed the Burn Dennet River (which I'm happy to say does exist), past a graveyard and through fields where shaggy Highland steers stood, stoic in their wet wool. I walked alongside the busy A5, past a cricket field and into the village of Ballymagorry. Graffiti scratched on a wall informed me that "Emma HEARTS Jerome." Fiona, Becky, Dara, Mad Dog, Jennifer and Carla had all weighed in on the matter, an improvement over the usual UDA and IRA slogans, I suppose—or the always popular FTP (meaning, um, "down with" the Pope, and usually matched with FTQ, meaning, "I wish to express my stern disapproval of the Queen").

A trio of teenage girls were waiting out the latest round of rain under an entranceway, and in spite of my cloak of invisibility, I stopped to ask them if there was somewhere nearby I might get a meal. My exact words were: "Excuse me, do you know where I could find a restaurant?"

"Res'durAHNN?" they said, mimicking my accent and breaking into fits of giggles.

Sigh.

One girl, the bravest of the three, said, "Well now, there's Floyd's, Floyd's—or Floyd's. They're all very good, but personally I recommend Floyd's."

Floyd's was right around the corner, and it was closed. Of course. So I went into a nearby bar instead, where I had a genuine "sarsaparilla moment." Remember how, in the old Hollywood Westerns, the hero will enter a saloon and everyone stops what they're doing: the bartender, poker players, dance hall girls, everyone? As silence envelops the scene, the hero will saunter up to the bar, spurs a'jingle, and ask for "sarsaparilla." This reveals him to be a right girl's blouse, and the shooting commences. Same thing in Ballymagorry. When I entered the bar everyone stopped, stared, hard.

It was smoky inside, but kids were running around shrieking with laughter nonetheless. They stopped, mid-shriek. Stared, as well.

I shook water from my jacket, went up to the lady behind the counter, spurs a'jingling, asked, "Do you have any soup?"

"Soup?"

"I would really like a bowl of soup."

At the sound of my accent everything shifted.

"Floyd's, you should go to Floyd's. Floyd's. Aye, aye." Everyone was in agreement on that.

"Floyd's is closed," I said and—make note of this—no one was surprised.

"Aye, so it is. Won't open 'til five."

They didn't serve meals, but I did get a cup of tea and a bag of crisps (Roast Chicken & Bacon). I followed this with a shot of gin strong enough to kick-start a cadaver. I then unfolded my maps and considered my options. I'd planned to end my day in Ballymagorry but, its Oirish name aside, I could see no reason now for stopping and decided to push on instead to Strabane, the next town down the road. An informal poll of patrons put the distance at "two miles, maybe more, possibly less." As I pulled on my rain gear, one of the fellows, the oldest and presumably wisest, said, "Aye, there's no such thing as bad weather, only the wrong clothes."

I thanked him for that piece of advice, took my leave.

A very persuasive stucco salesman had blown through Ballymagorry. The main street was sort of an "Ode to Stucco." One small house even had a stucco door and a stucco gate. Union Jacks and Red Hands. Signposts painted over with Loyalist red-white-and-blue out here on the farthest edge of British territory. The Protestants of Ballymagorry were staring down the Republic on the other side of the river. Tenacity didn't begin to describe it.

PROTESTANTS HAVE BEEN in Northern Ireland longer than Europeans have been in North America. This is their home. They're not going anywhere, and the idea that they could ever be bombed into a sense of brotherhood is an odd notion indeed. As odd as those famously belligerent Unionist leaders who feel they can bully Catholics into a sense of loyalty. "*Maybe if we just YELL at them loud enough, they'll learn to love the Queen.*"

The affinity to Britain among Ulster Protestants is, I suspect, born of strategy rather than true kinship. After all, the founding oath of that most Protestant of societies, the Orange Lodge, is "to maintain the laws and peace of the country and the Protestant Constitution, and to defend the King and his heirs *as long as* they shall maintain the Protestant Ascendancy." (Emphasis mine.) "Conditional loyalty": a contradiction elsewhere, perhaps, but not here. Prior to partition, during the rancorous debates on granting Ireland Home Rule, the Protestants of the North were fully prepared to go to war against Britain in order to remain British. They threatened to set up a break-away provisional government—threatened treason, in effect—in the name of loyalty. Logic doesn't explain it. A sense of siege does.

It's often said that an identity crisis lies at the heart of Irish Protestant culture; they know who they're not, but not who they are. I wasn't so sure that was true—they certainly seemed self-assured to me—but Catholic nationalists often wholeheartedly agree that the Protestants of Northern Ireland aren't "real" Irish. Nationalists do this quite consciously, in an attempt to diminish the Protestant presence, to deny Protestants a claim on a land they have spent centuries working, a land they've helped build, a land their ancestors are buried in, a land they have died defending.

When did Irish become a synonym for Catholic? And how exactly did Irish and Protestant become mutually exclusive terms?

Many of Ireland's great nationalist heroes have been Protestant: William Drennan, Belfast doctor, founder of the United Irishmen—the very man who coined the phrase "the Emerald Isle"; Theobald Wolfe Tone, iconic leader of the 1798 rebellion; Henry Joy McCracken, rebel leader, hanged in Belfast; old Napper Tandy, immortalized in the ballad "The Wearing of the Green"; romantic rebel Robert Emmet; Henry Grattan, founder of "Grattan's Parliament" and an unwavering champion of Catholic emancipation; wild-eyed Republican proselytizer John Mitchel; leader of the Young Ireland movement, William Smith O'Brien. Even the founder of the Irish Republican Brotherhood—forerunner of today's IRA—was a Protestant, one James Stephens. Charles Stewart Parnell, once known as "the uncrowned king of Ireland"—the list goes on. Lord Edward Fitzgerald, Sir Roger Casement, the Countess Markievicz. These were men and women who fought, and often as not died, for Irish rights. Protestants all.

The poets, playwrights and scholars who spearheaded Ireland's Gaelic revival were overwhelmingly Protestant as well, from Samuel Ferguson to Thomas Davis, from Standish O'Grady to Douglas Hyde, who founded Ireland's Gaelic League specifically to stave off—in his words—"the loss of our language." The first proper Irish-English dictionary, instrumental in preserving the Gaelic language in Ireland, was edited by an Anglican bishop. From George Sigerson to W. B. Yeats, from Alice Milligan and Anna Johnston to Ernest Blythe: those Gaelic road signs you see sprouting up everywhere, the revitalized Celtic arts scene, the modern image of Ireland as Gaelic—owes an immense debt to Irish Protestants. "Modern Irish nationalism," historian Robert Kee points out, "was invented by Irish Protestants." The linking of "Gaelic" to "Catholic" was a political, not a cultural, move, and the alienation of Irish Protestants from Gaelic culture is one of the most unfortunate aspects of the current approach to Irish identity—especially in the North, where the Ulster-Scots have such clear and deep Gaelic roots.

And even then, the term "Protestant" hides a far greater complexity than is generally acknowledged. The original Protestant Ascendancy, after all, was a ruling elite centred in Dublin, rather than Belfast—Church of Ireland Anglicans who could be as hard on dissenters as they were on Catholics. The Penal Laws targeted Presbyterians as well as Catholics. It was very late in the game that the Anglicans and the Presbyterians of Ulster came together as "Protestants." The first great exodus of immigrants from the North were not downtrodden Catholics but Presbyterians fleeing religious intolerance. (Oh, the layers of irony involved in that statement.) The formula would only later become simplified—oversimplified, in the eyes of many—to that eternal either-or, Catholic/Protestant rubric.

During my time in the North, I'd learned to "read" a pub, to know whether the bar I'd entered was Protestant or Catholic long before any portraits of the Queen or tributes to King Billy were spotted, simply from the atmosphere. Protestants seemed more … clenched. It was the siege mentality made manifest.

Unionism is about maintaining the status quo: "What we have we hold." It's essentially a defensive posture—*No surrender!*—and as such, lends itself more readily to pessimism, to bitterness. The Nationalist stance, in contrast, is one that looks ahead, to a time when a "united" Ireland will come together as one. *Chucky ar la!* (How said unity would be achieved in the face of over a million Protestant Unionists is something glossed over. As noted, the strategy so far— "We'll bomb 'em into a sense of unity"—hasn't exactly won people over.) The Nationalist position, fanciful though it may seem, is about claiming the future. It is essentially optimistic, more upbeat, and I had found this reflected in the nature of the various communities I'd walked through. Irishmen all, but the Protestants seemed more guarded, more *clenched*.

If my trip had uncovered a single paltry truth, though, it was this: the similarities far outweighed the differences. The people of Ulster, whether Protestant or Catholic, were resoundingly more like each other than they were like anyone else.

Old School Unionists may indeed be fighting a rear-guard action against the inevitable. But try as I might, I couldn't see how the "One Island, One Ireland" proposal was any more realistic. You started to suspect that the real failure had not been of the Republicans to win over the Protestant majority in Northern Ireland, or of the Unionists to convince the Catholic minority to join them, but of the Northern Irish as a whole to create a larger, overriding sense of Ulster identity, independence, even. Drowned in sheer stubbornness, I imagine.

WHEN YOU ARRIVE in Strabane you soon learn that the town was the birthplace of John Dunlap, printer of the US Declaration of Independence, and that the Woodrow Wilson ancestral home is nearby. After that, they pretty much run out of things to tell you.

Not a lot to see in Strabane.

Strabane was a border city, and as such had been hit harder than most by the Troubles. The unemployment rates were among the highest in the UK, and at one point Strabane earned the unenviable sobriquet of being "the most bombed city in Europe," an honour later surpassed by Sarajevo. The inevitable hunger striker martyr murals, IRA graffiti and high-flying Irish tricolours let you know which side of the equation you were on. There was a wry terseness to Strabane. And if nothing else, that trait was the source of one of my favourite moments in Irish history. During the sixteenth century, the Clan O'Donnell was grazing their cattle on land owned by the O'Neills. When the High Chief of the O'Neills heard about this, he sent a message: "*Pay me my rent or—*" The O'Donnell chieftain replied with an equally curt message of his own: "*I owe you no rent, and if ...*" The O'Donnells kept the land. Built a castle on it, in fact, and eventually wrested control of the area away from the powerful but fatefully distant O'Neills.

Overheard while I kicked around Strabane: "*Oh, he's a cheeky fokker,*" a phrase I took an immediate anthro-linguistic interest in, adding it to my already rich "feck, fook, fack" hypothesis regarding Ulster dialects.

There was a tatty, downheel feel to the city. When I went to the travel kiosk, they directed me to other towns instead—never a good sign. "*There's a nice place across the river* ..." My guidebook actively discouraged travellers from spending time in Strabane. "If you *have* to stay ..." A gangle of spotty-faced teenage boys, gawky and ungainly as teenage boys are the world over, tried their best to help, but they didn't know any B&Bs nearby either. I called around: here a fax line, there a parent out or relatives in. The only hotel available was waythefuck out of town, a long walk on my already tired legs. In the end, I allowed myself to be swept back into the gravity well of Derry.

I returned to Strabane the next morning on an early bus. Pale mist. Softer light. But Strabane was still Strabane. The only thing to do was leave.

THE POOLS OF PURGATORY

Sunshine on green hills greeted me as I walked into Sion Mills. If the name sounds vaguely Biblical, that's because it is—Sion being a reference to Zion—one that hints at the community's twin roots: gospel and commerce. Sion Mills began as a "model village" based around a linen mill, as laid out by the Bible-thumping Herdman brothers: John, James, George—and Ringo, I believe.

Like Cushendun on the Antrim coast, Sion Mills was originally designed almost entirely by one architect, giving it a consistency of style and its own overriding look. The newer town sprawled out along the highway—Sion Mills seemed doomed to become a bedroom community for Strabane's wealthier citizens, who were, quite sensibly, fleeing Strabane—but the heart of the old village was still there, distinct as ever, with its checkerboard row of streets and its low-roofed millworker cottages. Squat and solid, they crowded the sidewalks with their rough-textured, whitewashed walls, and though the cottages themselves were very modest, the cumulative effect was quite striking. Mind you, I didn't know how I would like living in one. I was sure they were quite cozy inside, but I also imagined you'd start to feel like a giant, ducking your head to enter and stepping out almost directly into the street when you left.

Past the town's half-timbered church, looking like a scene on a Swiss chocolate box, and beyond the modern Herdman Mill with its corrugated metal walls in olive green, looking more like a military instalment than a factory, you reached the low, grassy banks of the Mourne River. (Which is nowhere near the Mourne Mountains, I should note.) Where other towns ignored their rivers, Sion Mills had embraced theirs. Sliding soft beneath its sheltered canopy of trees, the Mourne was part of a centrepiece park. It was the village's main stroll, even if it was tucked out of sight.

Spanning said river was the famed Swingin' Bridge of Sion Mills (apostrophe theirs). Name aside, the Swingin' Bridge did not swing. Not in the 1970s wife-swapping sense nor in the "pivoting upon its axis" sense. It did bounce a bit. Though I imagined "The Slightly Bouncing Bridge of Sion Mills!" wouldn't have quite the same zing to it. It was a bridge built so mill workers on the other side wouldn't have to wade across the top of a nearby salmon weir. Today's wire-and-metal suspension construct was actually the third footbridge to be built across the Mourne. The mill owners kept building bridges, at ever higher levels, and the bridges kept washing away. The first bridge was built in 1871; the current one dated from 1988. It had survived— so far.

Below the Swingin' Bridge lay the river's whirlpools, one of them aptly named Purgatory Pool. *That in-between world, endlessly turning.* No Dantean travellers or depth-plumbing pilgrims here, though; this was the realm of fly fishers, men in waders casting perfect arcs into the water.

I followed the shore past Purgatory and the old salmon weirs, where trees draped their branches into the river like fingers trailing from the side of a boat. Herons glided low along the water. This beat bog walking any day.

Farmers, however, had a different feeling about hikers tramping through. I'd been warned they would oftentimes post "Beware of Bull"

signs to keep walkers out. So when I came upon one such sign—
Beware of Bull indeed!—I decided to call their bluff. The fields beyond
the fence were newly tilled; I didn't see any tracks, let alone any rogue
bulls, and I didn't imagine cattle would be grazing on freshly turned
loam. It was slow going, though, across soil soft and deep, and the
fence on the far side of the field seemed to get farther and farther away
the nearer I got. I kept my senses attuned, ready to flee at the first whiff
of bovine testosterone. *Flee, to where?* Hmm. Maybe centre field was
not the best place to be, so I veered toward the river instead, found a
path and followed it, feeling very clever. I should have been asking *why*
there was a well-trodden path along the side of the river. As I walked
along I realized, slowly, I admit, that I was following a cattle trail. No
sooner had this awful realization dawned than I came upon a mighty
and menacing cow flop. Still steaming, by the looks of it. A large flop,
almost virile, I'd say. The sort a bull might make.

He (*she?* please let it be a she) must have gone to the river for a
drink now and then. Sure enough, a few paces along, the bushes were
trampled at water's edge and the bank was pocked with hoofprints.
Who would guess bulls could be so nimble? I looked for potential
places to hide. Thorn bushes and nettles, mainly. If a bull charged
now I would be caught—in every conceivable way—on the horns of
a dilemma.

I'll end the suspense. I wasn't killed by a bull that day. I made it
through, nerves well rattled, and was never happier to see barbed wire
than when I reached the end of that stretch. A sign was posted in the
next field. *Beware of Bull.*

"You fokkers!" I shouted, at no one in particular.

Onward I skulked, through the next field and the next, until I
came at last to the Camus Bridge. Another bridge to nowhere. Very
existentialist, that, and suitably so, considering its name. It was an
abandoned railway span, with a bottom that had long since fallen out,
leaving a criss-cross of girders over open water. I crossed it as nimbly
as any bull. The girders themselves were wide enough, but they had a
staccato line of rivets running down the middle, which made my

footsteps wobbly. The winds were stronger now as well, and I found myself batted about, with my poorly packed gear swaying wildly, throwing my already uncertain centre of gravity off kilter. It's a wonder I made it across at all.

The ruins of a stone church stood in a quiet grove of trees, its parish now one of sheep and solitude. I had entered a forgotten valley, one scattered with derelicts, and the next bridge I crossed was so completely grown over as to be blanketed with grass. The rail tracks these bridges had carried no longer existed, but you could see memories of them in the grassy ridges running through the fields, could chart their path across the landscape. I was walking among phantoms in a place once humming with human endeavour: trains pulling in and churches letting out, love affairs and feuds. Guidebooks often comment upon how rural the North is. But they rarely mention how deserted so much of it is. With its abandoned cottages and forgotten valleys, Northern Ireland was not so much a farm as it was a ghost farm. Even its beauty was elegiac.

I SPENT the next three nights in Newtownstewart, which most experts would agree is three nights too long.

I'd been planning to follow an old rail line marked on the Ordnance Survey map, but the rains had begun bucketing down as in the days of Noah. Even I wasn't dumb enough to try that route in a downpour. Instead, I made the slog into Newtownstewart along the highway as traffic fanned past, dousing me with an accuracy that could hardly have been coincidental. I found a room—or rather rooms—at a modern self-catering holiday cottage and collapsed onto one of the beds, asleep by the second bounce.

It was a strange place, Newtownstewart, cleaved in two by the A5, which bottlenecked in the middle of town. Lumbering transport trucks careened down the main street, veering sharply as the road turned, with speeding cars and overloaded rigs cannon-balling by mere inches from children walking home from school. It was bizarre. Must have been like living in the middle of a freeway interchange.

Indeed, I urge you to drop whatever it is you're doing (reading a book, probably) and drive to the airport, get on a plane, fly to London, transfer onto a flight to Belfast and then take a bus to Newtownstewart, making sure to arrive late in the afternoon when traffic is at its screaming worst, just so you can stand, agog, and say, "Oh my god! He wasn't kidding."

This is a problem many towns and villages in Northern Ireland face. They weren't designed for the amount of traffic now being forced through them. Newtownstewart, though, was sad even without the bone-shaking traffic and the pall of exhaust that hung over the place. The buildings, a kaleidoscope of greys and browns, were afflicted with some sort of architectural eczema, paint and plaster flaking away in great dusty scabs. Housing estates had UDA, UVF, "No Surrender" written on them. There was the usual RUC fortress. The town seemed to loiter about, hands in its pockets, watching the trucks go by. It was one of the few places in Northern Ireland that made Strabane look good. (*Suggested tourist motto for Strabane:* "If you think we're dismal, you should see Newtownstewart!") Between the melancholy buildings you could catch glimpses of elemental green, of hills rolling. Away.

I ate my supper at Handy's Chip Shop Take-Away, where I tried the "Cow-Boy Supper" (fried potatoes covered in baked beans and topped with sausage. Always with the sausage). Back in my empty three-room apartment—which sounds grand but was actually quite lonely—I watched the local weather forecast with a guarded sense of optimism. They were calling for "wet tonight, clearing by morning." This cheered me up considerably, and I went to bed in an upbeat mood. When I woke the next morning, the forecast had changed to "clear now, with heavy rains by mid-day."

Why had I ended up in Newtownstewart? (Note the wording; no one *goes* to Newtownstewart; they end up there.) I ended up in Newtownstewart solely because the Ulster Way crossed the highway south of town. That was where I would pick up my original route—if the weather ever cleared. The telly was no help. It was either raining or about to rain; there were only ever the two forecasts in Northern Ireland. So why bother? Right? I might as well just set off up the next mountain, regardless. How bad could it get? Gusting winds, lashing rain, bone-cracks of thunder and lightning that backlit the sky in flashbulb bursts, that's how bad, and it struck me—not literally, of course—that standing at the top of a high hill beside a cairn during a thunderstorm might not be the wisest choice. Which is how I ended up in Omagh.

There were times I would think I should have braved the storms instead.

LACERATIONS OF THE HEART

Travel writers often refer to the "French" feel of Omagh—something to do with the old stone bridge, the warren of streets at the bottom of town, the French Gothic architecture and asymmetrical spires of Sacred Heart Church (modelled on those of Chartres Cathedral, it was said)—though I confess the Gallic flavour eluded me.

Omagh was attractive enough on its own terms, even in the rain. Built on a steep slope, its main street rose toward several grand architectural gestures: the twin spires of the Catholics, the single spire of the Protestants and between the two the Omagh courthouse with its Doric columns, and lion and unicorn presiding.

A trinity of rivers met in Omagh, and though the town was set apart from them, walking paths had been opened up along the banks. Quaint shops lined the High Street, and as I wandered about, I felt that familiar tug—*I could live here* ... It may not have been Paris, but after the freeway that was Newtownstewart's downtown, I was happy to be in a place worthy of a stroll.

Any Catholic church in Northern Ireland, whatever its size, was inevitably referred to as a "chapel." Cathedral-like Sacred Heart, with its lakes of stained glass and polished pillars, was still considered a "chapel." At a nearby church hall, I came upon a sign that read SAINT JOSEPH'S BOOKSHOP. NOW OPEN. "Open," of course, meaning "closed." I tried the door anyway and was about to leave when a woman whisked past. She saw me, stopped and came back, asked "Are you here for the Weight Watchers meeting?"

This was, as you might imagine, not exactly a high point of my trip.

"The meeting's around the other side," she said helpfully.

"No," I said, jaw clenched. "I'm not here for the Weight Watchers meeting. I'm waiting for the bookstore to open."

"Oh, it's not open t'day, I'm afraid."

"It isn't?"

"Oh, no."

"So this sign here, the one reading 'Bookstore Now Open,' would mean …?"

"Oh, that? That sign's always up. It doesn't mean anything." She tutted at me, as if to say, "*Everyone knows that. What's wrong with you?*"

So back I went, into the wet Parisian streets of Omagh.

WITH THE COSTS of my trip piling up—camping and youth hostels were no longer part of the equation, due to weather in the first case and age in the second—I considered fobbing myself off as a reporter and penning articles about my trip for the many lavishly funded regional newspapers back home. I'd already made a few exploratory calls. As I walked down the main street of Omagh, I thought maybe I should give it a try. "I could do a survey," I thought. "Ask people where they were that day."

I stopped to take a photo: a limp bouquet of flowers in the rain.

"The car was right there, right where you're standing. A red Cavalier, so it was." A lady from one of the shops had seen me with my camera.

I stood beside her in the doorway, and the only thing I could think to ask was, "Why?"

Why this? Why here?

"It's the County Town," she said. "The courts, the county office … it's busy. Full of life."

The bomb had destroyed the end of the street. The area was still fenced off, still under scaffolding. The men who did this had driven in from across the border, in cars that were later traced through cellphone calls. They chose Omagh, one of the few large nonsectarian towns in Northern Ireland and one of the few places where the two sides were trying to come together. The men in the cars were IRA—the *real* IRA, as they called themselves—and they were taking a stand against peace.

The 1998 Good Friday Agreement had just been signed. Britain had (again) renounced any economic or strategic claim on Northern Ireland, asserting that the North would remain a part of the UK only so long as a majority of its inhabitants supported the union. (This is called democracy, a tricky concept for some.) The agreement had passed with overwhelming support, and that had to be stopped. When you peddle in hate, you can't have people getting along. It throws the paradigm out of whack. The men who detonated that bomb were fighting to preserve the status quo: a status quo of sectarian divide and cyclic violence.

On a sunny Saturday in August 1998, the market town of Omagh blew apart.

Twenty-nine people died. Protestants and Catholic alike. Eleven of them children. A Spanish exchange student and a teacher from Madrid. Hundreds more injured, many severely so, some blinded, some crippled for life. One man lost three generations of his family in a single searing flash: the bomb killed his wife, their eighteen-month-old granddaughter and their thirty-year-old daughter, who was pregnant with twins. The Real IRA had managed to reach through time, kill generations yet unborn. Even now, the number of dead at Omagh is sometimes given as thirty-one. Among those killed was an eight-year-old boy on a class trip from Donegal. When the school bus made its long journey back to the families, his mother found half a packet of sweets on his seat, carefully wrapped in a tissue. He had saved them for the ride home.

On one of the last shopping weekends before school started, the Real IRA had parked a car bomb in front of a store that sold school uniforms. They then called in a false warning, telling the police that the bomb was planted at the courthouse at the other end. The crowds were duly moved down to where the Cavalier was parked. Apparently, the Real IRA had been hoping the RUC would set up a barricade at that end, so they could run up the body count. As it was, the bomb went off prematurely, and they had to be satisfied with just twenty-nine killed. It was Northern Ireland's worst single act of terrorism.

The Omagh bombing was met with universal condemnation. This time, there were no Republican apologists talking about "historical contexts" or "British occupation," no attempt at using the civil rights movement of the 1960s to justify mass murder today, none of that blathering shite. The photos of the victims, smiling toddlers and buoyant young mothers, fathers, brothers and friends, the funeral processions in Omagh, Madrid, Donegal: it was one atrocity too many, and it marked the last gasp of the Troubles. *With a bang and a whimper* ... What began in Derry in 1968 ended in Omagh in 1998. Thousands of lives squandered. For what?

To understand the enormity of the violence, consider the following: during the course of the conflict, more than 3,500 people died. Republicans killed more than 2,000 of these—civilians, soldiers, bystanders, police, Catholic and Protestants alike—and Loyalists killed another thousand. Most of those who died were civilians. Tens of thousands more were injured or crippled for life. The numbers are horrific enough on their own, but set them against Northern Ireland's small population base, and you see the true scope of what happened. Had comparable casualties occurred in the United States, the dead would have numbered 700,000, with eight *million* more wounded. Compare that to the number of people who died in the World Trade Center attacks and you get just a glimmer of what Northern Ireland has gone through. *Imagine eight hundred passenger jets hijacked, four hundred Trade Centers collapsing ...*

It was a war marked by appalling brutality on both sides. Loyalist paramilitaries often committed atrocities as horrific as those of the IRA, among them a bomb planted at McGurk's Bar in Belfast that left fifteen dead, including the owner's fourteen-year-old daughter. Without the clear targets of police and the army, Loyalists tended to favour random sectarian murders, killing Catholics after each IRA attack. The Shankill Butchers, a particularly gruesome UVF cell in Belfast, were little more than serial killers, tying up their victims and torturing them to death before dumping the bodies. The IRA generally went for the higher body counts and bigger media splash of "big bang" bomb attacks.

In Omagh, people were—in a sense—still counting the dead. A coroner's inquest was being held under heavy security, and an editor in Ottawa had emailed to say, "Send a report from the Omagh inquest, 800 words. We'll run it on the weekend."

I joined the long queue to get in, was searched and scanned, and took a seat in the public gallery as the coroner began going through the list of the victims, one by one, recording the cause and time of death.

"Punctures, bruising, internal bleeding, shrapnel injuries, left lower leg badly mangled, blistered skin, scorched flesh, base of skull fractured, extensive bleeding into the chest cavities, ribs broken ..."

Detail by detail by endless detail. He went on methodically, clearing up discrepancies and confirming post-mortems, as family members clutched damp Kleenexes like rosaries.

> NAME: Adrian Michael Gallagher, age twenty-one, known to family and friends as Aiden. He had followed the crowd down the street ...
> *A large, gaping laceration of the mouth. Spinal cord severed. Burns to the face.*

> NAME: Samantha McFarland, age seventeen. She was volunteering at the Oxfam shop when the bomb went off, and was killed alongside her best friend, Lorraine Wilson, who was also volunteering at the Oxfam shop that day ...
> *Internal hemorrhaging, broken bones ...*

A strange calm came over the proceedings. It was like a town council meeting, but instead of discussing zoning laws and store hours, they were detailing deaths, correcting birth dates and checking the spellings of the victims' names.

The coroner presiding was exceptionally kind. I noted how he addressed each family in turn, expressed his sympathy, assured them—if the person had been killed instantly—that there had been no suffering. If, however, a death had been a drawn-out agony, he expressed his admiration for the person who had died, how they had "clung to life, had tried their best to remain."

A mother sat weeping silently, rocking back and forth, back and forth, as though wanting to hold her child one last time.

Among the dead was a young woman whose school test results arrived a week after she was killed. She'd passed her A levels and would have begun the physiotherapy degree she'd always dreamed of getting. All those lives stopped short.

Shrapnel lacerations in the chest, puncturing the right carotid artery. Metal had pierced her right eye.

One by one, the details were read into the records. And one by one, the families appealed to those responsible to understand the suffering they had caused on that sunny Saturday in August.

I walked out onto the street, the competing church towers of Omagh rising above me. I spent the rest of the afternoon waiting for the rain to end.

It never did.

The coroner's inquest was set to resume the next day, so I returned to Omagh, but I couldn't bring myself to go back inside. I called the editor in Ottawa and declined the assignment.

At Bogans Bar, I ordered a sandwich and a bowl of soup, ate quietly. I knew I could walk for as long as I wanted, could walk through bog and forest, city and village, could walk until I had beaten a trough in the soil, but I would never be able to walk my way into an understanding of any of this.

"Everybody out!" It was a man in the bar's doorway, ordering patrons to leave. *"Now!"*

When the IRA plants a bomb, they have a secret codeword they give the RUC so that the police will know the threat is real, not a prank. You don't want amateurs and freelancers getting into the bombing business. You don't want students calling in bomb threats to get out of exams. You don't want people being frivolous about it.

Someone had called in a bomb threat for Omagh, had given the RUC the correct code. The streets were being emptied, and emptied quickly. I hurried out of the bar, down the main street with the rest of the crowd, my mouth dry, my throat tight. The police had the end of Market Street cordoned off, were moving people away, and we walked right past the scaffolding where the original bomb had gone off. I headed straight for the depot and caught the first bus back to Newtownstewart, where I holed myself up in my empty three-room apartment. I started to shake. Waves of tremors that I couldn't control. A delayed reaction, I suppose.

I hadn't paid for my meal: I woke up in the middle of the night with that realization. It seemed important to return and pay, to not use any of it as an excuse. So I went back to Omagh again.

The publican remembered me, was surprised. "An honest man," he laughed. "There's a rarity. T'tell the truth, we'd already written it off."

Another customer remembered me as well, an older fellow in a threadbare sweater.

"Poor taste, innit?" he said. "Ringing the police with a hoax like that. Of all a' towns to do that to, not Omagh. Not after wha' we been through."

"Why are they doing it, then?" I asked. So many of the questions I had in Northern Ireland began with *Why*.

"Part of the plan, innit?" he said. "To tear the community apart, turn it against itself. The worst part is"—there was a pause—"it's workin'."

Almost every Wednesday, he said, a bomb threat was phoned in from somewhere.

"In poor taste, innit?"

It was.

"You'll be wanting a drink, then?" This was the barkeep, and the way he said it, it wasn't really a question.

I nodded. "Yes, I believe I will."

HARVESTING AIR

On my final night in Newtownstewart I made the walk up to Harry Avery's Castle, twin half-moon towers above the town. The castle was built in the 1300s, and though its name sounded English, it was actually a Gaelic stone castle, rare in Ulster, Avery being an anglicization of the Irish name *Aimbreidh*.

It was late in the evening, and the castle towers were caught halfway between shadow and silhouette. I walked across wet fields to get there, and a big, floppy-eared dog came galumphing over to see if I wanted to be pals. I scritched him behind his ears awhile, and he went off, tail still wagging. When I reached the castle I was rewarded with a full 360-degree panorama of the valley and the white precision of windmills on the hills beyond, blades slicing air in karate-chop cartwheels. The next day, I would be walking right under those windmill blades. That was the plan, anyway.

WHEN I REJOINED the Ulster Way south of Newtownstewart, the rains had lifted, and the air was moist with the scent of green.

Ahead lay the heathery heights of Bessy Bell, with not a waymarker in sight. I struck out, aiming straight for the top, and soon came to an electrified fence—labelled as such, fortunately. A huddle of cows watched as I tried to climb over without coming into testicular contact with the wire. I knew there would be no aid available were I to stagger back into town clutching my balls and moaning, "*Help me, for the love of God help me.*" Ulster hospitality has its limits. Instead, I high-stepped across as though playing a life-sized game of Operation, using a crossbeam post and an outcrop of rock to deftly avoid contact.

I then plodded upward across steep, spongy fields. Four days of heavy rain had turned the landscape sodden.

The final stretch was across bracken fields and flattened bushes that *seemed* thick but offered no real support. I sank through with every tortuous, ankle-twisting step and ended up wading—almost swimming—my way to the top. When I reached the radio tower at the summit, I was exhausted and brimming with profanity. Bessy Bell was home to a well, a magical well. If you placed three white stones beside it, you would be granted your heart's desire. I hadn't thought to bring any white stones with me, unfortunately. Not that it mattered, because I couldn't find the well anyway, even though it was marked on the Ordnance Survey map and in the guidebooks. I left with my wishes unfulfilled. Just as well, really, because it spared the architects of the Ulster Way being struck down repeatedly by a bolt of lightning.

A gravel road ran down the other side of the hill, toward the chop and whir of the wind turbines. I was soon surrounded by them, their propellers dizzying to look up at, eerie to walk beneath. They were unnaturally quiet for such large feats of engineering; just the *whiff-whiff-whiff* of blades turning. I loved the idea of "wind farms," the notion that you could harvest air.

The road snaked into thick forest from there, and somewhere along the way I entered the private estate of the Duke and Duchess of Abercorn. The Ulster Way crossed the edge of their demesne. I considered filching some pheasant's eggs or perchance poaching a jolly trout from one of m'Lord's streams, but I decided not to risk a whack on the backside and transport to Van Diemen's land. I did practise my forelock tugging in the general direction of the lord's manor, though, just to be safe. (Forelock is a synonym for testes, yes? Kidding!) Although an anti-monarchist in principle, my main objection to the ongoing anachronism of landed gentry is the fact that I am not counted among their members. It really was an oversight, their not having included me. If anyone could whack a peasant properly, I could.

Soon enough I came upon a deer-crossing sign. This being a nobleman's estate, it showed a mighty stag in mid-flight. I didn't see any mighty stags, but I did hear two distant rifle shots: claps of thunder in the distance. And then—bolting across the road—several deer leapt past, appearing and disappearing in almost the same instant. I froze. More gunshots, closer now, and the sound of dogs baying. Let's hope it was a pheasant they were chasing—or even a peasant—and not those particular deer. Fearful of getting caught in the line of fire, I picked up my pace, expecting at any moment to see a fury of hounds come pouring out of the woods. None did, fortunately, and I was thus spared having my head stuffed and mounted over a fireplace as a conversation piece in someone's manor house.

A stone cabin stood at a fork in the forest, stag horns nailed above the door. Smoke was drifting from the chimney. In the yard, a doghouse—but no dog. Not something you like to see. The chain was lying on the ground, but the hound itself had slipped free. Even worse, the Ulster Way made a sharp turn at the Y, passing along the other side of the house and giving any unseen curs another go at me.

I made it by the cabin ungnawed and came to a country church, where I stopped for lunch among the graves of the various dukes and duchesses who had come to rest there over the years. The waymarkers after Baronscourt Church were a mess, pointing in every direction except the correct one, but I made it through and came out of the forest and onto a rise of hill. On the road below lay a cluster of buildings. This was Drumlegagh, I decided, and I walked down to meet it.

A graveyard and large Presbyterian church, and beside them, the true hallmark of civilization: a SPAR store, retail equivalent of an oasis. I dumped my pack outside, went in to stock up. The place was crammed with people, customers and visitors mainly—the line between the two seemed blurred—plus an annoyance of children from a nearby school.

"What's five pence get us then?" one of them shouted.

The lady of the store shooed them away like alley cats, clearing a path for me. In lieu of a pub, it would seem this shop was the communal living room of Drumlegagh.

"Tom Findlay? Was he sober enough to tell you?" one fellow was asking.

"Sure, he was working on a car."

"Doesn't necessarily mean he was sober now, does it?" came the reply.

The shop was an extension of the family's home; when I asked for a cup of tea, the lady poured me some from her own pot. When I asked her what I owed, she said, "Don't be daft. That's me good deed for the day."

From the SPAR store the road rolled down the hill past jumbled fieldstone fences and farmhouses falling into decay. In the distance, the wind turbines of Bessy Bell seemed small and quaint, children's pinwheels arranged along a distant hilltop.

The Ulster Way crossed the quiet trickle of Fairy Water, a stream more heard than seen, then ran up to a country crossroads. I looked around for a place to bed down for the night, saw nothing but squishy fields. Sleep in one of those and you'd wake up with the ground moulded around you and bog water seeping in. I looked at the sky, saw the usual foreshadowing. With a sigh, I was preparing to batten down for a miserable night when I spotted—in a shaft of heavenly light—a bus stop.

I waited almost an hour as the skies grew darker, but a bus did appear, and I was swept back along the road to Omagh as rain hit the roof like BB pellets on a tin can.

Ha! You didn't get me this time, you fokkers!

The driver was eyeing me in his mirror. I had said that last part out loud.

"The rain," I said by way of explanation. "It's been trying to get me."

CIRCLES OF STONE

I don't know how I ended up in Kesh. People living in Kesh must ask themselves that all the time. Kidding! It was a lovely town, actually, near the shores of Lower Lough Erne. It just wasn't on my itinerary. The Ulster Way went nowhere near Kesh, which made it something of a mystery, my having ended up there.

Personally? I blamed the monotony of planted forests, with their regimental formations and endless gravel roads. They put me in a mindless stupor. The architects of the Ulster Way had an inordinate affection for planted forests. Me, not so much.

The day had begun with a long walk up Bolaght Mountain. Sheep were grazing on the roadside, and I sort of herded them along, their uncropped tails flopping like feather boas. The road ended at open heights, where a trail ran across raised bog toward a hidden lake. It was a fisherman's trail, even if none were around that day. Fishermen, of course, come equipped with hip waders. Sure, the trail started off grandly enough, stone slabs clearly waymarked, but it quickly turned into a churned line through the muck. The saturation was so complete on Bolaght Mountain that my footprints almost immediately filled with water. The trail became an open stream running through the grassy hillocks.

Spend enough time picking your way across the bogs of Northern Ireland and you become attuned to the topography. You turn into an amateur botanist, studying the plants and the lay of the land, trying to second-guess the pitfalls (and possible pratfalls) that lie ahead, looking always for anchors to hopscotch across on. You learn to read the vegetation: bright green moss is a sure sign of squelchy water below; taller grass signifies drier ground, especially if it's on a slight hump. But the broad-leafed, dark grass you see is usually growing straight out of open water. Put your foot down there, and your boot will be swamped.

It was slow going, but eventually I reached the crest and saw below me Lough Lee, destination of the aforementioned hip-wading fishermen. Beside it was a small pond, little more than a puddle. And beyond that, forest. Planted forest. I followed the trail down, between pond and puddle, descending out of the wind but now facing another interminable stretch of forestry service, with all that entailed: the claustrophobia, the lack of a view, the numbing sense that you weren't really moving forward but were walking on a treadmill. As the hours dripped away, I walked and walked past: trees. Trees aligned and trees replanted, trees recently reaped and others lined up waiting in what was, essentially, an arboreal abattoir. If nothing else, my walk that day provided a study in forest management. If only forest management were remotely interesting!

When I reached the other side, the Ulster Way suddenly veered north, following an unnecessarily complicated route through private driveways and various farmers' fields. In doing so it missed—almost intentionally, it seemed—the Drumskinny Stone Circle. This was Ulster's mini-me version of Stonehenge, one of the most significant prehistoric sites in the North. I had no intention of bypassing it, so I turned south instead, making what was meant to be a short detour.

This took me past Rotten Mountain—which was, I should note, hardly rotten and not much of a mountain. Just a low, flat hill really, with a thick strip of forest running up the top and a few houses thumbtacked to its side. Still, it must be a great address. *"You can send it to me care of 'Rotten Mountain.'"*

The Drumskinny Circle was beyond Rotten Mountain, in a small clearing set back from the road. Thirty-nine stones, with a cairn beside them, in a circular arrangement that was both understated and astonishing. I walked out, stood in the centre and—I know this sounds flaky—it seemed somehow calmer, quieter inside the circle, as though the wind had stopped, as though the world were catching its breath. The Drumskinny site seems to date from the end of the Neolithic period and the start of the Bronze Age, but no one knows for sure. Nor does anyone know what these prehistoric circles represent, or why they were built. Blood and sacrifice? Calm reflection? Astrological calculations? Communal rites? Simple ornamentation? A meeting spot or rallying point, perhaps, for forerunners of the Orange Halls and Hibernian Lodges of today? Enter the Drumskinny Circle and you were standing in the middle of a four-thousand-year-old riddle, unsolvable, undeniable.

One thing I can say: the stone circles at Drumskinny are not an aid to navigation. Not in my case, anyway. My Drumskinny detour would prove fatal, you see, because once I went Off Route I was never able to get back on. Everything got turned around. There was a latticework of lanes in the area, and no matter how hard I frowned at it, the real world refused to conform to my maps. I shoe-horned it in nonetheless, deciding unilaterally that the line of trees *over there* was in fact the southern edge of forest marked *here* on the map. I crossed a couple of bridges that had apparently been overlooked by the surveyors and then strode off in precisely the wrong direction. At which point I stumbled upon a pub out in the country. Happenstance doesn't get much better.

That crossroads tavern, far from any town or village, made me think of the challenge James Joyce had once thrown down. "A good puzzle," he stated, "would be to cross Ireland without passing a pub." "Country pub" does not equal friendly, though, as I quickly discovered. It was another true sarsaparilla moment. I moseyed in to hard stares from hard men. They sat around a table, as rooted as any stone circle. I spotted the Gaelic Athletic Association paraphernalia on display and adjusted my repertoire accordingly, making a note to replace my jokes about the Pope with ones about the Queen.

I sidled up to the bar, as you do, and set about charming my way into the publican's good graces.

"Hello there," I said. "I've just walked over from Bolaght Mountain, and boy, are my—"

"What'll it be then?"

"Um, I'll have a half-pint of Har—"

And *bam.* I swear the glass was in front of me before I got to the "p." He waited, arms crossed, for me to finish it and get out.

Which I did, with a flourish of sleeve across my mouth and a satisfied *Ahh.*

"Guess I'll be going then!" I said to the others. Somehow they held back their tears.

I stepped outside, having shotgunned a glass of lager, feeling light-headed, yet oddly refreshed—and set off once again in exactly the wrong direction. The beer may have had something to do with it. I passed the Montiaghroe Catholic Church and, across from it, another cluster of standing stones aligned in a meadow. The day was becoming a Neolithic Easter egg hunt. Great fun, that, until I came upon a confusion of signs, none of which were for the Ulster Way.

As I walked on, I became vaguely aware that something was wrong. It was the bends in the road: there were none. I'd been walking straight when I should have been zigging and zagging. When I reached Drumskinny's rural post office (the post office *was* Drumskinny, apparently), I accosted a husband and wife who were just leaving.

"I'm a little confused," I said, trying not to weave on my feet; that half-pint had really hit me. "This is the road to Pettigo, yes? I'm a hiker," I explained, though they could probably have figured that out from the map, boots and backpack.

"No, not the road to Pettigo," they said.

I pointed the other way. "So that's not"—I checked the map—"Drumnagalliagh?" Now, I defy anyone who is not Irish to pronounce that correctly. Whatever it was that came out of my mouth dumbfounded them both; they cocked their heads at me like the RCA Victrola dog.

"Where're you to, then?" asked the husband.

"Pettigo."

They looked at me with sad expressions.

"This is the road to Kesh," said the wife. "You're nowhere near Pettigo."

"Nowhere near," said her husband, underlining the point unnecessarily, I thought.

"We'll run you down to Kesh," she said. "You can catch a bus from there."

Which is how I ended up not in Pettigo.

On the drive down we crossed the bridge at Tubbrid, and a Union Jack appeared, snapping cleanly above the local Orange Lodge. Beyond it, a solid grey church, looking more like a Norman castle than a place of worship, with a red-white-and-blue of its own flying above its turret. One road, two churches. It was only a mile or two from the Montiaghroe chapel to the church at Tubbrid, and yet a great divide had been crossed. Above the post office was Catholic, below it was Protestant. *This strange Eden.*

Soon after, we arrived in Kesh. I liked Kesh. It was quaint without being twee. A lazy river flowed along, wending its way down toward the convoluted coastline of Lower Lough Erne. But Kesh was nowhere near where I was supposed to be. I hadn't merely drifted off course, I had sailed.

The next bus was ages away from departing, so I took a taxi instead. It had been an expensive navigational error on my part.

ESCAPING PATRICK'S PURGATORY

A statue of a 1920s IRA man, his rifle pointed toward the border, welcomes you to the Republic. This was Pettigo. A river ran through it, and a border. The taxi had dropped me off on the UK side, beneath a giant oak tree that spread its shade over a small square, and I walked down from there.

Technically, the UK side of the river was not Pettigo but Tullyhommon, best known for a narrow escape it had during the 1980s, when an IRA bomb failed to go off during a Remembrance Day service attended by more than two hundred members of the local boys' and girls' clubs. The goal had been to wipe out an entire generation of Protestant children, but the detonator hadn't gone off, and the ceremony continued without anyone realizing the threat they were under. Only a faulty wire had stood between them and carnage.

I crossed over into the Republic, where the Quiet Man statue squared off with the border, rifle ready. On this side of the river the police stations were not fortresses, the IRA having shown a magnanimity to the Garda that they did not show the RUC. On this side of the river, there was no razor wire encircling the stations, no bolted doors, no watch towers.

I found a room in a guest house filled with joyously squabbling children and ongoing debates. As I was signing in, the lady of the house cornered one young boy and, with arms outstretched, corralled him in for a hug. "This one's the baby," she said as he squirmed to escape. It was a fine place, clean and spacious, considering the size of the family, but the plumbing was indecisive: in the bath the water was first cold, then lukewarm, then very lukewarm, then almost hot— then suddenly cold again. Looking back on it later, I realized the plumbing was simply a foretaste of the penance to come.

DEMONS PURSUED HIM, *flames seared his flesh …*

But the knight never wavered. Fuelled by his faith, onward he went, though his tormentors were many. Onward he went, across valley and plain, through prisons of sin where the souls of the dead were pinned by burning rivets to fiery wheels, were slow-roasted on spits and given Satanic baptisms of molten iron. Onward, until at last he crossed a bridge and came to an earthly paradise, a return to Eden before the Fall.

The Knight Owein had passed through purgatory. It was a story that would sweep through Europe, would capture the medieval imagination. Ireland in the twelfth century was on the outer edge of the world; beyond it lay only cold sea and silence. Lough Derg, the remote lake with its small island where the entrance to purgatory was said to be, was in Ireland's desolate northwest, the outer edge of the outer edge, and as such it lay in the borderland between this world and the next, a threshold, a portal to the afterlife.

The Knight Owein's journey, with its visions graphic and gratuitous, was one of the world's first potboilers, a medieval bestseller, transcribed and translated, passed on from monastery to monastery. It was a tale that would inspire Dante.

On medieval maps of Europe, St. Patrick's Purgatory—where the Knight Owein had made his journey to the otherworld—was often the only Irish landmark that appeared. It attracted pilgrims and adventurers alike. Some went mad from the experience; others were shattered, retreating into hermit-like solitude, never to smile again. In an early example of sensory deprivation, pilgrims were locked into the darkness of a cellar-like pit overnight, having first fasted and maintained a vigil. Lacking in sleep, and light-headed from hunger, they found the veil between this world and the next dissolving.

The Protestant Ascendancy condemned the pilgrimage as one of "superstition and idolatry" and several times razed the island, chasing off the monks and filling in the cave. By 1704, fines and public floggings were introduced for anyone making the pilgrimage. (Considering that they were coming to Lough Derg as penance, the threat of a whipping probably wasn't the dissuader the Protestants thought it would be.)

They continued to come by the hundreds, by the thousands, ferried across to that barren island on that distant lake. Today, the lurid visions of the Middle Ages are long gone, but the pilgrimage itself remains, an unbroken chain stretching back a thousand years or more. It is a rite of atonement, a purgatory not in the sense of a physical holding cell between Heaven and Earth, but in the sense of *purging* oneself.

Pettigo was the jumping-off point for Lough Derg, and I decided to make the trip, even though it wasn't on the Ulster Way. It was time to recharge my batteries, to bless my aching feet, anoint my calves. It was also time to discard the boots I'd been wearing. They had grown pungent. The treads were caked with dry clay, and no matter how much I gouged, they never came clean. I'd purchased a new pair of boots back in Derry, and I pulled them on now for the first time. I felt a pang of guilt at discarding the old ones—it was like saying goodbye to a faithful but faded servant. I ditched them in the Republic, then walked out along Lough Derg Road in squeaky new footwear.

It would be, I decided, a new start.

IT WAS FOUR MILES from Pettigo to Lough Derg; I decided to hitch. My luck with thumbing rides had been poor, admittedly, but this was part of a holy pilgrimage. Where there were pilgrims, there was Christian charity, and where there was Christian charity, there was an opportunity to take advantage of it.

Sure enough, I was picked up almost immediately by a mini-van filled with elderly ladies who giggled as I wedged my way in. A short hop, and there we were at the visitors centre on the shore of the lake. I thanked my benefactors, wiggled free of the van.

The waters of Lough Derg had a brownish-red tinge. Amid these blood-muddy waters were rocky outcrops. Serpent's Bones, as they were known. The original purgatory cave on the island had been closed down in the late eighteenth century due to the dangers of overcrowding and been replaced with a "prison chapel," so named because pilgrims were shut into it during their first night. This chapel in turn was replaced by an enormous basilica. With its unusual octagonal tower and copper-domed roof, the basilica dominated the cluster of buildings that crowded the island. The island itself had all but disappeared. From the shore, it looked like a medieval village floating on the lake, as if the buildings had been built upon the waters themselves.

One of the ladies I'd hitched a ride with was waving at me frantically, calling me to the dock where a boat was waiting. I scrambled on and we headed for the island, motor putt-putting us across. No one had asked me for a ticket. I should have noted that.

As we approached the island the ladies began removing their shoes, rolling off half stockings and carefully stowing them in their bags. This puzzled me. Was I going to be asked to wade ashore? Surely the island had a proper pier. It did, and I walked up it, dry of foot, while the barefooted ladies followed.

Curiouser and curiouser …

I wandered around. Ate an apple, took some photos. I popped a can of soda, stretched out at the water's edge, wondered idly when the boat back would be.

I entered a small reliquary where tiny shards of bones from twenty-nine saints were on display, including one from Saint Patrick himself. Visitors filed past fingering rosaries, mouthing silent prayers. Back outside, the others seemed to be following a strict circuit: kneeling, praying, turning. Me, I was rummaging in my pack for more food.

There are few archaeological sites on the island, largely because Protestants kept showing up and reducing everything to rubble and then—because Protestants are nothing if not thorough—carting said rubble away. But a cluster of stone foundations remained, marking the site of early beehive huts. These were Celtic monastic cells, known as "penitential beds"; pilgrims were required to circle them while reciting a litany of Hail Marys and Our Fathers. I knew this because I'd picked up a couple of booklets at the island's small shop and was now thumbing through them. The protocol of these stations was incredibly complex.

"Am I supposed to take my shoes off?" I'd asked the lady at the counter.

"Not on this pilgrimage," she said. "It's not required, but you can't really stop people, not when they're devout like that."

So I went back down to the water's edge, stretched out, read on.

Pilgrims are to remain on the island for three days and three nights and must maintain a strict fast, beginning on the midnight before their arrival and allowing no food except a single meal each day of dry bread and black tea brewed from the dark waters of Lough Derg. No other food is permitted. (I read this as I was eating a sandwich.) *No tourists or sightseers are allowed on island during the pilgrimage season, and pilgrims may not bring cameras, radios or musical instruments.*

I looked over at my camera, sitting beside my Walkman.

Pilgrims are required to pray continuously, following a set pattern of nine stations, circling the basilica and stony penitential beds on bare feet, standing, kneeling, praying, repeating. On the first evening they are locked into the basilica overnight to begin a 24-hour vigil without sleep.

I finished the last of my sandwich, swallowed hard.

Fasting? Kneeling on rocks? Sleepless vigils, endless stations, more fasting? Three days!

I panicked, dug deep into my pack, took an inventory: two power bars and a single packet of Prawn Cocktail potato chips, which I didn't even like. I couldn't survive three days on that! I couldn't survive three *hours* on that. And yes, it's a sad testament that my first thought was about food and not the divine retribution that was sure to follow from the fact that I was *not a pilgrim*. I was a stowaway, a fraud. Why had no one pulled me to one side and asked me what the hell I was doing eating sandwiches and taking pictures while the fasting faithful said prayers? They must have thought I was a journalist of some sort. I'd seen a radio crew earlier talking with one of the priests. They must have figured me for one of them. I ran down to the dock. No boat. The reporters were gone, and so was any chance of hitching a ride back to shore. I was trapped.

It. Got. Worse.

On some cue—a church bell? had I missed that?—everyone began filing into the main basilica. Hundreds of people moving as one, and there was me, being swept along. So I did what I used to do back in junior high, when I wanted to dodge a morning assembly: as everyone walked forward, I looked straight ahead—and walked backward. It worked. I backwalked out of there and slipped around the corner of the basilica.

The island was suddenly very quiet.

What to do? What to do? Too far to swim, and not enough open space to dodge the lightning bolt that was sure to strike at any moment. I ducked down a side passage, one lined with columns and—*dammit!*—ran right into a priest who was hurrying toward me, robes flowing.

"It's this way," he said, gently guiding me back toward the main door like the lost lamb he presumed I was.

"Um, I'll be along in just a minute," I said. "I'm, ah, looking for my friend." Lame, I know.

The priest had classic Irish features, red hair and pale eyes, and he said to me, "But everyone's already inside." And then: "American?"

"Um, no. I'm Canadian, and ah, you see, the thing is ..."

"Come, come," he said, trying to herd me along.

"Y'see, the thing is, I'm not actually Catholic."

"Oh."

"Technically, I'm what you'd call a Protestant. There's been some kind of mix-up, and well, the thing is … " My voice trailed off.

"I see." He smiled and said—this is a direct quote—"Not to worry. We welcome everyone, even," his voice dropped, "Canadians."

So I went in.

The interior was cavernous. Stained glass windows filtering light. Eight strong pillars supporting the dome. The basilica was where pilgrims kept sleepless vigil, and though the lady at the shop had assured me that this would not be one of those nights, I kept waiting for the doors to rumble shut, the lights to dim.

The pews inside the basilica were filled with worshippers. They watched me enter with the priest, saw him show me to a spot—the others in the row had to shuffle down to make space for me—all of which only added to the awkwardness I felt. Far from sneaking out, I had now become painfully conspicuous. My face burned.

Then the service began.

It was like a theological version of Simon Says. Everyone was constantly sitting down and then standing right back up, turning to one page in the hymn books, then another, answering the priest with set phrases. I was forever the odd man out, jumping up at the wrong time, sitting down likewise, giving the wrong answers, stumbling over the hymns, mumbling the prayers. The others in my row started to lose patience with me, casting stern sideway glances at me every time I fumbled a cue. I was, by mid-sermon, the pariah of my pew.

All the while, behind the altar, a crucified Christ looked down, arms outstretched, somewhere between surrender and embrace …

"Lord have mercy."

"Lord have mercy."

"Christ have mercy."

"Christ have mercy."

"This is the Gospel of the Lord."

"We believe in one God, the Father Almighty, maker of Heaven and Earth, of all that is seen and unseen."

The rote part of the sermon came to an end, and the priest began a more relaxed conversation with the congregation. He noted that there were five hundred and fifty in attendance. "We have people here from South America, we have people from Italy and Spain, we even have people here today"—his voice dropped—"who are not Roman Catholic."

Ah! That explained it. A wave of sympathy swept down my pew. People leaned over, gave me a smile, the way you might a particularly slow child who was trying really hard. They became very helpful after that as well, assisting me with my hymn book, finding the right page for me, directing me away from the Holy Communion line afterward. I was like their dim-witted mascot.

The service ended on a nice note, though, with everyone shaking hands and saying, "Pleased to meet you."

"*Pleased to meet you, pleased to meet you too*," I said, shaking hands all round. (It was only much later, when I told a Catholic friend about it, that I discovered I'd fumbled this as well. "Will, you eejit, it's *Peace be with you.*")

I headed straight for the dock, elbowed my way to the head of the line as if I were trying to catch the last helicopter out of Vietnam. Pilgrims constantly flowed on and off the island, and I was determined to get away before anyone decided to lock me in and take my food.

What is the nature of pilgrimage? What is the reason people make these journeys? I suppose it's to remove one's self from the everyday, from the sleepwalk of habit and routine, to step outside one's self, to take stock of one's life. Going on pilgrimage requires you to move beyond the comforts of home, to challenge yourself in body and mind, to endure. To go into the world—and return, renewed. It is an act of voluntary exile.

Only as we putt-putted back to shore did I realize I was caught in a pilgrimage of my own making as I walked the slow stations of the Ulster Way, penance without absolution. And I wasn't even halfway through. *Christ have mercy.*

Part Six

BORDERLANDS

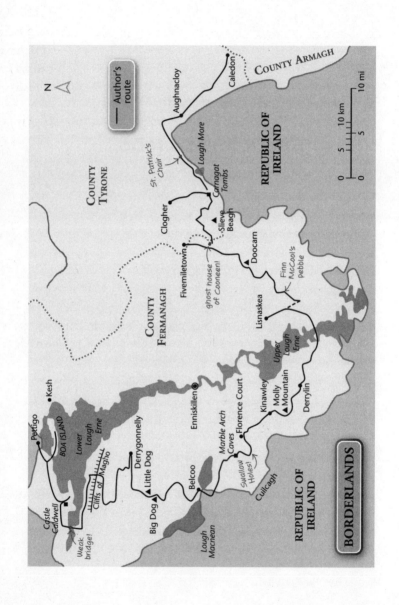

PETTIGO TO CALEDON
Along the Southwestern Border

Pettigo was asleep.

I walked out into the cold beauty of an Ulster mist, day pack over one shoulder, feeling refreshed and renewed. Clouds of fog were moving across the fields. Past sheep more spectral than real and cattle present only by sound, I followed a lane into a tunnel of trees.

I came to a fence that had been strung directly across the muddy path. A sign read "Beware of Bull." I had no intention of pushing my luck; in this fog, I might bump into the bull before I ever saw it. I turned back, made my way up onto the main road and walked down to a gas station. It had just opened, by the looks of it, and several young men in coveralls were standing about, ready to spring into action should a car with a cough pull up. *Bluff, or fair warning?* I decided to take a quick survey. "Do you think there really is a bull in the field over there? Or is that just to discourage walkers?" The sign was awfully faded; any bull might well be *using* a walker by now. The consensus? "Definitely not, absolutely no bull, so go on through. Unless of course there's a bull, in which case, absolutely don't go."

"So ..." I said. "The answer is definitely no, but possibly yes."

They nodded enthusiastically; agreement all round. I'd gotten a handle on the situation.

In the end, I stayed on the main road, the traffic shooting in and out of the mist as I walked along the side.

The haze melted slowly away, and details began to emerge, a landscape taking form. I crossed a bridge over the Waterfoot River. During the height of the Troubles, this would have been an armed checkpoint with border patrols. Now, there was only a small sign saying "Fermanagh" to let you know you'd entered British territory. It was deemed more noteworthy out here to have gone from County Donegal to County Fermanagh than it was to have crossed an international border.

I'd been looking forward to Fermanagh. This was Northern Ireland's hidden corner, a land of lakes and archipelagos, pagan idols and sixth-century monastery ruins. Most of the county was underwater. *"The paradise of Ireland"*: that's how a sixteenth-century poet had described the Fermanagh lakelands. Having suffered through the embarrassment of St. Patrick's Purgatory, I was ready for a bit of paradise.

I had skirted the outer reaches of Fermanagh at Kesh; now I was striking out for its very heart. My first inkling of the county's quiet neglect was the architectural Chia pet I came upon, a house so overgrown it looked like a strange DNA experiment, combining botany and engineering, part plant, part abode. *"Just add water and let grow!"* It was the sort of house a Hobbit would live in. The roof was a furry green cap, and trees—knotted trunks and twisted branches— had actually grown *into* the walls, making it look as though the house itself had sprouted from the woods.

Beyond Bilbo Baggins's hut, Lower Lough Erne came into view as a backdrop of sudden blue. I passed a stone church with cows grazing at the front door and saw beyond it the wooded sweep that was Boa Island.

The Ulster Way bypassed Boa Island just as it had the Drumskinny Stone Circle. I would not do the same. Although it wasn't named for the feathery wraps women fling over their shoulders, Boa resembled one nonetheless: a long froth of trees running parallel to the shoreline of Lough Erne, pinned to the shore at either end by causeway bridges.

Boa Island is also home to two of the most enigmatic artifacts in Ulster: the Janus Stone and the Lusty Man.

Named for the Celtic goddess of war, Boa Island was the site of one of the last Druidic cults in Ireland, one that survived long after Christianity had conquered the rest of the country. Pagan carvings now stood in a Christian graveyard, the palimpsest of Irish history very much in evidence. Many of the headstones were little more than moss-covered nubs. Others were freshly cut with the dates carved in polished granite. In the centre stood the Janus Stone and, beside it, the Lusty Man.

The Janus Stone, the more prominent of the two, is a carving that appears on the covers of guidebooks and tourist brochures, looking very much like a pagan garden gnome. The Lusty Man is similar, though smaller and more effaced. Coins were piled in front of both as an offering.

The Janus Stone has two faces, carved on opposing sides. Photographs don't do these faces justice; they tend to flatten out the features, render them two-dimensional and dull. But in person, the Janus Stone seemed almost … alive. The longer you looked at those faces, the more depth they revealed. The longer you looked, the more their personalities came to the surface. The face looking east seemed more at peace. The one facing west was more clenched, its cheeks bunched tighter together, its mouth open wider. It was a sterner, angrier god. Which is to say, of the two pre-Christian stone carvings, it was the Protestant one.

I ate my lunch among the graves and Gaels of Boa Island, then walked back to the shore. The air had a thick, tropical feel, and I could see heavily wooded islands, like tightly bunched broccoli tops, in the lough.

The coast road from Boa Island was fraught with Ulster drivers, and I was glad to escape to the wooded peninsula of the Castle Caldwell estate, a piece of shoreline that turned back on itself, forming an inlet all its own. This was once the property of Anglo-Irish elite from Scotland. (If you can figure out how a family of Scots can be considered "Anglo-Irish," you will have untangled a great deal of Ulster's history.) The Caldwells were a porcelain family—that is, patrons of the famed pottery in nearby Belleek. Near the entrance to the estate stood the Fiddler's Stone, a monument that was carved to commemorate a fiddler who got drunk and fell into the bay and drowned. Only in Ulster ...

Trees had taken root inside the roofless ruins of the Caldwell manor, and the woods surrounding it were everything that a forest should be. Mixed, shaded, deep. Old-growth stands and towering canopies. Everything that the regimented, replanted forestry zones were not. Leafy ferns, waxy ivy, mossy tree trunks. Sunlight filtered through the leaves, and evergreen needles blanketed the paths. A hundred shades of green. The rainforest disarray was both soothing and primal; leave someone in these woods long enough, and they would happily devolve, would soon be scaling the trees, swinging by their tails. (Yes, they would have sprouted tails.) Footpaths crisscrossed the peninsula, and I successfully squandered the rest of the afternoon there, wandering about the ruins, watching the swans float past on reedy waters.

It was only when I went to leave that I ran into trouble.

As I headed back toward the main road, my advance was blocked by a lieutenant of the Canine Territorial Army. It was the very Hound of Finn McCool. Back bristling, teeth bared, he now stood in my way. The caretaker's cur, it would seem. I'd walked past the cottage on my way in without hearing a murmur, but this, I realized, had been a set-up. I'd been cornered.

"*Hellooo!*" I called out to the cottage. Nothing.

The dog was growling low threats. I retreated, found a Lord Almighty great stick—a right feckin' log, it was, with a great knot on one end—and thought, "Right then, let's have at it." It was the Ulster in me coming out.

With a swagger born of desperation, I strode past, club ready, expecting a pounce and a snap to be followed by an inter-species sparring match. But none came. Instead, the dog barked angrily, then wagged his tail. Mixed messages, those. I made it through, looked back. He was still on the road, watching me watching him.

Before long, I came to a T. An unassuming intersection, but it was a significant milestone on my journey. I'd now gone as far west as my walk would take me. Had I continued on that road just a few miles farther, I would have reached Ireland's western shores, would have crossed the island. Instead, I turned, hostage to an itinerary, and headed south over the Rosscor Viaduct, marked WEAK BRIDGE, wooden slats rattling underfoot. I walked myself into darkness.

AN ULSTER HAIKU

The next leg of the Ulster Way involved heading straight up the side of a cliff. Carrying my entire gear, no less. Headlands pushed out toward the shores of Lower Lough Erne like the massive prows of iron ships. These were the famed Cliffs of Magho, and it was there that my day's hike began. An Ulster Way sign pointed in; it should have pointed *up*.

I'd never made such a straight ascent before, and I was soon wet with sweat—more condensation than perspiration, really. I was walking up into alpine jungle, and whenever I stopped to catch my breath, which was every two or three steps, a chill set in. Rough wooden stairs had been worked into the trail, and the wood was waterlogged and pliant underfoot. Slicked tree roots, wet scree, loose puddles along the way. *In Northern Ireland, even the cliffs don't drain.* My ears popped, then popped again, and I reached the top in a final thigh-straining burst, coming out triumphantly ... onto a parking lot.

A middle-aged couple in matching sweaters had laid out a picnic in the back of their open hatchback, which sort of took away from the "*I have scaled the cliffs of Fermanagh!*" mood. No matter. I felt I had earned the view. Lough Erne was spread out in bright, island-speckled blue below, framed by the distant Donegal hills. It was bloody friggin' marvellous, so it was. (A view like that brings out the poet in me.)

I followed the path inland, over soft raised bog. I still found it strange walking on ground that *bounced*. One of the books that captured my imagination as a child was the novel *Voyage to Venus* by C. S. Lewis, which depicted the planet as a world of water with entire continents of reeds floating on the surface sustaining life. I remembered vividly Lewis's descriptions of how it felt to walk on land that undulated underfoot. Now I knew. It felt like Ulster. I no longer wondered where C. S. Lewis had got his inspiration. He was from the North, after all. He would have known that sensation, would have known it well.

Someone had been running cattle through, and the trail was churned with pockmarks and cow flops. No actual cattle, though. (I half expected the ground to spit up a cowbell at any moment, with a burp and a low chuckle.) This sloppy trail skirted the edges of several small ponds among the trees, with cattails standing in their own reflections. In one pond, the sudden leap of a fish breaking the surface sent long, slow ripples circling outward: a perfect haiku moment.

I left unkempt woods, entered planted forests.

The Ulster Way headed toward a distant sweathouse, but when I finally reached the spot where the trail branched off toward it, I discovered that the section ahead of me had been clear-cut. A battlefield of branches scattered like soldiers' bones; tree stumps wrenched out and toppled on their sides: the path I was supposed to follow had been obliterated, and any waymarkers for the Ulster Way (if there had indeed been any) were now gone. I opened the Ordnance Survey map, plotted an alternative route down to the main road and up again from the other side. To my amazement, it worked.

I found the sweathouse on its heathery slope of hill: a round stone hut, rough-cut and hidden in a cleft feathered with ferns. Sweathouses like this were once used to treat rheumatism and other such complaints that came from living in a cold, damp environment. A turf fire was built inside, and when the brick floor was glowing red the fire was cleared and a mat of green rushes laid down for patients to crawl onto. It created an instant and intense sauna. I crawled inside myself and found it cramped yet comfortable. Mind you, I didn't have to share it with a bunch of sweaty people complaining about their rheumatism.

The trail continued down from there. At a lone house in the distance, a farm dog, territorial as always, appeared on top of a hill, woofing loud incriminations. My path skirted the dog's yard, and I hurried past only to find my way blocked by overgrowth. Not weeds or brambles, you understand, but full-grown trees with branches that were all but cross-hatched. Had anyone walked this trail in years? Or ever? The growth got thicker farther along; I could see that. So even if I'd managed to bushwhack my way in, I might never have emerged on the other side. Years later, they would have discovered a skeleton tangled in the briar. "*He appears to have died swearing,*" the medical report would read.

Forced to backtrack, I passed the same farmyard, and the dog now came down the hill in full attack. I ran, heart pounding, expecting to be hit from behind at any moment. When I finally swung around to face him, he had stopped at the magical force field that was the end of his driveway. The dogs of Fermanagh were a surly bunch, no doubt about it.

I followed a path through scrub woodlands and open bog, and then began my descent toward tiny Largalinny Lough, in a steep valley far below. The path quickly became a cascade, with water running down in step-like formations. I hopscotched when I could, waded when I had to. It was incredibly slippery, and I thought, *If I fell here, twisted my ankle, broke it, even* ... Some things were better not to think about.

I had imagined other hikers doing the Ulster Way, other pilgrims, a certain camaraderie on the trail. I hadn't expected this to be a solo slog along trails long neglected in a landscape well sodden. Northern Ireland wasn't a sponge, I realized, it was a wool sweater. It soaked the moisture up, wouldn't dry no matter what you did, and got cold as soon as it got wet. It even sort of drooped, too. Hiking Ulster was like walking five hundred and sixty miles in a wet sweater.

And then, in the midst of such moody thoughts, a tiny frog leapt out of my way. It was another small haiku moment, and I came up with a poem as I slurched along. (I'm sure "slurch" is a word. If it isn't, it should be.)

A frog, in a bog—waterlogged.
   —an Ulster haiku by Will Ferguson

For the full 5-7-5 effect, any extra syllables can be added by clearing the phlegm out of your chest.

Finally, after a great deal more slurching and the usual invective that came with it, I arrived in a wider valley. A wider *dry* valley, with sandy trails flowing through it and willows growing everywhere. In the distance, I heard the mosquito-like drone of a motorbike, and as I came around a bend, a young man on a motocross bike was filling the valley with noise: roaring up and down, up and down, turning, skidding. When he saw me he did a perfect double take—and then fled, leaving a waft of exhaust.

And there it was: the Ferguson Cairn.

I'd heard about this, knew it was on my route, and I was pleased for all the obvious reasons, even though my father was a Scottish Ferguson, not Irish. The cairn marked the site of the nineteenth-century farm where William and Elizabeth Ferguson—*William Ferguson*, no less!—had raised their twelve children: Catherine, Anne, John, Andrew, Elizabeth, Robert, William, another Elizabeth, Edward, Margaret, James and Henry. And those were *Protestant* Fergusons. Can you imagine what the Catholic Fergusons were getting up to?

I'd planned to get a photograph of me in front of this memorial, honouring as it did my coincidental namesake, but I was, of course and as always, alone, the kid on the motocross having long since disappeared. A sign on the cairn noted that at the time of its construction, there were more than three hundred living descendants of William and Elizabeth Ferguson. On the memorial was a line from

Longfellow: "Lives of great men all remind us, we can make our lives sublime, and departing leave behind us footprints on the sands of time."

Words like that, and you can't help but look over your shoulder at the path you've just come down, at the footprints you've left. Mine were barely visible and wouldn't survive the next rainfall.

ON TAKING THE GOD OF DARKNESS AS YOUR LOVER

I had a sign and everything. It said DERRYGONNELLY in friendly big letters, boldly writ. Fat lot of good it did me.

I'd hoped to hitch a ride to Derrygonnelly at the end of the day. It was the nearest town on the map, but traffic was sparse, and the few vehicles that went by didn't stop. The drivers wouldn't make eye contact with me even when I held up my sign and beseeched them with big puppy dog stares.

Once again, the Ulster Way had abandoned me in the geographical centre of—I checked my coordinates, to be sure—nowhere. Four miles to Derrygonnelly. Four miles off route, four miles on tired legs. If I added in the number of miles I had to walk at the end of these hikes, the journey would be six hundred miles, easily. I faced a long trek through shaggy farm lands. Fermanagh is underpopulated and slightly scruffy; those parts that are not underwater are covered in woods.

When I heard a vehicle approaching from behind I didn't bother turning, just kept walking. Sure enough, it rolled to a stop. A small pickup truck with an older man at the wheel. He rolled down his window, jerked his jaw toward the back without saying a word. (Why he needed to roll down the window for this was unclear.)

The sun was lying low in the southwest, angling in through the trees, striping the road with shadows, and we drove into Derrygonnelly through bar codes of light.

Derrygonnelly was a one-street sort of town. But a pleasant enough street: traditional storefronts with shops below and flats above, forming a continuous wall on either side. Nothing spectacular, but quintessentially Irish—Ulster Irish. Indeed, Derrygonnelly was almost a blueprint for the type of small town one finds throughout the North.

One street, four pubs: that too was Ulster. *Doogie's, the Cozy Bar, Old Pal's, Bar Knockmore*. I chose one at random, went in, and was welcomed almost immediately by the town drunk.

Sigh.

I'd picked up a paper at a newsagent, had a pint in front of me, a bag of Smoked Ham & Pickle potato chips freshly opened, and was trying to catch up on the news—while I'd been on the trail, the world had been getting along just fine without me, apparently—when a teetering old man with a spider's web of veins across his cheeks staggered over. He may have been challenging me to a fight, I wasn't sure. His accent required an encryption decoder of some sort. Jerking his jaw toward my newspaper (ah yes, the Ulster jaw-jerk: it can mean anything from "Climb in the back, I'll give you a ride in" to "What are you perusing, my good man?"), the old fellow leaned in uncomfortably close, said, "Oswell?"

"Oswell?"

"Inna whirl 'en? Oswell?"

"Oswell? No, my name's—Oh. Yes. Gotcha. All's well in the world, yes." He was referring to the paper.

And then, for no reason, he said, "I hit ya, ye won't see daylight for many days." He was weaving on the spot, defiantly maintaining his balance.

"Whatever you say, man. Just stop breathing on me."

"Nog nog o' fishing ya?"

"?"

"Nog nog o' fishing." He repeated this several times, and I slowly realized he was offering me a choice: "Knock-knock or a fishing joke."

"Um, fishing," I said.

Well, the effing joke took ten incomprehensible minutes to recite, with many reeking gusts of breath and invasions of body space. The punchline was, "*What do we call this river? Nothing. We don't call it. It runs right to you.*" He gave a long, dry husk of a laugh.

I grimaced in what I hoped was a smile-like manner. "Funny," I said. "Not ha-ha funny, but still ..."

"Wha's me hora'scope then? Pisces. Pisces is me." He was waving his hand at my paper.

The waitress shooed him back to his bench in the corner. "Pay him no heed," she said.

The waitress's friend had dropped by, and they were talking at length about so-and-so's wee boy who had won the "Bonny Baby" contest at that year's fair.

"Oh, she never bragged," the friend said. "Lord knows, I would have."

My drunken compadre across the bar gave me a wink and a nod, as though some unstated understanding had passed between us. I smiled tightly and tried to return to the story I was reading, but dammit anyway, I couldn't help myself. I flipped to the back of the paper, found the horoscope. *Pisces: Today is a good day to tell knock-knock jokes.* Well, no. But it was apparently a good day for Pisces "to make investments." I considered going over to him and whispering "Buy stocks," but thought better of it.

Perhaps because I'd come through the hills to get to it, Derrygonnelly seemed like a remote mountain town to me. I checked into a lodge, quiet now in the off-season, and watched the next day's forecast. They were calling for "scattered showers, clearing toward morning." Nine hours later, rain was lashing the streets and wind was rattling the windows. The fellow who had rented me my room said, "Another night, then?"

I sighed. (I was doing a lot of that since I got to Derrygonnelly.) "Another night."

DERRYGONNELLY to Enniskillen: eight buses a day, the first at 8:05 a.m., the last at 6:21 p.m.

I loved the exact nature of that, six-twenty-*one*, when in actual fact

I knew the last bus might show up anywhere between sixish and midnight. I staked out the bus stop, waited in the rain with a grim resolve. The bus arrived at *exactly* (and I do mean exactly, because I checked) six-forty-nine.

The rains hadn't eased, and after spending the day pacing up and down Derrygonnelly like a stir-crazy bear in a zoo, I'd decided to head into the city and wait out the weather there, taking all of my gear with me, knowing it might be a while.

I should note here that "city," "village" and "town" have very specific meanings in Northern Ireland. To be officially designated a city, for example, requires that you have a cathedral. Enniskillen had no cathedral, but to me it was still a city, and a fine one at that.

It sat on an island in the heart of Fermanagh, at a strategic bottle-neck between the Lower and Upper Loughs. The site had once been a stronghold of the Maguires, Gaelic lords of the lakes, who ruled Fermanagh's waterways in the way that the O'Cahans ruled the valleys or the MacDonnells the coast. After the Tudor conquest of Ireland, Enniskillen was planted with Protestant settlers, and when the armies of Catholic King James moved north on Derry, Enniskillen stood fast. It was never taken. Today, even though the city has a Catholic majority, Enniskillen stands alongside Londonderry and the Boyne in the Holy Triumvirate of Protestant Ulster mythology.*

Enniskillen's name appears to have come from that of a Celtic warrior queen, who took the god of darkness as her lover and later her husband. *Wedded to the night.* Another possibility is that the name was derived from "Inis Ceithleann," meaning Kathleen's Island, after another warrior queen, who ruled alongside Balor of the Mighty Blows. (If you're going to be a chieftain, that's the nickname you want. I was seriously considering introducing myself to people as William of the Leathery Feet.)

---

*The final victory at Aughrim is often included as well, forming what is sometimes referred to as "The Orange Quadrilateral."

The island nature of Enniskillen is not immediately evident—it's not like gondoliers are gliding by or people are shopping in sailboats—but take a walk in any direction and you'll soon come to a bridge leaping gracefully across open water with boats lined up along grassy banks. On the south side of the island sits the city's trademark castle, with its rounded storybook towers. Although most of the castle dates to the seventeenth century, sections of the original Gaelic stronghold have been incorporated into the current keep. Enniskillen Castle now houses a military museum, and I wandered in as the rain pelted down in a drumbeat tattoo outside. From the Boer War to the Gulf, past campaigns were duly noted and commemorated. Enniskillen men had stood tall at the Boyne, had served at the Somme. At Waterloo, an exasperated Napoleon had complained of the Enniskilleners, "They know not when they are beaten." Ulstermen, in other words.

As I walked the streets of Enniskillen, a miracle occurred. It stopped raining. I'd been warned that Fermanagh was wet—even by Irish standards. "Aye, they have webbed toes in Fermanagh" is what they tell you in Antrim. But now the skies had cleared. The city glistened. Awnings dripped with sunlight. Bicycles splashed by. Even the steam from the sewer grates seemed romantic.

I loosened my rain jacket, turned my face to the sun as it spilled into the city. I was unaware, you see, that the rain hadn't actually stopped but was in fact gathering strength for a second assault. It came back with the vengeance of an Orangeman pounding on a Lambeg. I ran for cover as the streets were strafed, dashed under a besieged awning, watched the air liquefy in front of me as I pulled my rain gear back on.

The man beside me said, cheerfully, "Nice patch there for a bit."

So I shot him.

Well, no. But at least he hadn't said—

"Mind you, there's no such thing as bad weather," he continued. "Only the wrong clothes."

So I shot him again.

OSCAR WILDE and Samuel Beckett were both educated in Enniskillen, meaning the city had given us the arch quip *and* the theatre of the absurd. Beckett, of course, revelled in existential angst, that gnawing awareness that we live in an arbitrary universe, trapped in lives that are meaningless and incoherent. He must have been a lot of fun at parties. It also makes sense that he would have studied in Ulster, the North being one big theatre of the absurd at times. Case in point: the friendly staff at the tourism office.

The rains had turned horizontal, were punishing the few pedestrians foolish enough to be caught outdoors. I'd stayed in a lovely but somewhat pricey hotel the night before, so I decided to seek out more reasonably priced lodgings. The staff at the Tourist Information Centre in Enniskillen were very friendly and *very* well informed. I knew I would be heading back to Derrygonnelly once the rains ended, and I was running short of money.

"Is there a cash machine in Derrygonnelly?" I asked the lady at the desk.

"Absolutely!" (She forgot to end the sentence, though. "Absolutely *not*," as it turned out.)

And was there anything nearby that might be cheaper than the Ashberry Hotel? Well, there was a motel, just across from the hotel, in fact. And how much would that be? "Oh, twenty-seven pounds." (Mark the telltale "Oh" at the start; she was just guessing.)

I did a quick, obsessive conversion in my head to dollars. My accommodations in Derrygonnelly had cost me only sixteen pounds, but I was in the city now.

"Okay," I said. And I marched out in the rain, arrived in the motel lobby dripping wet.

The woman at the counter was very sweet. "Forty pounds, please," she said.

"*What?*" I sputtered, casting water and aspersions in all directions. You could see what she was thinking: *"Bloody Americans."*

So, back to the Tourist Information Centre I went. I'm nothing if not indefatigable.

"You're back!" said the lady, chirpy as ever.

"The motel," I said. "You told me it would be cheaper than where I am now."

"It is," she said.

"But the hotel I'm staying in costs thirty-five pounds, and that includes breakfast." I considered drawing a diagram for her, explaining how forty pounds is actually *more* than thirty-five, but gave up. I had been bested, and I knew it. Back to the hotel I went, to check in for another night. I could hear my wallet whimpering.

FOR ALL THAT, I fell deeply in like with Enniskillen. I could see myself living there. It was beautifully situated, architecturally quirky, historically rich.

The clocks, as always, had either stopped or were running late. (Finding a clock in Northern Ireland that tells the correct time was a puzzle on par with Joyce's puzzle regarding pubs.) I was in front of the Enniskillen War Memorial trying to get my bearings. Several major roads braided their way through the city, creating all sorts of oddball pedestrian crossings, and I was attempting to figure out the best way across when I realized where I was standing. It stopped me cold.

If I could have folded back the years, if I could have collapsed time, I would have heard a bone-shattering crash and the sound of walls caving inward. Then silence. Silence, followed by the sounds of screams, of voices crying out in pain, of police sirens and terror. I was standing on the site of a mass murder, what had been, until Omagh, one of the worst massacres of the Troubles. I was standing on the site of the Black Sunday cenotaph bomb, set off by the IRA during Enniskillen's Remembrance Day service of 1987.

No one romanticizes Loyalist thugs, at least not outside of Northern Ireland and certain areas of Scotland. But useful idiots (as Lenin famously described the members of liberal democratic societies who defended Communist ideology) often romanticize the IRA, making endless excuses for them, twisting things around, trying to see some sort of "noble cause" in their atrocities. Among IRA apologists, the end *always* justifies the means. I wished I could drag those people here, to Enniskillen, to ask them where the bravery was in any of this. It didn't take a lot of courage to plant a bomb and then scurry away.

The IRA might have killed hundreds in Enniskillen—that was undoubtedly the intent—but on that rainy cold November morning, the Poppy Day parade had been delayed and the ceremony was late getting started. As it was, eleven people were killed and more than sixty others injured, some of them gruesomely so. One of the victims, a retired schoolteacher, was left a vegetable by the blast. He lingered in a coma for more than a decade before he too died, bringing the grim toll to twelve. Limbs and headless torsos were left smouldering on the streets. Trapped beneath the rubble, Gordon Wilson felt his daughter Marie take his hand and whisper something to him. Marie was a nurse, twenty years old, who had returned to Enniskillen from Belfast for a visit, much to her parents' relief. They were glad to get her out of that dangerous, strife-torn city.

Marie held her father's hand in hers. "Is that you, Daddy?" she asked.

"Yes."

"Are you all right, Daddy?"

He told her he was and said, "Hold on …"

"Daddy," she said. "I love you very much."

They were the last words she spoke.

And yet, Gordon Wilson refused to lash out after his daughter's death. He would have no part of any call for vengeance, any eye-for-an-eye retaliation against random Catholics by the UVF or their ilk. In an interview, he said instead, "I lost my daughter and we shall miss her. But I bear no ill will. I bear no grudge. Dirty sort of talk is not going to bring her back to life … She was a pet and she's dead. She's in Heaven and we'll meet again."

U2 frontman Bono was more visceral in his response. Sick of Irish-Americans in particular who romanticized the IRA, who spoke rapturously about the "resistance," about the "glory" of the revolution, Bono famously replied, "Fuck the revolution! Where's the glory in bombing a Remembrance Day parade of old-age pensioners, their medals taken out and polished up for the day? Where's the glory in that? To leave them dying or crippled for life or dead under the rubble of a revolution that the majority of the people in my country don't want. No more!"

Why Enniskillen? For the same reason Omagh was targeted. The city hadn't fostered the traditional bitterness between Protestants and Catholics you found in other places—and we can't have that. The borderlands of Fermanagh were Republican at heart. This was IRA country, and the Enniskillen bomb was built across the border, in County Leitrim. Some thirty different people are estimated to have been involved in planning and staging the attack. None of them has ever stood trial for the crime.

The statue at the Enniskillen cenotaph survived the blast. It always was a somewhat muted memorial, depicting a lone soldier standing with head bowed. After the bomb, bronze doves were added around the base: one for each victim, along with a plaque remembering those who had been killed. It is the only war memorial in the UK to include the names of civilians.

BIG DOG, LITTLE DOG

I returned to Derrygonnelly under sullen skies, checked back into the lodge, emptied my wallet for another night. As the fellow wrote up a receipt, I asked him, "So, where's the nearest cash machine?"

He said: "Enniskillen."

The next morning, I returned to the place on the trail where I'd left off, dragging all of my gear with me once more. I was about to enter Big Dog Forest. Considering the number of close calls I'd already had with the farm curs of Fermanagh, this did not bode well. As I would discover, though, dogs were the least of my worries.

I hiked through the countryside, down a quiet lane, past rural bungalows strung like laundry along the roadside. I was looking for the start of the next trail. I came up, over a small rise and—

There was a bull.

On the road.

He was tearing up grass on the side of the tarmac, chewing loudly, tail flicking, testicles swaying, sides knotted. A walking testosterone bank, all shoulders and neck. He lifted his heavy head, looked in my direction and snorted. He had a ring in his nose and everything. They say the human instinct at moments such as these is to fight or flee, but there is a third option, as I discovered: *freeze*. Which, ironically enough, was the correct choice. Seeing no movement on my part, the bull got bored and went back to his roadside repast, ripping out grass in great pulls.

The road was narrow, with fences on either side forming an unintentional cattle chute. My very own running of the bulls. Even worse, said fences had thin wires running along the top. Which is to say, they appeared to be electrified. It was the kind of a challenge they usually throw at James Bond. *"You may get past the Bull of Doom, Mr. Bond, but can you survive the Fence of Electricity!?!"*

What to do? I could see a cattle grate ahead, the type of corrugated road surface cattle aren't able to cross. In theory, anyway. This bull was clearly on the other side, though, so not only was I facing a bull, I was facing an especially agile bull. People get killed by bulls in Northern Ireland every year. I'd been warned about this, and the words came back to me now with an unsettling clarity. Slowly, I started to slink away, remaining as quiet as possible. I didn't so much retreat as ooze backward.

Once I was out of the bull's line of sight, I considered my options. There was simply no way to squeeze by him. I'd have to climb the (possibly) electrified fence. I touched the wire tentatively, my face in pre-emptive wince, but there was no debilitating surge of current. I threw my pack across, climbed over. I then strapped my pack back on and walked along the inside edge of the field, acutely aware that I would have to pass the bull farther along. He would be on the road, but on the other side of the cattle grate, and I figured no matter how nimble he was he couldn't simply bolt across but would have to tiptoe quickly if he wanted to get me. At which point I could scramble back across the fence. If he crossed again, I would do so as well. I was prepared to keep that up all day if I had to. It would be like a French bedroom farce.

As I approached the open gate the bull snorted, but he didn't paw the ground or even eyeball me as I passed. Instead, he went back to tearing up the grass, thinking no doubt, *"It really is greener."*

Once I got far enough away for my sphincter to unclench, I climbed back over the fence and hurried down the road. With every rustle of wind, every creak of fence, I jabbed a look over my shoulder, expecting to see El Toro standing on the rise of road behind me, backlit majestically. It never happened. Fortunately.

Heart still rattling in my rib cage, I went up to the next farmhouse, rang their door bell. I wanted to tell them, "Your bull got out." If it was their bull. Not that it mattered; there was no one home.

The adrenaline surge kept me on high alert as I walked on to where an Ulster Way signpost sent me directly through someone's yard. I checked and rechecked, but no, that was the route. Straight in. Having run the gauntlet of bull and fence, I was prepared for a farmyard dog to come flying out. First El Toro, and now Bowzer. Worst thing was, had I been attacked by a dog, no jury on earth would have convicted him. "So he was walking right through your yard, the very yard you are sworn to protect!?" Dog, replying: *"Woof."* Lawyer: "No further questions!"

I crept along the driveway past the house. A woman hanging clothes stopped and watched me, baffled, as I passed. I steeled myself for the inevitable dog to appear, hurried through. Some countries would call this trespassing.

It's a test of one's mettle, walking the Ulster Way. Mettle and chutzpah.

BIG DOG FOREST. There was a Little Dog as well. Together they formed a pair of heathery hills, Finn McCool's hounds, it was said, turned to stone by a sorceress's curse.

The forestry trail I eventually arrived at led me down to twin lakes, striking in their symmetry. A road ran between the two, as a causeway, but a secondary trail, tramped down in tall grass, led to Little Dog. I climbed stone-cut stairs, slippery with moss, through wet heather all the way to the top. Looking back, I could see the dense forest I had just crossed; looking ahead, I could see the dense forest I still had to face. A depressing view, actually.

Big Dog lay directly across from Little Dog, but the path between them was flooded, so I returned to the main trail instead and came out on asphalt. I followed that road down to the next stretch of forest, passing a dead badger along the way. It was encrusted with flies, ribs flattened. This wasn't the first such carcass I'd come upon. You get to see a lot of dead animals when you walk through a country. No leprechauns, but lots of road kill.

Lough Formal was a clean circle of water. No holiday parks, no speedboaters slicing across the surface. Just perfectly pooled, quietly neglected beauty. I stopped for lunch, the inevitable SPAR sandwich, then followed the road to where a natural spring was trickling across the road. Hanging from a branch, and stretching myself out, I cupped a hand into the water, drank from my palm. It was so cold it chilled my teeth. It had the faint taste of peat, yet was clear as glass. I emptied my canteen of its tap water, filled it there instead.

Beyond the lake I crossed the rubble of yet another forestry clear-cut. Occasionally a single tree had been left standing, like a flagpole of surrender, but everything else had been felled. The excess debris had been tidied up, however. It was as though someone's fussy Irish mother had come through and swept it into large piles that were even now awaiting a giant dustpan.

I was walking with a wall of evergreens on one side of me, open obliteration on the other. The front row of trees had toppled backward, uprooting earth as they fell—only to be propped up by the trees behind. It was dramatic in its way, passing these fallen giants with the dirt still clinging to their upturned roots. You could see how shallow their grip on the earth had been. Why had they fallen—

strong winds? Weak roots? Whatever the reason, it seemed like a metaphor for something.

Here's the thing about forestry roads: they have a habit of splitting, of branching off without permission, blithely forming intersections that never quite line up with what is marked on the maps or described in the guidebooks. At some point, I took a wrong turn and never quite recovered. Each choice I made after that seemed only to lead me farther astray.

I could feel the first whisper of dusk. Even worse, the cotton-ball clouds and shafts of sunlight that had so artfully enhanced my views of Lough Formal were gone. Darker clouds had appeared, heavy, even bloated, I dare say. As the ceiling of sky began to lower, the first few drops appeared, much like a sniper finding his range. I heard a distant crack of thunder—or maybe it was a tree toppling over. I wasn't sure.

I knew that if I kept on a downward slope, I would eventually come out at the bottom. That was my strategy, flawed though it was. Another T-intersection, another wild guess in the falling dark. I came to a dead end, was forced to retrace my steps. *I should have been marking my way as I went, scraping arrows in the dirt.*

No sooner had I resigned myself to spending a long night in a wet forest than I came to a kink in the road. In the distance, I could see a brooding mass of tabletop heights, and soon after, a broad expanse of water. Lough Macnean. I hurried down, out of the forest onto a road, Off Route, but no matter. I'd made it through; I had crossed the Fermanagh interior. *Huzzah!* It immediately started to rain. Great chamber pots of it, pouring down, washing across the road, blurring the landscape.

I began the long walk into Belcoo.

A lorry barrelled past, drenching me head to toe (though, admittedly, I had probably already reached the scientific saturation point by then). Headlights appeared and disappeared, watery and yellow, as the cars crept by. It's a hard rain indeed that can slow down an Ulster driver.

At the Holywell crossroads outside Belcoo, I came to the ruins of a medieval church. A wart well was tucked into a rainy grove beside the road, but the trees provided no shelter and I slogged on. Four separate Ulster Way signs, all within sight of each other, gently guided walkers in toward the only town around. I arrived just in time to catch the last bus to Enniskillen.

Time spent getting to Belcoo: seven hours. *Time spent in Belcoo:* seven minutes.

DEATH BY SAUSAGE

Enniskillen. In a pub. In the rain. Again.

The stooped old man at the table next to me was slurping his soup like a moose drinking pond water. *Sluuurp, sluuurp.* It was all I could do not to walk over and shove his face directly into the bowl with a cry of "There you go! Eat up!" He eventually got to the bottom of the bowl—and then began sucking on his teeth. Oh, it was a cornucopia of sound effects, all right.

I was in a miserable mood. (You've probably already figured that out.) It wasn't the rain or the slurping of soup or the fictitious nature of Britain's "longest waymarked path!" Okay, it was all of that. But it was also a sense of deflated expectation. I had pictured myself striding into Irish pubs at the end of a day's hike, walking stick in hand, sporting knickerbocker pants (which I don't even own) and a tweed hat (ditto), to be welcomed by a hearty chorus of shamrock greetings. Folks would gather, fawn-like, around my feet as I shared with them tales of the places I'd been, the vistas I'd seen. They would offer me flagons of wine and bags of rubies and their daughters' hands in marriage—which I would of course decline, gentleman that I am, much to the regret of said comely lasses.

But in truth, after a hard slog through mud and moor and endless forestry trails, I was usually so tired, so soul-achingly tired, that at day's end I wanted only to sit in a corner and nurse a wounded beer. Everything had begun to annoy me, the slurping of "*today's soup du jour*" being only the latest. (I'd tried to point out the redundancy of the phrase "today's soup du jour" to the pub's owner but had failed.) The soup in question was, of course, vegetable.

Then, when I thought things could only get worse, they did.

I'd ordered a plate of pub fare, something-something-and-sausage, and as I ate, I noticed a different taste, one I hadn't come across before. A herb of some sort? What was it they put in turkey stuffing? Sage? Thyme? No, that wasn't it. I had consumed more sausage since I came to Northern Ireland than I had in all my previous lives combined, but here was a nuance I hadn't yet encountered. What was it? Ah, yes, *botulism.*

I made my way back to the hotel, stomach gurgling, and had a long shower. I fell into bed and was instantly asleep only to lurch awake again because—well, hell, someone had entered my room while I was sleeping, had shoved a fist down my throat and was now punching my stomach from the inside. I ran to the washroom, retched into the toilet until my jaw ached and my eyes began to water. My stomach spasmed and then, just as suddenly, my bowels loosened. I grabbed up the washroom bin, sat on the toilet—just in time—and huddled there, retching from both ends, as it were.

And so passed a very pleasant night.

I'd joked about Death by Sausage, and now I was facing the very possibility. I couldn't get out of bed. I was feverish and weak and racked with the sort of pain that comes from having your intestines knotted like balloon animals at a children's birthday party. When the maid came knocking I moaned her away, crawled to the telephone and called down to the front desk to book another night.

I'm going to die here, I thought. This was, I now realized, karma in action. Back at the pub in Glenarm, I'd been served the drowned corpse of what was purportedly chicken while the lady who owned the place chatted with me, only to discover I'd once lived in Japan.

"You speak it, then?" she'd asked me. "Japanese?"

"A bit," I said, as I poked at my meal with a fork. It was definitely flesh of some sort.

The lady had heard of the mythical Japanese tourist. Said tourists moved in orderly queues, never got pissed to the gills and broke the furniture, paid top dollar for everything, were unfailingly polite.

"Here, I wouldn't even know what to do if any showed up," she said.

Surely a recipe isn't THAT hard to follow, I thought as I poked at my chicken. And what kind of recipe begins with *Boil for 48 hours*?

"How would I welcome them?" the lady asked. "The Japanese. You know, 'Make yourself at home,' that sort'a thing. Kin ye teach me? Would ye mind?"

I thought about some poor Japanese traveller wandering into this pub by mistake. "Well," I said, "I suppose the best thing to say would be '*Kiwotsukete, kono tabemono abunai yo. Tabenai de. Nomimono dake.*'" (Which can be roughly translated as: "Be careful! The food here is dangerous. Don't eat anything. Just drink.")

She'd carefully written it out, practised the pronunciation. And now, weeks later, I found myself in a hotel in Enniskillen with my guts turned inside out, paying a heavy karmic price for what I'd done. The Chicken of Glenarm—*that* hadn't killed me, but the sausages here almost had.

I faded in and out of consciousness for the rest of the day, the bedding soaked with sweat. Several friends I hadn't seen in years dropped by to say hi, as did my old high school shop teacher, who wanted to know when my project was going to be handed in.

The front desk called up to see if I was okay, but there was little the staff at the Ashberry Hotel could do except get the next night's fee up front.

And the whole while, through the window of my room, I could see blue skies …

SWALLOW HOLES AND CELEBRITY TREES

I returned to the village of Belcoo, weaker but wiser. Like Enniskillen, though on a much smaller scale, Belcoo sat astride a strategic bottleneck between loughs. The village had the airy feel of a summer cottage, even with the bracing cold wind coming in off Lough Macnean. A crisp day, it was. September had slipped away, and autumn was creeping in on cat's feet.

Traditional storefronts faced a wide swath of green: Belcoo's Cottage Meadow Park, with its fountains of trees and pool-table lawns. An ornamental pavilion with a rooster weather vane and decorative clock tower stood at one end—hands stuck at 11:24, this being Northern Ireland after all, where time has stopped. Across from the pavilion, and marring the view, was a grim RUC fortress with watchtowers, razor wire and the unblinking eye of a security camera. Several RUC officers had once been killed on the park's common, blown apart by an IRA boobytrap, and even now the station remained under near lockdown.

Oddly enough, though situated on a lake, Belcoo had no real shoreline; the park ended not at the water but at a row of trees. On the other side of them lay an unkempt grassy area, clumped with bouquets of bushes, clutches of shrub. I mention this mainly because this hidden area was wide enough to make a surreptitious bivouac in the very heart of Belcoo possible. Not that I am recommending such a course. Especially with the RUC station perched nearby, floodlights at the ready. But—if someone were, say, to slip *behind* the trees at the *other* end of the park, near the bridge, for example, and then walk down, no one would be able to see them. They would find many good places to pitch a tent, in among the bushes. Which I'm told is highly illegal. And thus, not to be recommended. I slept very well, though, with the sound of the lake lapping nearby.

EARLY MORNING in Belcoo. Mist coming in off the water. Birds trilling. On the far side of the lake, cold steam was rising. Distant cliffs were taking shape. A landscape exhaling ghosts.

I walked out onto the Cottage Meadow common as Belcoo stirred and woke. The shops lining the main street, windows shuttered for the night, now yawned and stretched, came slowly to life. As I pushed my way through the bushes, I startled a lady walking her dog; it must have seemed as though I were emerging from the lough itself.

Belcoo is on the border. Cross the bridge at the other end of the village, and you enter Blacklion, Belcoo's mirror community. The border of Northern Ireland is about as porous a divide as you could hope to find, which is strange considering what a cultural and psychological chasm it represents. Etched in blood and yet so ephemeral as to feel nonexistent. I wondered whether Britain's failure to secure its only land border lay in a certain island mentality: coastlines are real, concrete, whereas imaginary lines drawn through fields and farmyards must seem hopelessly abstract.

So convoluted was the borderline that no sooner had I walked into the Republic than I walked back out again, re-entering Northern Ireland a half-mile down the road. The jagged cliffs of Hanging Rock moved closer with every step. They pushed in, juniper and yew trees leaning out over sheer-drop rock. A massive boulder, netted in vines, sat beside the road, having rolled from the heights years before. I might have walked right past had I not noticed a stile. *When you see a stile, there's always a reason.* I climbed over, and the sheer size of the roadside boulder soon became evident. Trees had sprouted from the top, ferns were layered across the sides. It was a Chia boulder. You certainly wouldn't want to be caught under it. Which is what had happened to one unfortunate man and his donkey.

This was the famous "Saltman" stone, named after an itinerant trader who was riding along during a storm so violent it sent a huge chunk of cliff crashing into the valley. The saltman had been travelling the area collecting money, and he was never seen or heard from again after that night. The morbid assumption was that he and his donkey now lay beneath this behemoth of a boulder. (Either that, or he had been remarkably quick-witted, seen the cliff collapse, disappeared with his funds, migrated to America, with donkey in tow, and made his fortune in the New World. Stranger things have happened.)

I leaned in across the nettles to knock on the boulder's side. "You okay under there? Can I get you anything?" Then, in a sudden spine-tingling moment, I heard it … *the bray of a donkey! The ghost donkey of Fermanagh!!* I'm lying, of course. But wouldn't that be a terrific ghost story? Even better, I think, would be to wedge a pair of boots under the boulder and then hide behind a bush and moan "Little help?" as people went by.

I followed the Ulster Way—waymarked, this time—into the gorge at Cladagh Glen. Trees had fallen along the path, great whales of biomass wet with rot, and the river churned through in a white noise echo, over moss-furred boulders and driftwood entanglements. Waterfalls were spilling across rounded rock, unravelling like silk into the pools below. These woodlands were a tiny remnant of what had once been a vast forest covering much of Ireland: damp ash woodland, one of the last stands in Europe. I passed under overhangs of limestone rock that seemed ready to give way at any moment. It was a prehistoric landscape. A pterodactyl might swoop past; a brontosaurus might suddenly emerge from the water, vines dripping in its mouth.

I came at last to the Marble Arch. This had been part of a cavern, but most of the roof had collapsed during the last ice age, leaving behind today's limestone span. (The stone looked so polished it was initially mistaken for marble, and the name stuck.) The path I was following crossed the arch on wooden stairs that had metal mesh for grips, and it brought me out at the Marble Arch Interpretive Centre.

Limestone is remarkably porous. Water will eat away at it, following fault lines, worming passageways through, forming underground caves. At Marble Arch, those caves ran 165 feet deep. Flat-bottomed boats usually ferried visitors across underground rivers, but the heavy rains had brought the subterranean waters dangerously high, and I was restricted to visiting only the first sections of the caves. I had the place to myself, though. Just me and an older fellow who worked there and who followed me down to make sure I didn't trip and impale myself on a stalagmite or, more likely, to ensure I didn't snap one off as a souvenir.

Inside the caves, sounds were amplified. Every drip and plonk of water echoed. I had gone from hiker to spelunker, and in the dank cathedral of Marble Arch, chambers and passageways disappeared into cold underground pools, emerging unseen on the other side. Hidden flyovers and crawlspace connections led from chamber to chamber, past curtains of stone. Fleshly folds. Slow eruptions of cauliflower calcite. Stone, made fluid. Castles were growing upside down from limestone ceilings. Stalagmites reaching up, stalactites dripping down, had fused over the slow course of millennia to form pillars and columns. A devil's anvil. A porridge pot. Calcium, textured like bone marrow. And always, the plonk of water.

I emerged from the Marble Arch Caves like a hero in a Jules Verne novel, refreshed and smelling slightly of the otherworld. After that, however, I faced the sheer and unavoidable mass of Cuilcagh Mountain.

A dark tabletop, rising straight out of the surrounding moors, Cuilcagh's height is given—in metric measurement—as an ominous 666 metres. The Ulster Way offers you the choice of skirting the hem of Cuilcagh's vast blanket of bog or striking off directly toward it and right over the summit. The latter course is not for the faint of heart, and guidebooks are replete with warnings about trying to tackle Cuilcagh. It's the kind of mountain people die on in bad weather. It's the kind of mountain that is always in the shade, even on clear days. The kind of mountain that seems to stand in its own shadow.

I chose the option that didn't involve going over the top. Instead, I followed a route that would pass a series of "swallow holes," hidden pits covered in peat where the bogwater drained into underground caverns. The water disappeared, even though the holes themselves were not visible. It sounded a lot like sending someone through a minefield, but apparently the swallow holes were easy to spot. They'd be large muddy patches in among the other muddy patches. "Try not to fall into one" was the helpful advice I received at the Marble Arch Interpretive Centre.

Over a fence, swinging wide around the bare-knuckled rise of

Gortmaconnell Rock, I followed a faint line of guideposts stuttered across the landscape. Over a hump of hill, and the moors suddenly spread out before me, unbroken for miles as they swept toward Cuilcagh Mountain. During the last ice age, Cuilcagh would have been an island in an ocean of ice, a hardcapped rise spared the grind and scour of glaciers. A cloak of thick peat now surrounded the mountain, nine feet deep at places. These were the "blanket bogs" of Cuilcagh, among the most extensive in Europe, with a sludgy soil that is known as black butter.

As I walked across the moist rot of these moors, the view of Cuilcagh went from ominous to outright threatening. I could see dark clouds roiling up behind it, could see the winds snaking along the grass. As the weather moved toward me, I could almost chart its progress. In Fermanagh, storm clouds from the North Atlantic are pushed in from the west and forced up into the hills, whereupon they collapse into rain and sleet. The sharp edge of the Cuilcagh summit is particularly effective at catching the undersides of clouds and tearing open their bellies. The slopes of the mountain receive more than six *feet* of rain every year, and very little of that drains off. I'd seen my share of bog since I came to Northern Ireland, but in front of me now was the Mother of All Bogs.

I began to hurry, stumbling as I went. The dark clouds were now spilling over the top of Cuilcagh Mountain and tumbling down the front, erasing the line between mountain and sky. The wind was whorling in, sculpting the grass; I was now racing the weather. I could see pond-sized puddles ahead, the famed "swallow holes," I presumed, just as I felt the first spray of mist. No time to investigate the sink holes; I had to reach Florence Court Forest before it rained. Just as well, I suppose. One really shouldn't be poking around in bogs looking for sink holes. That's what insurance companies politely refer to as "death by misadventure" (only because it sounds better than "death by stupidity").

I reached a limestone hollow just as the first volley of Cuilcagh-chilled rain hit. No downpour followed, though, and I was blown into

Florence Court Forest as much as anything. In among tall stands of trees, I entered the seventeenth-century estate of the Earls of Enniskillen. The challenge would be to get through without being shot on sight as a poacher. I'm kidding, of course. The earls were long gone, and Florence Court was now owned by the National Trust. And as far as I know, the National Trust has yet to shoot a single poacher, or even wing one, really. (They're terrible shots.)

I came out onto a gravel path as a pair of power walkers swept past, pace as brisk as the weather. Other couples appeared, and soon after that an elderly woman came along with her dog, a small rickety creature excessively groomed (the dog, not the lady). It was such a jarring leap to go from the ragged edge of the Cuilcagh bogs to the world of manicured forests and Sunday strollers.

I found a park bench, fumbled with the various dominatrix-style straps that held me in bondage to my backpack. A spitting wind, spiteful but largely impotent, was shaking the treetops. I had won the battle, if not the war.

As I sat there, floppy-limbed and fatigued, I slowly realized I was looking at history, arboreal fame, as it were. The large shrubby tree in front of me was a yew, but not just any yew. It was a celebrity yew. The most famous in Ireland. The Mother of All Irish Yews, in fact. According to the historic marker I was now reading, the tree in front of me had been discovered on the slopes of Cuilcagh Mountain in the mid-1700s and given to the Earl of Enniskillen as a gift. The Irish yew can't propagate by seeds, so cuttings were taken instead. The Irish yew trees throughout the British Isles, in the courtyards and churches and garden estates, all came from this single parent tree. I don't know why I found that so fascinating, but I did. As another pair of power walkers swifted by, I said "Famous tree!" which only caused them to pick up their pace and avoid eye contact.

This Mother Yew had spread out in her dotage, as we all do, had grown more open, less columnar. She maintained a powerful dowager presence, though, and as I creaked back onto my feet, I bid her adieu. Yes, I was talking to trees now.

I followed a path to an equally regal vista. Across open meadows, atop the fanning slope of a baronial lawn, lay the manor home at Florence Court, a pre-eminent example of the Big House in Ireland.

I've always admired Georgian architecture, more so than the self-consciously twee Victorian sensibility that followed, charming and über-British though it may be. Even when writ on a grand scale, Victorian always seemed to be trying too hard. It was the architecture of city halls and antique shoppes. Georgian was the architecture of refined tastes and classical homes, of inherited wealth and the stolid sense of self-worth that came with it. I admire the *confidence* of Georgian architecture, the certainty of it. There was a symmetry to Georgian homes that reflected a world where everything was aligned, where the crusty-nosed peasants knew their place, where wax-moustached gentry dallied with their milkmaids, neglected their embroidery-adorned wives, and conspired to raise emotionally consti-pated children. A wonderful, wonderful age, in other words.

Florence Court was a testament to this Georgian love of symmetry, an approach that often went so far as to create false doorways inside simply to balance real ones. (The bane of drunkards, I'm sure, struggling with door handles added purely for aesthetic purposes.) If there was a faith embodied in this architecture, it was the faith of watchmakers, of everything having its place and its assigned protocol.

Unfortunately, I had arrived at Florence Court out of step and out of season. The house was now on autumn hours and wasn't open that day. If nothing else, this spared me the spasms of envy that overtake me on such tours. I plodded on in my muddy boots, just one plebe among the many.

WALK INTO KINAWLEY and the first thing that welcomes you is a pub. My kind of town, Kinawley. Saint Naile came here in the sixth century and rolled a large rock down a hill. Where the rock stopped, he built his church. Saints were always pulling stunts like that, throwing a spear or rolling a boulder, declaring, "Where it lands, there shall we raise our church." Do you think the builders were getting a little tired of this?

"From whence this sling lands, so shall a great and mighty church be …"

"Um, the rock landed in the middle of a bog."

"Fine. *Where this javelin strikes, so shall we construct a steadfast and imposing house of worship, built of stone, with a tower that soars as high as—"*

"It landed in a pond, m'Lord."

Long pause. "Must you always be so negative?"

The ruins of a medieval church still stood, a single window and two side walls, inside the town's ancient graveyard. Saint Naile founded a monastery at Kinawley as well, and the town boasted a wart well of its own. Always with the warts. Did they not get cancer back then? I'm just saying, if you're going to ask for divine intervention in the laws of nature …

The pub of Kinawley was calling to me, cooing softly, running its hand along the nape of my neck, nibbling gently on my ears. It was getting dark, though, and I needed to check the bus schedule first, to make sure I didn't get stranded. The nearest place to stay was back in Enniskillen, and the bus times were posted across the street from the church, heartbreakingly close to the pub's warm and inveigling entrance. The last bus to Enniskillen had already left. The only one after that was to Derrylin at 6:25 p.m. From there I could either change buses or take a taxi. I checked my watch. It was twenty past six. I suppose I *should* have been wiping the sweat from my brow with a theatrical "whew!" at having made it to Kinawley just in time for the last bus, but truth be told I could already taste The Pint That Got Away.

A pub, but no time for a drink. Cruel punishment. I was tempted to go in anyway, grab a quick gulp, maybe pick up a packet of Spring Onion & Aged Cheddar chips, but with my luck the bus would actually be on time. So I maintained my vigil as the minutes ticked by and the sky darkened. The bus pulled up at three minutes past seven. I checked.

ISLAND HOPPING

Molly Mountain was the gentlest swell of a hill. Fields curved up and over. Sheep and cattle grazed at impossible angles. And me with just a day pack, having left the rest of my gear back in Enniskillen. When I first daydreamed about walking the hills of Ulster, this is what I'd imagined, not the wet barrens of the Sperrins or the heathery exhaustion of Bessy Bell, but the soft shoulders of lovely Molly. As always, the mountains were hills, and the hills, mountains.

As I walked up the side of Molly, large lorries rumbled by, elbowing me off the road and dusting me in a fine chalky pall. I passed one quarry and soon came to another, this one straddling the road. Large trucks on cartoon wheels were pulling in and out amid the crunch and fall of bedrock.

Molly was still a beautiful mountain, though. It was also another milestone. Having gone as far west as the Ulster Way would take me, I had now gone as far *out*; this was the farthest point from Belfast I would reach. After Molly Mountain I would begin my slow return, reeling myself in, back to Belfast.

Winds were sweeping across, feeding turbines on a distant hill. I now had my first clear view of Upper Lough Erne. In contrast to the wide-open waters of the Lower Lough, the Upper Lough was crowded with islands. Drowned drumlins. From these heights, the lake looked more like a river running through a maze of hills. It's a convoluted landscape, Fermanagh's lower lakeland: more land than water, more forest than field.

As I walked down, the lake slipped out of view, and the community of Derrylin appeared. Unfortunately.

Derrylin was the sort of place where, as you soon as you enter it, you want to leave. A nerve-racking place. The main street was basically the highway, with traffic firing through constantly. A village built on a road that became a freeway, it must have been a hell of a place to live. The simple act of crossing the street required an impeccable sense of timing and a certain steely nerve.

The Ulster Way bisected Derrylin, cutting across and heading into farmland. At an hourglass squeeze in the Upper Lough, a road hopscotched across Trasna Island to the other side. Other than Enniskillen, the Trasna Island shortcut provided the only crossover point anywhere along the lakes. Because of this, traffic was heavy. Trucks and cars funnelled through with the express purpose of splashing pedestrians. A downpour had just ended (in Fermanagh, a downpour has always just ended), and the sun was lighting up the water and casting prisms in the air. It struck me then how similar the Ulster landscape was to Woody Allen's memorable description of sex: "Even when it's bad, it's still pretty good."

The bridge to Trasna Island was thick with green fur: fungal growths draped in Daliesque style. The second bridge, on the other side of the island, was also dripping. A sign designated the second bridge as a public fishing spot, listing "trout, pike, perch, rudd, bream, & eels" as allowed catches. I had no idea what "rudd" or "bream" were, but even I knew what the sign meant: *The waters here are jumpin' with fish.*

The route marked on the Ordnance Survey map had me following the main road; the guidebook had me following the shore. Always up for a shore walk, I chose the latter. I should have known better: there was no shore, just a reedy interface of water and land, and I found myself pushing through progressively boggier patches, with the water almost over my gaiters at times. Cattle had filed through recently, their hooves punching holes in the earth, and those holes having filled with water. I tried sticking to outcropped tufts of grass, but even that became impossible. I was island hopping on a smaller and smaller scale until, at last, I was stranded in the middle of open water. I thought: *How deep can it be?*

Answer: pretty fuckin' deep.

My boots instantly filled with water and I splashed through madly like a man fleeing piranhas. I could see a sailing club of some sort but couldn't get to it; the way was blocked with barbed wire as high as my head and strung as tightly as a lute. Even without the standing water and the pockmarked mud, there was no way I could have followed the route laid out in my guidebook. These were the sorts of things that undermined one's confidence in the advice one was receiving.

I followed the barbed-wire fence into thorn bushes, cursing all the while, my mood having shifted as quickly as the Ulster weather. *There is no path along the north shore! It's a swamp, fenced off at the far end. Godammit.* It took me forever to untie the knots of my wet laces and then work my feet free. I wrung out my socks and dutifully pulled on a fresh pair, which just as dutifully soaked through the instant I pulled my wet boots back on.

And so, feet burning from swamp water and friction, I limped onward. I passed a family holiday camp that was ringing with laughter and joy. I considered going in, finding someone to accost and rant at, but decided against it in the interest of international relations.

At this point you're probably thinking, "Oh, c'mon, Will. It's not so bad. At least you haven't run into any junkyard dogs yet."

That wasn't from lack of trying.

I soon came upon a yard littered with the bones of dead automobiles: rust-bucket relics with 4-Sale signs slapped on. A large notice was posted out front. BEWARE OF GUARD DOG. NO LIABILITY ACCEPTED WHEN GATE IS CLOSED. The gate, of course, was open. *Ha!* I thought, as I walked past on feet of fire, *at least they'll be liable if I'm attacked. That'll teach 'em!*

Bogs, barbed wire and junkyard dogs. Come, experience the majesty that is the Ulster Way.

FOR A PLACE of worship, Aghalurcher Church had a very turbulent past; battles had been fought at its gates, men slain at its altar, prisoners taken, feuds settled.

Today all was quiet. The ruins lay tucked in beside a country lane, and you entered through the graveyard. A few Celtic crosses had been raised, but what really set Aghalurcher apart was its wealth of skull-and-crossbones graves, eighteenth-century headstones carved with reminders of human mortality. You know, in case the graveyard itself wasn't reminder enough. Hourglasses, coffins, funeral bells and lots and lots of skull-and-crossbones. *Here lyeth the body of Daniel Magilroywh died 1726.* It was like entering a pirates' burial ground.

The church fell to ruin in the 1600s, but the cemetery did not. In Ulster the dead had greater longevity than the living, and the Aghalurcher graveyard was still being used. As in the Janus Stone cemetery on Boa Island, there was a deep continuity at work.

The name "Aghalurcher" meant "the field of the cast" and referred to how the site had been chosen, by the sling of a stone or the toss of a spear, depending on which version you read. "*Where this spear lands, a mighty church will rise ...*" This was also the burial ground of the Maguires, Lords of the Lakeland. The Maguires were an erudite clan, true patrons of the arts, and Aghalurcher was in the heart of their territory. In 1484 one of the Maguires was killed here, right at the altar, no less, and by his own brothers. (Though well read and learned, the Maguires were also what you would call a dysfunctional, or "Irish," family.)

A stone vault, still intact, held the mouldering remains of the Balfours of Castle Balfour, the Plantation family who pushed out the Maguires, replacing Gaelic rule with that of the Anglo-Irish.

From Aghalurcher, a mile or so of tarmac took me into Lisnaskea, where I would once again catch a bus back to Enniskillen. A sign outside the town welcomed visitors in English, Gaelic, French and German (I considered going into the town office and complaining loudly in Japanese), and the main street was lined with shops and humming with life. It seemed to glow with commerce and optimism.

The next bus wouldn't be for a while, and though my feet were now raw with incipient blisters (who knew that callouses could blister?), I walked over to the town's castle, sitting proud on its rise of hill beside a church. It was built by the Balfours in or around 1620 and burned down by the Catholics in or around 1641. It was then rebuilt. Then re-burned. Repaired, and then burned again—this time by accident, though you never know in Ulster.

Balfour Castle was a ruin, but a very solid ruin, one built in the Scottish "strong house" style with spiral-staired turrets, high-pitched gables, tall chimneys and a stone fireplace, still extant. I walked through the dungeon-like vaults at the bottom, followed a metal stairway up and then looked out upon the peaceful hills of Ulster.

As I was leaving, a torrent of schoolboys rushed past me into the central keep. I could hear their feet clanging on the steps, and I smiled. What must it be like to grow up playing inside castles? Among towers and turrets? Then, just as I started to feel some of that magic myself, I heard the sound of breaking glass and a child yelling, "Feck *off!*"

Sigh.

I walked back down to the bus stop, waited there in the falling dark.

NOAH'S MOUNTAIN

I had entered again the rolling world of drumlins, a landscape that undulated over rise and hollow so much it seemed to be in motion. Ah, drumlins: the joy of photographers, bane of long-distance walkers, so lovely to look at, so exhausting to walk across. This was the miniature Northern landscape that had inspired Jonathan Swift's tales of Gulliver, Lilliput being Ulster writ only *slightly* smaller.

A Neolithic standing stone was marked on my map. It was an important Ordnance Survey reference point, and when I couldn't find it I started to worry. I wandered up one road, down another, returned to the crossroads, frowned at my map. It was while I was standing there that a silver-haired farmer came trundling down the lane on his tractor. He stopped, climbed out, came over.

I had been poking about the edge of his property, and he wanted to know why. (He was clearly memorizing my features for the police report he would file later.) "Lost, are ye?" But when I explained what I was doing, an easygoing smile emerged.

"The stone is it yer looking for? Is just there." He pointed behind me, and sure enough, there it was, performing its balancing act in a small grove right at the crossroads. I'd been looking for something set dramatically against the sky.

He pointed past one of the fields. "I live just there. The stone, it came from up *there*." He pointed ahead to a rise of mountain. "From the top of Doocarn, flicked like a pebble by Finn McCool. At least, that's what me da always told me."

Another tale was attached to the standing stone as well, one involving a roving thief and a stolen sheep. "Me da told me about it, how a robber had taken a sheep. This robber, he dragged that sheep away on a rope, so he did. Came here, an' he hid among the trees, fell asleep like, leaning against the stone w'the sheep still tied to his wrist. During the night the sheep circled him, then run over the top. Fell down on the other side and was hanged. And the rope? Well, it had gone round the robber's neck, y'see, and it choked him too, so it did. Next morning, they found the both of them, dead on either side of the stone, killed by same rope." He pointed to an indent on the side of the boulder. "That's where the robber was sittin'. That's the imprint his back made." He smiled. "That's the story me da told me, anyway."

THERE WAS MIST among the hedges, like wisps of cotton tangled in the briar. I followed a side lane into the hills, above the main road and parallel to it. Bungalows lined the way, and a sign beside an open gate read "Beware of Dog." No sooner had I spotted this than the dog in question came bolting out, a black and white blur barking loudly, snapping at me with feint after feint. I had my rain jacket tied loosely around my shoulders, and I used it now like a toreador's cape, dancing backward, trying my best not to get bitten. A shirtless man appeared at the front door and yelled, "*What the feck are you doin'?*" I really didn't know. Truth be told, it was a question I'd been asking myself a lot lately, but still. It was a bit much, what with me walking on a public road. I was about to reply in kind, saying, "I beg your pardon, but I happen to be walking on a public road and am perfectly within my rights!" when the man yelled "*Get the feck inside!*" That only confused me more, until I realized he'd been yelling at his dog all along. The dog loped back toward the house, throwing me one last dirty look over his shoulder before disappearing.

I knew a series of small lakes were strung like pearls along the valley below: half a dozen or more, paced out and neatly labelled by the Ordnance Survey. I'd been hoping to use them as reference points, but the lovely bird's-eye view presented by the maps was lost down here among drumlin contours. Lakes curled behind wooded hills, spilled into hollows, played hide-and-seek among the trees.

After several false starts, I found the road I was looking for: a private drive, or rather, a public lane that was slowly being expropriated. Several farmers had built sheds and barns that all but closed the lane off to traffic. They were using it as a sort of communal driveway and parking lot. A farmer was working on his tractor—farmers must spend more time with their tractors than with their wives—and had the engine pulled apart, with pieces scattered across the road. He stopped, watched me pass, a pipe clenched in his jaw, not saying a word. He may have been worried about my safety, if not my sanity, because farther up, a German shepherd lay dozing in a driveway, chest rising and falling, ear twitching as I approached. A large WARNING GUARD DOG ON DUTY sign was posted above. The curtains in the house behind were drawn, and no vehicles were parked out front, so there was no one home to call the dog off if he attacked. I slipped past, holding my breath, then hurried into a clumsy gait once I'd cleared the last house.

Into planted forests: steeply uphill, through the usual regimented evergreens, out onto a tarmac road and then back in again.

I now entered the depths of Doon Forest (which I initially misread as "Doom"). I'd been walking more or less uphill since I'd left the standing stone, and I arrived aching and out of breath at a lake in among the trees. This would be Lough Corry. I still found Ulster's summit-top lakes very odd, sitting high on their crests of hill, refusing to drain, proudly defying gravity and common sense. It was the intransigence of these lakes that I found so striking.

A cement jetty speared the water. And there, standing on the dock—a fisherman! Leaving! Don't leave! He was an elderly man of slight build. A scooter was parked beside the jetty, the kind Audrey Hepburn might drive through Paris, scarf flapping, *diem* perfectly *carpéd*. The man was reeling in his line, packing up his tackle box. Stay! I wanted to say. I'd been walking in the woods for hours with only the song "Da Doo Ron Ron" stuck in my head to keep me company.

"Any luck?" I asked with an unnatural interest in the subject.

He was startled by my presence. "Luck? No, I've had none of that. Brown trout, but not a nibble, it's why I'm leaving." He pulled on his helmet.

Don't go! I wanted to say. I have sandwiches! We can talk! About fish!

It was no use. He puttered off on his Audrey Hepburn scooter, leaving me to trudge, as always, ever onward.

OUT OF DOON FOREST onto open heights.

Ahead of me, almost at eye level, lay the summit of Doocarn, a mountain of truly mythic proportions. You've heard of Noah and how his ark came to rest on Mount Ararat? Piffle. Noah's ark landed *here*, on the charred heights of Doocarn. It was here on this bleak mountaintop that the animals filed back off the ark, it was here on Doocarn that the world was reclaimed, that God's covenant was reaffirmed. That was one version. Another, even better version, one recorded by the Bishop of Clogher in the 1600s, was that Noah's grandson Beith had landed here in an ark of his own. This second ark (not actually mentioned in the Bible, an unfortunate oversight) contained the thirty most beautiful women in the world, as rescued by the quick-thinking Beith. They landed here, on Doocarn, in the borderlands of Fermanagh. Hence the beauty of Irish women as celebrated to this very day.

Any lovely maids had long since departed, alas, and I was left to admire Doocarn alone. Barren, with tufts of scrub grass and a flat summit pocked with hollows and rocky outcrops, soil the colour of burnt peat, Doocarn certainly felt Biblical, though I couldn't vouch for the theological soundness of any of it. I could vouch for the beauty of said women, though. Perhaps it came from spending so much time alone in the hills, but whenever I descended into the towns below, it was something I noticed.

From those lonely Biblical heights, I followed a tarmac lane downward, past another small lake. This would be Lough Na Bull, or, as I read it, Lough No Bull.

At the crossroads of Eshywulligan, I parted ways with the Ulster Way temporarily, setting my sights on Fivemiletown, the nearest place with food and lodging. It would add an extra four miles at least, by my tally, but would save me having to dine on bark or sleep under a bush. I was walking off the map again, pushing another Ordnance Survey sheet behind me with every step, as the forests gave way again to drumlin farms, the fields graceful curves of green. The road rose and fell, rose and fell.

Cooneen had been my first choice for a sleepover, but I'd been advised there were no shops. "Just churches." Sure enough, the domed tower of the Cooneen Catholic church rose up, looking almost Byzantine, its dome glowing pale in the light of early evening. Over the Colebrooke River, and the stone tower and sharpened spire of the Protestants rose up. It was a valley cleaved in two, Northern Ireland in a nutshell. Round maternal domes and tall uncompromising towers: a Freudian would have a field day with those competing ecclesiastical forms.

Churches aside, Cooneen was little more than a loose gathering of houses. Considering it had inspired one of the most famous ghost stories in Ireland, it was also remarkably unspooky. Coming around a bend in the road, I found my way blocked by cattle, as a long line of livestock shuffled across the road like downtrodden pre-revolutionary workers in a Soviet propaganda film. I waited it out. Dozens of cows with black-on-white patterns moved across, a procession of Rorschach tests herded along by a young man in a jeep. He gave me a perfunctory Ulster nod as the last of the cows passed.

Soon after, I came to an abandoned house with holes in the roof and windows emptied of life. So I walked back to where the cattle had crossed, asked another fellow, the father perhaps, who was now closing up the gate, "Is that the Ghost House of Cooneen? Just over there?" It certainly looked like a ghost house.

"No," he said, after a long hard stare. "That's farther back."

"Do you know where?" I asked.

"Wouldn't know anything about tha'," he said, turning his attention back to the gates.

I was long past Cooneen, so in retrospect, it was a stupid question. But the boundaries of Ulster townlands were amorphous at the best of times, so you never really knew where one ended and the next began. His reaction suggested it wasn't the inanity of my question he wished to ignore but something else.

COLD TEA

On my way into Fivemiletown, I passed an invisible castle. I'm assuming it was invisible, because I went right past it without seeing a thing. This was irksome. How could I have missed a castle?

It had been a long enough day as it was, just getting to Fivemile. The skyline of the town floated above the drumlins as you walked toward it, yet never seemed to come any closer. When I finally staggered in, like a man stumbling toward a mirage, the town was bright with promises of shops and showers, of pubs and frosty pints of lager, maybe even a few of those ark-borne beauties to whittle away the night with. A boy can dream.

On the way in, I'd crossed back into County Tyrone, and truth be told, I was glad to put the cul-de-sac of Fermanagh behind me. A beautiful county, to be sure, but a hard one to walk. It was really the realm of sailboaters, not hikers. Perhaps it was the promise of pubs that beguiled me, but somehow I'd managed to walk right past the ruins of Agheeghter Castle—which I'd circled forcefully on my map—without noticing.

I had stopped outside a shop in Fivemile and was trying to refold my map in proper accordion fashion when a stocky fellow in a ratty jacket came over with his friends.

"American, then?" He must have heard me earlier, when I was inside. "Y'look lost."

"Not exactly lost. I seem to have misplaced a castle."

"Aye?"

"Aye."

"Give us a look then."

We huddled around, and I pointed it out to him on the map: *Agheeghter Castle, outpost of the Maguires.*

"Oh, *tha'*," he said. "It's back that way."

"Aye?"

"Aye."

But note this: he only remembered the castle *after* I'd shown it to him on a map. That would turn out to be significant; the map had conjured the castle into existence, not the other way around. It was, he assured me, about two miles or so back along the road I'd walked in on, past the creek.

Two miles at the end of a long day is a long two miles. "Is it worth seeing?"

"Oh, aye!" On this there was agreement. Nods all round. Aye, worth seeing.

So off I hobbled, looking for the Ghost Castle of Agheeghter.

I reached the creek in question, saw only fields and a few farmhouses. It was baffling. I eventually flagged down a BT Telephone repair van. The man inside was wary. He kept his door locked when I approached and talked to me through a crack in the window. Once he caught my accent, though, my non-aligned identity was revealed, and he relaxed, lowered his window, even leaned his head out to look at my map.

"The Halls family owns all of this," he said. "Both sides of the road. If there's a castle on their land, it's sure they'd be the ones to know about it." He gave me a lift to the next lane, and I walked down to meet a farmer, who was also wary.

"Castle?" he said. "No, no castle. Hasn't been for years. The council widened the road."

I looked at the narrow lane I was standing beside. So this was what a widened road looked like in Northern Ireland.

"An' anyway," he said. "Was only a few stones lyin' about. Wasn't much to see to begin with."

I trudged back to Fivemiletown, muttering darkly all the while. I was getting awfully tired of being lied to right to my face. Sure enough, the man I'd spoken to was where I'd left him, holding up the wall with his friends.

"Did you find it?" he asked. "The castle?"

"It. Doesn't. Exist," I said through clenched teeth. "Or rather, it exists only on maps and in the fertile imagination of Ulstermen."

He was shocked—shocked and appalled! "You must have missed it," he said, waving his hand back the way I'd come, trying to trick me into going out again. There was not a chance in hell of that happening.

One of his friends piped in. "You should ask at Halls. They're the—"

"I did," I said, teeth still clenched. "I was told ... what were the exact words now? Oh, yes. He said, and I quote, '*It doesn't exist.*'"

"Impossible!"

"And yet, somehow true. Now then," I stepped closer to the man. "You said you knew it well."

"Aye. My father told me about it when I was a wean."

Mark that. His father *told* him about it—when he was a child. He was *at least* forty-five, so I asked, "And that was, what? Thirty, thirty-five years ago?"

"Oh," he says, "at least."

"So you haven't actually seen it? You just heard about it—thirty-five years ago?"

"Aye."

"And this entitles you to go about blithely handing out directions, sending unsuspecting visitors tramping about in fields looking for landmarks that don't exist, does it, you wee bastard?" But of course, that's not what I said. What I said was, "Oh. I see."

"Welcome to Fivemile!" he said.

THE UNION JACKS at Fivemiletown were frayed along the edges and tattered, the red, white and blue having faded to pink, grey and pale sky.

I entered the Carrick Rock Café, ordered a tuna sandwich and the day's soup du jour. It was vegetable. Of course it was vegetable. In Northern Ireland, *du jour* had, at some stage, been mistranslated as "of vegetable." Perhaps they should be calling it "soup of the year" or "soup of always."

As I muttered and chewed and stirred my soup, the local crazy lady came in, speaking in a shriek and babbling away merrily about ... stuff. I forgave her her sputterings because I knew that I was only one misdirection, one herd of cows, one bowl of soup away from ranting at strangers myself.

Later, I took an informal survey of the cafés, pubs and coffee shops on Main Street, stopping at every spot that advertised "Soup of the Day," "Chef's Choice" or "du jour." Vegetable, every one. Vegetable, vegetable, vegetable. It probably was the lack of variety among the soups of Northern Ireland that drove that lady over the edge. One type of soup and five hundred kinds of potato chips.

And yet, for all my vexed musings over matters weighty and pressing (soup and missing castles, mainly), I liked Fivemiletown. True, it had a surfeit of traffic rumbling through, but it also stood on the edge of beauty, above the wide pastoral tapestry of the Clogher Valley. The site was originally known as *Baile na Lorgan*, "village on the long ridge," but this was later changed to mark the exciting fact that the village was situated exactly five Irish miles from each of the neighbouring towns of Brookeborough, Clogher and Tempo. "*Welcome to Fivemiletown! We're equidistant from several other communities!*"

The Clogher Valley Railway had once run right through town. How they could have squeezed a locomotive down Main Street puzzled me until I learned it was a single-engine pup, a trolley that ran along tracks much like a taxi, stopping on request. I knew that nearby Round Lake (named with the same creativity as the town) had a picnic area and a campsite, but though I'd promised myself I would camp whenever possible, what I really needed was a long bath and a pillowy mattress. I found a small B&B in behind Main Street.

"Would you like some tea?" asked the gentleman of the house as I filled in the registration form. He was a soft-spoken pensioner.

"Sure," I said, "if it's not too much—"

"Because I'm afraid my wife is out just now. She'll be back after seven, she can make some tea then."

You know, if the two of us put our heads together, I bet we could figure out how to do it ourselves. "Seven will be fine," I said.

The lady of the house did indeed return, and did indeed make us a nice cuppa. Her husband and I had been waiting very patiently.

"I was up in Omagh," she said by way of explanation. "Some shopping to do."

"Oh," I said. *Omagh.*

She poured me another cup, offered me a plate of shortbread cookies. "You've been to Omagh?" she asked.

"I have."

"Family?"

"Um, no. Not exactly."

"Oh." She straightened the doily on the table. "We were there, you know. At Omagh, George and I. When it happened."

They'd been moved down the street by the police, she told me, had walked past the corner where the car bomb was parked. "I was going to meet our son Jim at the Presbyterian church. That was our meeting spot. We passed someone speaking Spanish, and I said to George, 'Those will be foreigners. They're visiting.' We thought that was so kind, somehow. Them visiting us. And then, when we got to the library, oh it was awful—the dust and smoke. The cries. I can still hear it." She looked at me, as if maybe I would know the answer. "Why would someone do such a thing? That was a Catholic holiday. Everyone was in

Omagh—Protestants and Catholics. They were all in Omagh that day. It was a beautiful day, a lovely day. Why would they do something like that?" She wasn't looking at me anymore.

The tea grew cold, and the silence hung in the air like an accusation.

FOLLIES, ARCHITECTURAL AND OTHERWISE

The day started with ghosts and ended in an open grave.

I'd returned to Cooneen as an overcast sky descended, grey upon the land. A cold morning, threatening rain. Appropriate weather, considering I was on the hunt for ghosts.

Ghost House was right. It might have been invisible as well, because I'd be damned if I could find it. Even the taxi driver seemed skittish, dropping me off at the Cooneen crossroads with a vague wave of his hand. "Down tha' way," he said. And he was gone.

I asked at one of the few houses around, a whitewashed cottage where an elderly lady was puttering about in her yard. "Oh," she said, brushing back an errant strand of hair. "It's the Murphy house is it, you're looking for?"

Was it really haunted? I wanted to know.

She laughed, a warm, dry chuckle. "Ghosts? *Nae*. Was just the older people would say, 'Aye, there's a ghost here and a ghost there, one in the lane, one by the brook, one by the bridge.' The way I see it, t'was just to keep the young ones in at night. No dalliance was possible when the girls were scared to go out." She laughed again. "Not scared today are they, though?"

A trim man in his sixties, her son from the looks of it, joined us, curious as to who I was and why I was poking around in Cooneen. "The ghost house?" he said. "Aye, that's left after the river, where the road branches off. It's in the woods." He had his own explanation. "Was before indoor lighting, y'see. Ghastly dark at night. Every sound, every shadow would scare you deeply. Now we'd go and investigate. The imagination doesn't run wild as it once did."

I wasn't so sure. My imagination still had a tendency to panic and bolt like a team of runaway mustangs. Still—I was determined to visit the most haunted house in Ulster, and so I set off on my task.

The tale begins in 1913, at the homestead of the widow Murphy and her six children. Mrs. Murphy had purchased an isolated farmhouse not realizing it was already inhabited. The spirit of a murdered soul, it was whispered. Footsteps at night. Tap-tap-tapping on the walls. Soon enough, the family realized they were not alone. The poltergeist began tossing pans and cups from the cupboards, pulling the bedclothes off sleeping children, taking human shape under the bedding only to have emptiness revealed when those same covers were flung aside. The haunting of the widow Murphy and her children made the national news. A priest sent to investigate witnessed children's clothing, laid out on a bed, starting to move, rising and falling as though someone or something were inside, breathing.

The Murphys eventually fled, abandoning the house and emigrating to America—only to discover, to their horror, that the ghost had emigrated with them, had disembarked as well at Ellis Island. It followed them through New York City and beyond, through several rooms and hovels before simply … disappearing. The Murphy house at Cooneen, now on forestry lands, had been left empty ever since.

The skies were rumbling and the road ahead was one long stretch of empty. No houses, just dark forest pressing in from both sides. I'd located the Murphy house on the Ordnance Survey map, but when I got to that spot there was nothing there. As I stood, map in hand, a car rolled up, came to a stop.

The woman inside lowered her window. "Lost?" It wasn't really a question.

"I'm trying to find the Ghost House of Cooneen."

"It's not signposted," she said. "But it's in there all right. You have to cross the ditch, duck under. It's in the trees—here, follow."

She drove ahead a hundred feet or so and then waited for me to catch up. "In there," she said, pointing to a wall of trees with no clear entrance.

"Really?"

"Duck under," she said. "You'll find the lane. But be careful." And then she too was gone, hurrying away, or so it seemed.

Now, I'm not sure how one goes about girding one's loins, but that's what I did. I could see a faint break in the underbrush. I took a deep breath—and then jumped across the murky ditch. I then crawled in, under low-lying branches, and sure enough, I came out onto an abandoned lane. The surface was thick with layers of wet leaves—it was like walking on mulch—but I followed the lane, and it took me into a secluded grove.

And there it was, rife with nettles and clutched at by vines: the Ghost House of Cooneen.

It was a solid building. Made of stone. You could walk right through it if you were so inclined, in one empty doorway and out another, and though sections of the wall had fallen away, the house was still very much intact.

A wind was moving through, searching each room in turn. I hesitated at the doorway, then went in. The floor was mossy and sprouting mushrooms; sections of the ceiling had caved in, and the attic above was open and dark. The fireplace had been used recently, judging from the blackened scorches I saw, and a few beer cans lay scattered about.

The story of the Ghost House resonated because it was one of departure. The family fled not to Dublin or Belfast but to America, to the New World, a fresh start, and yet were pursued by old ghosts and bad memories. Ireland's history is one of exile, of wild geese and defeated earls, of famine victims and Protestant dissenters; it is a tale of ships disappearing into the distance. I came from the other side of the story, that far shore, where those ships reappeared out of the mist: the fundamental divide between New World and Old. My grandfather's story ended on a dock in Belfast, began anew on a pier in Halifax. It was an *absence* that made the Ghost House of Cooneen so eerie, not a presence. A house emptied of everything, even its ghosts.

Unless …

A thought trickled down my spine.

The poltergeist that had pursued the Murphys across the Atlantic stalked them through the New World, until one day it simply— disappeared. A metaphor, no doubt, of how the past fades with new beginnings.

Or …

Maybe the ghost was homesick. The ballads and lore of Ulster were filled with a longing for the green sod, from Ossian to St. Patrick. Maybe the ghost *came back*.

I crashed out of the undergrowth and onto the road, panting, then turned and headed down the tarmac at a very brisk pace. So brisk, indeed, that it may have looked to the untrained eye a lot like someone fleeing.

SLIEVE BEAGH forms a great splotch of brown on the map. Three counties and two nations converge atop it.

I spent the rest of the day creeping around the outer hem of Slieve Beagh, wishing I could strike off straight across it instead. The Ulster Way followed a complex course of side lanes and back roads, circling the mountain from one intersection to the next, and I spent more time immersed in the map than on the trail, it seemed, retracing my steps, trying to sort out which zig was followed by which zag. As long as I kept the mountain on my right, I would eventually get around it. Problem was, Slieve Beagh—all 1,247 feet of it—had vanished, lost in the overcast. It was a presence all the more imposing for its absence. A ghost mountain.

I followed the trail until I came to Golan Big, where an Ulster Way waymarker congratulated me for having made it through. Golan Big was only a small cone of a hill, grassy and unremarkable. "Golan Big?" I thought. "More like Golan *Small*. Ha ha." Then I realized I had said this out loud, and the suspicion again took hold that I was starting to lose my mind. "*He walked into the hills of Ulster, came out the other side a babbling imbecile.*"

If nothing else, Golan Big (or small, ha!) was a welcome break from the forest. The summit of Slieve Beagh was still playing it coy. A shy mountain, as they say; you spend the day circling it but never really get a good look at it. I came at last onto open slopes, and as I turned to begin my descent, the Clogher Valley reappeared in a misted panorama of hills and rolling fields.

On a distant rise I could see a tower sticking up like a thumbtack, unmistakable even from here: Brackenridge's Folly, labelled more charitably as "Brackenridge Monument" by the Ordnance Survey. It was a mausoleum—a very conspicuous mausoleum—built by a nineteenth-century squire who, not accepted into local society while he was alive, was determined to get noticed upon his death. In other words, he built it to piss off his neighbours. It was another thirty years before the squire packed it in. He was buried deep inside the mausoleum and upside down, as per his instructions. Mr. Brackenridge was convinced the world's magnetic polarity was going to reverse, and apparently he wanted to be flipped right side up when it happened. All of which may have been an extended practical joke, because when the crypt was opened years later, it was empty. Another version had it that the grave was raided and his bones scattered. Either way, it now sat vacant. The Brackenridge Monument was only a mile or so off route, so I decided to get a closer look. How often does one get to see an empty mausoleum built out of spite by an upside-down nineteenth-century Ulster squire?

The folly sat (squatted really) atop a grassy hill. It was a square tower, three stories high, telescoped in style with each floor narrower than the one below. It was also on private land; you were not allowed to go up to it, and there was a warning posted to that effect. What a waste! It was such a curiosity and would have been an easy attraction to promote. It's not even as if visitors would be disturbing a real grave; the squire's bones were long gone, if they'd ever been there— though his ghost was said to haunt the hill, if you can call strolling about in top hat and tails "haunting." (He really should have been getting lessons from Cooneen.) The Tourist Board could arrange access, I thought, build a fenced pathway up to the mausoleum, hire someone to dress up as a squire, maybe sell some T-shirts. I know, I know, a North American through and through. But when the day came for the world's magnetic poles to reverse, this was where you'd want to be.

THE PROMISE OF RAIN was now palpable. The Ulster Way used to run right to the border, where a tea room had once offered warmth and sustenance to travellers, but the tea room had been closed down after the road into the Republic had been blown up. There were several such gaps on my Ordnance Survey maps: roads cratered by the army to control the number of border-crossings available. Most of these gaps had since been rebuilt; one of the first acts after the cease-fire had been to re-establish land links with the Republic. The tea room, however, had never reopened.

I followed another route instead, to a hill where the chambered graves of the Carnagat Court Tombs lay hidden amid a scraggle of trees. A Neolithic site used well into the Bronze Age, the tombs were originally covered by stone slabs, but these had been pulled off during excavations in the late 1800s and never replaced. Archaeologists had combed through the tombs looking for gold and bones, but any treasures or kingly corpses at Carnagat had long since been looted, and the graves yielded only a flint arrowhead, a Bronze Age archer's wrist brace and many unanswered questions.

Carnagat is a dual tomb, with the two set back-to-back, forming a rudimentary stone maze laid out in the shape of a human body, it seemed to me. With the stone ceilings gone, you could walk through the chambers, kicking up God knows what sort of wraiths and stirring up God knows what sort of curse. The tombs at Carnagat date back five thousand years or more. I thought again of the graveyard in Dungiven and the headstone of the martyred IRA hunger striker. I thought of the woman I had met there, who had said of Dungiven Priory, "You think that's history? History began in 1968." But she was wrong. I wanted to bring her here, say to her, "You think the highway across the border, blown up during the

Troubles, you think that's history? This is a history deeper than all of that."

The cairns at Carnagat were once the haunt of wild cats. They were also, it was said, a "trysting place of fairies." As always, when one heard stories of fairies in Ulster, it was well to keep in mind that these were rather sinister creatures, part magic and part memory of pre-Celtic tribes pushed out by the invading Gaels. Fairies existed in a dark, parallel world, one best avoided. (In any encounter between fairies and humans, humans always come out the worse for it.) Having outwalked the willies I got at Cooneen, I now found myself tramping about a fairy lair. Ulster is haunted.

The only people living in Carnagat were the dead. I saw not a flicker of life, no homes on the hill; the only abode of any sort was the chambered tomb. Maybe the fairies and the feral cats had chased everyone off.

As I walked back toward the main road, I thought, *Gosh, wouldn't this be a terrible place to get caught in the rain?* It came down, first in a whisper, then in a shout.

It was well after dark by the time I finally made it back to Fivemiletown. I staggered in wet and exhausted, but the lady of the house and her husband were relieved to see me just the same. I'd told them I was going to Cooneen to track down the Ghost House, and they were worried when I hadn't returned. Perhaps the spirits had got me? But no, it wasn't the spirits. It was worse than that. It was Ulster weather.

ON NOT GETTING KILLED

The rain had eased, was now just a falling mist, and the beautiful border lake of Lough More was rendered in a pastel blue. The Lough More shore I was walking along was in Northern Ireland; the other shore was in the Republic. A line drawn in water.

St. Patrick's Chair lay hidden among stands of Sitka spruce and Douglas fir. A trail ran along a forested ridge to where a tumble of boulders was jumbled across the path like dice of the gods. Soft with moss, thick with clover. St. Patrick's Chair was among them, a boulder shaped like a seat where, if you perched to make a wish, your dreams would come true. Worn down by a thousand years of bums and wishful thinking, St. Patrick's Chair was unfortunately filled with cold water the day I went through. I decided against scrambling up and dipping my posterior into it, thus forgoing my allotted wish. (It probably would have just involved soup anyway.)

From St. Patrick's throne, steps led down to a wooded grove where a holy stone was located. Flat, with a small dish-shaped hollow on top, it was pooled with water that never ran dry. A miracle, or so they said. I looked up through dripping branches to skies wet with forecasts of further rain, then back at the water cupped in the stone. A miracle? Really? The miracle would be if it *did* dry up. That, I would be impressed with.

The path beyond St. Patrick's Chair ran along the bottom of a gully, and eventually came out onto tarmac. It was a quiet enough road—at first. Little did I know that it would almost be the death of me.

I passed a row of bungalows lined up with the forest at their backs. A little boy playing with trucks in one of the front yards looked up, surprised at the sight of me. "Hello!" he shouted.

"Hello," I replied.

"Where are *you* going?" he asked.

"Belfast."

"Is tha' far?"

I thought about this. "The way I'm doing it, yes."

I could see the curtains move in the window behind him. Someone was keeping an eye on me. You can't linger at the roadside with children, not when you're a scruffy male on the tramp. Which was a shame, because I could have used the company.

"Where'd you come from?" he asked.

I pointed back down the road. "St. Patrick's Chair," I said.

"Did you make a secret wish?"

"Maybe."

"What was it?" he asked.

"Well," I said, "if I told you, it wouldn't be secret."

I was starting to think I had really squandered an opportunity. St. Patrick at my beck and call, ready to alter the fabric of time and space at my invocation, and I had lacked the foresight even to wish I could reach the end of the Ulster Way before the snows flew.

"Well," I said, wary of the surveillance from behind the curtain. "I'd better go."

"Will you come back again? I have a new digger."

Will I be back this way? No.

"Maybe," I said. And off I went, feeling sad for the both of us. When I looked back, he was still waving.

I PASSED farm cottages, long since abandoned, and ate a late lunch among the ghosts of a derelict stone house on the side of the road. It must have been a prosperous home in its day; someone had invested a lot of pride in its stonework windowsills and stately fireplace. The house had been built to last generations, and now trees were growing inside. I left feeling wistful. Vignettes of quiet ruin tend to lull one into a state of introspection, to turn one's thoughts inward, to—*shit!*

In my stupor-like walk, I had come to the A28 where it made a sharp turn through the trees. I decided to cross it to avoid the blind corner, which was really stupid, because just in front of a blind corner is the one spot where you *shouldn't* cross. (What was I thinking? I wasn't: see note above.) A lorry came flying around, full-throttle. The driver didn't have time to honk or even hit his brakes; he swerved, with a violent jerk of the wheel. You've heard the phrase "a miss is as good as a mile"? That's bullshit. The vehicle missed me by mere inches—I felt the suction of its passing, was slapped with the air as it went past—and that was nowhere as good as a mile.

I fled back to the side of the road. My throat was tight, and I could feel my arteries constricting in the side of my neck. I'd had close calls before—was once almost clipped while hitchhiking at an off-ramp in Japan—but this was worse. My walk around the

Six Counties had nearly ended with me smeared across the pavement. And here's thanking the gods above that the driver of that particular lorry was neither hungover nor talking on his cellphone nor fiddling with the radio. I heard no distant crash of metal, no dying gasp of *"Y' wee fecckkeeerr ...,"* so I assumed he had survived our close encounter as well.

Still shaken, I retreated to a nearby church and sat there till the worst of my tremors subsided. It was Saint Mary's Church of Ireland, with a dainty, almost decorative tower and a meadow out front. Had the local minister chanced upon me, I would have been an easy touch for a donation. For one mad moment I even managed to convince myself that it was the presence of the church that had saved me. This is how converts are made. No one chooses religion based on a careful weighing of the evidence. You are either born into it—or chased.

I started back out, crossing the Blackwater River and climbing into the countryside, leaving the highway behind. I came to Cullenbrone, which consisted of a single intersection and a large stucco house. No pub, which was just as well, because after almost getting hit earlier, I might have crawled into the bottom of a pint and never come out. A different sort of salvation.

The quiet of the countryside ended when I spotted traffic hurtling by on the A5 ahead. Fortunately, the Ulster Way turned right and followed a parallel road instead. *Unfortunately*, the route was not signposted. Fortunately, it seemed quite simple; last lane on your right before you reached the A5. This would take me to Old Chapel Road, which in turn would take me into Aughnacloy. *Unfortunately*, the lane in question didn't exist.

I got all the way to the A5 without finding said lane. I retraced my steps to a cluster of farm buildings, where a pair of muddy farm dogs came out and watched me, heads tilted. I had the feeling they would have helped me if they could. I checked my maps again. The lane running parallel to the A5 was clearly marked. Surely the Ordnance Survey wasn't inventing roads now?

Unless ...

I should have known. It was another case of "appropriation by stealth." The farm's driveway was actually part of a public road. Pieces of equipment and bits of machinery lay about it, projects started and abandoned, repairs on hiatus awaiting parts and so on. Just beyond, a narrow Beatrix Potter sort of lane continued into the countryside. I tiptoed through holding my breath. Never mind that this was a public road; in Ulster terms I was trespassing. As long as Mr. McGregor didn't come roaring out with a shotgun, though, I'd be fine.

TRUE BLUE

Aughnacloy's main street, the widest in Ireland, was almost comically vast. So wide, in fact, that it curved *up* along the middle. Aughnacloy felt more like two separate towns, facing each other across a border.

My feet walked me into the first pub I came across. The rains had started to sputter and spit, and a cold wind was stirring, but a barrel of lager and a big bowl of du jour were all I needed. I was ready to face whatever the elements threw at me.

I found a room in a guest house on the edge of town. The bed had deep pillows, soft, inviting blankets and a portrait of the Queen staring down from above (which is a terrific dissuader when it comes to masturbation, by the way, for any B&B owners out there).*

The next morning, the rains had stopped but the winds had grown. Blackbirds were huddled above the streets like a Hitchcock motif, squawking their tuneless squawks. A blustery day, but the Aughnacloy Market was in full swing, with the stalls hunkered down against the elements.

"It was a real market in days gone," I was told by the woman at one stall. "Now there's not even any livestock for sale."

"Oh, and here I was hoping to pick up a pig, maybe a couple of cows." I was joking, but she missed that and took me instead for a livestock dealer.

---

*A portrait of the Pope works equally well.

"He's come all the way from America," she told another customer. "And here they're not even trading livestock anymore."

Livestock no, but tchotchkes, yes. Tchotchkes and trinkets and Taiwanese-made toys, power tools and tea towels, carpets and WELLCOME (*sic*) mats, flashlights and oven mitts, doodads and thingamajigs, plants and pots, and potted plants, and pans and plates, and plates and pans—all strung up and swinging wildly in the wind. And the clothing on display that day? A veritable parade of polyester. Outfits that had apparently been sealed in an air-tight container since 1972 had been brought out like treasures from a time capsule. The clock above the Northern Bank had stopped; time had frozen in Aughnacloy, as had the fashions.

And if Aughnacloy was home to Ireland's widest main street, it was also home to its worst drivers. Or should I say, *parkers*. I had never seen so many vehicles so sloppily angled, this way and that, two deep at times, every which way except as marked. The cars of Aughnacloy were parked almost entirely on impulse, it seemed. Indeed, the town's spacious main street resembled nothing so much as a used car lot manned by drunkards with ADD and poor depth perception.

"Aye," said a man in the market when I mentioned this. "We don't park our cars in Aughnacloy, w'jest abandon them."

THE FOLLOWING DAY, I set off on what would prove the longest, least enjoyable and most unmemorable slog of the trip: Aughnacloy to Caledon, in the rain, along the A28. This was the same highway that had tried to kill me earlier. Luckily, the A28 out of Aughnacloy had a wide, grassy verge alongside it, so the worst I faced was constant spray and occasionally dousings from the flow of traffic. That was bad enough, though.

The Ordnance Survey showed the Ulster Way making a beeline for Caledon. Guidebook versions had it twisting through the countryside like an alley cat with Alzheimer's, adding a good ten miles to the trip. A scenic detour, perhaps, but not in this weather. I stuck with the routing marked on the maps.

The rain was pouring down. Cars were snowplowing water ahead of them as they went, and I was worried the RUC might pull over, pick me up for walking on the side of a highway. By the end, I was hoping for it. They never did, though, the bastards, and I was left to forge on.

I ate my lunch inside a phone booth. That pretty much sums up the day.

When I finally got to Caledon, there was nowhere to go but back. I waited under an awning for the next bus and was returned to Aughnacloy along the very road I had just walked. I reeked of wet boots and bad moods.

Plonked back in Aughnacloy, I found a quiet bar and a publican who made the mistake of asking me how I was doing. "How am I doing?" I said. "You want to know how I'm doing?" I told him, at great length, about being lost in the Sperrins and poisoned in Enniskillen and almost being killed on a blind corner.

"Why do it, then?" he asked, reasonably enough.

I thought about that a moment. "I don't really know," I said. "Just stubbornness, I suppose. I'm not going to let the Ulster Way beat me. I'm in this till the end."

He smiled. "Spoken like a true Ulsterman."

"But I'm not," I said. "My grandfather was."

"Aye. It's in you. Kin see it yer eyes. True blue Ulster."

That night as I sloshed back to my B&B, I thought about my grandfather, about what was gained and what was lost by his leaving Belfast. I thought about the photograph of him as a young boy on that grand estate. I thought about the various versions of his past, murky and unresolved.

What I didn't realize was that my Uncle Don in Seattle had decided to come at the past from a different angle. If the government records were lost, what about those of the orphanage? The Dr. Barnardo's Homes had long since shut down, but a charity still existed under that name, and they might have files of their own. Indeed, they did. The information had come back, and Don had forwarded a copy to my mother. She sent word to me that the information was now on its way, care of the guest house in Belfast.

And thus, in a suitably roundabout fashion, information about my grandfather's past was winging its way toward me even as I splashed past the Aughnacloy RUC station. The truth would be waiting for me when I got to Belfast. *If* I got to Belfast.

Part Seven

BANDIT COUNTRY

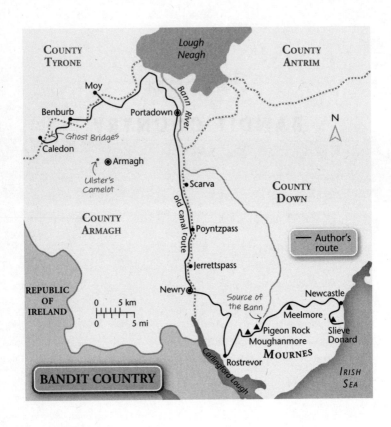

COUNTY
TYRONE

Lough
Neagh

COUNTY
ANTRIM

Moy

Benburb

Portadown

Bann River

N

Ghost Bridges

Caledon

Armagh

Ulster's
Camelot

COUNTY
ARMAGH

Scarva

old canal route

Poyntzpass

COUNTY
DOWN

Author's
route

Jerrettspass

REPUBLIC
OF
IRELAND

Newry

Source of
the Bann

Newcastle

0   5 km

0   5 mi

Meelmore

Pigeon Rock
Moughanmore

Slieve
Donard

Rostrevor

MOURNES

Carlingford Lough

IRISH
SEA

BANDIT COUNTRY

CALEDON TO NEWCASTLE

via Lough Neagh and the Mountains of Mourne

Armagh City, in County Armagh, is Ireland's answer to Canterbury. The ecclesiastical capital of the island, it was chosen by St. Patrick himself and is claimed by Catholics and Protestants alike.

There is an undeniable elegance to Armagh City. Built among seven hills, with its twin cathedrals, its rows of terraced homes and its tree-lined mall—the largest common in Ireland—Armagh has just a whiff of snobbery about it, accessible and aloof in equal parts. It is one of the most beautiful inland cities in Ireland, a showcase of Georgian architecture, but what makes it truly distinct is the way it overlays a far more ancient street plan. Armagh is one of the few cities in Northern Ireland that predates the Protestant Plantation. Derry may radiate a Renaissance world view, but Armagh follows an older, more internal logic. It is the logic of a city that *grew* rather than was planned, one that evolved slowly to meet the needs of peasantry and ecclesiastical processions, earthly commerce and stately altars, marketplace and High Mass, livestock and learning. The architecture may be eighteenth century, but the blueprint is medieval—at times even older than that. Castle Street, which curves around the grounds of the Anglican cathedral, actually follows the line of a prehistoric defensive work.

The city's name is from *Ard Macha*, "Hill of Macha," an ancient site dedicated to the warrior queen Macha, who gave birth to twins after being forced into a foot race against horses. Patrick came to Armagh as Paul had gone to Rome, to strike at the heart, to convert at the core. Armagh was an important centre of pagan society, and when Patrick arrived in AD 444 he built his church on the very spot that had once been Queen Macha's stronghold.

During the Dark Ages that enveloped the rest of Europe, Armagh helped keep the flame of knowledge burning. It is the oldest episcopal see in the world outside Rome, the religious focal point of Ireland, a centre of worship for more than 1,500 years. As the cradle of Irish Christianity, it was also a plum target for marauding Vikings, invading Normans and Gaelic rebels. (Shane O'Neill even showed up at one point to torch the place.) Heroes are buried here as well. The body of Brian Boru, High King of Ireland, who broke the Viking hold on Ireland at the Battle of Clontarf in 1014, lies in the grounds of what is now the Anglican cathedral.

One city, two cathedrals, both dedicated to St. Patrick. I walked toward the Anglican Church of Ireland Cathedral, on the site of Patrick's original church. It didn't dominate the skyline the way the Roman Catholic Cathedral did, but like the city, it followed a medieval floor plan. Regimental banners hung inside, and among those honoured was one Thomas Osborne Kidd, "who fell, pierced by a rifle ball, whilst serving in a Naval Brigade before Sebastopol." I couldn't think of a more perfectly imperial way to die than by being pierced by a rifle ball at Sebastopol.

Across from the Protestant cathedral, on a lower hill but reaching higher, the French Gothic spires of the Catholics spiked the sky. The interior was magnificent: Italian marble, mosaic tiles, stained glass artistry, angels at vertigo heights and strong, almost muscular pillars, holding up a central tower that was never built. It had its oddities as well: a collection of cardinals' hats decaying into dust, and a regrettable 1960s kitsch altar, but, like the Protestant cathedral, it enclosed space, imposed silence. My footsteps echoed. A few parishioners were confessing sins, original and otherwise, and an elderly woman was murmuring prayers to herself. A coin clanked into a candle-offering collection box.

Other towers, other spires. The Armagh Observatory, founded in 1790 by the city's Anglican archbishop, sat in a landscaped park near the centre of the city, its dome-topped telescope trained at the stars. One of the leading astronomical research centres in the UK, it was part of a larger "Astropark." The Astropark *("Where Heaven comes down to Earth")* featured a planetarium and an outdoor orbit path, where you could walk the elliptical routes of various planets, as well as a grandly named Hill of Infinity, which took you along a path at a rapidly accelerating scale, across the planets and beyond our solar system, through distant nebula and far-off galaxies, until you arrived at the very edge of the known universe! (otherwise known as the top of the hill) and found yourself on the brink of the Big Bang itself. From the top of Infinity, I could see the city's skyline angling upward. And at that moment, the entire city seemed to be aligned toward the stars, fixated on Heaven.

I walked through the mall, kicking leaves as I went, past cricket fields and cannons captured in the Crimean War. Sun was slanting warm across the city, stretching out shadows as families and slow strollers ambled by. A big, dopey dog chased squirrels through the trees— *"Where'dhego? Where'dhego? J'aseem? Did'ja? Did'ja?"*—while his owner ran after him waving a leash.

SNIPERS AT WORK; JUNKIES BEWARE

I used Armagh City as my base camp for the next series of walks, and it was a distinct pleasure to fall back to the city at the end of the day. I could see myself living quite happily in Armagh City, had the cards of life fallen differently.

The Ulster Way didn't go through the city. In fact, it barely entered County Armagh, choosing to skirt the border instead, running north, bypassing the interior and—more to the point, I suppose—giving the southern reaches of Armagh as wide a berth as possible.

In a land of Janus countenance, Armagh is the most riven county of all. The north is staunchly, rabidly Loyalist, home to the killing fields of Portadown and Lurgan, where Catholics were targeted by an especially brutal branch of the UVF. North Armagh is the birthplace of the Orange Order. And South Armagh, just down the road? Another world altogether. Known as "Bandit Country," South Armagh has always been a lawless frontier. Staunchly, rabidly Republican, it was home to some of the most ruthless men the IRA ever produced.

It had always been so. During negotiations for the partition of Ireland, there was heavy pressure to give South Armagh to the Republic, and as late as the 1970s British administrators were trying to come up with a way to hand the region over. They even floated an "acre for acre" swap of land in South Armagh for adjoining areas of northern Monaghan. Nothing came of it, though, which was a shame, because it might have saved everyone a great deal of heartache and bloodshed. Instead, the wild borderlands of South Armagh remained under British rule—*nominal* British rule. It had become the Wild West, or rather, the Wild South, where the RUC and the Territorial Army faced almost daily ambush. At the height of the conflict, the IRA posted signs similar to "Men at Work" or "Children at Play" that showed silhouettes of a masked gunman holding up an Armalite rifle, under the heading "Sniper at Work." Soldiers stationed in South Armagh likened it to being "ducks in a shooting gallery." The SAS were sent in, and the IRA's South Armagh Brigade took them on as well. The bomb that killed twenty-nine people in Omagh was built in South Armagh, as was the one that blew up the Docklands in London and the one that tore apart a regimental parade of horses in Hyde Park, to name just a few.

Armagh City, with its duelling cathedrals and competing claims on the truth, was caught physically and spiritually between North and South. The Ulster Way, however, dodged the issue. This was understandable, I suppose. When the Ulster Way was laid out, the Bandit Country of South Armagh was at its worst. It is one thing to send walkers through raised bogs and down trails that lack proper waymarkers; it is quite another to send them down roads signposted "Sniper at Work."

Before I rejoined the Ulster Way, though, I went to Emain Macha, just outside Armagh City. Now known as Navan Fort, it was once the site of Ulster's ancient capital. Celtic cosmology divided Ireland into five provinces. In the middle was Meath, with its capital at Tara, and around it were the "four fields" of Ireland:

> In the east, Leinster
> In the south, Munster
> To the west, Connacht
> And to the north, Ulster

Each in turn was associated with a season:

> Leinster was spring
> Munster was summer
> Connacht was autumn
> And Ulster was winter

and a time of day:

> Leinster was dawn
> Munster was midday
> Connacht was dusk
> Ulster was midnight

You may have noticed a pattern: Ulster as winter, Ulster as midnight. Each of the provinces was also a political abode with its own realm:

> Leinster was wealth
> Munster was music

Connacht was wisdom
And Ulster? Ulster was war.

If Armagh City was Ireland's Canterbury, then Emain Macha was Ulster's Camelot. Before its destruction in AD 332, Emain Macha had been a stronghold of the northern Celts for six hundred years. An ancient seat of kings, the spiritual and political centre of Ulster, it was also home to the Knights of the Red Branch. The Ulster Cycle sagas predate those of King Arthur, and have been compared to the *Iliad* in their scope and themes. The stories are centred around Emain Macha, with tales of King Conor, the Knights Twelve, Deirdre of the Sorrows, Morrigan the Witch and the great warrior Cuchulainn, who once single-handedly held back an invasion from the south led by Maeve, Queen of Connacht, who was intent on stealing the Brown Bull of Cooley.

Emain Macha was at its glory hundreds of years before Christ. Excavations unearthed the skull of a North African Barbary ape, an exotic pet presented to one of its kings and evidence of Emain Macha's reach. Today, little remains. The site was essentially one drumlin among many, the Mother of All Drumlins, as it were, not in size or scope, but in the depth of its history. In 95 BC, a massive temple, 122 feet in diameter and supported by more than 200 axe-hewn oak beams, was raised atop Emain Macha—and then burned, intentionally it would seem, as a sacrificial offering. The mound from this enigmatic act of arson is visible on Emain Macha even now.

Imagine a drop of water, or blood, landing in green fields, rippling away, and Emain Macha was the swell at the centre. The hill once rang with the sound of sword on shield, of battles won and wagers lost, of kings blinded by lust and lovers star-crossed—but today what comes to mind instead is a haiku by the poet Bashō:

Summer grasses,
all that remains
of warrior dreams

I'd taken a taxi out to Emain Macha, but decided to walk back along the Navan Fort Road, which followed an ancient Celtic route. I passed a factory that made cinder blocks, stoop-backed men laying them out to dry like grey dominoes along the ground. A conveyor belt dumped gravel into machinery for crushing. Dust lay across the hedges like flour, and the puddles on the road were thick with chalky grey slush.

I came to the outskirts of the city, found a path that ran along the edge of a housing estate. It came out at a crumbling cement stairway overgrown with weeds, where a pile of rubbish smouldered, the burning flakes of paper cartwheeling away. The smell of feces and urine. Sodden cigarette butts. Crushed Pepsi cans. A handpainted sign that read "Shoot the JUNKIES." And beside that: "All junkies—WATCH OUT." A disembowelled mattress lay flopped across the path, and an unravelled condom had been discarded nearby.

But this was Ulster, and even in Junkie Alley there was legend and lore. I hadn't followed this path by accident; I was looking for a holy well said to overflow once a year on the Feast of Saints Peter and Paul. It had been an important pilgrimage site and was marked on my Ordnance Survey map.

Some young teens were hanging beside a chain-link fence, watching me as I came along.

"Is there some sort of holy well around here?" I asked.

I expected a surly shrug at best, a thumping at worst, but they became immediately animated. "Aye. Saint Patrick's Well. Hard to get at, youse hafta jump tha' fence."

The fence was very high.

"Or you kin go all away around, like," they said.

They showed me the way. You had to thread through a back alley, past IRA graffiti, across broken glass, to a pocket of shrubs. Somewhere in the middle of that was a well. My disappointment must have been evident.

"I think council's gonna put a wee fence around it, an' a sign," one of them said. "Make it an attraction, like. Should come back then."

They were waiting for me to do something, so I took a picture, nodded my appreciation. "Well," I said. "Thanks."

"Y'is American?" they asked.

"More or less." I'd long learned not to bother trying to explain the concept of "Canada."

"Is it like here, then?"

I thought about Emain Macha, about the competing cathedrals, the "Sniper at Work" signs, the mythic landscapes and neglected holy wells. "No," I said. "It's nothing like here."

Walking back toward the cathedrals of Armagh, I considered coming back again on the next Feast of Saints Peter and Paul, to see if that well did indeed overflow with water, or whether the miracle of it had long since run dry.

GHOSTLY BRIDGES

The Ulster Way passed through several small towns on its way to Lough Neagh. I started at the stone village of Caledon, an arrangement of stately Georgian homes clad in sandstone, though "stately Georgian" is probably a redundancy of sorts. Among architects, Georgian is almost a synonym for "stately." What I really wanted to see in Caledon was the Bone House, an eighteenth-century folly constructed entirely from the knuckle bones of cattle. It was somewhere in the wooded recesses of the privately owned Caledon Estate. This struck me as profoundly unfair. If you were going to construct a building out of cow bones, you owed it to the public to let them have a decent gawk.

I walked alongside the walls of Caledon Estate, jumping up now and then, trying to catch a glimpse of the Bone House, puzzled, as always, as to why I was on this side of the wall instead of the other. I would have made a terrific aristocrat. I look quite fetching in a cravat, I have an unshakeable belief in my own self-worth, and I can pop a monocle out of my eye socket at the damned effrontery of plebeian presumptuousness with the best of them. And you can bet, if I owned a building composed entirely of knuckle bones, I would have let the great unwashed in for a peek.

From Caledon, the Ulster Way ran along the Blackwater River, on the border between County Armagh and County Tyrone, following half-forgotten country lanes where grass grew down the middle of the tarmac. The route felt like a river itself as it curved through fields, following the contours, splitting around drumlins. Recent rains had left the fields an even deeper shade of green, if such a thing was possible—comparing greens in Ireland was like comparing superlatives. Sunlight filtered through leaves, drowsy and warm, chlorophyl and chloroform in equal parts, it seemed. I was almost sleepwalking, with billows of green on either side.

I came into Wilsontown. Or rather, Wilsontown *Upper*. I counted four buildings, not one of which was a pub. Scandalous! Still, Wilsontown (Upper) did contain an odd attraction: a ghost bridge. It stood in a field where a canal had once flowed. Four or five of these ghost bridges appeared along this one stretch, among them the one at Wilsontown.* *The hills are boggy and the canals are dry. This entire country is built upside down.*

Having experienced the excitement of Wilsontown Upper, I couldn't wait to get to Wilsontown Lower. Sure enough, I came to a T-intersection, turned left and—yes!—there I was. Wilsontown Lower was much larger and far more cosmopolitan than Wilsontown Upper. Where Wilsontown Upper had four houses, Wilsontown Lower had at least six. (And you just know the people in Wilsontown Lower really rub that in.) Black circles were burnt into the tarmac, a testament to small-town boredom, the rubber skid marks all but shouting, "Get me out of here!"

In the next hollow was a clutch of homes named, reasonably enough, the Hollow, which was, by my estimate, somewhere *between* Wilsontown Upper and Wilsontown Lower in terms of size. The road beyond wrapped itself around a factory and then took me in to

---

*Upper

Milltown, where a disused linen mill on the banks of the Blackwater housed the Benburb Heritage Centre. A sign in the window read OPEN. I tried the doors anyway. No one was about. The site included a youth hostel, and a few unconscionably young backpackers were kicking about, but other than that, no one. Just the OPEN mill, a chimney stack and a lock-keeper's cottage.

The path along the Blackwater ran past canal locks and old stone buildings, then up above a driveway marked with exasperated hand-painted signs: "Private!" "Keep Out: Private." I felt like walking down, tapping on their door, saying, "What you really need is a 'Beware of Bull' sign," but a pair of yippy dogs were yapping away at the bottom of the drive, and I decided not to stir up any more animosity.

The Blackwater was not black; it was a deep, peaty green. I followed a side path down to where the water was breaking over contoured rock. It even *tasted* green. It was a beautiful walk, through shafts of sunlight, on a trail of beech and pine. I passed a house-shaped block of vines along the way, realized that there must be a building in there somewhere. The sound of the waterfalls along the Blackwater was amplified by the forest. Birds were debating bird matters, and an insomniac owl somewhere in the forest hooted his sleepiness.

I crossed the river on a footbridge, by a sign that warned would-be waders of "Deep, fast flowing water." A castle lay ahead. It was a strange sensation, coming across a seventeenth-century fortress at the edge of a forest. I imagined there were no trees obstructing the castle's sight lines when it was built, and its cliff-top perch must have given it a commanding view of the river. But I was so used to seeing castles above sea coasts or high on open hills that the one at Benburb felt almost like a hidden fortification, defended not by might but by misdirection. It was hard to tell where cliff ended and castle began, but as I followed the path around, the walls slowly took shape. A round tower came into view and, beyond that, a red-brick priory above a sweep of lawn.

Benburb Castle stood on the site of an older Gaelic fortification built by—who else?—Shane O'Neill, "the Proud." (Shane O'Neill was the whack-a-mole of Ulster history, forever popping up at different spots and different times.) The strange thing about Benburb Castle was that only *the walls* were protected for their heritage value, not the grounds within. There was a house sitting inside the walls—not a manor, you understand, but a regular home with a car parked out front and kids' bicycles scattered about. A handsome stone cottage, a little pocket of middle-class comfort, inside the walls of a seventeenth-century castle: it was one of the most incongruous arrangements I'd ever come upon. Imagine kissing your spouse goodbye every morning, then walking out to your car as bug-eyed people (such as myself) peered in through the front gate. You'd certainly feel safe within those thick stone walls—if your neighbours ever rolled up with battering rams and siege towers, you'd be ready—but it must have felt like a fish bowl at times.

Up the hill and past the priory lay Benburb proper. Like Sion Mills with its millworkers' abodes, the heart of Benburb village was its apple peelers' cottages, squat strong buildings that gave the village a feel both quaint and solid. I had entered apple country, County Armagh being the "orchard of Ireland."

My day's walk—more an extended stroll than a hike—ended in Charlemont, and I was soon in deep among the orchards; the drumlin hills bristled with them. Charlemont was once a key military location on the frontier of Gaelic resistance, where the English maintained a massive fortress. Today the village was little more than a sleepy line of shops along the side of the road.

It was hard to imagine that this quiet stretch of the Blackwater River had been the site of two historic clashes. The first was in 1598, when Hugh O'Neill, now allied with the O'Donnells and the Maguires, clashed headlong with the English at Yellow Ford, just south of the river. The battle ended in a resounding victory for the Irish; the English were cut down, their forces scattered and their commander killed.

The second battle was waged in 1646, just outside Benburb. Once again the Irish used topography to their advantage; once again the English—or the Scots, in this case—marched into a trap. Although outnumbered and outgunned, Owen Roe O'Neill, nephew of the late great Hugh, rallied his men "in the name of the Father, Son and the Holy Ghost." Under the cry of *Sancta Maria!*, the Irish destroyed the Scots army. The Scottish general fled so quickly he left his wig on the battlefield. As many as three thousand Scots were killed, compared to just three hundred on the Irish side. It was the greatest defeat ever suffered by the British in Ireland, and the clashes at Yellow Ford and Benburb would go down as the two greatest victories the Gaelic armies ever achieved. And yet they were barely remembered in Northern Ireland. They certainly hadn't been immortalized the way Londonderry and the Boyne were. No doubt that was due largely to the fact that Yellow Ford and Benburb were *Catholic* victories, but there was more to it than that, I thought.

Londonderry and the Boyne were watershed moments in Irish history. Yellow Ford and Benburb were not. In neither case was the victory followed up; in both cases the larger conflict ended badly for the Irish side. They won the battles, lost the wars. Hugh O'Neill and the other Gaelic nobles would abandon Ireland, sailing away for good in an event that became known as the Flight of the Earls. It was the death knell for Gaelic rule in Ireland, opening up the rebellious North for the full-scale plantation of Protestant settlers. It was against this plantation that Owen Roe O'Neill fought during the uprisings of the 1640s, to no avail.

So the victories at Yellow Ford and Benburb proved hollow. The Catholic faith was all but outlawed. The Penal Laws were brought in. Catholics were forbidden to teach school or preach in chapels, purchase land or hold public office, vote, join the navy or army, or take part in parliamentary proceedings—restrictions that would remain in effect, albeit fitfully enforced, for a hundred years. There is such a thing as being a sore winner, as the Protestants demonstrated.

I CROSSED THE BRIDGE from Charlemont into Moy ("The Moy," as it is known). Laid out in the 1750s, the village was modelled after the piazza of Marengo in Italy. Chestnut trees stood in circular stone beds on either side of a wide boulevard. The shops, set back from the main road, were spared the usual bathwash of exhaust, and even with the traffic firing through, Moy had a serenity to it. The village was about as Italian as Omagh was French, but still. It was a pleasant, summery spot, even in those first cool breaths of autumn, and I quickly added it to my list of Alternative Lives. *"He walked into The Moy one day, never came out ..."*

The Moy church, on a hill above the boulevard, presented a strange view: its front entrance had been walled in. Local lore traced that to one of the ladies in the congregation who kept complaining about a draught. (A true Ulster solution. *"Feckin' cold, is it? Aye? Well, I've got an answer fer tha'—Jimmy, hand me those bricks."*) I'd also read that it was to keep the devil at bay, though I suspected what was kept at bay was more likely the odour of horse manure, which must have once permeated the village. For more than one hundred years, Moy was the heart of Ulster's equestrian culture, providing the best of cavalry and carriage horses across the British Isles. Its fairs would have been held in the square right below the church, where the warm aromas would have undoubtedly wafted upward. *"Ye find it smelly, d'ye? Well, I've got a solution fer tha'."*

I ate a splendid meal in a splendid café and considered spending the night in The Moy whiling the evening away—but my main gear was back in Armagh City and much as I liked The Moy, I couldn't see renting two rooms, one for me and one for my backpack.

RETURN OF THE GREAT DIVIDE

On its slow march to Lough Neagh, the Ulster Way crossed the M1 dual carriageway, and I found myself on an overpass as cars fired through below. Those heading east would be in Belfast before I made it to the next small cluster of homes on the map. I too was going to Belfast. I was just taking the long way, is all.

The landscape began to flatten after I crossed the M1 freeway. I had left the drumlin belt behind, and I now entered the orchards and lowlands of Lough Neagh. I was approaching at last the vast fresh-water sea in the heart of Ulster, a pie chart of boundaries in which five of the Six Counties converged. Over the course of my trip, I'd learned what a versatile term "lough" was, and by "versatile" I mean "madden-ingly imprecise," referring as it does to ponds, bays, salt-water inlets, sea channels, fjords and oversized puddles. Neagh, largest lake in the British Isles, was also a "lough." The Ulster Way circled it, turning a wide, slow mandala, and yet the route ran beside the lake for only a few miles and even then never actually reached the shore.

The air changes the closer you get, and long before you see Lough Neagh, you can feel it. The lake was created by Finn McCool, who scooped up the earth to hurl it at his Scottish rival. He missed and it landed in the Irish Sea instead, where it formed the Isle of Man. (There were also some fanciful geological explanations for Lough Neagh involving low-lying sedimentary basins, but no one put much stock in those.)

I followed a lane down. In my effort to be as up to date as possible, I'd been consulting the 1854 *Hand-Book to the Antiquities and Scenery of the North of Ireland* by J. B. Doyle, who assured readers that "the shores of Lough Neagh are celebrated for their pebbles." Alas, the shoreline was reedy along the edge and squelchy underfoot. If there were any pebbles present that day, celebrated or otherwise, I failed to find them.

Farther down, I climbed a gate with a sign that read "No Shooting" but failed to mention trespassing; taking advantage of that loophole, I tried again to walk to the water's edge but was turned back, this time by open marsh. A few cattle lay resting nearby, legs folded under them (either that, or they were stuck flank high in the muck). I could see clear across the lough, which surprised me, considering what a great splash it formed on the maps. The Sperrins rose beyond the far shore.

Waves were lapping in. Seagulls reeled above, and a few swans floated past, bobbing on the water. I could see what may have been eel boats anchored offshore, eels being a delicacy of Lough Neagh. (Not that anyone eats them; they just catch them and sell them to the Dutch, who, let's face it, also serve pancakes for supper.)

Another quiet lane led down to the River Bann, the same river I had tried unsuccessfully to hitch a ride across with a fisherman at Portstewart. Here it emptied into Lough Neagh, apparently to re-emerge on the other side of the lake and continue its journey to the sea. A small ferry had once carried cars and pedestrians across the river—it was a short hop, barely a road's width—but the service had long been discontinued, and the ferry road simply ended, dropping off directly into water. In lieu of guard rails, they had posted warnings with pictures of cars falling into the river. I ate a late lunch, soaked up a rare bit of sun. A pair of fishermen sat on lawn chairs on either side of the Bann, dangling lines into the current, chatting across the river to each other. It was such a narrow divide. *Get a running start, and you just might clear it* ... But no, once again the Bann had blocked my progress. A metaphor for something, I was sure. I retraced my steps, turned south instead. And that was the last I ever saw of Lough Neagh.

I PASSED A LONELY Ulster Way sign pointing the wrong way, could hear the traffic on the M1 drawing near again. Protestant homes with Protestant flags, Protestant farms with Protestant fields. Another solitary Ulster Way sign, this one pointed drunkenly toward Heaven, showing me the one direction in which I knew I wouldn't be going.

Orchards sound more bucolic than they really are. I was deep among apples now, amid the fruit of original sin, walking past rows of bad-tempered trees gnarled and knotted like bent-backed Old Testament prophets.

The telephone poles began to sprout Union Jacks, and soon enough I could see the sharpened beacon of a church steeple rising above the fields. Drumcree. In a land of church steeples, this one stood out, because Drumcree was the site of holy clashes during the mid-1990s that almost led to civil war in Northern Ireland. In a land of flashpoints, Drumcree was the phosphorous flare that had lit up the night.

I walked up the road to the church grounds, a heartbreakingly pastoral scene on the outskirts of Portadown. Portadown was the heartland of Orangeism. The order was founded in a village just outside the city, and Portadown remained its bastion. It was also, not coincidentally perhaps, the most militantly Loyalist town in Northern Ireland, even more so than Larne or Carrickfergus. Portadown was ground zero of the Loyalist cause. It had been called, ironically one assumed, the "Vatican of Loyalism."

During the Catholic uprisings of 1641, Protestant settlers—men, women, children—were herded with pikes onto a bridge near Portadown, where they were stripped, speared, shot with muskets and driven into the river. Those who survived the assault drowned, and for months afterward a ghostly figure appeared above the water, a woman, pale and naked to the waist, hair dripping, eyes blazing, crying out, "*Revenge! Revenge!*" That was more than three hundred years ago, but the Protestants of Portadown talked about it as though it had happened just last week.

During the Troubles, Portadown was part of the Loyalist killing zone, the mid-Ulster "murder triangle" where Catholic civilians were targeted by a branch of the UVF that eventually broke away from the organization because they felt it was getting too "soft." Although not Orangemen themselves, these breakaway Loyalists aligned themselves with the lodge in a very public manner. *And with friends like these …*

In Northern Ireland at that time, the various Loyalist groups and Protestant orders—Orangemen, Royal Black, Apprentice Boys and the like—staged roughly 2,500 marches every year, compared to 300 Nationalist marches. Why you would need 2,500 marches a year to affirm your identity is something best left for another day, but the fact remains that most of these pass peacefully. A dozen or so parades were flashpoints, however, and none more so than Drumcree, in the middle of Orange Country. (Ironic, considering that this is apple country, but never mind. One shouldn't mix apples and Orangemen.)

The Orangemen had been walking down what is now Garvaghy Road for almost two hundred years, but as the demographics shifted, Garvaghy became a Catholic neighbourhood, and opposition to the annual marches grew. The two sides clashed headlong every year; it was like their annual rugby match, played by Ulster rules, with the RUC in the middle, a referee at a riot. The Catholic community said the marches were antagonistic and triumphalist. The Orangemen countered that the current Drumcree march, held in July during the run-up to the Twelfth, did not celebrate William's victory over Catholics but rather honoured the memory of men who had died at the Battle of the Somme. Garvaghy was a public road, and they felt they had the right to walk it, free assembly being a basic democratic right. Catholics just as adamantly pointed out that an alternative route was available, arguing that the only reason to run a Protestant parade through a Catholic community was malice. All the talk about democratic principles and cultural traditions was just a smokescreen, they contended, and the marches were really just a way to remind the Catholics of Portadown that they lived in a Loyalist city and had better not forget it.

The RUC were ordered to push the parades through, and they were attacked and demonized by Catholics in Northern Ireland for doing so. After several years of violent confrontations, the parade was finally banned, and the RUC were now ordered to block it. This they did, with the same resolve they had shown earlier, throwing barricades across the road, unrolling barbed wire, digging trenches. The British Army was flown in to back them up as running battles raged across the church grounds and the cemetery. The RUC was now attacked and demonized by the Protestants. Following similar clashes the year before, an off-duty police officer, recognized at a pub in Ballymoney, was kicked to death by a Loyalist mob. Catholic churches burned across Northern Ireland and Orange halls were attacked in kind, as the rioting spread. Northern Ireland teetered on the edge of outright anarchy. It ended in the saddest way possible, with a petrol bomb lobbed into the home of a single-mother Catholic family in a Ballymoney housing estate. Chrissy Quinn escaped, but her three little boys, Jason, Mark and Richard, aged eight, nine and ten, burned to death. Their charred remains were discovered curled up in fetal positions. They died, it was pointed out, in an Orange flame. After that, the glorious Siege of Drumcree didn't have quite the heroic resonance of Londonderry or the Boyne. The protests continued, but any sympathy the Orange Order might have inspired was severely damaged, irreparably perhaps.

Protestant pensioners on Park Road, at the end of Garvaghy Road, found themselves thrust into the frontline of sectarian attacks, their street tagged with Loyalist banners and Union Jacks. Under constant siege by their Catholic neighbours, they were forced to close themselves in at night behind metal shutters. Neither side held the moral high ground at Drumcree.

The Orange Order might have said, "We don't wish to cause offence; there are other routes we can follow." The Catholic community might have said, "We respect the traditions behind your march and your right to walk a public road." But this was Northern Ireland, and neither side was willing to be the bigger man.

I walked the quiet church grounds, where the steeple stood high against the dying light: a beautiful spot, really. *If you didn't know, you would never have guessed.*

FOR ALL ITS GRIM REPUTE, Portadown remained a thriving centre of commerce. "Business and bigotry" was how the city's two specialties were explained to me before I arrived. It was also a city known for its roses, those beautiful and notoriously prickly flowers. The Ulster Way did its best to avoid South Armagh, but you didn't need to go there to reach Bandit Country. Portadown had bandits to spare.

I showed up at a guest house not far from Drumcree, but they were booked solid, and no amount of sad eyes or awkward pauses on my part could convince them to boot someone from a bed to make room for me. "*They gave you our number? Really? The Tourist Board? Because we're booked all week, so we are.*"

The husband felt bad. "There's a nice wee sports club in town. Bannview. It's very large, sure they'll have room for you there."

But when they realized that I didn't have a car, would in fact be walking, the lady of the house exchanged looks with her husband. The sun was going down, darkness was seeping in, and I would have to go down Garvaghy Road and across Park to get there.

"You know what? I'll just run ye in," he said. "That would be—better."

And so I was swept into Portadown, along one roundabout and then another. The husband came in to the sports club with me to make sure they had a room.

"Aye, we kin help you out," said the beefy fellow at the desk. He looked at my benefactor, said, "And where is yer guest house, then?"

The husband hesitated—just a heartbeat, but that was enough. He told the clerk the name of his B&B.

"Oh, aye," said the fellow at the desk. "That's up on—" and he named a street.

The first fellow nodded.

A tight smile. "Well, that was very kind of you, thinkin' of us."

The husband nodded, left quickly.

Something had passed between them, four hundred years of divisiveness, perhaps, thirty years of Troubles, five years of Drumcree confrontations: I couldn't begin to know. It must be such a burden to be weighted down by tribal allegiances like that.

My room was very clean, very bright. I washed out some socks and T-shirts, hung them in the window to dry, then wandered out into the dark city. I stopped at the first shop I came to, asked for directions to the nearest restaurant. The shop clerk and one of the customers then proceeded to have a detailed debate about which one they should send me to. People in Northern Ireland went out of their way to help in cases like this. Unfortunately, they usually started off by giving intricately detailed explanations of which way *not* to go. "Aye, there's a wee cathedral on the corner, and there'll be a bicycle lyin' on its side next to a tree, right where the lane curves slightly to the left—not completely, ye unnerstan', but jest slightly, like—and that's where you'll see a huge wee house wi' green shutters." Friend, cutting in: "Not green, black. Sure he painted 'em." "Aye? Still green, last I saw." "Nae, black." "Okay, let's just say *greenish-black* then, anyway, youse follow that road, past the church, by the bicycle, it will take you to a wee bridge. Cross that, and you will soon be lost. So whatever you do, don't go tha' way. Now. The way you *want* to be goan ..." (*Note to Ulster readers*: You can deny this all you want, but it's true. Ask a simple question, get a complicated answer: it's the Ulster way.) This applied not only to directions, but to history as well. Ask "So when was this church built?" and you were treated to a forty-minute dissertation, after which you would still not know the answer. Meanwhile, someone who pulled a drowning child from a canal, when asked about it, would say, "Was nothin' really," if he answered at all. He might just shrug it off. I suspected the unique interplay of Scots and Irish influences in the North had created this strange dichotomy between modest understatement and lengthy explanations, which often obscured more than they elucidated. But I honestly didn't know. (And you'll notice how concise my own disser-tation was on this matter.)

Anyway.

I had asked for directions, so it was my own fault. I left the shop with my head good and full. I had no idea which way I was supposed to go. The streets were dark and eerily quiet. When I stood under a streetlamp to get my bearings, the curtains in the house across the way moved.

Broken glass and graffiti. Litter on a wind, scuttling across the road. I'd obviously taken a wrong turn somewhere. The road ahead curved under a darkened overpass. Homes were flying tattered Union Jacks, and as I started to cross the street, I stopped. Cold. The other side was lined with Irish tricolours, and the graffiti went from LVF to

IRA. I thought, *This can't be good*. Ahead of me, in Republican territory, I could see what looked like storefronts, their lights pooled on
empty sidewalks. My stomach grumbled. I was hungry and—was that
a chip shop ahead?

I looked at the billowing flags on the opposing sides of the street.
Houses on both had surrendered to sectarian threats, were shut down
and boarded up; some were even bricked in. A factory nearby had
been abandoned as well. A thin stream, a mere trickle of water,
separated the red-white-and-blue from the green-white-and-orange.
The night seemed to have grown *thicker* somehow.

"Y' look lost."

It was a voice behind me. An older man in an undershirt, cigarette
glowing like a firefly. He was leaning on his gate watching me. A
Union Jack moved on the streetlamp above him.

"I was, ah, trying to find a place to eat. I can see some lights up
ahead but …"

He shook his head slowly. "Those'll be closed, aye." He put out his
cigarette. "Tourist, are ye?"

I nodded.

With an almost beatific smile, he said, "You really shouldn't be
down here."

A small red car pulled up just then, window down. "Get in," said
the driver. He was talking to me.

Pardon?

"C'mon," he said. "You were back in the shop earlier."

I remembered him. I remembered the clarity of the directions he
had given. "You're going the wrong way," he said—somewhat redun-
dantly, I thought.

The driver and the other man nodded curtly at each other. Neither
side wanted some boneheaded Yank wandering about tripping wires.
As I climbed in, the driver turned to me. "Chippy okay?"

I nodded. "A chippy would be fine."

When I got back to my room, the laundry I'd hung up had been
taken down and the curtains pulled closed. Some sort of evening

turndown service, I supposed. My clothes were still a bit damp, though, so I had to hang them back up.

I slept in and made it to breakfast just before last call. I gave the woman my room number, ordered everything save the sausage and found I had been seated beside an American businessman who was involved with a local Portadown factory that made—I forget. He was a fine fellow nonetheless, and the woman who brought out his breakfast gave him a warm smile. Very warm. You could have toasted marshmallows on that smile. She then turned an icy gaze on me. "Tea or coffee." Not a flicker of warmth. So I smiled, really big. "Tea, please!" Immune to my charms, she left without a word. Even my tablemate picked up on this.

"Wow," he said. "She really doesn't like you."

The service in Northern Ireland had been so unerringly friendly that I found this jarring.

"Do you think it's because I got here just before breakfast ended?" I whispered to my dining companion, after the lady in question had returned to drop my plate in front of me. Apparently she and I were feuding.

"Hey, I arrived just before you did," he said. "And she was nice to me."

"Maybe she thinks I'm American," I said.

"Could be. Or maybe she knows you're Canadian."

Having endured an unprovoked cold shoulder, I slunk out into Portadown by day, past Union Jacks and Orange Lodge banners and murals showing vicious RUC constables beating down angelic Orangemen, then into a Nationalist enclave and past another mural showing police beating down angelic Republicans. Both sides aspired to the coveted position of the downtrodden. The message was the same either way: *We are under siege, not them. We are the real victims, not them.*

I walked down Garvaghy Road. A working-class neighbourhood surrounded by a sea of Loyalists. A little boy with Thomas the Tank Engine runners was sitting on a front step chewing sugar candies off a string. I thought about the pensioners under siege on Park Road, about children burning, about off-duty police officers dragged from pubs and kicked to death, about the watery cries for "*Revenge!*" As I walked toward the shopping plazas in the city centre, I saw a McDonald's at one end, its golden arches catching the light—and I felt a sudden surge of relief. I walked toward the arches, rested my forehead on the cool condensation of its windows, the glass like ice on a fever. It was so comforting, the polished surface, the lack of memory, the lack of any larger context.

ON TRAPPING THE DEVIL

The Newry Canal, connecting Lough Neagh and the coal fields of the Ulster interior to Carlingford Lough on the Irish Sea, was Britain's first true canal, built more than one hundred years before the Suez. It predated the Industrial Revolution. Construction began in 1731 and took ten years and many lives to complete, with workers cutting a trench eighteen miles long armed only with picks, shovels and spades.

The Ulster Way followed the old towpath from Portadown to Newry. Though once the primary economic artery of the North, the canal had been replaced by rail lines and highways. It was now a quiet corridor through the countryside, a footpath for Sunday strollers and long-distance walkers.

I left Portadown with just a day pack, heading out into a mist-chilled morning along a tree-lined path softly lit in muted colours. Cattle were grazing along the banks, and in the still morning air the sound of them ripping up their clumps of grass was unnaturally loud. The last of the wildflowers were starting to fade, golds giving way to brown, pinks turning to rust. Swans drifted by with their usual pageantry, shock-white atop the algae green of the canal. A train rattled across the far side of the field.

I came to the first of the canal's fourteen locks, Moneypenny's, which formed a bridge across the water, with the old lock-keeper's house restored and sitting pretty alongside. The locks formed a systematic stairwell, raising and lowering water levels to bring ships up and over, from Lough Neagh to the sea. Through a paddock of skittish young steer, and over a fence smeared with fecal matter, I came out onto the main road, crossed another bridge. The trail beyond was mucky. Entire stretches of it were swamped, and the canal itself was brackish, with duckweed and surface slime. I kept expecting to see crocodile eyes drift in.

"Stay positive," I told myself. "This swamp water will help wash the cow shit off your boots."

Farther up a dredging operation was under way, the digger feeding on the bottom and coming up with mouthfuls of mud and vines. Lumps of the putrid guck had been dumped beside the path. It smelled worse than cow manure, worse than horse shit, worse even than pig poo, and I hurried past arm over mouth, like Bela Lugosi behind his cape.

Once I got past that part, the trail became firmer and drier. Some sections had even been surfaced, and I soon came upon a work crew unrolling sheets of rubber, which another group of men was raking gravel over. At the next lock I ran into a pair of engineering consultants who were standing beside a silver Jaguar with maps open.

"We'll be finished by spring," they said. "A bicycle- and footpath, surfaced all the way through. You're probably one of the last to walk it in its rougher state."

The question I really wanted to ask was, "*A Jaguar? Really?*" Who knew that bicycle- and footpath engineering was such a lucrative field?

The trail ran past potato fields pregnant with yield and along the crumbling walls of an old railway bridge buttress. A smattering of new houses appeared on the other side of the canal, and across a stone bridge stood the church steeple of Scarva. The homes along Scarva's main street had overspills of flowers hanging from baskets. The village felt like a garden. It was wonderful, like walking into spring. It was as though autumn had been held at bay at the town limits. A sign announced that Scarva had just won a Britain in Bloom Award, and the year before an award for "Best Kept Small Village." The clock above the parish hall in Scarva was stuck at exactly 10:10.

It was a good place to have a rest, because Scarva's great claim to fame was as a resting spot. It was here that William and his army had encamped before marching off to victory at the Boyne. The village now staged an annual recreation of the battle between James and William, with local farmers playing the role of the battling kings. I certainly left Scarva feeling refreshed enough to take on any uppity usurpers to the throne.

An army surveillance helicopter choppered by, prowling the landscape from above. To the east of Scarva lay the earthwork of the Dane's Cast, a pre-Christian defensive mound that caterpillared across Ulster's southern border, filling in vulnerable gaps between the bogs and mountains, blocking invasions from the south. The Dane's Cast was a reminder that Ireland has never been unified, has always been at war with itself, even under high kings like Brian Boru. Historians often cite the lack of a single overriding monarchy as the cause for many of Ireland's woes. The English didn't need to divide and rule; the island was already divided. It was just a matter of playing one chieftain off another. The 1598 rebellion launched by Hugh O'Neill of Tyrone probably came the closest to achieving a united Irish front, but by then it was too late. The army helicopter hovered a moment, then flew away. The echoes were a long time fading.

I came into Poyntzpass on a path of loose shale, to shrieks and shouts of children in an unseen schoolyard. I left the canal, went up Railway Street and past a small pub. The name: I'd heard it before. The Railway Bar in Poyntzpass. Why did I know that name?

Poyntzpass was considered a mixed community, even though it had roughly the 70/30 Protestant majority you found in Portadown. Here, though, the two sides were known to get along well. It was the sort of town where Union Jacks went up on the Twelfth, only to be happily replaced with Irish Gaelic football banners a few weeks later. As if to illustrate this, an unusual convergence of streets occurred at the inter- section past the Railway Bar, where the town's two main streets,

Chapel and Church came together—"chapel" signifying Catholic, "church" signifying Protestant. I was taking a photograph of this unlikely crossroads when a woman walked past.

"Wondering about that, are you?" she laughed.

I was.

"Well, the story told is that they're named like that because there's a church on each of the four roads into Poyntzpass. A priest, when he first arrived, he said that was so the devil couldn't get in." She laughed again, a warm, loosely thrown laugh. "After many years, though, when it came time for him to leave, this same priest said he realized that the devil was already *in* Poyntzpass. But with a church at every exit, he couldn't get out."

She invited me back to her home for tea and more local history— "My husband can tell it better than me"—but the day was ticking down, so I had to say no. I still regret that. I'd taken an immense liking to Poyntzpass based solely on that one story and her laughter.

It was only much later, when looking through some books, that I realized why the name of the Railway Bar had sounded so familiar. It was something that had happened there a few years earlier. Two men had stopped in for a chat. Philip Allen was Protestant, Damian Trainor was Catholic. They were lifelong friends—had more or less grown up together—and Philip had asked Damian to be best man at his wedding. They were at the pub talking about the upcoming nuptials when masked gunmen entered. Loyalists from nearby Banbridge. The gunmen opened fire. Damian died instantly; Philip was rushed to a hospital in Newry. He died on the operating table. There would be no wedding, no best man. Only a pair of funerals. The whole town turned out for both.

In Northern Ireland, there was a church at every exit. The only hope was that someday, somehow, the devil would find a way to escape.

THE CANAL BEGAN to run clearer after Poyntzpass. I passed through another Valley of Lost Bridges. Sloping fields and rounded hills, shapes like figures lying beneath green satin, here a shoulder, there the curve of a hip. *And don't drumlins look like the soft swell of young breasts.* You know you've been alone too long when the contours of the land start to turn you on. The sudden crash of a pheasant egg-beating its way out of the underbrush shook me out of my reverie. Just as well; they might have found me rolling in the grass, making love to the landscape.

The day's hike was coming to a close, and I left the canal at Jerrettspass. The bus stop there had a schedule posted, but I didn't bother checking. I knew that there was only a coincidental relationship between the times posted and the actual departures, so I stretched out instead for a nice long wait. Not a soul was stirring in Jerrettspass that day.

I'd booked another night back at the Portadown sports centre, much to the obvious displeasure of the woman in charge, the one I'd met that morning. "You want to stay another night?" "Yes, please." "Another?" "Yes." This was followed by a long pause. "You want to stay another night?" "Um, yes?" I thought about trying to find a room somewhere else, but I'd already washed more of my socks and had hung them up from my window to dry. Sunny days needed to be seized. Clothes stayed damp here for such a long time, and I'd often been forced to hike in clammy shirts and moist socks.

It was after dark by the time I got back to Portadown. By now, the man at the front desk had joined the ranks of people who had taken a dislike to me. "Hello," I said cheerfully. "I walked the canal from Portadown to Jerrettspass. It was great. Tomorrow I'll be doing the walk into Newry from—"

"So you'll be checking out then?"

"Sorry?"

"You'll be checking out tomorrow."

"Um, yes?" They were in such a hurry to get rid of me.

Back in my room, my laundry had been taken down and laid flat on the bed. Dry, fortunately, so at least I didn't have to hang my socks up again. I did, however, have to repack, which was always like trying to stuff a large pillow into a small pillowcase. It was while making a final sweep of the room that I found it, under the bed: a note from the lady of the establishment. I still have it. It reads:

> *It would be appreciated if the curtain rail was NOT used as a clothes line. Laundry is not permitted in the rooms. A laundry facility is available on request.*
>
> *Thank you.*

She must have slid it under the door that first day ...

Here I had been engaged in an ongoing war and hadn't known it. I left the next morning as quickly as possible. With my luck, Bob and Marge would have shown up too.

THE BOYS FROM BELFAST

I followed the canal into Newry. I had entered the Gap of the North, the traditional invasion route into Ulster, where the Red Branch warrior Cuchulainn had once held back an entire army single-handedly. The Celtic El Cid, Cuchulainn, wounded in battle and no longer able to stand, asked his chariot driver to tie him to a boulder, sword in hand. The mere sight of him had cowed Queen Maeve's men. The Gap of the North had seen it all: ancient battles, last stands, defiant acts of Ulsterheadedness (a term I coined that is fairly self-explanatory). To this list, I added a folly of my own: that of an Ulster Way trek.

It was still early in the day when I arrived in Newry. Jonathan Swift famously summed up Newry as "High church, low steeple, dirty streets and proud people." That was before the canal brought prosperity, though. Newry today was a city braided with water, the canals and rivers winding through, bridges leaping back and forth. Handsome homes and hotels lined the canal route, providing a water-reflecting study in the enduring strength and symmetry of Georgian architecture. The Newry City Hall itself was an act of architectural derring-do, balanced on pillars over the canal, one half of the building in County Armagh, the other half in County Down. Suspended above the water, it gave Newry a distinct "Venice of Ulster" appeal—more so even than the island city of Enniskillen.

For Unionists, however, Newry had a pungent reputation. This was a Catholic Nationalist stronghold, one of those places, like Derry, that probably should have been ceded to the Republic. Newry looked to the south, turned its back on the North for the most part. The unofficial "capital" of South Armagh, this was where the bandits came to relax. And Newry had seen its share of killings during the Troubles, most notably a mortar attack on the city's police station that left nine officers dead.

Thanks to its proximity to the border, Newry was also a popular cross-border shopping destination, one that boasted glossy plazas and Marks & Spencer wares. I sought out the cathedral instead, with its ornate interior, lambent stained glass and forests of columns. Intricate altar pieces in wedding cake arrangements, the stone as pliant as candle wax. Marble, perpetually cool to the touch, drawing heat away from your hand. A heart entwined with thorns. Ireland.

I sat on a back pew, feeling wistful. Not for any existential or philosophical reason. It was more petty than that. My birthday had passed unmarked somewhere along the canal between Portadown and Newry. The odometer had rolled over, once again. Middle age taking one more Mother-May-I step forward. Alone on my birthday in a city where I knew no one, I decided, tired or not, I would go out, would *do something*.

I checked into a fine guest house, the likes of which I hadn't seen since Derry, and as dusk settled on the city I set out in search of Newry's tawdrier side. It wasn't hard to find. I came upon a string of down-at-the-heel establishments, boyos clustered in conspiracies of booze and broken glass outside. I went into one just off the canal that promised "Live. Music." (Period theirs.) Live—and kicking, as it turned out. No standard Oirish fare this; drummer and bass player were locked in mortal combat when I came in, unable to find a rhythm they could agree on and intent on battling it out at maximum volume. It was the thump-thump-*whap* of a fat man falling down the stairs forever. The singer, meanwhile, a woman high on helium, was wailing a tune that bore no relation to what was going on behind her.

The second bar was subdued to the point of morose; any potential laughter was lost in a beery haze of cigarette smoke. I finished my pint, went to the next bar. Which is to say, I had entered a downward spiral. I ended up in a crowded pub where I was adopted by a gang of rowdy men from Belfast. *Avoid rowdy men from Belfast:* that's a good general rule of thumb, but it was my birthday, and I needed the company. Not that I would use that to try to gain sympathy and/or free drinks.

"Yer birthday, is it?" they said. "Next round's yours, then."

Sigh.

When they found out I was walking the Ulster Way, I became a star. A minor star, to be sure, but a star nonetheless. They were fascinated by the far-flung places I'd walked through, even though all of them were a day's drive from Belfast. "Strabane? Never been there, always wanted to. How was it?" Wet. "And the Sperrins?" Wet. "And Fermanagh?" Very wet.

I wanted to say, *"I know your country. I have felt it in my bones, in the aching of my muscles, the grinding of my knees, the swelling of my tendons. I have felt Ulster in the boredom of its forestry trails, the bogginess of its bogs, the beauty of its landscapes."* But all that came out was "Wet, very wet."

The ringleader, a bull-faced young man with cauliflower ears, leaned into my ale-fogged depth of field, asked, "Been t' the Falls?"

"Sure," I slurred. "Tons. Up in Antrim. And at Marble Arch. There was this one waterfall that was—"

"No," he said. "In Belfast, like. Falls Road. You hafta come see us when ye get in." He raised a pint of Guinness. "Chucky ar la!"

This triggered a round of similar salutes from his tablemates. "Chucky ar la!" in turn became "Up the 'Ra!" a Republican football slogan—*'Ra* being the IRA.

And I said to myself, "Self, maybe you should be going." *They find out I'm a Prod …*

One of his friends was appalled at the route the Ulster Way followed, swinging up, as it did, and missing the best part of County Armagh. "Slieve Gullion, like. It's brilliant, so it is."

"Aye, aye," the others agreed. "Feckin' brilliant."

"And Crossmaglen, where my uncle's from, it's lovely, like. The market and all."

"Oh, aye," the others agreed. *Feckin' lovely, so it was.* On that they concurred.

Crossmaglen lay at the very core of Bandit Country. Crossmaglen was where the "Sniper on Duty" shooting gallery was invented. Crossmaglen was the main Republican base of the South Armagh IRA.

"I haffa go now," I said, mumbling it more to myself than anything. I staggered to my feet, lurched first toward the toilets and then headed for the door. I stumbled my way along, and a very slow-motion escape it was, like a man with one leg that was asleep. Outside: cold air, no rain. Thank god for that. My knees buckled, and I held out my hands to steady myself as though I were surfing the sidewalk. Took another step, stumbled again. This drew the attention of some fellows loitering nearby.

One came over, clamped a hand on my shoulder, said—something. It felt as if I were at the bottom of a well and he was hailing me from the top. He clamped his hand tighter on my shoulder. Grinned fiercely at me. His head was … *square.* Well, a cube, really. It had corners.

He began to steer me toward an alley. I could only make out bits of what he was saying. "This way now … C'mon then …"

I could see two of his friends farther down, waiting on either side. Somewhere in the innermost recesses of my reptilian brain an alarm was sounding, faint but insistent. I pushed away from him.

"What the fuck are you fuckin'—*I don't know you!*" I roared.

"Sure y'do." His friends were waiting.

I was three parts sloshed, true, but three parts drunk is still one part sober, and I slipped away again, shouted in my best John Wayne American, "Don't screw with me, asshole!"

He laughed.

"C'mon," he said, "sure we're all friends here." And he started steering me down the alley again.

And then—a spill of light from the door behind me, a tumble of voices and—"There y'are! Thought we lost you."

It was the Belfast boys come to rescue me.

The fellows in the shadows melted away, and I was stagger-walked back into the bar by my Falls Road protectors.

"We'll get you home," they promised. And they did.

CROSSING THE MOURNES

I left Newry in the early hours, head throbbing, as dawn cast a cold gold light across the church towers.

Stray mongrels nosed through last night's trash. I rolled by PATRICK MURPHY & SONS, POULTRY, RABBIT & GAME EXPORTERS and then walked uphill, past an altar to the Blessed Virgin. Beyond the graves, sunlight was filling the valley.

The walk to Rostrevor contained all of the elements I'd come to expect from the Ulster Way. High hedges and narrow lanes. Loughs pooled in picturesque valleys. Territorially attuned farm dogs. A trail overgrown with thorn trees. A long detour over squelchy fields with much muttering and increasingly inventive blasphemy.

The road ahead rolled across the crest of Craignamona. Fieldstone fences and a smattering of sheep. A few final wildflowers in dabs of yellow, flecks of faint purple. Heathery heights, a flattened summit and the wind, always present.

I had entered the Kingdom of Down, as it was sometimes known, the last of the Six Counties. Down is where the drumlins gather. Imagine your hand running across a tablecloth, and Down would be where the folds bunch up. It was often described as a "basket of eggs," with its rounded hills tightly packed, but the Ulster Way didn't run through County Down's drumlins; it followed the coast instead. Before I could reach the coast, though, I had to get across the Mournes.

Craignamona was only a warm-up for what was coming, but even from there the views were expansive: the Mournes ahead, the sea channel of Carlingford Lough below, the dark mountains of the Republic behind. A mazework of stone fences worthy of the Minotaur criss-crossed the slopes. Cows moved across the open fields above, sheep picked through the labyrinth below. The smell of manure was on the wind, the body odour of a landscape. The road twisted its way down into the valley's cleft. Farmhouses were huddled on the windward side, and a secluded mountain stream was having a conversation with itself. The stream became a river, and the road I was on crossed it, then turned sharply, almost meeting itself on the way back.

An Ulster Way signpost, sun-bleached and half-forgotten, steered me into the next valley, one which opened out onto Carlingford Lough. I could see thick forests on the flank of Thunders Hill, the bald rise of Leckan More behind it. It was Ulster laid out in one sweeping view: barren heights, deep forest, green pastures and the sea.

I passed an assortment of derelict farmhouses in various stages of decay—derelict farmhouses also being a key element of the Ulster landscape. Newer homes began to appear, and the hedges became sculpted, the fields more cultivated. I followed the bungalows in to Rostrevor.

ALTHOUGH SITUATED on the shores of Carlingford Lough, Rostrevor was more of the forest than of the sea. It had an alpine air about it. I liked Rostrevor because it had no flags, no strident, shouting loyalties. The streets were filled with amblers, and the pubs were brightly painted, looking sunny even in the shade. Oak trees in the town square. Church steeples behind. A clock that actually told the correct time, and a "local boy does good" monument on the edge of town that honoured the officer from Rostrevor who was credited with burning the White House during the War of 1812. You had to love a town that took pride in something like that.

Stone homes were draped in elegant understatements of ivy. A stream tumbled through the town's aptly named Fairy Glen. Just beyond lay the wide wooded common of Kilbroney Park. It was wonderful. Families were picnicking on the grass like vignettes in a Victorian photo album. But the Mournes were breathing down my neck, looming in the background. It was distracting, like trying to enjoy high tea knowing that a water buffalo was lurking behind the curtains.

I stayed in a splendid room with cumulus pillows and crisp, clean sheets. The following morning, armed only with a day pack and my own indomitable spirit, I set out to cross the Mourne Mountains. It would be the longest single walk of my trek: overland from Rostrevor to Newcastle, across the roof of Ulster. Twenty-four miles. The days were getting shorter, so I would have to move quickly as well.

Autumn lay heavy across the hills, and a few errant leaves spiralled downward as I entered the forest. Tall cedars creaked on a cold wind, but I was sheltered from the worst of it. Not for long, though. I crossed a stream, felt the path turn steeper. When I came out onto exposed heights, I discovered just how powerful the wind had grown. Clouds in various shades of bruise—jaundiced yellow, dark blue, deepest purple—boiled inward.

I startled some sheep grazing in the ruins of a stone farmhouse, and they scattered, galloping away in full flight. Sheep will gallop if you scare them badly enough—who knew?

The trail plunged into the windbreak of higher forests, but I knew this was only a temporary reprieve. I made an awkward leap across one stream, crossed another on a fallen tree and came out at the stone barrier of Batt's Wall, which ran over the top of the Mournes like a small-scale Great Wall of Ulster. I would rejoin it later. Now, however, I pushed on.

The landscape beyond Batt's Wall grew more rugged. At Mass Stone, where slabs formed a rough altar, I stopped for a communion of chocolate-covered wafers and bottled water. During the dark days of Cromwell, and again under the Penal Laws, Catholic priests had often been forced to perform the Eucharist in secret locales, at altars such as this one.

The stream above Mass Stone looked clear. I was tempted to fill my canteen from it, but you never knew when a bloated dead sheep might be wedged into the water upstream. I'd found my magic tablets, but they gave everything a bleachy taste that defeated the point of the exercise: to drink from the earth-chilled streams directly.

I entered sparser forests, stands of Scotch pine, and finally faced the Mournes head on. Past Rocky Mountain, a broken-toothed pile far from the sensuous curves of drumlins, bedrock slabs now showed through the heather like bones through a hide. I crossed a fence, ran out of trail.

Rain clouds were gathering strength on the far side of the sky. Ahead lay the saddleback of Windy Gap, and beyond that, summit after summit. I headed for the gap as the wind pushed back. I came to a fast-running stream, barely made it across on slip-wet rocks, and there, in this unmarked sea of peat was an Ulster Way signpost—the first I'd seen since I set out that day.

Batt's Wall swooped down through the hollow in Windy Gap, then ran straight up Slieve Moughanmore. Narcissus Batt, my guidebook informed me, was a nineteenth-century Belfast merchant who had planted most of the Scotch pine I'd passed through earlier. Why he built his wall remains something of a mystery, but it did provide a certain clarity to the route. As I followed Batt's Wall across the next two humps, I came to admire his stubborn resolve, his steadfast refusal to acknowledge the lay of the land. I passed sheep bones and ram horns, bleached like Viking helmets, but no actual sheep. Bog must have got them.

The summit of Slieve Moughanmore marked the highest point reached along the Ulster Way, just shy of 1,840 feet. From the top I could see the suture line of Batt's Wall running up the next mountain. The black clouds that had been brooding on my left were now on the move, so I hurried on, boots gummed up with an oily peat that added extra heft to my gait as I threaded my way down, down, down and then up, up, up. The highest and second-highest peaks on the Ulster Way, back to back: Slieve Moughanmore and Pigeon Rock Mountain. I reached the top of the second summit, 1,755 feet, out of breath and wet with sweat, face flushed in spite of the cold.

Around me the muscled mountains of Mourne, all biceps and triceps, shoulder and pectoral, lay knotted and flexed. Slieve Muck, probably the most appropriately named mountain in the range, now lay directly in front of me, with a thin road winding through below. I'd been looking for the Spelga Dam, which was a prominent point of reference on the maps, but it wasn't visible from up here. *These are mountains that can hide a dam in plain sight.* I came down into the valley, and only then did the Spelga reservoir slip into view. Here, the headwaters of the River Bann were "impounded." Having encountered the river first at the sea, and then at Lough Neagh, I had now arrived at its source.

I ate a late lunch, trudged on to the edge of Fofanny Forest, where a waymarker pointed me toward a path that didn't exist. I followed the outer reaches of evergreen to a second smaller dam, where I tightroped across metal pipes just as the first crack of thunder sounded. Beyond Fofanny, a trail cut across the grassy flanks of Meelmore Mountain where a black and white sheepdog was bringing in a herd to his owner's whistled instructions, the sheep flowing like water. I could see snatches of green and a few brave farmhouses below. If it started to pour, I knew where I would be heading and which doors I would be knocking on. The storm clouds had been fighting among themselves, but suddenly, through a tear in the overcast, the sun broke through, disconcertingly low in the sky, drawing colours from the hills: blood and rust, orange on green.

I reached Tollymore Forest just as it was getting dark. Rule #314 of long-distance walking is *Avoid entering forests at dusk.* But an Ulster Way signpost was urging me on, and I had to get through this final stretch of woods if I wanted to reach Newcastle, the seaside resort town waiting for me on the other side.

Among the stands of cedar in Tollymore lay the King's Grave, a Neolithic tomb encircled by trees, their roots twisting around the piled stones to form a crown of thorns all their own. It was said that if you stomped on the King's Grave you would hear an echo come back across the centuries. Rather than disturb any slumbering spirits—it was getting late, and I was alone in a dark forest—I decided to take that on faith. Especially as Tollymore was also the realm of the Blue Lady, a ghostly figure said to haunt the woods above Newcastle.

I reached a clearing and the sun was now a glowing copper coin, low in the sky and about to disappear. The Mourne Mountains are said to have inspired C. S. Lewis's vision of Narnia, that mythical world parallel to our own. I believe it. As the sun dropped into its slot, the mountains seemed to swell, soaking up the last of the light. I had entered Magic Hour, that time of day when the land seemed to be emanating its own illumination. Light without shadows. I had entered Narnia.

The path led back into the forest as I fumbled for my flashlight, hurrying along what I hoped was the right trail, sweeping the flashlight back and forth as I went. It picked up a pair of eyes. A fox? The King's Ghost? Ice Queen of Narnia? The Blue Lady? I swallowed hard, pushed on in what was now a sort of restrained panic. I didn't have my tent with me or my sleeping bag or supper. If I got lost out here … ˙

I crossed two bridges in quick succession and then—lo!—came to an arrow with a sign indicating a "Car Park" ahead. *A car park it is!* Like the wardrobe into the hidden kingdom, the car park would take me out again, into the mundane but comfortably familiar world.

A deer appeared, then another, crossing the trail with dainty steps. In the woods ahead I heard a low grunting noise. When was the rutting season for deer, exactly? The grunting calls grew nearer. I didn't fancy a nightfall encounter with a hormonally enraged stag. Stags can kill. I picked up my pace, hoping I could avoid becoming the object of his affections.

There was a crash in the underbrush, and when I rounded a corner there he was, like a coat-of-arms emblem. I clicked off my flashlight.

Stood perfectly still. He stood still too, blocking my path. The wind was in my favour, a good thing, because I was close enough to hear him breathing. I waited, but he didn't move, so I looked for the nearest patch of thicket should he charge—you don't want to face a stag in the open—then leaned down, quietly scooped up a handful of pebbles, and tossed them toward him as hard as I could. Like a trip wire sprung, he bolted back into the woods.

It really is remarkable: first, that nature would put such enormous antlers on animals that regularly run through the forest, and second, that the animals would do so with such aplomb.

I reached the car park, could see the lights of Newcastle shimmering below, could see the wide arc of beach and the moon caught in the sea beyond.

When I arrived, Newcastle was ablaze with laughter and crowds of people milling about, charting their pirate plans for the evening. Stags of a different order. Newcastle was a holiday town, rife with cafés and hotels, and after the solitude of the Mournes it was like being swept into a carnival. The Joyland Arcade was life itself! The bells and dings and ricocheting pings were a symphony after the empty hills I had crossed to get there. In Newcastle, night was banished. I'd done it: I'd crossed the Mournes from Carlingford Lough to the Irish Sea, and that was cause for celebration. Celebration, of course, being a code word for "more beer!" I needed to get back to Rostrevor somehow, but first there would be burgers and chips and endless pints of lager delivered as if on a conveyor belt. I might just be the first person to walk five hundred miles and gain weight.

"I just got in," I said brightly to the publican as he drew my first lager. "Just now."

"Is that so?"

"From Rostrevor. I walked. Overland."

He looked at me. "There's easier ways, you know."

ONE LAST MOUNTAIN

Newcastle billed itself as the gateway to the Mournes, and the town itself sat in the granite shadow of Slieve Donard, a massive rise of rock, at 2,789 feet the highest peak in Northern Ireland.

Returning to Newcastle with my full pack the next afternoon, I found a room in a widow's guest house. Debated tackling Slieve Donard. The Ulster Way didn't go up Donard, but how could I come this close and not?

My knees were shot, but after a full Ulster Fry and a mummy-wrap of tensor bandages around my various aching joints, I was ready to reach for the very top of Ulster. Donard would be my farewell mountain. After that, it would be mainly coastal paths and road walking all the way to Belfast. So I hobbled forth at dawn, through streets wide and narrow, moaning "Muscles so sore, alive, alive-o." A cold wind was coming in off the bay, and Newcastle looked like a living room after a party, but no matter—I was heading for loftier climes.

Something was wrong.

I sensed that right away, because when I got to the head of the trail I saw—*other walkers*, the first assembly of hikers since that pocket of backpackers in Dungiven. I was taken aback. There were Australians being boisterous and Frenchmen being droll. There were Americans being American, and Englishmen smiling tightly, fixated, as always, on the behaviour of the Americans. There was a band of Spaniards and a loose affiliation of Scots. There was a gathering of Germans with crisp boots and walking sticks (you just knew their laces were exactly the same length). And there was me. I was, undoubtedly, the least enthusiastic person there.

I set off ahead of the pack only to be passed, one by one, by every single person who was at the car park that day, including members of the Pensioners Rambling Association of Some Such. The Germans were particularly German about it, crowding past me at the first bottleneck available, all but elbowing me to one side as they strode off into the forested valley ahead. I slogged on, my knees and back creaking. Too many miles. Too many years, as well. If I were a car, the warranty would have long ago expired.

Another pair of hikers shot past, men my age, walking at a light-footed pace, with aluminum walking poles swinging. The years had been easier on them. I hadn't even seen these guys at the car park. They were probably just waking up when I embarked on the trail.

And I was on a trail, a real trail, not an imaginary line on a map, but a route well marked and well maintained.

As I came out of the forest, Donard was startlingly close. It was a damp, grey day elsewhere, perhaps, but I could see a halo of light behind the mountain, and I picked up my pace, determined to catch the sun before it was swallowed by clouds. I spotted the two hikers who had passed me earlier, resting before the final assault. They watched me approach and then, just as I drew near, they swept off again. It was like a particularly lopsided game of tag. *Slow and steady never won this race, I can tell you.* With every twist of the ascent, as I tortoised along, I would catch a glimpse of them ahead—and then they would be gone.

Leaning into the mountain, ears popping, wind stinging my eyes, I neared the final stretch. A pair of hikers poked their heads over the edge, spotted me below. A young couple, wind-creased and grinning. Scottish, from the accent. The boy was wearing a jester's cap.

"Come up!" they cried. "Loads of room. It's brilliant!"

And it was. The last bit almost did me in, but I made it. I stood atop the highest peak in Ulster in an operatic mood, chest squared, jaw to the wind.

"You just missed it," said the Scottish girl cheerfully. "Sun was out. It was pure dead brilliant."

But even in the wet grey, the panorama was—comprehensive. All four nations of the United Kingdom were visible: Scotland, England, Wales, and Northern Ireland. It was a heady, almost dizzying view. All four pieces of the puzzle, with Ulster at my feet, the Republic at my back and the hammered silver of the Irish Sea and the North Channel below. It was the high point of my walk, in every sense.

The two hikers I'd been pursuing, in the much the same way a bear on a unicycle might pursue a pair of gazelles, were waiting at the top. They waved me over.

"You made it," they said.

I nodded and folded myself into a sitting position. Chugged some water.

"You've been up Slieve Donard before," I said, more as an accusation than anything.

"We have," they admitted. "Aye."

We shared some squares of chocolate, marvelled at the view. John and Charlie were curious about why I was hiking alone. When I told them I was walking the Ulster Way, was on the final lap, they congratulated me.

"We've seen those signs," they said. "Have often wondered about that. What's it like, then?"

"The Ulster Way?" How to sum it up? "Well," I said. "To give you an example, there's a beautiful walk by St. Patrick's Chair. And there's another beautiful path along the Blackwater River between Milltown and Benburb Castle. In between those is twenty-five miles of road walking."

"Aye?"

"Aye. I think the people who designed the Ulster Way were so enamoured of the idea of one continuous, unbroken circuit that they tried to force everything into a single route, even when it didn't fit. And yet—" In spite of the scabies and the food poisoning and the endless soul-numbing planted forests and the near-death highway encounters, in spite of all that—I thought of the rolling hills and undulating landscapes, the unspoiled beaches, the scenic valleys, the windswept heights. *To walk Ulster?* Yes. Absolutely. *To walk the Ulster Way?* That's a harder question to answer.

I looked across to the distant Sperrins. "This is a beautiful country," I said, aware of how inadequate that was. I thought about the sectarian gang tags, the broken bodies, the UDA, the IRA, the police barracks and the military watchtowers. "It's—it's a land of contrasts,"

I said. But that too seemed inadequate. It was more than mere contrast, it was—"Jarring," I said. "That's the word I'm looking for."

"Jarring?"

"Yes," I said. "You walk into some picturesque little village, and you think, 'What a lovely spot,' and then there's this godawful monstrosity of an RUC station with razor wire and everything." I had to laugh. "I mean, Jayzuz, can you imagine being a cop in Northern Ireland? What kind of crazy does it take to sign up for that gig?"

They nodded. "Aye, it's unfortunate. No choice, really, with the RUC under fire like that."

"I suppose. So what do you guys do?"

"We're police officers."

Shit. "Really?"

"Really."

"RUC?"

They nodded.

Double shit. "I mean, you sort of have to, don't you?" I said, backpedalling like mad, fully aware that I was atop a mountain with nowhere to go. "Barricading your police stations, right? I mean, it's understandable, it's just, you know, for people who aren't *used* to seeing that kind of thing, it's just sort of—"

They laughed. "Don't apologize. You were just being honest."

John, the leaner of the two, had been with the RUC for twelve years, and before that the air force. He was in his thirties, married with two kids. His friend Charlie was more solidly built, a few years younger than John, married with two children as well. Charlie was now stationed in central Belfast, and I had the feeling that the hikes they went on were John's initiative, that Charlie would have been just as happy spending his days off at a pub. I had the utmost sympathy. Neither of them seemed like the sort of slobbering monsters that Republican hardliners liked to depict. The whole time I talked to John and Charlie, I didn't see them bayonet a single baby—or even poke one, for that matter.

"How'd you two meet?" I asked.

"Just bad luck, really," John replied. "We met in police training. We were stationed together in Newry."

I did the math in my head. They had joined the force *after* the mortar attack at Newry killed nine officers. That hadn't dissuaded them. No wonder the IRA couldn't win. They were up against their fellow Ulstermen: an immovable object against an implacable force. I realized as well that just a few nights earlier I'd been drinking with men who might well know of, or even be related to, the people who had launched the Newry attack. I thought it wise not to mention this to John and Charlie. I did mention Drumcree, however, and how the Ulster Way avoided South Armagh. Strangely enough, they were as disappointed to hear this as the patrons at that Republican bar in Newry had been.

"That's a shame," they said. "There's beautiful countryside in South Armagh."

And as for Drumcree?

"That was really a no-win situation for us," said John. No matter what the police did, they were attacked for it, with each side convinced the other was being favoured. "Aye," said John. "I knew people who set their alarm, woke up early, and drove twenty miles just to be offended."

I was talking with members of one of the most embattled, honoured, vilified and highly decorated police forces in the world. A force that had been targeted by INLA and the IRA, had been attacked by Loyalists and Republicans alike, had been on the front line of an undeclared civil war. And yet they seemed so blasé about it. If I was looking for lurid, I wouldn't find it with John and Charlie.

"Don't think I've ever even drawn my gun," said Charlie. "Let alone used it."

John couldn't remember ever drawing his gun, either. Though he did remember a funny domestic dispute in which a wife had smashed a bottle of Worcester sauce against her husband. The broken glass had hit the man's neck, and it looked serious. Looked like an artery. "Turned out it was mainly the Worcester," he said.

It was easy to forget, with the fortresses and armoured cars and the constant threat of attack, that the RUC was still a working police force, and that the everyday crime rate in Northern Ireland was among the lowest in Western Europe. Officers with the RUC had to be trained in heightened awareness, nonetheless, had to hone their observational acumen. They had to be able to make an immediate assessment of a situation, no matter how innocuous it might seem, and they had to do it in a heartbeat. How had they read me? I wondered.

"Did I look kind of suspicious?" I asked. "Maybe a little rough? Did you think, *Better keep an eye on this guy*?"

They laughed. "No."

Oh. "Well, did I at least look like a seasoned hiker, a man from the hills?"

No. They figured I was a first-time visitor. "You were taking photos of everything, not just the views."

They had noticed my erratic pace as well. Slow and laboured, instead of well timed and well oiled. They certainly hadn't pegged me as someone who was about to complete the Ulster equivalent of Mount Everest.

I was crushed. "Really? I don't look like a hardened long-distance hiker?"

"Well." They decided to go easy on me. "Maybe." But they were just saying that, I could tell.

We parted ways at the top of Slieve Donard. They gave me a contact number for when I got to Belfast. "We'll buy you a Guinness, celebrate your victory."

John and Charlie returned the way they'd come. I went down the other side, following another fieldstone wall toward a sea the colour and texture of pockmarked pewter. Picking my way over rocks the size of fists and footballs, I entered a geometric landscape, one composed largely of right angles: an abandoned quarry cut from the cliffs with a waterfall misting through. Here's a word we need: one that describes the inwardly smug feeling you get when meeting someone who is just setting out, huffing and puffing, as you come down.

"Hello."

"Hi."

"Hello."

I arrived at Bloody Bridge, site of an early religious massacre (all of Ireland is the site of an early religious massacre), and I followed a trail through thorny bracken out onto the coast road. I had crossed Slieve Donard, front to back, top to bottom.

Unfortunately, I now faced a long walk back to Newcastle under wet skies. I started along, not bothering to hold out a thumb, expecting no favours and receiving none. Then a van pulled over. "Newcastle, *ja*?"

When you are forced to rely on the kindness of Germans, you've reached a nadir of sorts, I suppose. Still, they were very sweet, and they dropped me off right at the front door of my guest house. The whole time, I didn't see them bayonet a single baby.

HORSESHOE BAY

I'd been thinking about pieces that don't quite come together, that don't quite fit, whether they be the pieces of a puzzle, the countries of a kingdom or the events of a life.

The photograph of my grandfather at the estate, before the orphanage—how did that figure in the larger picture?

On the open plains of the Canadian West, my grandfather had found a larger canvas on which to paint his life. Clean air, hefty meals and old-fashioned farm work had caused him to shoot up in stature. He later moved to the city, enrolled in night courses, lived at the Y, drove taxis, slaughtered beef. He took up swimming, learned to dive from great heights and toured the prairies with the YMCA sports teams—soccer, basketball, gymnastics. He even sold Fuller brushes to farmhouse wives for a while. In fact, it was on one such trip that he met a girl of seventeen. A smile, a fluttering of eye contact. I've always thought my grandmother had the loveliest of names: Lily Fair.

She was cooking for the threshing crews on her brother's farm when Dick Bell from Belfast showed up. My grandmother always remembered the moment she first met the thin Irish expat. "I was cooking farm meals, and here was this beautiful man, filled with graces."

The travelling salesman and the farmer's daughter. Except this was a story that ended not in a ribald punchline but in seven years of courtship, and then marriage.

My grandmother was acutely aware of the contrast between Dick and her own family, and she remembered how mortified she felt when he first came for dinner. His manners were impeccable, her nine siblings not so much. Her brothers were particularly bad, jostling in, grabbing the food as soon as grace was said. "Now, boys," said their mother. "We have company." They stopped. One of the brothers offered my grandfather a bun off his plate. "Sorry. Here you go."

Seven years of courtship. Seven years and hundreds of love letters. Bundled together, bound with ribbon, these were letters my mother and her sister would carefully untie and read, secretly, for years afterward.

Lily Fair got her teaching certificate, and Dick Bell gained his papers as a telephone engineer, which put him at the cutting edge of technology.

They were an upwardly mobile young couple, pitching woo at the height of the Roaring Twenties. It was a good time for courtship. Bumper crops and dance halls, and telephone wires going in everywhere. Lil and Dick danced the Charleston. My grandfather was so tall he could swing his leg clear over her as she went under, a fancy dance move helped by my grandmother's small but curvy frame. "I had Mae West's measurements," she used to joke. "But not quite the height."

My grandfather always took it as a point of pride that Lil was the first and only girl he ever kissed. Years later, when one of my brothers asked our grandmother if the same was true for her, she just smiled, said, "No." She'd been kissed before.

Those Charleston dance hall days ended in drought and economic collapse. My grandparents were married, had two daughters a few years apart. It was just before their second daughter—Lorna, my mother—was born that my grandfather lost his job. The telephone company he'd been working for folded, and he and his young family found themselves in the worst of all possible worlds: the dust bowl of southern Saskatchewan, in the sun-baked centre of the Great Depression. The despair was parching. The promise of the New World had turned to dust and blown away, topsoil spiralling into the skies. There were times my grandmother feared her husband was becoming suicidal.

It might have ended there, with a lonely loss of fortune, another family laid low. But like the *deus ex machina* he so often was, my grandfather's brother Bill sent for him. *Come west, farther west*, was the message. Bill was now in British Columbia, on the misty shores of the Pacific Northwest. Why, the climate was almost Irish!

Bill and his wife helped Dick and Lil get back on their feet. My grandfather bought an interest in a small tugboat, took up a life of beachcombing, started scavenging the coastlines, hauling in logs that had broken free from booms. One of my mother's earliest memories was of living on a boat at East Hope Wharf in Burrard Inlet. And there was her poor mother, Lily Bell, daughter of the drylands, not knowing how to swim.

My mother almost drowned between those boats, slipping through a gap as my grandmother lunged for her, catching hold only of the little red hat my mother was wearing. It was tied under her chin and it held for a moment, then slipped off. My grandmother lunged again, grabbed hold of her daughter's collar. She was straddling the gap between two boats, trying desperately to pull her child out of the water as the boats moved apart. My mother's six-year-old sister was screaming for help on the deck, while under the water, eyes wide open, my mother watched her little red hat float away. She was four or five years old, and she loved that hat. She stretched out for it, slipped away from her mother, sank to the bottom, lungs filling with water ... Two men had heard the screams and they came running, hooked my mother with a pole, brought her up dead. One of them knew enough about artificial resuscitation to clear her lungs, though, and my mother spewed up salt water, then passed out.

When her father returned, he held her. "I saw an angel," she told him. Today, my mother no longer believes angels brought her back. She did see a light; she remembers that clearly. "A near-death experience leaves a great imprint on you," she says. "But it leaves an even greater imprint on your parents."

Perhaps it came from his having almost lost her, but she and her father had a deep bond after that. She was always, I suspect, his favourite.

World War II found my grandfather's training back in high demand. As a qualified telephone technician, he was hired on by Bell Telephone and quickly became their top troubleshooter. Soon after, he bought his wife a proper house in North Burnaby, at 4219 Triumph Street. *Triumph Street*. I often wondered: if my grandfather could have gone back in time, found that sickly orphan sobbing as his brother's ship left Belfast, if he could have found that child, told him that one day he would live in Canader, on Triumph Street, would it have assuaged the pain?

Just seven days after they arrived on Triumph, my grandmother gave birth to twin boys. My grandfather was eventually promoted to regional supervisor, and he oversaw the installation of automatic phone exchanges in the Vancouver area. The first direct-dialled phone call in the City of Vancouver, without an operator as middleman, was a test call from my grandfather to my grandmother. He often took one of his kids along with him when he had to work on the phone lines. They remember him doing intensely delicate, very precise repairs with his huge hands.

The Bell Telephone Company magazine once ran a cover that featured portraits of all the Bells who worked for them. Among them was my grandfather. But was he really a Bell? Wasn't that simply the name the orphanage had assigned him? Or was there more to it than that? Was the name "Bell" some kind of clue to who he really was?

If my grandfather was originally a gypsy street urchin, he was a very well-mannered one. Although good-humoured by nature, he insisted that his children eat their meals with their backs perfectly straight and both feet flat on the floor. They had to use the proper cutlery with the proper dish, had to pass plates from left hand to right, then chew slowly, with hands folded on their laps. He sometimes used a yardstick to check his daughters' posture. (In direct response to this, my mom let us eat like wild jackals. I still don't know which fork is for salad and which is to scratch your head with.) Sometimes, when their mother had baked a pie, he would cut it in purposely uneven pieces and then hand them out. If he caught one of his kids checking to see who got the bigger piece, he took that child's piece of pie back.

"The lesson he was trying to teach," said my mother, "was never to compare what you had to others, never to feel sorry for yourself—or to crow about good fortune."

My grandfather sang, had a beautiful, velvet voice. "He could always make us cry," my mother told us. "All the sentimental Irish tunes, 'Danny Boy' in particular." He loved language as well. "We had this big dictionary. It was more important than the family Bible. It had its own special table. After dinner, Dad would open it up, and we would look up words, make sentences."

Although his clothes were always neatly pressed, my grandfather didn't own a lot of them. He had only one good suit. It was the suit he was married in, the one he wore to his children's weddings, the one he was buried in. "He never really changed in size or shape," my mother said.

My mother got involved with a man much less immutable, someone who changed size, direction and alibi almost daily. She was in Edmonton, alone with her baby Danny, when she heard that her father's health was fading.

"I had been having dreams that he was going to die," my mother recalls. "I borrowed money and flew out, spent a month with him."

Her last memories of her father are of him hugging her goodbye as she was about to board the plane back to Edmonton, of choking back her tears, of wishing she could be in two places at once.

After his daughter left, my grandfather became nostalgic. "Let's revisit old places, Lil," he said to my grandmother. They took a ferry from Horseshoe Bay to Bowen Island, visited beaches they hadn't been to in years.

On a Saturday, two weeks after my mother got back, the phone rang and she knew. She knew before she even answered.

My grandfather died just a few days before his birthday. He was turning fifty-seven, and my grandmother was in the kitchen decorating a cake for him. Bill and his wife were coming over for an early celebration, and she was hurrying about getting ready. My grandfather had been in the garden, but he came in and sat down in the living room. He was making strange noises; there was a rattle in his chest. My grandmother came out, realized he was trouble. She ran for the phone. There was a fire station just a few blocks from the house. She called, and they were there within minutes, but it was too late.

On her last visit, my mom and her dad had talked late into the night about life and what lay on the other side. "He said he didn't think it mattered whether Heaven or Hell existed, that it was what we did here that mattered. The effect we had on others, on our children, our children's children," my mother recalled.

Bill was devastated by his brother's death. My grandmother returned to teaching.

"She missed Dad," my mom said. "Toward the end of her life, she was dreaming about him a lot. She was looking forward to seeing him again. You have to realize, she was a widow a heck of a lot longer than she was ever a wife."

He wasn't the first boy she kissed, but he was the last.

Part Eight

THE INNER SHORE

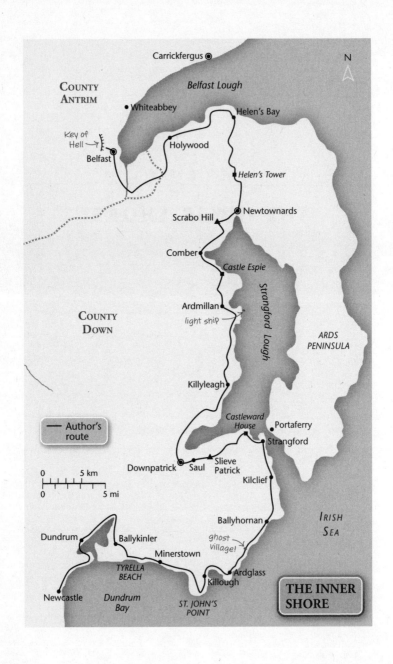

Carrickfergus

COUNTY
ANTRIM

Belfast Lough

Whiteabbey

Helen's Bay

Key of
Hell

Holywood

Belfast

Helen's Tower

Scrabo Hill

Newtownards

Comber

Castle Espie

Ardmillan

light ship

Strangford Lough

COUNTY
DOWN

ARDS
PENINSULA

Killyleagh

*Castleward
House*

Portaferry

Author's
route

Strangford

0   5 km

Downpatrick

Saul

Slieve
Patrick

0   5 mi

Kilclief

*IRISH
SEA*

Ballyhornan

Dundrum

Ballykinler

*ghost
village!*

Minerstown

*TYRELLA
BEACH*

Ardglass

Killough

Newcastle

*Dundrum
Bay*

*ST. JOHN'S
POINT*

N

**THE INNER
SHORE**

NEWCASTLE TO BELFAST
via Strangford Lough

It was good to be back on the water.

Since turning inland at Castlerock, I hadn't walked beside the sea again till now. Thunder-sighs of waves rolled in. Seagulls reeled, and the air was heavy with the cold promise of rain. High tide on loose shale. With Newcastle huddled low along the shore, and Slieve Donard pressing in from behind, I followed the coast to the sand dunes and marram grass of the Murlough Nature Reserve.

The advancing sea pushed me up into the dunes and onto a moist jungle track thick with mossy trees and rampant growth of buckthorn and heather, the air cool and steamy at the same time. A forest built on sand. Remarkable. We think of sand as representing the transitory nature of things, yet many of these Murlough dunes, rising sixty feet or more, were at least six thousand years old.

I came to the estuarine alcove of Dundrum's inner bay, a tidal lagoon connected to the sea by the narrowest of channels. I could hear the sound of gunfire, dull thumps followed by duller echoes. *Surely people aren't hunting in a nature reserve?* A muddy sheepdog appeared with a red-faced woman trailing behind, trying her best to keep up. It wasn't immediately clear who was taking whom for a walk.

She smiled.

"Brave day," I said, still not sure what that meant.

"Aye," she said. "If only they'd stop shooting."

An army firing range was located on the other side of the bay. "Target practice," she said. "Not hitting many of them, by the sounds of it."

"Is that what that was?" I said. "Here I thought someone was hunting ducks with a cannon."

A beautiful, three-arch stone bridge took me across the inner bay and onto a tree-lined avenue, which led into Dundrum. I entered under an honour guard of oak and passed the Rapunzel tower of the St. Donard Church of Ireland.

Dundrum was a fine place, even with the firing range nearby and the coastal traffic that funnelled through. The shops were tasteful and understated, the shopkeepers here having shown more restraint than those in Newcastle, where garish illuminated plastic signs had often been slapped up onto long-suffering Victorian storefronts.

The great attraction of Dundrum, though, was its medieval castle, dramatically situated on its hill above the village. This was one of a string of coastal fortresses built by the Norman invaders during the Conquest of Ulster. My old friend John de Courcy had built the first stronghold at Dundrum in 1180 only to have his position—and his castle—usurped by his sometime ally and oftentimes rival Hugh de Lacy. (John de Courcy and Hugh de Lacy had a "stormy" relationship, much like Shane O'Neill and Sorley Boy MacDonnell.)

The round central keep was a rarity in Ireland, where most castles were square and solid, and though the stone cylinder of Dundrum Castle was now a hollow shell, stairs spiralled up to the highest edge. Feeling dizzy and precariously poised, I looked out from the top of the walls to the contoured coastlines below. A splendidly strategic location for a castle. Those Norman invaders, they knew what they were doing.

Across the bay I could still hear the muffled thumps of the firing range ordinance, sounding like weapons of older wars. A strange continuity was at play.

Fine day, if only they'd stop shooting.

SEA AND FOAM

The beaches of Northern Ireland must be among the best-kept secrets in Europe: slender arcs of soft, blond sand, shallow waters, unspoiled, unruffled.

Having followed the deep inlet of Dundrum Bay along the trail of an abandoned rail line, past fences dripping with dulse left there to dry, I came to Ballykinler, which was essentially an army base with a town attached—though "town" might have been too ambitious a word for a collection of stucco homes, a beauty parlour, a Chinese take-away and a gas station/convenience store/post office. That gas station combo more or less *was* Ballykinler. The guns, however, were much closer now.

Beyond the bungalows of Ballykinler lay Tyrella Beach, a mile and a half arc of sand with waves rolling in. And not a soul around. Tyrella was admirably underdeveloped: public washrooms, a handful of holiday cabins in the grassy dunes nearby, a faded sign for the summertime Punch and Judy Show, and that was about it. No towering hotels, no tourist emporiums, just sand and sea and sky— and the ever-present mass of the Mountains of Mourne behind. *And yes, they really do sweep down to the sea.*

It was a blustery day. I'd moved my base inland, to Downpatrick, and was now travelling light. I slipped off my day pack, feeling unencumbered, unconstrained. But having a beach all to yourself is not as romantic as it sounds. I took off my boots, peeled off the socks, turned up my trouser legs, waded through cold water, felt lonelier for having done it. Only one set of footprints along the wet sand.

I would have continued along the beach at Tyrella, but I could see the rocky headlands of Rathmullan Point blocking the way, and I was forced back onto the road instead. At Minerstown, the houses were strung along the road like laundry on the line. Minerstown had a tavern but no school, and no church or post office as far as I could tell. They had their priorities right in Minerstown. Unfortunately, the bar was not yet open, so I pushed on. I could see the barbershop pole of the St. John's Point lighthouse ahead, and I set my trajectory accordingly. St. John's Point, a knot of land that caught the current as it swept past, creating undertows and dangerous eddies, had littered the sea floor with shipwrecks. Waves were coming in, higher now, marble-veined with foam, curling up, crashing in, spraying the shore road with a fine mist. Rooftops along the way were wet with moss and mould.

On the stone-strewn coast, I came upon a small grey church looking miserable and damp, with a salt-eaten, sea-stained graveyard beside. A rusted wrought-iron Celtic cross stuck out of the grass like a sword handle.

The road curved into trees, but even that offered no respite from the wind. The hedges were brow-beaten by it; younger trees were cowed in supplication, the older ones breaking like dry bone. A crack of limbs sent branches onto the road in front of me, and soon after a tractor trundled past, pulling a full load of earth-brown potatoes. The tractor veered to avoid the debris, and a potato bounced off, rolled across. I picked it up, turned it over; it had bruised green where it hit. It was an image that has stayed with me ever since: a country that bruises green.

At a T in the road, a warning was posted beside an open gate: "Beware of Dogs." I noted the use of the plural, not dog but *dogs*, and I shovelled myself past, leaning into the wind, sure that any guard dogs would be huddled inside their guard dog homes, but not wanting to take any chances. Out of the trees, I was back into the full brunt of it.

I ate my lunch—such as it was—among the ruins of an ancient pre-Norman church, using the rubble-fit walls as a windbreak. An ancient *bullaun* stone, flat with oval hollow, provided the font for a holy well. From the ruined church, I pushed on toward the end of the peninsula, where a lone farmhouse stood. The road beyond was private, running down to the black and yellow bumblebee stripes of the lighthouse on its rocky headland. The Ulster Way turned left to follow the coast along a public footpath.

The land was coming undone, a tapestry unravelling. When I stumbled, rocks rolled down like human heads. But wind without rain is exhilarating, and I picked my way along the storm-raked coast enjoying the cymbal crash of waves. Lightning strafed the sky, soundless in its distance. I could feel static electricity tingling the hair on my forearms. The sea was alive. It swelled and fell, heaved and rolled. Mountains moved along it. Large ships disappeared, then reappeared.

With my face billowing like a test pilot in a centrifuge machine, and me almost lifting off at times from sudden gusts, I became aware, in a vague sort of way, that boats were streaming toward the harbour, hightailing it in, it would seem, and the thought occurred to me that perhaps a steeply exposed headland was not the wisest place to be when a gale hit. I picked up my pace—or tried to. With the wind against me, it was like running in deep water. I felt like a bad street mime. *Man, falling off a cliff.*

Land and sea were arm wrestling, and I was caught in the middle, trying not to choose sides. The path ran low to the water, and the cymbal crashes were coming in faster and higher. Waves were foaming the air. One seethed onto the path, swirling around my boots. The next one hit me hard, almost took my legs out from under me, and I scrambled straight up the embankment, figuring a possible tumble was better than a certain dousing. When I got to the top I flopped down, heart racing. Below, the path I had been on was submerged. The water churned over it, then slid away. The path reappeared. I looked out, saw a wall of water bearing down. It slammed into the cliffs below. It would have hit me full force in the chest had I still been down there, would have, undoubtedly, dragged me into the sea. The next wave came in even higher.

"Holy shit," I said softly.

I looked out at the sea, tried to picture where I would have been right about now, arms flailing in the undertow, mouth open, swallowing sea water. I wondered how long it would have taken for my body and day pack to wash ashore. *Death by misadventure.* I had avoided it not by guile or a cunning sense of timing but through sheer, unadulterated dumb luck.

"Think I'll stay up top," I said.

IF YOU'D ASKED your granny to knit a town, she would have knitted Killough. Even in heavy wind, it reminded me of a doily: small cottages with leafy sycamore trees lining the main avenue.

Having narrowly escaped being swept away, I'd walked across the fields until I found an old coastguard station, then followed what was known as Fisherman's Row down to Killough harbour. It was a pretty village with several pubs. I stopped in at a shop, picked up a pamphlet, discovered that Rex McCandless, "inventor of the McCandless flying Autogyro," was buried in the Killough cemetery, and asked the clerk if there was anywhere I might get a cup of really strong coffee. Having survived St. John's Point, I needed something more than milky tea.

"Your lucky day," he said. "It's our annual coffee."

Annual coffee?

"For charity. Buns and sweets, at the hall at the end of the street. Coffee for cancer."

They were indeed selling sticky buns and homemade treats, along with dainty hors d'oeuvres of cheese and fish pinned to bread like edible brooches. Muddy of boot, wild of hair, with two days' stubble and a wind-seared face, I felt like Caliban at a cocktail party. The ladies of Killough were very gracious nonetheless, waving away my offers of money. I was "an out-of-town guest" who had come all the way from America just to attend. The awkward self-consciousness I felt was the price one paid for free coffee and buns, sweetly proffered.

A young woman with chestnut hair and the most amazing dimples—dimples a boy might fall into and never come out of—laughed when I told her I'd walked in from St. John's Point. "You're mad," she said. "There were warnings. You shouldn't have been out there." She thought it was funny as well that I had arrived on what she described as "the highlight social event of the year" in Killough.

Martina worked at the town's oyster farm but lived farther north, on the other side of Strangford Narrows. When she found out I still had to walk over to Ardglass and then somehow get back to Downpatrick, she offered me a lift.

"I'll pick you up later in Ardglass," she said. "At the harbour."

She had to get back to work, and I had to finish my walk. I zipped up, pulled on my backpack and walked out into gale-force winds. She was still laughing when I left.

THE WALK FROM the tidal harbour of Killough to the deep-water inlet at Ardglass took me past a small middle cove, one known as Coney Island (confusingly so, as the hook of land was still attached to the shore). In Ardglass, the bay was sloshing about like a load of dirty laundry. In spite of its ruggedly famous golf course, Ardglass was a working fishing community, one of the few left in Northern Ireland, and its shops and homes were jumbled around its steep harbour with no real central square. The bay, I supposed, served as one. The golf course had cliffs that plunged directly into crevices, where many lost balls—and on occasion, players—had fallen.

Ardglass also had no fewer than seven castles.

"Just tower houses, really," said the man at the shop when I asked about it. "Most of 'em are quite small, y'know."

But still, seven castles? Why wasn't this being promoted more? *SEE the AMAZING Seven Castles of Ardglass!!*

"Well," he said, "would hate fer tourists to come an' be disappointed, like. Quite small, most of 'em."

I spent the blustery afternoon checking off the various castles, and I can say the cumulative effect was quite stunning. True, the "castle" perched right at the harbour was more of a guardhouse than a proper fortification, but overall the castles of Ardglass attested to the importance the harbour had long held. The centrepiece of the collection was an intact fifteenth-century tower house known as Jordan's Castle. (The distinction between a castle and a fortified tower house is largely semantic. This was very much a castle—compact, but a castle nonetheless.) In 1429, as English control crumbled along the outer edges of the Pale, Henry VI offered a ten-pound subsidy to any loyal liege who would build a castle on his land. These "ten-pound castles," as they were known, were built to a standard pattern: square or rectangular, three or four floors high, with doorways guarded by turrets and overhanging "murder holes," a windowless ground floor used for storage, open-roomed living quarters above, narrow-slit windows and latrines fitted into the corners of the walls—long-drop toilets, as it were. Compact and easy to defend, these were "no frills" castles; just inner keeps, really, standing on their own without a moat or outlying walls. The tower houses of County Down dot the coastline even now, Jordan's Castle being among the best preserved.

Jordan's and the harbour guardhouse aside, Ardglass's other castles, of various ages and lineages, included King's Castle, which was now a seniors' residence; Horn Castle, which had been incorporated into the golf course clubhouse; Cowd Castle, which was perched nearby above the links; Margaret's Castle, which was a B&B; and finally Isabella's Tower, a nineteenth-century folly I'd passed on my way in, set on a grassy mound outside of town.

With rain now spitting and winds still raging, I ducked into the marina—and found myself in the middle of a drama unfolding.

The people inside the main building were watching the harbour, waiting for word from a ship that hadn't made it in. The skipper was young, I gathered, and in the snippets of conversation the tension was palpable.

"Winds were bad, aye, but that squall came out'a nowhere."

"He lost his net and shelter, is what I heard."

"He's only eighteen."

"Was ten miles out when he radioed in. Haven't heard a peep since."

"On the fritz, maybe."

Waves were lashing the far side of the bay, even with its protective seawalls.

"Aye, ten miles out, last I heard. And caught in this, mind."

And then: "*There!*"

A small boat appeared, limping into port as if from battle.

"Conrad's in!"

The wave of relief that followed brought tears and smiles to the crowd. *Conrad was in.* I had been caught up in it as well. The man next to me clasped my shoulder and grinned at me, and I grinned back just as wide.

Martina arrived soon after. Still teary-eyed and smiling, I stuffed myself into her car. I was soon whisked to Downpatrick. Martina had gone well out of her way, so I offered her dinner to say thanks, though truth be told I was aching for company; I'd been dining alone for quite some time now. We had a splendid meal in an old coach house restaurant, but I fear the wine and the sheer novelty of having a dining companion may have gone to my head. As the evening wore on I heard myself speaking at great length about every manner of topic, waving my hands and expounding away. I'd like to think that Martina was as concerned as I was about the appalling lack of waymarkers on forestry roads in Northern Ireland, but I am harassed by doubts. Because Martina lived on the other side of Strangford Lough, she had to make sure she caught the last ferry over, though I imagine by the end of the meal she was prepared to swim if she had to.

I'd been using a guest house on Scotch Street as my base, and it was late by the time I got in. When I did, I entered another intense drama, this one involving me. The lady of the house came hurrying out when she heard my key in the door, breathing a huge sigh. "Oh thank goodness," she said. "I was just about to ring the police. Cyril said not to worry, but you'd mentioned you would be walking St. John's Point."

I assured her, "It was far too windy. I didn't go anywhere near the coast. I stayed well back."

I mean, really. Did I look like an idiot?

A SENSE OF INTRUSION

The Famine of 1845–49 was Ireland's Lamentations and Exodus rolled into one. A million died during the Great Hunger. A million more fled, most of them to America, in a mass migration that still stands at the core of the Irish diaspora.

The *scientific* cause of the disaster was a fungus that rotted potatoes in the fields, turning them into black mush and filling the air with "a fearful stench." The *cultural* cause was poverty—and a rural population that was overwhelmingly dependent on a single staple. Grains were cash crops; potatoes were left to farm workers to feed their families on. The *political* cause was ideological. It was an age of laissez-faire economics, of faith in a magically self-correcting marketplace. These three elements—fungus, poverty and ideology—came together to devastating effect.

Following the armed rebellions of 1798, Ireland had been forced into a full political union. This new "United Kingdom," born in 1801, would provide great benefits to Ireland, tying the island to the enlightened affluence of Great Britain. That was the claim, anyway. But as the devastation of the famine spread, London's hostile indifference to the plight of the Irish became cruelly evident. The market must run its course, with minimal involvement from the government. As the very man in charge of Irish Relief put it, "Ireland must be left to the operation of natural causes."

What began as a potato blight ended in mass graves and bodies abandoned on the roadside. Entire families starved to death, their mouths bleeding green from them trying to eat grass. Landlords began to evict the poorest of them, knocking down hovels and leaving people to die in the ditch or to crowd into poorhouses where disease and epidemic were rife: typhus fevers, starvation deliriums, dysentery, gangrene, blindness, cholera. "Sorrow, suffering and mute despair seem to have taken possession of their souls. Their feelings are blunted, their ideas confused and their energies paralyzed ... They have more the appearance of ghosts than living beings." That was how one report described the effects of mass starvation on the people. Others spoke of "emaciated creatures," "moving skeletons." And all the while, food was *leaving* Ireland by the shipload. Only the peasant staple, the potato, had been blighted; grains continued to be exported, sent to English ports, often under armed guard. It was the "invisible hand" of the marketplace in action, and a shining example of the many benefits of Union.

A million dead, a million more gone. But numbers alone do not convey the horrors of the Great Famine; numbers never do. The Famine Village above Ardglass provided a haunting testament to what had happened. I'd heard about it from the shopkeeper in Ardglass, who had circled the spot on my Ordnance Survey map.

I did the next leg of the Ulster Way in reverse, walking south so that I could end the day in Ardglass rather than on some exposed stretch of coast far from any public phone or bus service. The sea had settled down, was no longer actively trying to kill me, and I picked up the trail at Ballyhornan, which was really just a pub and a scattering of fishing cottages turned into summer homes. On the green plateau of Gun's Island, cattle grazed beneath a lighthouse.

It took me several hours to reach the Famine Village. I made my way from one jagged cove to the next, past derelict fishing shacks on sea-blackened rocks below. The tide was out, and the coast was tortuous and tricky. I came to Benboy Hill, a windy tuft of grass above the serrated shoreline, and then climbed up to the abandoned village, coming out on an eerie emptiness: buildings silent amid tall grass, windows like empty eye sockets. I had to wade through grass and thorns to reach their walls. I was walking among ghosts, surrounded by family hearths overgrown and barns in slow collapse. Stone silos and a muddy trail. Another clutch of hollow homes beyond. It felt like a graveyard looted long ago.

I followed a farm lane past the ruins of an old windmill to where a pale crucifix stood, pinned like a butterfly above a pool of murky water. Beyond the crucifix and the hilltop remnants of a medieval church, I joined the main road and then headed back to Ardglass. I didn't stop, though. I kept going.

The sun was low across the water and the distant Mournes were catching gold by the time I crossed the bridge into Killough. I had decided to drop by and say hi to Martina, make amends, maybe convince her I wasn't the babbling lunatic she had no doubt taken me for. (And no, I wasn't simply trying to wrangle another lift back to Downpatrick.) It was a real treat, coming into a town where I actually knew someone. Unfortunately, it had taken me so long to get to Killough that by the time I arrived Martina had already left. (Either that, or she saw me coming.) So I waited for the bus to Downpatrick feeling forlorn, as the skies darkened and the first inevitable drops of water hit. A skinny kid with spotty skin was holding forth to a sloppy, heavily mascaraed girl who was enthralled by the breadth and wit of his anecdotes. He recited to her how he'd told that fokker this, and this fokker that, and how he'd set that fokker straight too. After twenty minutes and no bus, I'd had enough.

Out of the rain and into a morbid pub. Old pickled men in old pickled tweed. The smell of soggy ashtrays. A woeful air and a sense of intrusion, as if I'd walked into the middle of a funeral. It was a pub full of people adrift in thoughts of past defeats and yesterday's dreams and how it had all come to nought.

I sat at the bar, behind an oversized jar where pickled eggs were suspended like eyeballs in formaldehyde. A packet of Roast Beef & English Mustard chips and a shot of rum, and I was ready to brave the wet streets of Killough again. I got as far as the next pub.

VIKING STRAITS

The only thing better than a fifteenth-century castle perched on the shores of a picturesque bay is a fifteenth-century castle perched on the shores of a picturesque bay that has a sex scandal attached to it. Bonus points if the scandal involves a cleric.

A cluster of "ten-pound castles" gathered near the entrance to Strangford Lough. One of the finest was at Kilclief. Constructed even before the official 1429 edict, Kilclief Castle was built by John Cely, Bishop of Down, for his mistress, the lovely Letys Thomas. When the archbishop caught wind of this, he sent a strongly worded rebuke to Cely. And when Cely decided to move in with Ms. Thomas, the archbishop ordered him back to the official residence. Bishop Cely ignored the order, carried on. So the archbishop had him excommunicated. Bishop Cely ignored this as well. Eventually the Pope had to step in, stripping Cely of his office and making the excommunication unequivocal. The ex-bishop and his lover stayed together, and their original medieval "love nest" was still standing on the shores of its picturesque bay. (Though I'm not sure how scandalous a long-term monogamous relationship really is, even if it is not sanctified by the church. Compare this, for example, to Bishop Hervey up near Castlerock, with his string of lovers and the attempted seduction of his young cousin.)

A sign outside the castle read OPEN.

Damn. I was hoping to go in. Dark windows, a bolted door. I tried the handle anyway, looked up, realized I was standing beneath a dropgap "murder hole."

I walked north along the coast to the entrance to Strangford Lough, a vast sea inlet where tides are forced through a bottleneck, creating some of the strongest currents in Europe. On the Cloghy Rocks offshore, seals were said to frolic and play, swimming and diving and basking—and riding unicycles and juggling, for all I knew. Because the rocks were pretty much submerged when I went through, any seals that were out there had put away their unicycles for the day. A notice board advised that the best time to view the Cloghy Rock seals was between 9 a.m. and noon. I checked my watch. It was ten to three. I considered hanging around for another eighteen hours and ten minutes to see if the seals reappeared but decided against it, on the grounds that no seal, unicycle-riding or not, was worth that sort of wait.

I could already see the pretty town of Portaferry with its windmill on the other side of the lough. The sun broke through, catching Portaferry in a spotlight, and for a moment the buildings seemed to blush.

Across the Narrows from Portaferry lay the equally pretty village of Strangford, creating a mirrorlike reflection. Between the two was the channel the Vikings had named "strong fjord." There was very little left of the Norsemen in Strangford itself, but the village did have a certain Nordic feel about it, with small, tidy houses painted in light, bright colours, modest and proud.

Certainly, the bearded giant with the red hair who stormed the castle for me had Viking coursing through him. I'd walked up to the Strangford tower house, had found a sign reading CLOSED. By which they meant "Open, on request." A hand-written note tacked to the door said you should knock at 39 Castle Street and ask for Mr. Seed. He would have the key. Which is what I did. Which is how I met the Viking giant of Strangford.

"Um, Mr. Seed?" I asked.

"One of 'em!" he said—boomed. "Y'll be wannin t'see the castle, then?"

I nodded.

"Aye." He grabbed the key, pulled on his jacket.

We walked up in the rain. Mr. Seed opened the door. We had to duck to get in—a reminder of how short the sword-wielding knights of lore were. Squat men with crossbows, hunkering behind thick walls. Inside, over cobblestones, then up along stairs in the near dark, we made our way through a rough stone interior, past archers' windows and fireplaces where the recessed stones had been charred black from centuries of peat. It must have been a miserable place in the winter. But with the open floor plan—the castle was essentially three rooms stacked on top of each other—it must have been convivial as well. Which sort of described Ulster as a whole, really.

The Ards Peninsula, on the other side of the channel, may have been a tableau of gentle rolling hills, but the current between it and Strangford was anything but. The tides forced their way through like a fast-running river—one that changed directions twice a day. I bought a ticket, took the ferry across, felt the current catch the boat, felt the boat push back. For a moment we seemed to stand still, motor straining, as eddies and swirling patterns broke around us. And then, suddenly, we were through. I took a rainy stroll through Portaferry, which had a striking tower house of its own, then caught the ferry back to Strangford as the currents once again tried to fling us out into the Irish Sea.

The Ulster Way went past the Strangford tower house, then around a hook of land and into the next bay. The street ended in a narrow gap, where a tight rising pathway known as Squeeze Gut continued. (The various places around there all had names like that: the Narrows, the Squeeze, Strong Fjord.) The path wedged its way through between walls, then turned into a wet wooded trail, mucky with mulch and leaves. I came out onto a stunning three-castle view of the lower lough. If I was reading my map right, and I wouldn't bet the rent on it, that was Portaferry Castle, Audley's Castle and Old Castle Ward in one expansive sweep.

Islands were scattered across Strangford Lough—one for every day of the year, it was said—and before me was at least a week's worth. I followed the shore to a small inlet, where I came upon an old bathing house, its walls wreathed in ivy. A path led me down to where ladies in bloomers had once soaked their decorous derrieres in the salubrious waters of Strangford Lough. Seaweed was clotted along the shore, and the inside of the building was now junked up with beer cans and broken bottles. The pool itself was brackish—almost congealed—thus dashing any hopes of a quick skinny dip. Just as well, because no sooner had I walked back up to the main trail than a woman strolled past with a Dalmatian.

"Brave day," she said, and I agreed.

Beyond the bathhouse I ran into the sort of trouble I thought I'd put behind me. The tide was now swollen, and the lough itself was lapping at the trail, swamping it at times. Tangles of wet dulse had been pushed up onto the path; it was like walking on entrails. With the final stretch all but impassable, I was forced to cut across spongy grass instead, boots squelching. I wasn't wearing my gaiters because I had—foolishly—assumed my days of bog walking were done. Boots and pant legs were soon soaked through and, in a nasty case of déjà vu, I found my way blocked by barbed wire. I snagged my pant leg in the process of climbing over, ripping the fabric and drawing a thin slice down my thigh like a run in a stocking.

Having soaked my way around the peninsula above Strangford, I came crashing out onto the main road in a flurry of invective.

A car immediately pulled over.

Inside was another of those bright young women who seemed to find my very existence amusing. I was no longer invisible, at least.

"Peppa," she said, laughing.

Pardon?

"My name, it's Peppa. I saw you come out just now, thought you could use a ride."

Pepper—for that was her name (only slightly less odd than Peppa, now that I think about it)—was from England. She was in Northern Ireland working for the National Trust. "I'm on my way to Killyleagh," she said, "but I can drop you off in Downpatrick."

And so, I was taken from swamped fields and bloodied barbed wire back to my cozy guest house on Scotch Street. The lady of the home was happy to see me back so early; at least she knew I hadn't been swept off any cliffs this time.

SAINTS AND LESSER MEN

The solid magnificence of the Castleward manor on its rise of hill was a domestic dispute writ large—an architectural metaphor, as it were.

Lord and Lady Bangor did not have a particularly rosy marriage. He had married upward, into greater wealth, and she never let him forget it. When the day came in the 1760s to build their Big House, the Lord and Lady disagreed on everything, from the overall plan to the style of the drapes. It was a battle fought to a standstill, resulting in one of the most striking oddities of the era: a two-faced house, built in two completely different styles, inside and out, under a single roof. It was a His and Hers mansion, divided right down the middle, with Lord Bangor's half rendered in Classical and the Lady's in what was then the latest trend: Gothick.

Classical design, with its pillars and pediments, drew upon the clean austerity of Greek and Roman architecture. Gothick was more playful, with pointed windows and church-like corridor entrances that harkened back to the cathedrals and castles of medieval times. To this, Lady Bangor added her own often eclectic touch.

Castleward House, combining stolid sensibilities on one side with outright whimsy on the other, featured square, manly doors inside that opened directly onto curved, ladylike arches. (And not to pick sides or anything, but it is worth noting that the Lord's tastes, though a bit plodding, have stood the test of time, while the Lady's seem awfully dated and almost kitschy now. To stand beneath the rounded Arabian tent–like plasterwork ceilings of her boudoir was, in the words of one visitor, like being "under the teats of a great cow.") That said, the Lady's half of the house was much more *fun*, and far more memorable.

Lord and Lady eventually parted ways—not surprisingly, I suppose—and ended their years living apart, divorced in all but name. Their estate, however, lived on: a Venus and Mars, he said/she said, two-faced Janus kind of place.

Beyond Castleward House lay the reflective plane of Temple Water, a canal-like pond with shivering palm trees beside and islands of lily pads atop, their edges now curling from the cold. Swans, tucked in on themselves for warmth, slid past, and tendril branches moved like curtains on a wind.

Temple Water was known for its artful use of a "borrowed view," the lines of the pond leading the eye to Audley's Castle, a stone tower set against the sky above a forest of thorns—the sort the prince hacked his way through to get to Sleeping Beauty.

From Castleward, I worked my way back to Downpatrick, across the camel-backed landscape of Down. My route took me past Slieve Patrick, with its landmark statue of the saint atop looking like a massive chess-piece bishop. I made the brief climb up—and was taken aback by the view. Such a reward for such little effort! Slieve Patrick must be the most perfectly located drumlin in Ireland, offering panoramas comparable to what I'd earned atop the Mournes—but requiring just a short, jaunty stroll. The towering statue of St. Patrick looked out to mountains in the distance and cathedrals near at hand, with inlets and islands below. The Slaney River curled through, emptying into Strangford Lough and marking the very spot where Patrick began his mission: a slave boy returning, called back as an adult to the land of his captors. "*Come again and walk among us.*"

When Patrick and his small band of disciples came ashore at the mouth of the Slaney River in AD 432, they were met by a startled swineherd, who ran to tell his chieftain, Dichu, about their arrival. Dichu hurried over and set his hounds on Patrick, only to have Patrick calm them by reciting a psalm. (Anyone who can soothe an Ulster hound is a miracle worker indeed. I made note of it, for the next time I tangled with a farm dog: *Stay calm, recite psalm.*) Like his wolfhounds, Dichu too "became gentle." He was baptized by Patrick and in turn gave Patrick the use of a stone barn as his first church. The conversion of Ireland had begun.

The crossroads at Saul was where that first Gaelic-barn-turned-Christian-chapel stood. The name sounded suitably Biblical, with its "road to Damascus" overtones, but was actually derived from the Irish *sabhall*, for "barn." Patrick often returned to the monastery at Saul during his wide-ranging travels, and it was to Saul that he came as an old man. It was at Saul that he received his final rites, at Saul that he died, peacefully, on March 17, AD 461. (On St. Patrick's Day no less. What are the odds of that?) A stone church and round tower marked the spot where Dichu's barn reputedly stood, and even now it was said that anyone who died in the Parish of Saul went directly to Heaven, bypassing purgatory. (Mental note: *When the time comes, book a flight to Saul.*)

After his death, Patrick's body was placed on a cart yoked to a team of oxen. In the manner of spears flung and rocks rolled, it was decided that wherever the oxen stopped Patrick would be buried and a church would be built. Why an unguided pair of oxen would walk *uphill* remains something of a mystery, but stop they did, and the site they chose was now occupied by Downpatrick's Anglican Cathedral.

I walked into town under a late blaze of afternoon light. Downpatrick-among-the-drumlins: the town was draped over several round hills, with roads curving through. Like Armagh, Downpatrick was an ancient Gaelic stronghold recast as a Christian centre. And like Armagh, Downpatrick had a dual ecclesiastical skyline: the spiked corners of the square-towered Protestant cathedral and the sharpened spire of the Catholics, each claiming a drumlin of its own.

In Downpatrick, English, Irish and Scotch came together. True, it was just a convergence of street names, but still, it was a start. I walked down Scotch Street and up English, toward the Protestant cathedral and the bones of St. Patrick himself—and those of St. Brigid and St. Columba. (Columba was to Scotland what Patrick was to Ireland.) Three saints in a common grave, or so the story went. No one was exactly sure who was buried beneath the slab of Mourne granite beside the cathedral.

We do know that it was during the reign of the Norman invader John de Courcy, *Conquestor Ultoniae*, "Conqueror of Ulster," that the cult of St. Patrick took root. It was de Courcy who defeated the Irish chieftains and rechristened the town "Downpatrick." It was de Courcy who dug up the bones of the saint, along with those of Brigid and Columba, and then had them reinterred in a common site, thereby fulfilling an ancient prophecy. (And, not coincidentally, allowing de Courcy to claim an almost divine right to rule.) Ulster was a land rich in bones. The warrior-poet Ossian, the High King Brian Boru, St. Columba, St. Brigid, St. Patrick: they all occupied plots of land in Northern Ireland.

In the cathedral grounds I came at last to the granite slab itself, marked simply PATRIC. It was a strange moment. I felt as though I'd been following Patrick ever since I first spotted Slemish Mountain from the Antrim heights and had now finally caught up to him.

I was about to catch up to my own family's past as well. And as it turned out, I didn't need to go to Belfast for that. Belfast came to me.

A SMALL FAMILY

When I phoned the guest house in Belfast to let them know a package was being sent to me there, it had already arrived. So I asked them to forward it to me in Downpatrick, which is where it found me.

I sat on the bed in my room on Scotch Street, holding the envelope in my hands. I had been chasing this moment since I started on the Ulster Way as surely as I had been chasing St. Patrick. I turned the envelope from Barnardo's Homes over in my hand, peeled back the flap.

Inside was a scandal worthy of an Irish bishop. No war heroes; no young wife dying of heartbreak. Instead:

> With regard to your request for information regarding
> William and Richard. Both boys were admitted to
> Barnardo's on 1st July 1910 with the surname Press. Their
> mother was Anne Press, age not given, of Belfast.

> It is said that the boys' father, Richard Belshaw, led a double
> life, maintaining two families. He is believed to have
> bigamously married their mother using the name of Bell.

Bell, from Belshaw. Anne Press had died in October 1909, the letter said. The boys had then moved in with their father, his wife and their half-brother and half-sister.

> In May 1910 Mr. Belshaw was admitted to the Royal
> Victoria Hospital in Belfast, where on the 11th June, 1910
> he died of dropsy, asthma etc. As a result of their father's
> death, application was made to Barnardo's by Mr. Belshaw's
> wife for the admission of William and Richard. It was said
> that both boys were quite well behaved.

Not the Boer War, but bigamy. The letter went on to outline how William had been shipped to Canada three months after they were admitted; Richard had been kept behind due to ill heath and had spent his time "in various children's homes" before ending up on Jersey Island. I went downstairs in a bit of a daze, had a cup of tea.

"Are you okay?" the lady of the house asked.

I asked for the Northern Ireland phone directory, flipped through the listings, ran my finger down the page. Belshaw and Press were relatively small families, thankfully. At least I wasn't trying to trace a line of O'Neills, say, or Johnsons. And then, because life is nothing if not strange, when I told the lady of the house about the letter, she said, "Press, is it? There are Presses in Downpatrick. You should talk to Hugh Press, the estate agent. His office is just at the end of the street."

So I did. Still in a daze, admittedly.

Mr. Press was a silver-haired gentleman, well dressed and well mannered, dapper really. Considering that I just sort of showed up, he handled it well.

"The Press family came over in the 1600s," he said, "from England, with the Wards."

"The Wards—of Castleward? Lord and Lady Bangor of the two-sided manor?"

"That's right. Castleward was their estate."

Had I walked right past my familial landing site?

"The Press family were craftsmen, carpenters," Hugh explained. "They worked for the Wards. Some of their later handiwork can be seen inside Castleward House. A Press cabinet, I believe. We're a small family, connected mainly to Castleward and the area around it. Most Presses would have been baptized at Ballyculter Church. The records will still be there. I can ask my cousin Raymond to help you with that. He lives not far from there."

"So," I said. "You and I, we're sort of ..."

"Related?" He smiled. "Maybe. The records at Ballyculter will tell us. My father, he always thought the name Press might have been Czechoslovakian, from *Prezcht*, which is a surname over there, I'm told."

"Czech?" I said.

He nodded.

How did an Eastern European family end up in England four hundred years ago? Then the penny dropped. "Would they have been itinerant workers?" I asked. "Originally?"

"Possibly."

"Gypsies?"

"Perhaps."

Not possibly, not perhaps. *I knew.* I knew as surely as I knew anything.

There was one last question. It needed asking.

"Not a Catholic name, then?"

"No. Although there may be Catholic Presses as well. The church records will answer that."

Unfortunately, they didn't. There was no record for Anne Press for the dates I had been given, not at Ballyculter Church, anyway. If Mr. Press and I were related, it was very distantly. Though I must say, his manners and overall demeanour reminded me uncannily of the stories I'd heard about my grandfather.

WINTER BIRDS

My walk took on a renewed urgency. I needed to get back to Belfast, needed to trace the family records for Anne Press and Richard Belshaw.

I left Downpatrick, crossed the River Quoile, into County Down's "egg-under-a-blanket" landscape, a Lilliputian world of stone farmhouses draped in ivy and fields sewn together as though from patches of extra cloth. No doubt about it, God built Down on one of his better days.

A waymarker pointed me toward Castlewilliam. A fine name, and one I should give to my own manor house, I decided, once I'd tracked down the deed to my birthright. Much as the idea of gypsy origins appealed to me, I hadn't given up on the legend of a lost family estate; the double life of Richard Belshaw hinted at secrets as yet uncovered.

Castlewilliam, however, was little more than a country lane with a few houses thrown around. An Ulster Way sign tried to send me down a lane marked "Private Road: Trespassers Will Be Prosecuted" with a profile of a German shepherd posted beside it. Had it been the silhouette of a bichon frise, I might have considered it. Instead, I backtracked, then followed a higher road into the next inlet. Cottages were clustered along the high-water mark, as though washed up by the tide.

The road ran up and over, into Killyleagh Harbour.

Homes in powder blues and soft yellow, pale green and pinks, lined the shore, were reflected in the water. Killyleagh seemed like a reflection itself, a watercolour rendering more than an actual village. One could imagine oneself there, living a water-coloured life along water-coloured streets, raising water-coloured children in a water-coloured home.

Even the castle looked like something clipped from a storybook. Ask a child to draw a picture of a castle, and they will draw the one at Killyleagh. A Loire Valley–style chateau with round towers and conical rooftops, it looked almost Disneyesque, but in fact dated to the 1600s, with parts of it older still; some sections were from the original Norman keep of 1180. Killyleagh Castle had been in the same family for four hundred years, and it remained a private residence—the oldest inhabited castle in Ireland, according to the guidebooks. One could peer in through the main gate and marvel at what it must be like to live inside. Damp, I imagined, and expensive, and haunted, apparently, but still. A castle.

As I walked down the slope of High Street from the castle, a young woman swept past a band of admiring boys with a regal flip of her hair. She was an aristocracy of one, a haughty house cat fed on caviar and compliments, the Queen of Killyleagh. I wondered if growing up under the backdrop of a castle like that affected your outlook, added confidence to your stride, a certain self-importance to your posture.

It dawned on me then that I knew someone in Killyleagh, and she wasn't haughty or self-important at all. The Dufferin Arms seemed to be the town's communal living room, so I asked there.

"Has Pepper been in today?"

The barkeep looked at me blankly.

"Peppa," I said.

"Oh! Aye, Peppa." He called out to some customers down the bar. "Have youse seen Peppa?"

"Nae, Peppa's away," they said. "Won't be back till Monday."

Either that, or she saw me coming. No matter. I rented a room, ordered a pint. Considered the many versions of the past, buried and otherwise.

Overheard at the Dufferin Arms that night: "He's ruffled enough feathers to build himself a bloody ostrich."

I drank my lager, wondered idly if the Lord of the Castle ever came down to enjoy an occasional tipple amongst the common folk. I knew I would.

KILLYLEAGH was one of the more attractive towns I'd come across, but where earlier I might have lingered, I now barely broke my stride, leaving first thing in the morning, full complement of gear on my back. I had to get to Belfast, find out if there were castles of my own to claim.

I left Killyleagh on a day soft with rain. Sleepy-stepping children filed past on their way to their water-coloured school. Birds were relaying messages from treetop to treetop, and in the harbour the sailboats were rising and falling like someone breathing in his sleep. Up along High Street and past the castle, through a stone tower-gate, I followed the road into Shrigley.

Shrigley was Killyleagh's backlot, its shed, so to speak, the kind with dusty mason jars in the window and rusty wheelbarrows parked beside. There was a factory with porridge-grey walls, some row housing, brown on brown, and a High Victorian monument off to one side, sadly neglected and fringed with litter. The Shrigley

Monument was a strange construct: arches and columns and flying buttresses with no real central structure. And no indication of who it commemorated or why it was built; any inscriptions had long been effaced. Broken glass speckled the ground around the base, and the graffiti was half-hearted—FUCK THIS and FUCK THAT—with not an original thought or pithy turn of phrase to be found. The statues on the monument were headless. One of them was labelled FAITH, which I found ineffably depressing.

Fortunately, the Ulster Way soon left Shrigley, climbing the hill behind the monument past a mill pond. Ducks, prone to panic at the best of times, formed an airborne stampede as I approached, lifting off in tandem. I was squeezed in by hedgerows—hedged in, as it were—which made the occasional burst of traffic down that road an enlivening matter. After so many miles, though, I was now sidestepping teen-driven tractors with a matador's studied ease.

A series of country lanes took me north, along the inner shore of Strangford Lough, and at times the quiet beauty of the landscape almost overpowered me. It was as though all of Ulster had been pushed into this one last corner: billowing fields and curving coastlines, drumlin islands and thatched-roof cottages, hills rounding like the swell before a wave forms, valleys falling away, the white gold of sunlight through rain, hidden bays and endless inlets, the deep blue of the lough, the vigorous green of the land. Summer was a long time dying in Ulster.

It's been said that we don't remember days, we remember moments. I've often wondered if Heaven isn't simply a giant REWIND button, one that lets us replay the softest and finest moments of our lives: sunlight at a certain angle, the smell of a sleeping child in our arms. If it is, and if I make it there, I imagine I'll see more than a few fleeting images of Northern Ireland move past.

At Quarterland Bay, the tide had pulled out like a tablecloth parlour trick, leaving sloops stranded on tidal flats and slivers of water catching the sky. Over another curve and down to another bay, where the water had filled the hollows between drumlins. Another hip of hill, and I was on the road to Whiterock, where the stone ruins of a tower house guarded the causeway to Sketrick Island.

On Sketrick Island, just behind the tower ruins, was a well-known seafood restaurant, closed when I came through. The advantage of travelling after the season is that there are no crowds. The disadvantage is that there are no crowds. Shops and restaurants no longer needed to extend their hours, least of all in the hope of landing a lone long-distance walker.

Past the causeway harbour and its forest of masts, the Ballydorn Lightship lay permanently docked beside the shore, with a gangplank leading down. Although now the private property of a yacht club, the lightship had once guided fishing boats in, its comically large, top-heavy light-bulb beacon making it look like a boat that has just had a brilliant idea.

My day's walk from Killyleagh was supposed to end at the Castle Espie Wetlands Interpretive Centre. But first I had to get through Ardmillan. This seemed a simple enough task; Ardmillan was a tiny smudge of a village with only two roads out. The downtown was essentially a phone booth and an Orange Hall.* There were chickens on the street and a hall clock that lacked a minute hand, meaning the time in Ardmillan would always be "ish" (eight-ish, nine-ish, noon-ish). A quiet place, Ardmillan, and one that I could have gotten through handily had I not made the mistake of following the directions given in my guidebook.

I knew firsthand the bouts of wishful thinking that comprised a great deal of the Ulster Way, but this was something else again. The route, as described in the guidebook and abetted by waymarkers, followed the left-hand exit out of Ardmillan. Sure enough, there was an Ulster Way sign right where they said it would be, pointing in the correct direction, too: down a wooded lane behind a row of country homes. I strode in with the sprightly step that comes from knowing you are on the right track. And then the lane began to narrow. Thorn

---

*The phone booth was, of course, marked on the Ordnance Survey map.

brambles pushed in from either side, knotting themselves above my head, forcing me to crouch lower and lower. I felt like Alice, growing ever larger until any pretext of a path ended. The trail surrendered itself to chaos and left me facing a tangled wall of thorns. Forced to backtrack, I found a break in the hedges and crawled my way out, risking death by a thousand scratches, onto an open field.

Baffled, I followed the trail I'd been on from the outside for a while, saw it disappear irrevocably into a swampy thicket. It wasn't that the trail was overgrown; it didn't exist. I trudged up a grassy hill, scattering sheep as I went, saw a lone farmhouse on the other side and walked down toward it. The farm was marked on the Ordnance Survey, so I knew exactly where I was. It just didn't make any sense.

As I approached the gate, a large dog came out and challenged me to a duel. I declined. Had I known any psalms, I might have recited one then, but I decided instead to stay on the other side of the fence, especially as a smaller, over-caffeinated canine was now egging the first dog on. The yappy little sidekick was small enough to get under the fence, but he too stayed where he was. It was an Ulster standoff. Fortunately, the commotion brought out the lady of the house. She apologized, even though I was an incipient trespasser, as she dragged the dogs back inside.

I told her I was very sorry to bother her. "It's just that I'm lost. Well, not lost. I've been lied to, you see."

She nodded knowingly. "You're looking for the Ulster Way?"

"Yes!"

"Well, as I unnerstann' it, used to go over that hill there—" She pointed behind me. "Down to this wee road, here." She was referring to the tarmac lane that ran from her house downhill toward the main road.

"So there was a trail at one point?"

"Was. But a farmer ploughed that all in, like."

"When was that?" I asked. "Because it's still waymarked on the other end, and it's in my guidebook."

"When did the farmer plough under the old trail?"

"Yes."

She thought about this. "Oh, we've had this house thirty years now, and that trail was gone before we bought it. So I'd say ... forty years?"

"Forty years?" I sputtered. That was before the Ulster Way was laid out! Someone had plotted this section on a map, someone else had pounded in a waymarker, someone else had written it up in a guide-book, *all without ever having walked it.*

God*dammit.*

I sighed. Took a deep breath. "Can I cut across?"

"Of course," she said, opening the gate. She was a very sweet woman. She really was.

"Do you get many walkers coming through your yard?" I asked.

"Aye, a few."

"All as confused as me? Looking for a forty-year-old trail that doesn't exist?"

"No," she said. "Most are locals. They know about cutting over the hill. There were a few were askin' about the Ulster Way, though. Walking it, are ye?"

"I am," I said. "In theory."

THE NAME was a bit of a mystery. There was no castle at Castle Espie, though a dwelling on a nearby hill did have some suspiciously castle-like stones in its foundation. *"Castle? What castle? We didn't see no castle."*

Ironically, later industrial undertakings—quarries and kilns, seawalls and reclaimed swampland—all now abandoned, had helped turn the area into a conservation zone. They provided a perfect water-fowl habitat.

Today, Castle Espie was home to a Wildfowl & Wetlands Trust bird sanctuary with walking trails and ponds and an unbelievable assortment of birds. Many of the species that wintered over and bred at Castle Espie were endangered. Others were just plain fascinating: White-faced Whistlers and Bar-tailed Godwits, Red-breasted Geese and Spotted Redshanks, Whooper Swans and Pennyface Bewicks,

Mallards and Moorhens, Carolling Wood Ducks and Lesser Yellowlegs, Grey Plovers and Northern Cinnamon Teals, Kingfishers and Sandpipers, Greylag Geese and Hawaiian Nēnē. Now, to be perfectly honest, I had no idea which of these were actually splashing about at Castle Espie that day—I don't know a Grey Plover from a White-faced Whistler—but I did love their names, as I did their wild racing stripes and feathered hues. I loved the sound effects even more. It was a regular avian jamboree, with all manner of squawks, quacks and trills filling the air. Manic laughter and high-pitched whistles. Dry, ironic chuckles and monkey-like cries. Sudden machine-gun bursts and a noise like a leaky faucet dripping into water. There was even one bird that said *"Oooooh"* in the manner of a Monty Python sketch.

I hobbled on sore feet along the various boardwalks and to the different waterfowl-viewing sites. There were freshwater lagoons, saltwater marshes, a lough-view trail and even a platformed swamp walk above bayou-like waters. Though they should probably have called that one the "mosquito and midge walk," at least when I went through. The water was thick with the murky green of pooled algae, and I once again expected to see crocodile eyes floating in.

Among the most notable visitors at Castle Espie was the Light-bellied Brent Goose, which migrated from the Canadian Arctic every year, a journey of some three thousand miles. Fifteen thousand Brent Geese descended on Ireland annually, and three-quarters of those came to Strangford Lough. Hundreds had already arrived by the time I went through, their epic flight now over. Unlike my own.

I made the long walk into Comber at dusk, the streetlamps of the city a lightship calling me in.

THIS WEE MIZZLE?

I'd been walking toward it for two days, had seen it as far back as Sketrick Island, a stone tower perched on distant heights: Scrabo.

It was a perfect Rapunzel tower on a perfect Rapunzel hill, but I had one last gauntlet to run before I could reach it. I followed the divided highway—or "dual carriageway" as they are known—out of Comber. A wide walking path ran alongside it, luckily, and I soon came to a gravel road that rolled uphill toward the tower. A listless Ulster Way signpost assured me this was the route I needed to take, but no sooner had I taken my first step than a large dog sauntered out onto the road ahead, flicking a coin and chewing on a toothpick. Past him was another home with another driveway and another dog waiting on the road. Even if I managed to talk my way past the first hound, I might find myself trapped between the two, like a runner caught between bases.

With a sigh, I retreated. Studied my map. This wasn't the main road to Scrabo, fortunately. That was a little farther up. I gave the dogs a hearty wave (okay, it may have been a middle finger) and then headed off.

I'd made the right choice. Motte Road was tarmacked, hound-free and tirelessly direct. I leaned into the hill and walked straight up. I arrived feeling out of breath but buoyant: this was the last major hill of my hike. Scrabo Tower was built in 1857 as a memorial to the Third Marquis of Londonderry, and from its strategic heights I could see everything ahead and behind: Slieve Donard and the Mournes, Strangford Lough, which narrowed into a dagger of water below, the Irish Sea and the coast of Scotland prowling nearby. And to the north, Belfast. I could see Samson and Goliath, and the Key of Hell heights beyond. In the far distance, dark clouds over Donegal. A cold wind was blowing in, ruining my mood.

No time to linger. I followed a scrambly footpath down the brackened back of Scrabo Hill. The towns were coming closer together now and the Ulster Way took me directly through the Newtownards main square, past a handsome town hall and arts centre, where the insouciant young loitered about, carefree and loose-limbed, as I creaked past with my backpack.

I ate a late lunch in a quarry north of town, beside the chimney stack remains of what must once have been a large-scale operation. The quarry was now part of a wooded park, one criss-crossed with paths and dotted with ponds. Sheltered from the wind, young families walked along at the littlest one's pace. Older couples with fifty years of shared walks in their rhythm nodded to me. A few motocross bikes buzzed in the distance. So charmed was I by my own walk in the park that I missed my turnoff—it wasn't waymarked—and ended up alongside a golf course, where a pair of ladies were laughing uproariously at their lack of talent. They were trying to chip a ball out of a tricky bit and were succeeding only in spraying themselves with sand.

"Having fun?" I asked.

"Oh, aye," they said, weak from laughter.

Retracing my steps, I eventually found the right trail, and I followed it to another memorial tower, this one hidden in the woods and dedicated to Helen, Lady Dufferin, by her son. It didn't dominate the landscape the way Scrabo Tower had, was almost secretive in its wooded cul-de-sac. Past a pair of ponds, with the usual czarist swans and proletarian ducks, past a sawmill and an old schoolhouse, onto a hedgerow lane: it felt as though I were walking on a giant globe at times, turning it with my feet, rolling the landscape toward me.

As the sky darkened with threats of rain, I entered the soft beauty of Clandeboye Avenue, which formed a wide footpath through the trees. Rabbits hopped away, white tails bobbing. I was walking over layers of fallen, damp leaves. I was walking over autumn. The skies may have been in full Valkyrie advance, but down below, on half-forgotten Clandeboye, all was calm.

Alas, the Clandeboye Avenues of our lives must always come to an end, in this case at the Devil's Carriageway. I came out of my pastoral reverie headlong onto the thundering A2. If you leave Comber in the morning, as directed, you are perfectly timed to arrive at the highway at rush hour. The architects of the Ulster Way hadn't bothered putting in a footbridge or an underpass. What they had done was post a sign absolving themselves of responsibility:

DANGER: Please note that this section of the Ulster Way
terminates in six metres at the Bangor–Belfast dual carriageway. The next section commences on the opposite side of
that dual carriageway. Persons who decide to continue are
warned of the danger from traffic using that dual carriageway. They should exercise extreme caution in crossing this
busy thoroughfare. The Council accepts no responsibility
for loss, death or personal injury.

There was a loud rending sound, and the clouds above me
collapsed. The rain hit so hard it ricocheted up like shrapnel; it almost
seemed to be falling in reverse. Cars and trucks raced by, wipers
flailing, without so much as a tap of the brakes. I faced another
sudden-death round of Frogger. With loins well girded, I ran out onto
the asphalt, and ran just as quickly back. A satanic truck driver had
spotted me; he *sped up* when he saw me, I swear. Swiping the rain
from my face and sputtering, I waited for another gap, ran back out.
Bursts of traffic on either side now trapped me on the meridian. You
don't want to get caught between a commuter and his or her drive
home; in any encounter between hiker and car, the advantage goes to
the car. So I waited. Quite a while. But eventually another gap opened
up, and I bolted across to the other side. *Why did the chicken cross the
dual carriageway? Because the Ulster Way left him no choice.*

I followed a ribbon of trees north. The rains had gone from kettle-
drums to steady tom-tom, and a cement trail led me over a trickling,
makes-you-want-to-pee stream to the Helen's Bay train station. I
would have called it a day, caught the next train out, but I was so close
to the finish line that I pushed on, through residential streets, to the
shores of Belfast Lough.

Signs warned of "unexpected rogue waves," advising that "extra
vigilance is required." The rain was falling straight down, hammering
the lough into submission. Nonetheless, I decided to be extra vigilant
along that stretch, even though I still didn't know what the procedure
for "unexpected waves" entailed other than yelling, "Fuck, no!" And I

wasn't sure I wanted those to be my final words. *Here marks the spot where a minor writer was washed away, never to be seen again. Legend has it that on stormy nights his girlish shriek can yet be heard. "Nooooo! Fuck, noooo!"*

To hell with it. St. John's Point hadn't killed me; I figured I could handle Belfast Lough. I rounded the headland and, through the rain, I could just see the castle at Carrickfergus and the rainy outline of the County Antrim War Memorial. I could even make out the pale church at Whiteabbey, where this foolishness had all started.

It was getting dark. I left the shore, found a pub and sat in a puddle of my own making, with a pint in front of me and 546 miles of Ulster behind.

The publican looked at my backpack and damp maps.

"Yer walkin'?" he surmised.

I nodded.

"In this?"

I took a deep swig from my glass. "This wee mizzle?" I said. "This isn't rain."

THE IDEA OF GUINNESS

No triumphal arches had been raised in my honour, no cheering crowds lined the streets, no bevy of ark-borne beauties awaited my arrival. No Key to the City—or even Hell—was offered. There was just me, slogging in under heavy rains. I'd been walking toward this moment since I set out, but now that I'd finally reached Belfast, all I felt was empty. The Ulster Way entered the city in a roundabout fashion, swinging wide along the banks of the River Lagan. In the pounding downpour I abandoned it, following Ormeau Road toward downtown instead.

The guest house that I'd stayed in back when I'd first arrived was now overrun with students. Feeling old and irritable, I didn't even bother trying for a pity bed, though I did thank the staff for forwarding me the information from the Barnardo's Homes. The young man's cast was gone, his broken bones having mended quicker than it had taken me to reach Belfast again.

"I remember you," he said. "Goin' on a wee walk, were ye?"

I nodded.

"And how'd that work out?"

"I'm still not done," I said.

I found a room instead in a rambling hotel that had extended itself in stages, invading adjoining buildings, adding doorways, expanding into mazes of crooked stairwells and jerry-rigged corridors. I threaded my way through this warren of partitions and ad hoc rooms of dubious fire safety, key in hand, up and down hallways on threadbare carpets, until by trial and error, I finally reached the sad little cubby-hole that was my room. The bed took up almost the entire space, and it was a small bed. No matter, I was at last in Belfast. I crossed my room in a single step and flung open the curtains dramatically. I was faced with an alleyway and a dumpster overstuffed with refuse and spackled with bird shit. The walls of my room were saturated with sighs; the very wallpaper was heavy with them. Now I knew why. Guest after guest had tramped through these hallways, had threaded their way to this "room," had flung open the curtains—and had sighed. I couldn't even leave the window open to let a breeze in, because when I did the reek of garbage immediately filled the air. It was the last room available as well, which meant I couldn't insist on finer quarters either.

"So," I said to myself. "There are places worse to sleep in than a bog."

Apparently, the alleyway outside my room, as well as being a prime dumpster-diving spot, was also one of Belfast's DESIGNATED ARGUMENT SITES, and throughout the night a steady procession filed by: angry lovers, drunken mates, livid neighbours. They lined up patiently, in a queue, I imagined, just below my window, waiting their turn. Punctuated by the occasional breaking of glass and rowdy verses of conciliatory song, these arguments continued until, oh, about half past madness.

When the arguments faded, cats took over. Right below my window, a pair of felines were either making love or trying to kill each other. It was hard to tell, what with cats being the S/M connoisseurs of the animal world. The caterwauling worked its way into my subconscious, where it resurfaced in dreams of claw marks and the plaintive cries of love and pain. My sinuses were congested, or rather, *half* congested, which is always worse. And so, between bouts of cat love and Belfast discourse, I spent the night rolling from one side to the other, shifting things like a bubble in a carpenter's level, trying to find some kind of balance.

I missed the hills.

I COMPLETED the Belfast sections of the Ulster Way over the next few days, along the shore to Holywood and then down past Stormont, a massive brick of a building on its enormous sweep of parkland, which housed that Northern parliament, so often suspended, so recently revived but never very stable, in spite of the solid imperial certainties the building embodied.

I'd promised myself I'd kick up my heels, calloused though they were, and sally forth into the city's nightlife once I'd arrived in Belfast—maybe catch a donnybrook or a brouhaha. (I wasn't really sure what the difference was between a donnybrook and a brouhaha, but if anyone had charted these out in exact gradations, it was the Irish of Ulster.) Before I did, however, there was one last set of heights to scale. Which brings me to my next topic:

How to be a hero, in five easy steps, Irish version.

For those wishing to attain immortality as a romantic Irish hero (a triple redundancy, I know), the best procedure is to (a) be completely unsuited to lead an armed uprising, (b) lead an armed uprising, (c) fail brilliantly, (d) be captured and executed (by the English, preferably), but not before (e) making a passionate declaration from the docks as you are being led away in shackles.

The United Irishmen of the 1798 rebellion were the apotheosis of this. Under the leadership of Protestants such as Theobald Wolfe

Tone, they had met in secret on Cave Hill, high above Belfast, where they affirmed their desire "to unite the whole people of Ireland, to abolish the memory of all past dissensions and to substitute the common name of Irishman in place of the denominations of Protestant, Catholic and Dissenter." ("Dissenter" at that time meaning Presbyterian.) There are few happy endings in Irish history, and the United Irishmen Rebellion concluded, as most Irish stories do, in bloodshed and ballads. The rebels did make some fine speeches before they were executed, though.

Under dripping skies, I made the long walk up Key of Hell. It was a farewell performance played to an empty house and an abandoned stage. I stood looking out across North Belfast with its patchwork of competing paramilitary territories and interlocking tribal identities, where one's loyalty can be charted street by street, house by house. Beyond the city, Belfast Lough opened onto the sea. And somewhere in the mist below, Samson and Goliath were battling it out still.

HAVING FINISHED my walk, I rang up John and Charlie, the RUC officers I'd met on the top of Slieve Donard, to remind them of their offer.

"Oh aye," they said. "We'll take you out to celebrate."

But out meant in. As police officers, John and Charlie couldn't talk freely in public, so they took me to an RUC drinking hole instead, one located deep inside the corrugated metal walls of the Central Belfast Police Station. It was a sight as strange as that home inside the Benburb Castle grounds. It looked just like a regular Ulster pub, the kind you'd see anywhere, except that it was surrounded by razor wire and watchtowers.

"Guinness?" John asked, as we found a table.

"Lager," I said. "Harp, if they have it." And we raised our glasses to folly and new friends.

I never did acquire a taste for Guinness, try though I might. I liked everything about it—the long pull, the rich peaty darkness, the slow rise of foam, its deep history and long traditions—everything except the actual taste, with its fermented molasses kick and yeasty afterbite. I liked the *idea* of Guinness more than the Guinness itself. There were times I felt that way about Ireland as a whole.

EMPTY GRAVES

I arrived at the newspaper archives dripping with rain. I shook out my umbrella, dried myself off and signed in. The newsprint pages from 1910 were as dry as papyrus and crumbling along the edges. I found what I was looking for on page 5 of the *Belfast Evening Telegraph*:

> BELSHAW—June 11, at the Royal Victoria Hospital, Richard Belshaw. The remains of my beloved husband will be removed from his late residence on to-morrow (Sunday) afternoon, at 2:30 for interment in the City Cemetery. Friends will please accept this (the only) intimation.
>
> MARY A. BELSHAW

Beloved? This was a man who'd kept two families, had brought the children from his second liaison into his home after their mother died. Divorce was all but impossible in pre-partition Ireland—the laws of Britain hadn't been fully applied—but still. It must have been hard on Mr. Belshaw's legal spouse. She certainly didn't wait very long after he died to send William and Richard to an orphanage.

I found no obituary for Anne Press, but I had put in a request at the General Register Office when I'd first arrived back in Belfast, and I stopped in a few days later to collect a copy of her death certificate. On it, her name was given as "Annie Bell, wife of John Bell." She had died of TB on October 28, 1909, at age thirty-four. She'd been twenty years younger than Richard Belshaw. The birth certificates for her sons confirmed that the name "Bell" was one they had been born into, half Belshaw as they were. Their names were given as William Carson and John Richard Bell. But their mother's name had changed between the two births. On William's birth certificate, no father was listed, and her name was given simply as "Annie Press." By the time my grandfather was born, she had taken the name "Annie Bell, formerly Sloane" and listed the father as "William Bell."

That unexpected aside—"*formerly Sloane*"—opened up another possibility: that Annie had married into the Press family, had been widowed or abandoned, and had then gotten involved with a married man.

I asked at the desk. "Is Sloane a Protestant name or a Catholic?"

"Could be either," said the clerk.

In the various archival records I sifted through, two addresses in Belfast emerged: 71 Wilton Street, where my grandfather had been born, and 32 Ambleside, where Richard Belshaw had lived with his first wife and their children, and where William and Richard would have stayed during the eight months between their mother's death and their father's.

At the Public Records Office in the south end of Belfast, the 1901 Census of Ireland was available on microfiche. My great-uncle Bill had been mistaken; the records had not been destroyed by fire. I found the entry for 32 Ambleside easily enough.

Each house had its own page in the census, and the categories of information listed were revealing: "Head of Family" and the names of all residents and their "religious profession," as well as their age, gender, level of literacy, place of birth and marital status, whether they spoke the Irish language, and whether any of them were "deaf or dumb." There was also a checklist for "imbeciles," "idiots" and "lunatics." Although these terms had specific meanings at the time, it brought to mind a family sitting around a kitchen table, an enumerator filling in the forms as they mused among themselves, "*Now, w' Uncle Jimmy, d'ye figure he's an idiot or an imbecile?*" "*More of a lunatic, really.*"

Richard Belshaw had a son and a daughter. His wife, Mary, came from County Armagh; she could read but not write. He was an engineer, worked in a linen mill—as did half of Belfast at that time.

Between linen and the shipyards, you had the core of Belfast's economy.

The Belshaw family were listed as "Primitive Methodists." If there had been any religious divide crossed between Mr. Belshaw and Annie Press, it would show up on the census page for her address at 71 Wilton. The entry would also tell me where Anne Press was originally from, whether she had been married and what her religious affiliation was—which would help me narrow down the baptismal records. But when I went to find that page in the census, it wasn't there.

"There's a page missing," I said, bringing the microfiche to the front desk.

The woman at the counter smiled. "We're closing in five, sorry to say. But you come back first thing Monday, it's sure someone here'll be able to help you."

It was the end of the work day on Friday. My flight was on Sunday. The clock had officially run out.

I visited the Wilton Street and Ambleside addresses the following day. Both streets were in the Shankill. Now, that name either means nothing to you—or it means everything. Shankill Road and the surrounding side streets are the backbone of Loyalism. It's an infamous area if you're Catholic, a hard-knuckled street where the UVF and the UDA reign and unconvicted killers dwell. It is also the main business street of working-class Protestants, and as such has a certain raw vitality to it. I walked Shankill Road, with its crowded sidewalks and tattered shops, past Loyalist murals and small pubs, dusty fruit stands and chip shops. The smell of car exhaust and fried food hung in the air while pregnant women in sweatpants, cigarettes dangling from their lips, forced their prams through.

The Shankill is old; it predates the city. The first church in what is now Belfast was founded here by St. Patrick himself. *For God and Ulster*, the murals read. I turned onto Tennent Street, side-stepping broken glass and smears of dog shit, and came to a grim RUC fortress at the end of Ambleside. I walked down past row houses, looking for number 32. It was gone, but the footprint of the original "two-up-two-down" Victorian buildings could still be seen in today's flats.

Seventy-one Wilton, just a few blocks from Ambleside on the other side of Shankill Road, was gone as well. Mr. Belshaw had kept his two families close, would have been able to step out of his house after dinner and reach Annie's door quickly at a brisk walk. But here even the footprint had been erased. Wilton Street had been reconfigured into cul-de-sacs and tidy red-brick bungalows. I paced it out: 67, 69, 69A. The road turned, and, near as I could tell, the lot where my grandfather had been born was now covered by a layer of asphalt.

"Are youse lookin' for someone?" It was a lady in her middle years, leaning on her front fence.

"My grandfather," I said.

"Aye?"

"He was born on this street, spent his early childhood here."

"It's all changed, so it has," she said. "Used to run straight through. There was a wee playground, like. Would'a still been there when yer granda was a wean." And the image flickered past like a Zoetrope, silent pictures in black and white of my grandfather as a young boy, laughing, running. I thought of my own son, and of how long I'd been gone.

I took one of Belfast's black taxis down to City Cemetery, where the staff gave me a map and a single number: M2-302, the Belshaw plot. But when I paced it out, any headstone or marker that had once been there was gone. I didn't know whether the grave had been fenced in with wrought iron and had since been looted, or whether it had simply fallen into neglect, but either way, any trace of Richard Belshaw was gone. The headstone in the adjoining lot read "John Clarke." But on that only piece of Ulster I could lay claim to—the only one I knew for certain contained traces of my DNA—there was only grass. *The past is an empty country*. I'd been searching for missing landmarks all along. I took a photo, then made the long walk up Falls Road.

The boys from Belfast, the ones I'd met in the pub in Newry, had been from the Falls, though I couldn't remember which part exactly. Falls Road is a name that means nothing—or everything. The Falls, and the streets along it, form the backbone of Republicans. It's an infamous area if you're a Protestant: a hard-knuckled street where the IRA reigns and unconvicted killers dwell. As the main business street of working-class Catholics, though, Falls Road has a certain raw vitality. I walked along its crowded sidewalks, past tattered shops and Republican murals, past small pubs and dusty fruit stands. The smell of exhaust and fried food hung in the air while pregnant women in sweatpants, cigarettes dangling from their lips, forced their prams across broken glass.

Evening was settling on Belfast as imperceptibly as dust, and I decided to go back to Wilton, take one last walk through my grandfather's past.

Wilton Street was only a block or two above Falls Road. I turned left, up a side street—and hit a dead end. A corrugated metal wall, several stories high, blocked my way, cutting off Falls Road from the Shankill, separating me from Wilton. They call these walls "peacelines," and they slice the city up, keeping the two sides segregated. I looked at this barrier, thought about the many borders it represented: borders of the heart, borders of the past, of the present, of tribal demarcations and family divides.

It was time to go.

Home.

Part Nine

BEYOND BELFAST

BEYOND BELFAST

A Postscript

Belfast, 2008, July Eleventh.

It's the marching season in Northern Ireland. It is always the marching season in Northern Ireland.

Across Belfast, bonfires will be burning, massive fists of flame uncurling into the night. When William landed at Carrickfergus, fires were lit to guide him. Three hundred years later, those fires are burning still: Protestant orange in a sea of green. It's nearing midnight in Northern Ireland, and the Glorious Twelfth is about to start.

My return to Belfast had begun with a message left on my phone back home. "It's Mom calling. You remember the photograph, the one of my dad in front of those stone stairs, the one I photocopied for you when you made that long walk?" She paused, waiting for an answer, even though she was talking to my voice mail. "Well, I decided to get a proper reproduction made," she said. "When I peeled the photo out of the album, there was something written on the back. It might be a clue."

And so.

Here I am, back in Belfast, with the original photo this time. It is inscribed on the back, in India ink, with the name of an estate.

Unable to sleep, I wander out from my hotel into the Protestant night.

"YOU ARE NOW ENTERING LOYALIST SANDY ROW," a mural on a gable wall informs you. A working-class street in the middle of Belfast, Sandy Row is just a stone's throw from the Europa, once the most bombed hotel in Europe.

In a vacant lot on Sandy Row, a beehive of wooden pallets had been stacked several stories high, a bonfire waiting to happen. Flying atop this tower of pallets was an Irish tricolour, and for one heady moment I thought, "Wow. The Prods on Sandy Row are trying to be inclusive." Oh, right, I then realized; when the bonfire was lit the Irish flag would go up in flames.

A noisy throng of people were wedged into the street, and a makeshift table had been set up to sell "battles" of beer to the crowd out of a cooler. I bought a battle from a smooth-skulled man adorned with tattoos, slogans mainly, cryptic shorthand, the skin as canvas, tribal art. When he caught my accent, he grinned, said, "Welcome to Belfast."

The crowd surged forward on some unspoken cue, squeezing through a fence into the vacant lot where the tower of wood stood. Songs roared up spontaneously. "*King Billy's on the wall, King Billy's on the wall ...*" A cargo cult dedicated to the memory of a long-dead Dutch prince, it was oddly poignant, somehow; they had held the line, had kept the fires burning. "*He shines so bright and stands so tall, King Billy's on the wall ...*"

They lit the bonfire with Molotov cocktails. Fiery pitches at midnight, hurled by young men, exploding on impact. Wild cheers from the crowd and then—nothing. The flames sputtered, seemed to die. I thought maybe they'd have to try again, but then slowly realized that the towering structure in front of me was burning from within. A light appeared deep inside, became a flicker. Flicker became a flame. Flame became bonfire. Bonfire, a conflagration. Blast-furnace heat pushed the crowds back, faces lit up, pale eyes glowing.

Music blared from loudspeakers at a volume set so loud it distorted the sound, as the crowd shouted out their loyalties, singing their bloodlines into the night. Fireworks began popping like gunfire across the city. The fire crawled its way toward the Irish flag.

A mother was fretting over a child sitting on his dad's shoulders, worried about the heat, but the young father brushed her concerns aside. "He needs ta get used t' it."

One side of the tower suddenly caved in, and the whole structure came down, sending sprays of embers and burning lumber toward the crowd. They shrieked, fell back, some laughing, some panic-ridden. One young man, forearm over forehead, ran forward, braved the heat to rescue the flag from where it had fallen. Carefully, almost tenderly, he untangled it from the smouldering debris—and then flung it onto the fire as a roar of approval went up.

I pointed out to the fellow next to me that the orange on the Irish tricolour was in fact the orange of King William, that it was their own colours they were torching. "You're almost burning your own flag, in a way," I said. This did not endear me to him. He gave me a hard Belfast stare that reached into my chest, pulled out my heart and squeezed, after which I beat an unseemly but well-advised retreat.

From Sandy Row I walked down Donegall to Roden Street, where I'd been told an even bigger bonfire had been built. "Biggest in Belfast! They throw furniture innit, sofas and ever'thin. God bless 'em, it got so high the fire department had'a step in, stop them from makin' it any bigger."

I passed the City Hospital, where an earlier tower had fallen and been doused with foam by a nearby fire truck. The brick row-house walls facing the bonfire had been sprayed down as well and were still steaming from the heat. It must have felt like living in a kiln.

Over a bridge painted with murals of World War I soldiers marching off toward sunset at the Somme, I came to Roden Street. I could see the fire long before I arrived. It was reflected in the windows, as though the buildings were burning inside, as though the homes had trapped the fire within them. A startling optical illusion. Or was it?

I came around the corner at the end of the street, and there, in a debris-strewn vacant lot, was a pyre of apocalyptic scale. I'd never seen anything like it. The heat was immense; it stung my eyes, kept the crowds well back. Fire trucks were on standby, hoses at the ready, but fortunately, big as it was, the fire had nowhere to go. Built like a Mayan pyramid, it could only collapse in on itself.

"This isn't anti-Catholic," one of the women in the crowd explained to me. She was at the bonfire with several of her friends in tow, along with their children of various ages and heights. "The Twelfth, it's a highlight for the weans. This is about us as a people, about something we did together."

"It's a celebration, like," one of her friends said.

"Aye," she said. "A celebration. It's pro-British, not anti-Irish."

I looked at the tricolour going up in flames atop the Roden Street bonfire as the crowds cheered. "And yet," I said. "You can see how they might take it that way."

The top of the pyre suddenly imploded, sending up a fountain of sparks and folding the Irish flag into its inner inferno.

"Why is this fire so big?" I asked. "I was at Sandy Row, and it wasn't nearly as big as this."

They laughed, the way someone affectionately indulgent of her own foibles might. "Y'see tha' wall?" they asked, pointing to the end of the street.

"Yes?"

"The Catholics are just on the other side a'tha'. We want to make sure they kin see it."

"Those are your neighbours," I said.

"Aye," they laughed. "And w' want so themmuns can enjoy it too, you know. Just being neighbourly, like."

I walked back down Donegall Road at two in the morning while the carnival staggered to its drunken finale. Mad rambling mobs of young men sang their way down the sidewalk. Pools of warm bodily liquids. Splattered beer and broken glass. On Sandy Row, a knot of hard-staring men stood outside the Glasgow Rangers Club, pints in hand, eyes scanning the streets. My footsteps crunched underneath as I passed.

Those fires would smoulder for days. My clothes smelled of smoke, even after I washed them.

ON BATTLES, SHAM AND OTHERWISE

I slept late, woke on the Twelfth to the sound of flutes. The fall of feet, the joyous rattlebang of drums. Protestants on the move. Not the sort of thing you'd want to face with a hangover. Stumbling out of my hotel, I followed the music down. Bands marched by in row and rank, endless and relentless, coming in waves. Many were rousing, others melodic; more than a few were blood-and-thunder, kick-the-Pope bombast—the musical equivalent of hectoring someone from a pulpit. Men in bowler hats and orange sashes. Scottish flags and Red Hands flying. Union Jacks and burger stands. Kids on shoulders, watching the parade wide-eyed. *It's always the marching season in Northern Ireland.*

I knew there'd been a move of late to turn the Twelfth into a wider cultural event, "Orangefest," one that was more open, more welcoming. In Omagh, the local Catholic priest had been invited to walk alongside the start of the parade, an event unthinkable even a few years before. At another march, the Chinese community was included, and they took part with gusto, delivering a flamboyant dragon dance to the festivities, something later condemned by hardliners within the Orange Order. "This isn't about *cultural tourism!*" a former deputy grand master of the Orange Order bellowed from the bandstand in Ballyclare, all but spitting out those last two words as the TV cameras rolled. "This is about Britishness! This is about Protestantism!" The fact that such awkward constructions as "Protestantism" and "Britishness" rolled so smoothly off his tongue was a testament to the verbal dexterity of Ulstermen. The Chinese dragon dance was denounced just as vehemently by hardliners as nothing more than "paganism." (Northern Ireland must surely be one of the last jurisdictions in the English-speaking world where the term "paganism" is still used in public discourse.) Nothing had changed. And yet, everything had changed. The dragon dance, the Catholic priest in Omagh, the IRA's declaration that the armed conflict was over, the UVF standing down in turn, the power-sharing Parliament that had brought hated/beloved Republicans into government with their hated/beloved Unionist foes. The ground was shifting. *And the devil might yet escape from Northern Ireland.*

ONCE I'D ARRIVED in Belfast, I'd placed requests for wills, estate titles and other deeds with the various offices and archives. And while I waited for the holidays to end, I took a train out to Scarva to see the annual Sham Fight between Kings William and James.

I remembered Scarva, between Portadown and Newry on the old canal towpath, as a pretty little village, but if I was expecting a small, summery festival, I was soon corrected. It was like a Protestant Mardi Gras, minus the skimpy costumes and topless girls drunkenly carousing, alas. Scarva wasn't just overrun, it was invaded. A crush of people pushed in along the village's main street and then up into its commons. Later reports put the number of people at Scarva that day at well over *one hundred thousand.* This in a village of 318 people. To put that into perspective, the combined armies of William and James at the Battle of the Boyne totalled just over sixty thousand, meaning more people showed up for the re-enactment than had been in the actual fight itself.

As always, at events like this, one ran a gauntlet of food stalls and burger-and-chip vans selling "bacon on a bap," mini donuts and other such delicacies. An aura of warm grease hung over the proceedings. I bought a can of Coke and a clump of soggy, salt-encrusted, vinegar-doused fries, ate them, elbows in, among the mob, my lips as puckered as an aunt going for her favourite nephew. Union Jacks were everywhere. It was a veritable sea of Britishness, an ocean of Protestantism. Tea towels and marching-music CDs, plastic gewgaws sold to parents whose resolve had been worn down, miniature Orange sashes for the kiddies, Taiwanese-made toys and cartoon balloons. Sunglasses with Union Jacks splashed across the lenses coloured everything you saw, allowing you to look out at the world through a starburst of red, white and blue.

The bands squeezed past the pensioners who lined the route in lawn chairs. Accordion bands and flutes, bagpipes and brass, drums beaten to the point of breaking, banners flying Biblical scenes: Moses taking dictation, Adam and Eve being expelled. Many of the scenes depicted seemed obscure—"Hiram at the Temple," "Rahab and the Two Spies," "Elijah fed by Ravens"—until I realized they were from the Old Testament and as such not readily familiar to me. Protestant Ulster has always been an Old Testament sort of place, a Promised Land, one of righteous armies and vengeful gods, Canaanites and angry prophets, a chosen people. It was a reminder as well that in Northern Ireland history is not so much chronological as it is thematic, grouped around certain leitmotifs: endurance, betrayal, justice, revenge—and oh how often those last two are confused in Northern Ireland.

The music thundered onward. It stirred the blood, quickened the heart. The bands had come from every village in Ulster, it seemed— and more than a few in Scotland as well. They had names like *Pride of Ballinran* and *The Portadown Defenders*, while others walked behind banners honouring fallen brethren, lost friends: *In Memory of Hunter Moore* and *Lest We Forget*. As rousing chorus followed rousing chorus, as rolling drums followed rising flute, and rising flute followed rolling thunder, it all started to blend together: *Pride of Memory of Defenders of* _____, staying faithful and true to an empire that no longer existed, that may never have existed, an empire of widowed queens and doughty defenders forever answering a call to duty.

Hosted by the Royal Black Institution, the parade at Scarva was more of a family event, without the broken bottles and hooligan boys you found in Belfast. Children swarmed onto go-cart tracks and bouncy-castle jumping pits, as kiddy trains snaked past stomach-lurching, human-slingshot bungee rides. (The best offering by far was an inflatable slide in the shape of the *Titanic*—sinking. Kids scrambled up the side and then slid down the deck, as if into the Atlantic. The most famous ship in Belfast, forever sinking. *It was fine when it left.*)

And then, riding in on horseback above the crowds: William and James, in wigs and tails and tri-cornered hats, their jackets red and green respectively. The white horse and the brown.

I'd almost forgotten about the battle. The two kings, as played by local farmers, tethered their horses and then gathered their men: four on each side. *This* was the clash of mighty armies that had settled the fate of Ireland? I'd been expecting an American Civil War–style re-enactment; I hadn't expected this. As the two "armies" fell in, people began yelling out mock wagers, laying bets on the outcome, with the odds, naturally, in William's favour. One fellow declared he was going to bet on Jimmy this year. "He has'ta win sometime!" Seemed reasonable enough, law of averages and all. But this was Northern Ireland, and the law of averages didn't apply. The man remained undaunted, though. "I've got a tenner on ye, Jimmy! Doan be lettin' me down!" I suspect he knew Jimmy. I suspect they all knew Jimmy. No doubt Jimmy was a neighbour of theirs.

The two kings and their armies were soon lost in the crowd. I heard gunfire, saw a skirmish down the hill, not far from the bouncy castles: cap-gun rifles popping and the two competing flags waving wildly above the mob. The final battle would take place in a small paddock behind the main stage. The crowds had pushed in tight, but I knew what to do. I looked around for a band of bored-looking men touting cameras with oversized lenses. The media, in other words: the ones who covered this every year, who reported the same outcome every time. Sure enough, they started to move, and, with my own camera ready, I followed them up onto the stage and over, dropping directly into the paddock. I was now standing on the battlefield itself—I may well have ended up in the news clips and photographs from that day. *"Now, who the feck is that eejit?"*

Billy and Jimmy entered the ring to cheers and boos respectively. It was surprisingly tongue-in-cheek, considering this was the Holy

Victory of the Boyne they were celebrating. The two armies aimed a few more loud pops at their rival's flags as the kings squared off, whacking away at each other with swords. Jimmy took a swing, and Billy slipped. "*Oooooh*," went the crowd, but Billy was back up, and down went Jimmy. "*Hooray!*" On it went, amid tattered flags and gunshots, to laughter and jeers. On it went till victory was secured for another year. Jimmy lay down for a photo op, with Billy pressing his sword into his chest (even though, in real life, Jimmy fled to France). The photographer beside me said to no one in particular, "That's him, then."

Jimmy brushed himself off, shook hands with Billy. "Don't worry, Jimmy!" someone in the crowd yelled. "You'll get 'im next time!" "Aye," came another shout. "We'll see yis next year, Jimmy." They would.

And on it goes with Billy knocking down Jimmy all through eternity.

The battle, lasting all of twelve minutes, provided only the barest of pretexts for the festival; of the one hundred thousand people at Scarva that day, maybe, *maybe* four hundred of them saw the actual battle. The organizers could probably skip the fight entirely and no one would notice. The festivities would continue merrily without them. Jimmy and Billy could go to the pub and have a pint instead, and no one would be the wiser.

I squirmed my way down Scarva's multitudinous main street, feeling claustrophobic. I wrenched myself out of the flow and onto a path running past the village. Suddenly, I was back on the Ulster Way. I'd walked this very path. It had been sloppy and wet at the time. Now it was fully surfaced and well maintained: a fine bicycle/footpath from Loyalist Portadown to Republican Newry. I followed the canal awhile, feeling nostalgic and half expecting to see myself coming down the trail toward me.

A father and two young children bicycled up, stopped at the sight of the crowds ahead and the sounds of festivities in distant fields. The father looked concerned.

"Kin we go in?" asked the youngest, a girl of nine or ten.

"Kin we, Da, please?" asked her brother.

"No," the father said. "We can't." And they rode off, bypassing the village of Scarva and its battles ongoing.

ON LOSING THE ULSTER WAY

Still waiting for my document requests to work their way through the system, I took a sentimental journey into the Ulster countryside—by car this time. I was surprised at how small a place it was. Small, yet astoundingly varied. The green glens of Antrim, the jagged northern coasts, the swaths of soft beach, the dark mountains, the Fermanagh lakelands, the rolling drumlins of Down. *Drumlins! God, how I missed those.*

The villages and small towns I'd tramped through had hardly changed. And yet, there were new dynamics at play, a higher energy. More shops, better shops, and shops that stayed open later. There were more people on the streets, and it wasn't simply a matter of the season. There was an excitement here I hadn't felt before, and I thought, *This must be what it feels like when a siege has been lifted.* New restaurants had appeared, some in the most unexpected places, and with menus that featured more than one kind of soup. (When I ordered "today's soup du jour" and was served something other than vegetable, I was flabbergasted.) There were still five hundred flavours of potato chips, though, with more being added all the time. New flavours of potato chips—these are all real—included Thai Sweet Chilli, Oven Roasted Chicken with Lemon & Thyme, and Roast Ox.

In County Armagh I stayed with John, the RUC officer I'd met on top of Slieve Donard. John's children were visiting their grandparents, and I was given a guest room. I met John's lovely wife, was treated, as always, with the unconditional kindness one finds when travelling in the North. The world had changed since I'd met John on top of that mountain. The Royal Ulster Constabulary had been disbanded and then reorganized. John was now a member of the PSNI (Police Service of Northern Ireland). Where the RUC had a force that was only eight percent Catholic, the PSNI, through aggressive recruiting and quotas, was now at twenty-four percent and climbing. It helped that the IRA had promised not to kill any Catholics who signed up. The PSNI was officially a "police service" rather than a "police force," a politically correct gesture, perhaps, but one with impact. The transition had been an administrative headache, as attempts at affirmative action always are, and many senior officers had left, just as many young, inexperienced Catholic officers had been hastily recruited. But a good number of the fortress-like RUC bases had been dismantled and most of the military watchtowers removed. Police stations in Northern Ireland now often looked like, well, like police stations, rather than military encampments. The PSNI had begun patrolling in regular police cars rather than armoured Land Rovers, even—and this was staggering, almost beyond belief—in South Armagh's Bandit Country, where the IRA had once posted its "Sniper at Work" signs.

Nationalist enclaves in Northern Ireland still harboured disgruntled freelance Republicans, "dissidents," as they were known, who couldn't accept that the war was over and who were still vowing violence against the authorities, police officers in particular. These dissident IRA groups had already made dozens of attempts on PSNI lives by mid-2008.* For the most part, though, police in Northern Ireland were finally being allowed to do their job without being labelled "legitimate targets." A good thing, too, because with the breakdown of paramilitary control, crime had actually increased: bank robberies, extortion, attacks on immigrants and ethnic minorities, and inner-city drug dealing had all seen a marked rise. The overall rates were still far lower than in England, say, but were worrisome nonetheless.

---

*Sadly, in 2009, they would succeed, killing two British soldiers and a senior PSNI officer. Instead of pushing the two sides apart, though, the killings brought them together, with Unionists and Nationalists, Loyalists and mainstream Republicans joining in their condemnation of these murders.

"Aye," John noted. "We have our work cut out for us."

Police in Northern Ireland still operated in a charged political environment, where every action was taken as either a slight or favouritism by one side or the other, but slowly politics was being taken out of policing. "I even get to walk the beat sometimes," John said. "I really enjoy that. You feel you're part of the community, you get to meet people." He was sociable by nature. Barricades and siege towers didn't suit him.

John and I considered taking a day off to drive down to the Mournes, maybe hike to the top of Slieve Donard again for old time's sake, but the weather intervened, and we ended up in a pub instead. He still drank Guinness. I still couldn't.

I continued tootling about in a rent-a-car, following my old routes. The roads in Northern Ireland were generally good, if a little narrow—which wasn't a problem except when some bumble-headed walker veered into sight hogging the side of the road. Bloody pedestrians.

There was, I am happy to say, a cash machine in Derrygonnelly now, and a wide bypass around Newtownstewart as well. Traffic still rumbled through Derrylin and Aughnacloy, though, and the Sperrins were still cloaked in rain. The castle at Dungiven had been transformed into a four-star hotel—as it should be; that castle was wasted on us backpackers—and the INLA and IRA signs in Dungiven and elsewhere were starting to fade. In their stead, polished black obsidian memorials to brave volunteers who died "fighting the British" were now appearing, signalling a shift among Republicans, a focus more on the past, on looking back, mythologizing and eulogizing, rather than engaging. I'll take that over random killings and car bombs any day.

The bridge across the mouth of the River Erne was still marked WEAK BRIDGE. It still rattled when you crossed it. And Strabane—well, Strabane was still Strabane, only more so. But even there good omens were evident; for one thing, the city now boasted a large, defiantly optimistic Tourist Information Centre. "*Did you know that Strabane is the birthplace of John Dunlap, printer of the US Declaration of Independence?"* they ask when you stop in. *"And that Strabane is also the site of the Woodrow Wilson ancestral home?"*

The family SPAR at Drumlegagh was a sleek new Vivo. Expensive condos had spread along the shores of Lower Lough Erne, and everywhere, it seemed, on every hill and every crest, wind farms had popped up like mushrooms after a rain.

Kim no longer lived in Glenarm, and the town's police station, far from being a fortress, now looked positively Californian, facing the bay as it did, catching the sun on its palm trees, a tall, almost decorative fence having replaced what was once corrugated steel. I went back to Carnlough to find Moscow Joe, only to learn he had died several years earlier. The local council had since cleared out his yard, and his bungalow, if it still existed, was now indistinguishable from the rest. There were no more jawbones of dinosaurs or hubcaps filched from Berlin motorcades, no "wee rubbishy irish cottage" to be astounded at or puzzled by.

I wanted to see Ulster from up high and decided on impulse to climb the Garron Plateau—not to cross it, but just to reach those heights once more, to feel the wind fill my lungs. The route was blocked, however, and a sign had been posted: "Ulster Way closed. No access permission beyond this point."

When I tried to make the walk up the Lough Navar cliffs, that trail was closed as well, this time due to rock slides. The trail down to Big Dog/Little Dog, where I'd encountered a bull on the road, was closed off too, the waymarker removed. I remembered the lady hanging laundry, staring at me as I backpacked past, and I wondered if I had had something to do with it. Even the sole Ulster Way signpost in Dungiven was gone. There was still a flurry of them pointing you in toward Belcoo, though. If the trail had decayed, it had done so fitfully.

"The longest waymarked trail in the British Isles" was gone. I may very well have been one of the last people to walk it as originally mapped. That didn't fill me with swagger, though, but only a strange sense of loss. I felt wistful about it, which was odd. How many times had I cursed the Ulster Way while walking it, and now here I was missing it.*

It had been ten years since Omagh. The smoke had finally started to clear; the madness had finally started to subside. Flashpoints still existed, still flared up, but they were anomalies now, and Northern Ireland's thirty-year slugfest had ended, not so much in victory but from mutual exhaustion, like two punch-drunk boxers propping each other up in centre ring.

BELFAST HAD more walls than ever, true—more peacelines had gone up since I first came through—but you could now walk directly from Republican Falls Road to Loyalist Shankill in one go. You could cross that great divide without any army checkpoints to brave or razor wire to cross. I discovered that almost by accident when I returned to the city after my car trip. I planned to visit the Public Records Office and the Linen Hall Archives the following day—the answer to the riddle of my grandfather's photograph was now within reach—so I went for one last walk down Falls Road. The corrugated metal peaceline that had blocked my way when I'd tried to walk from my family's grave in City Cemetery to my grandfather's childhood street below the Shankill was still there. But this time the gate was open. The sight took me aback. Had there even been a gate there before? They would shut it at night, no doubt, and during riots, but still. The gate was open. It was mainly for traffic, but pedestrians could walk through it if they wanted to. Which is what I did, mainly for the novelty of going directly between the two most sectarian streets in Ulster—in the UK even. Falls Road to Shankill, direct. A no man's land of vacant lots and rubble lay on the other side of the wall, but beyond that was a tidy

---

*As this book went to print, it was announced that the Ulster Way would be relaunched with a new route, improved signage and an emphasis on promoting shorter, "quality" sections. Connector segments would be included, to keep the appearance of a continuous path, but the Ulster Way would be promoted instead as a series of shorter walks of more "reasonable length."

arrangement of red-brick bungalows. Wilton Street, where my grand-father had grown up, was in there. It all but butted up against that no man's land.

A five-minute walk, but one that leapt a chasm as surely as the bridge at Carrick-a-Rede. Ulster might never be at peace, but it was at least no longer at war. I whistled happily, hands in pockets, as I crossed toward Wilton, though the thought did occur to me: *I wonder if Loyalists watch that gate, looking for people dumb enough to come over from the other side?*

I was back on Wilton Street, where Anne Press had raised her children. *Annie Press, who were you? Were you even a Press at all?* Who was Anne Sloane? And why was that page in the 1901 Census missing?

During my original trip, I'd stopped by the *Telegraph* office in Belfast and spoken with one of the columnists there, hoping he might help put the word out about my attempts to track down the Press and Belshaw connections. I'd tried to be discreet, couching my words tactfully, aware that I was revealing one-hundred-year-old infidelities. But when the story appeared, long after I'd left Northern Ireland, it ran under the headline "A Sorry Secret Story of Bigamy and a Double Life of Shame." *Well*, I thought, *there goes any chance of someone contacting me*. But not long after that, I got a phone call at my home. The voice on the other end said, "We may be related."

He didn't have an Ulster accent. He was a geologist, calling not from Belfast but from the very city where I lived. He was the only member of his family not in Northern Ireland, and he was just a ten-minute drive from my house. I had crossed the Atlantic only to find my closest connection right back where I'd started.

We met, had a coffee. He looked a lot like my Uncle Don. Odder still: his name was John Clark, the same name that appeared on the headstone beside my great-grandfather's empty plot in Belfast. John and his wife, Trish, invited my wife, Terumi, and me and our two sons to their house. We met their sons as well, became friends, maybe even family. The actual lineage remains unclear, but on his grandmother's side, John appears to be descended from the legitimate, non-adulterous line of Belshaws.

Through John Clark, further Ulster connections had opened up: his sister Paddy in County Antrim, her husband, Roy, their children, their children's children. When Paddy heard I was coming back to Northern Ireland, she and Roy invited me to an after-wedding get-together for their son Fergus and his bride, Kate. I swung by during my rent-a-car journey. It was held at Castlerock, within sight of the Mussenden Temple I had walked by years before. I'd been moving among relatives back then and hadn't known it. And here I was, back at Castlerock, among cousins both distant and near at hand. Third, fourth, fifth? Once removed? Twice? Did it even matter anymore? At the Castlerock gathering, the rhythms, the humour, the turns of phrase … it all felt very *familiar*.

LORD DERAMORE TO YOU

In Belfast, the requests I'd submitted to the Public Records Office under the names "Sloane" and "Press" had turned up nothing that connected my grandfather to the estate depicted in the photograph. Oddly enough, Killyleagh, down on Strangford Lough with its fairy-tale castle, had been the birthplace of Sir Hans Sloane, Royal Physician, whose collection of manuscripts, plants and animal specimens had helped found the British Museum. But any attempt at connecting Annie Sloane (née Press) to the Sloanes of Killyleagh had also come up empty. The mystery of Anne Press refused to resolve itself. She didn't appear in any church records, seemed almost to have been erased from the books.

I went back to the Public Records Office one last time. That was where the missing page in the 1901 Census had thwarted me earlier, and I scrolled through the microfiche again, searching variations on the names and addresses given, sifting through similar-sounding streets. Nothing. The staff at the office were convinced I was just being thick, and one of them sat down beside me, as though I were an especially slow child in need of guidance, to run through the records himself. "Hmm," he said.

Hmm, exactly.

"I'll pop in the back," he said. "Check the original census books." He returned with a puzzled look on his face. "You're right," he conceded. "That page—it's been removed."

There was only one family per page, so whoever had torn that page out knew it was the information for Anne Press/Anne Sloane that they were removing. I'd hoped to arrive at the estate named on the photograph armed with sheafs of public documents asserting my ownership, but that plan had come to nought. I was left with only a single image with a cryptic inscription on the back.

I thanked the staff at Public Records and was pulling on my jacket when I thought to ask, "I'm trying to locate a family estate. Bell—I'm not sure if I'm pronouncing this right—Bell*voh*, Bell*vow*."

"Beaver," they said. "It's pronounced 'Beaver.'"

"Beaver?" I said. "It can't be. There's an L in there, and an O."

"Belvoir," they laughed. "But it's pronounced *Beaver*. It's a public park now."

I never did figure out the Ulster accent. "Is it far?"

"Walkin', are you?"

I nodded.

"Well, it'll be a long walk, if yer up for it."

I smiled. "I'm up for it."

"A nice wee walk, though," one of the staff said as they opened up a map to show me the way. "A fine day for it, too."

The route was crushingly familiar; it was along the Ulster Way. When I had entered Belfast in rainy non-triumph at the end of my trek, I had turned and followed another street in instead. In doing so, I had missed entering my family's long-lost lands.

From the Public Records Office, I followed Balmoral Avenue down a lane lined with sculpted hedges, past landscaped yards that looked like golf courses. The estates of the wealthy lay hidden behind gates. I began to hurry, my excitement mounting as I neared the entrance.

The air was fragrant, green-scented. A footpath bridge crossed the River Lagan, and I entered the forested and fern-festooned realm of the Belvoir Estate. Uphill beneath generous oak leaf canopies, feeling almost giddy, I came at last to a sombre stone-and-ivy arrangement: an old stable house, now an information centre, closed for the day.

Stables, yes, fine, but where was my manor house?

Belvoir Forest Park covers 75 hectares along the south bank of the River Lagan. I was reading this from an interpretive sign. *The estate was first enclosed by the Hills, a Plantation family, in the 1740s.* The Hills had long since decamped, so where did that leave me? It was maddening to be this close and not know.

A coin-operated telescope nearby provided an unintentional haiku in the form of the instructions it gave:

POINT THE TELESCOPE
   OBSERVE THE VIEW. AND AT NIGHT THE MOON.
     DON'T LOOK AT THE SUN.
      HOLD CHILD ON STAND.

The next day, I went to the third floor of the Belfast City Library to talk to a research librarian. She pulled out some information for me regarding the Belvoir Estate, sometimes spelled "Bellvoir." As in, Bell.

"Is there a manor house somewhere on the estate?" I asked, trying not to sound too eager.

"There was," she said. "It was blown up."

"Blown up?"

"Yes, in—let's see—1961."

"IRA?"

"Territorial Army. It was derelict. They took it down for safety."

Damn. "And was there any, y'know, *title* associated with the estate?"

"There was. The Belvoir estate had passed from the Hill family to the—"

Please say Press. Please say Press.

"—Bateson family. The head of that family, Thomas Bateson, was made Lord Deramore in 1885. His wife would have been Lady Deramore." The name apparently came from a great tree that grew on the Belvoir estate, *Deramore* being Irish for "big oak."

"The estate is now public lands?" I asked.

"It is. Lord Deramore was in ill health, and he died soon after. The family no longer resided at Belvoir after that. It appears to have changed hands several times. The house fell derelict after that. The vaults were looted for their lead coffins. The army took it over during the Second World War, built huts. It was demolished, as I said, in 1961."

"So the family line has died out?"

"It would seem. The records aren't clear."

"So if someone had a claim on the estate, through photographic evidence, say …"

"I imagine the government would have to return the property. But I'm not really an expert on—"

"And the title? Lord Deramore? That would come with the estate, right?"

"I imagine."

Hot damn! It was all I could do not to leap in the air. I'd come to Ulster as a mere commoner, grandson of an outcast orphan, but I would be returning as Lord Deramore! Friend and foe would be forced to curtsy at my passing. They'd have to tug their forelocks well and good, would have to avert eye contact and leave the room backward bowing when I dismissed them.

Then a crushing realization hit me: I was the fourth of six children, with three brothers older than me.

If nothing else, I understand Shakespeare much better now, because my immediate—immediate!—reaction was: "*I kill Dan, Ian, Sean—and the estate is mine.*"

I was mulling this over—"*How to get them together in one place without arousing any suspicions? And how to make it look like an accident?*"—when something else began to niggle at me. The spelling.

Even with the double L's, "Belvoir" did not look like what my grandfather had written on the back of that photograph. The "Bell" was the same, but the last bit looked different.

"Is there another estate," I asked, "one connected with the Press family, or perhaps the Sloanes or Belshaws, one that's named—" I took the photograph out now, the one my grandfather had carried with him all those years, turned it over. "Bell*vue*, maybe?"

She frowned. "Not that I know of. Except …"

"Yes?" I asked.

"The zoo."

"The zoo?"

"The Belfast City Zoo. It used to be known as Bellevue Gardens."

She opened a book of historic photographs, found an early one of the zoo, passed it across to me. And there they were—the stairs in my grandfather's photograph, the same ornamental urns.

Not a lost estate. A trip to the zoo. As quickly as they'd arrived, dreams of Lord Deramore slipped away.

It must have been one of the few warm memories my grandfather had of his childhood. Before his mother died, before he and his brother William were shipped off to an orphanage, before they were separated on a Belfast dock—before any of that, there was a trip to the zoo. That was what he had kept with him all those years. A trip to the zoo.

KEY OF HELL

I emailed my brothers back home. "Good news! I've decided to let you live."

"No estate?" Ian emailed back.

"Just the zoo. The photograph was taken on what was probably a Sunday outing," I wrote.

"The zoo?" Ian wrote back. "Excellent! Get in there and clear the trespassers out, set up a booth, start charging admission. That's our estate! And dibs on the monkey pens!"

I didn't set up an admissions booth, but I did take my grandfather's photograph with me to try to find the spot where he had stood smiling into the camera that day. But that too was gone. "Oh, I remember those," said the taxi driver when I showed him the ornamental urns in the picture. He was an older gentleman, and he slowed down to point out where the original gates to the zoo had stood. Like the missing headstone at City Cemetery, the redrawn street plan on Wilton, the rebuilt homes on Ambleside, there was nothing tangible, nothing real to tie me here, only faint echoes, fast fading.

I thought again about that missing page in the 1901 Census. I thought about who might have wanted it removed, who might have wanted to hide the past, might have preferred tales of a Boer War hero over base bigamy, might have wanted to shelter from his brother the truth, to cover up the fact that they were castoffs. I thought about my namesake, my great-uncle Bill and his trip to Belfast, of him returning to tell my grandfather that, sadly, the records of their family had been destroyed in a fire. Bill would have been old enough to remember the address on Wilton Street and would have been able to find the corresponding records. He had always watched out for his little brother, had always protected him. He was a good man.

As the afternoon turned to evening, and evening turned to dusk, I walked up Cave Hill from the zoo, looked out again across the city. The harbour below was half asleep, the cranes and dockyard towers silhouetted like medieval weapons of war. Beyond Belfast, I could see the dark Mournes in the distance, and down below, in closer, the lights of Whiteabbey, shimmering. And it hit me: I hadn't finished my original walk. I'd started at Whiteabbey, had ended at Cave Hill, but had never connected the two, had never closed the circle, had never completed the Ulster Way.

It was getting dark. I had an early flight the following morning, back home to my family. It was getting dark, and yet—the urge came over me to thread my way down through the housing estates and the competing loyalties below, down to the shores of Belfast Lough and then out along it to Whiteabbey, to finish the walk I'd started so long ago. The feeling was overpowering, and it came upon me like a voice, whispering.

"Come back again and walk among us."

SOURCES

The background on Northern Ireland and the Ulster Way comes from the following sources. For a sense of the beauty of the Ulster landscape, see the stunning aerial photography of Esler Crawford in *The North from the Air*, published by Blackstaff Press of Belfast.

Adamson, Ian. *1690: William and the Boyne*, Newtownards 1995.

Akenson, Donald Harmon. *God's Peoples: Covenant and Land in South Africa, Israel, and Ulster*, Montreal & Kingston 1991.

Bardon, Jonathan. *A Shorter Illustrated History of Ulster*, Belfast 1996.

Barker, A. J. *Bloody Ulster: Ballantine's Illustrated History*, New York 1973.

Beattie, Geoffrey. *We Are the People: Journeys through the Heart of Protestant Ulster*, London 1992.

Bryans, Robin. *Ulster: A Journey through the Six Counties*, London 1964.

Busteed, Mervyn. *Castle Caldwell, County Fermanagh: Life on a West Ulster Estate, 1750–1800*, Dublin 2006.

Campbell, Maureen. *Armagh: City of Light and Learning*, Donaghadee 1997.

Carmody, William Patrick. *A Guide to Cushendall and Its Neighbourhood*, Dublin 1904.

Corbett, Gail H. *Nation Builders: Barnardo Children in Canada*, Toronto 2002.

Cunningham, John B. *Lough Derg: Legendary Pilgrimage*, Monaghan 1984.

Curran, Bob. *Across the Roe from Bann to Faughan*, Donaghadee, 2006.

——————. *North Antrim: Seven Towers to Nine Glens*, Donaghadee 2005.

Dallat, Cahal. *Antrim Coasts & Glens: A Personal View*, Belfast 1990.

Day, Catharina. *Cadogan Guides: Northern Ireland, the Province of Ulster*, London 1995.

Dillon, Paddy. *The Complete Ulster Way*, Dublin 1999.

Donnelly, Maureen. *The Nine Glens*, Coleraine 2000.

——————. *Saint Patrick and the Downpatrick Area*, Downpatrick 1995.

Doyle, J. B. *Tours in Ulster: A Hand-Book to the Antiquities and Scenery of the North of Ireland*, Dublin 1854.

Duffy, Joseph. *Lough Derg Guide*, Dublin 1980.

Duffy, Sean (ed.). *Atlas of Irish History: Second Edition*, Dublin 2000.

Edwards, Ruth Dudley. *The Faithful Tribe: An Intimate Portrait of the Loyal Institutions*, London 2000.

Elliott, Marianne. *The Catholics of Ulster*, New York 2001.

Evans, David and Marcus Patton. *The Diamond as Big as a Square: An Introduction to the Towns and Buildings of Ulster*, Belfast 1981.

Evans, Rosemary. *The Visitor's Guide to Northern Ireland*, Belfast 1998.

Fay, Gerald. *Proud People: Newry Anthology*, Newry 1994.

Fermanagh District Council. *The Ulster Way in Fermanagh*, Enniskillen.

Flanagan, Laurence. *Irish Wrecks of the Spanish Armada*, Dublin 1995.

Fletcher, Martin. *Silver Linings: Travels Around Northern Ireland*, London 2001.

Flynn, Laurence J. *St. Patrick's Purgatory: Lough Derg, County Donegal*, Norwich 1999.

Forde, Hugh. *Round the Coast of Northern Ireland: Antrim, Derry and Down*, Belfast 1928.

Gallagher, Lyn. *Discover Castle Ward*, Downpatrick 2003.

Garrett, Rosemary. *Cushendun and the Glens of Antrim*, Ballycastle 1956.

Golway, Terry. *For the Cause of Liberty: A Thousand Years of Ireland's Heroes*, New York 2000.

Hanna, Denis O'D. *The Face of Ulster*, London 1952.

Harnden, Toby. *Bandit Country: The IRA & South Armagh*, London 2000.

Hayes-McCoy, G. A. *Irish Battles: A Military History of Ireland*, Dublin 1997.

Heatley, Colm. *Interface: Flashpoints in Northern Ireland*, Belfast 2004.

Hennessey, Thomas. *A History of Northern Ireland: 1920–1996*, New York 1997.

Holmes, J. M. *The Real St. Patrick*, Ballyclare 2002.

Jackson, Jack (ed.). *Cooneen: The Road to the Hills*, Enniskillen 1994.

Johnson, Paul. *Ireland: Land of Troubles, A History from the Twelfth Century to the Present Day*, London 1982.

Keaveney, Eamonn and Noel Parker. *Twenty-Five Walks in Fermanagh*, Edinburgh 1997.

Kee, Robert. *The Green Flag Volume One: The Most Distressful Country*, London 1989.

————. *The Green Flag Volume Two: The Bold Fenian Men*, London 1989.

————. *The Green Flag Volume Three: Ourselves Alone*, London 1989.

————. *Ireland: A History*, London 2003.

Lacey, Brian. *Discover Derry*, Dublin 1999.

Lawson, Leonard. *Twenty-Five Walks in Down District*, Edinburgh 1998.

Litton, Helen. *The Irish Famine: An Illustrated History*, Dublin 1994.

Llewelyn, John. *Cushendun Conservation Area*, Coleraine 1996.

Lundy, Derek. *The Bloody Red Hand: A Journey through Truth, Myth and Terror in Northern Ireland*, Toronto 2006.

MacDonagh, Oliver. *States of Mind: Two Centuries of Anglo–Irish Conflict, 1780–1980*, London 1983.

Mac Uistin, Liam. *The Táin: The Great Celtic Epic*, Dublin 1989.

McBride, Jack. *Traveller in the Glens*, Belfast 2004.

McCaffrey, Carmel. *In Search of Ireland's Heroes: The Story of the Irish from the English Invasion to the Present Day*, Chicago 2006.

McCann, Eamonn. *War & Peace in Northern Ireland*, Dublin 1998.

McCreary, Alf. *An Ulster Journey*, Antrim 1986.

McCusker, Breege. *Fermanagh: Land of Lake and Legend*, Donaghadee 1999.

McDaniel, Denzil. *Enniskillen: The Remembrance Sunday Bombing*, Dublin 1997.

McDonnell, Randal. *Touring in the Glens of Antrim*, Coleraine 1999.

McGarry, Mary. *Great Folk Tales of Old Ireland*, New York 1972.

McGuinness, Joseph. *Lough Derg: St. Patrick's Purgatory*, Dublin 2000.

McKay, Susan. *Northern Protestants: An Unsettled People*, Belfast 2005.

McKeever, Patrick J. *A Story through Time: The Formation of the Scenic Landscapes of Ireland (North)*, Belfast 1999.

McKillop, Felix. *Glenarm: A Local History*, Belfast 1987.

Madill, Harry and Margaret Manley, Finbar McCormick, Christine Walsh. *Killough: The Church on the Lough*, Killough 2000.

Martin, F. X. and T. W. Moody (eds.). *The Course of Irish History: Fourth Edition*, Lanham 2001.

Mitchell, Brian. *Derry: A City Invincible*, Eglinton 1999.

Moran, Jon. *Policing the Peace: Politics, Crime and Security after the Belfast Agreement*, Manchester 2008.

Murphy, Dervla. *A Place Apart*, London 1978.

O'Brien, Maire and Conor Cruise. *Ireland: A Concise History*, London 1997.

O'Connor, Ulick. *Irish Tales and Sagas*, London 1985.

Rankin, J. Frederick. *Down Cathedral: The Church of St. Patrick of Down*, Belfast 1997.

Robinson, Philip. *Diamonds in Stone: Twenty-one Years of Conservation Area Designation in Northern Ireland*, Antrim 1994.

Rogers, Richard. *Ulster Walk Guide*, Dublin 1991.

Ryder, Chris. *The RUC: A Force Under Fire*, London 2000.

Shaffrey, Patrick. *The Irish Town*, Dublin 1975.

Spencer, Graham. *Omagh: Voices of Loss*, Belfast 2005.

Sutton, Malcolm. *An Index of the Deaths from the Conflict in Northern Ireland: 1969–1993*, Belfast 1994.

Tóibín, Colm. *Walking Along the Border*, London 1987.

Warner, Alan. *Walking the Ulster Way*, Belfast 1989.

Watson, Philip. *The Giant's Causeway and the North Antrim Coast*, Dublin 2000.

Watson, Sandy. *Old Antrim Coast*, Ayrshire 2004.

Waugh, Edwin. *The North Coast, 1869*, Ballycastle 1990.

Wilson, Anthony M. *Saint Patrick's Town*, Belfast 1995.

Wright, Peter. *Ulster Rambles*, Antrim 1993.

Acknowledgments

I would first like to thank the people of Northern Ireland for the kindness they have shown me during my travels. In particular, I would like to thank Roy and Paddy Bailie of County Antrim, and John and Brenda Pentland of County Armagh, for their help and hospitality. I would like to thank Hugh Press, Raymond Press, John Press and Joy Wilkinson of County Down for their assistance in trying to track down my Press family connections. I would also like to thank John and Charlie, the police officers I met atop Slieve Donard, formerly of the RUC, now with the PSNI. And in Belfast, I would like to thank the staff and research assistants at the Public Record Office, the General Register Office, the Linen Hall Library, the City Library and the *Belfast Telegraph* newspaper archives.

Back home, I would like to thank my mother, Lorna Bell, daughter of a Belfast orphan, for keeping the stories of her father alive; and my brother, journalist Dan Ferguson, for the hours of interviews he conducted with her for this book; and my neighbour Jackie Ford for the hours she in turn spent transcribing those interviews, as well as the twenty-six hours (!) of tapes I recorded during my walk. I would like to thank my wife, Terumi, for her support and understanding, and for transcribing some of those tapes as well, and my uncle, Don Bell, for the information he obtained from Barnardo's. I would like to thank John and Trish Clark (John in particular for providing a template for the maps I submitted)—and my two great kids, Alex and Alister.

I would like to thank Penguin Canada and everyone who was involved in producing and promoting *Beyond Belfast*: my editor, Barbara Pulling; editorial director Andrea Magyar; VP of sales Don Robinson (who took a call in a Dublin pub from me about this very book); publisher David Davidar; VP of publicity and marketing Yvonne Hunter; managing editor Karen Alliston; copy editor Tara Tovell; Daniel Cullen, who designed the cover; Deborah Crowle, who created the maps; senior publicity manager Debbie Gaudet; senior publicist Barbara Bower; senior marketing manager Lindsey Lowy; senior online marketing manager Christina Ponte; and all the many booksellers I have met over the years. It's been a pleasure! *May the winds o' the heather be lashin' the Mournes afore the devil shakes yer sausage.*